AF255648

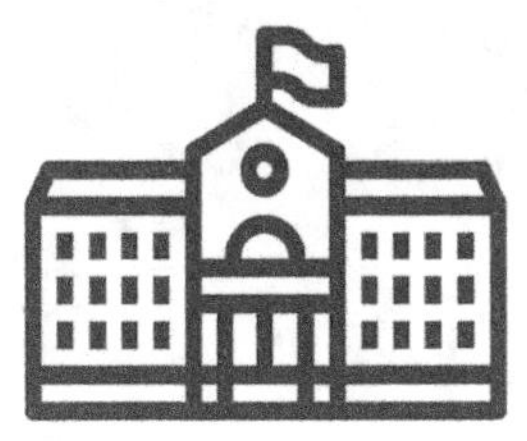

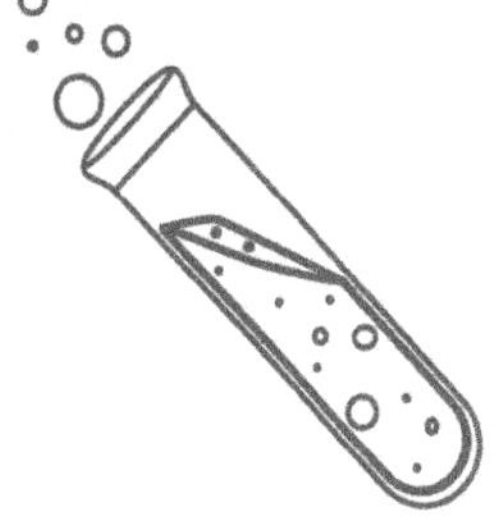
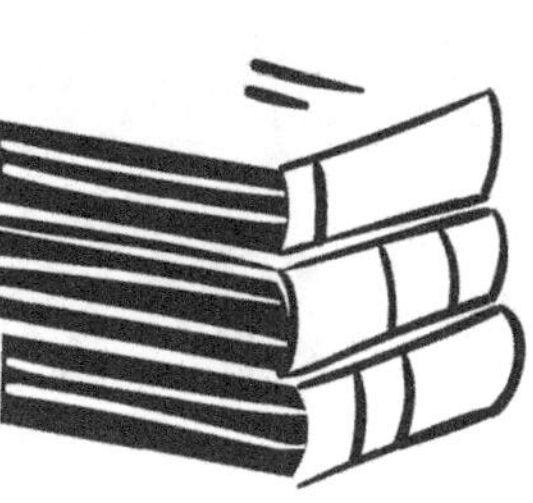
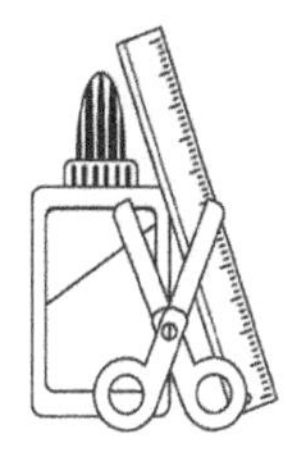

HBCUs: A **Leg**acy of Black Exc**e**ll**e**nce

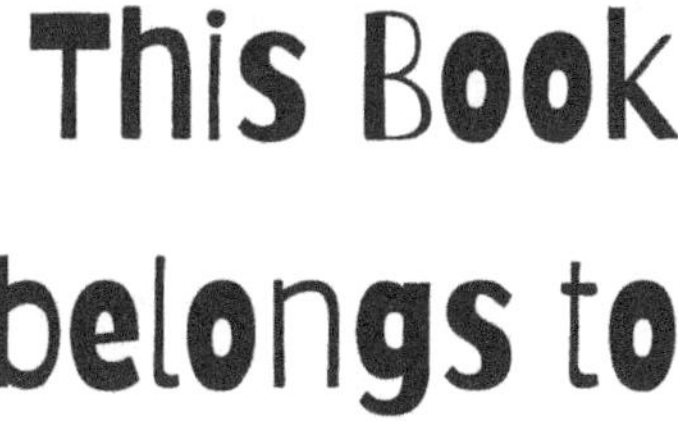

This B**o**ok bel**o**ngs to

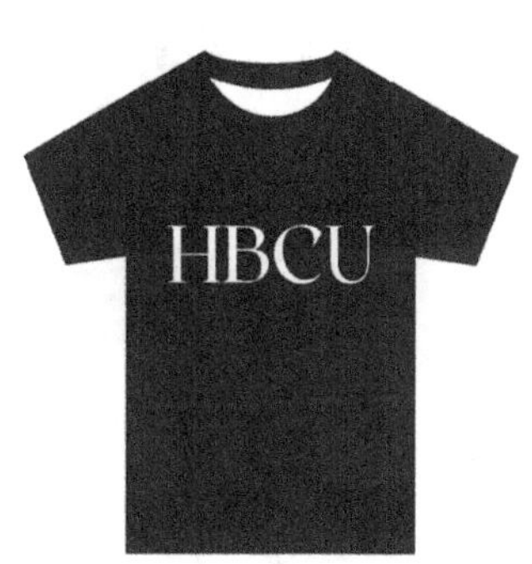

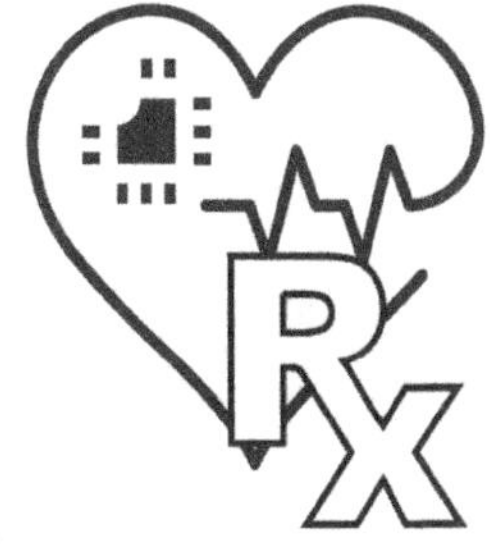

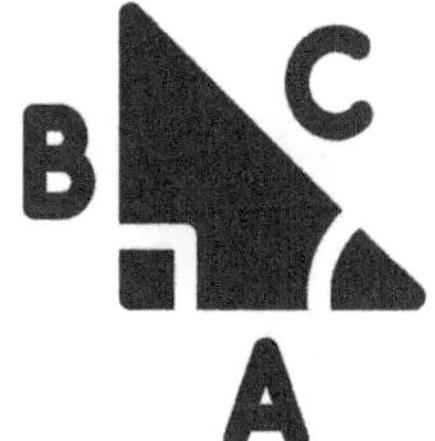

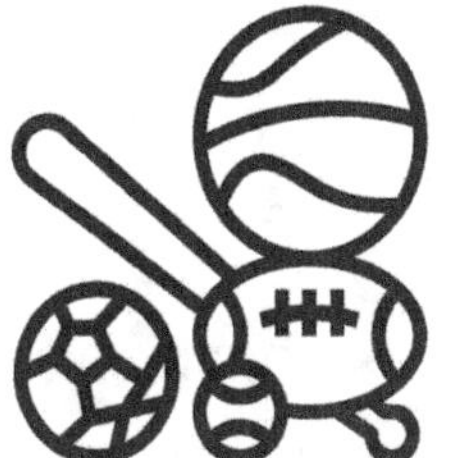

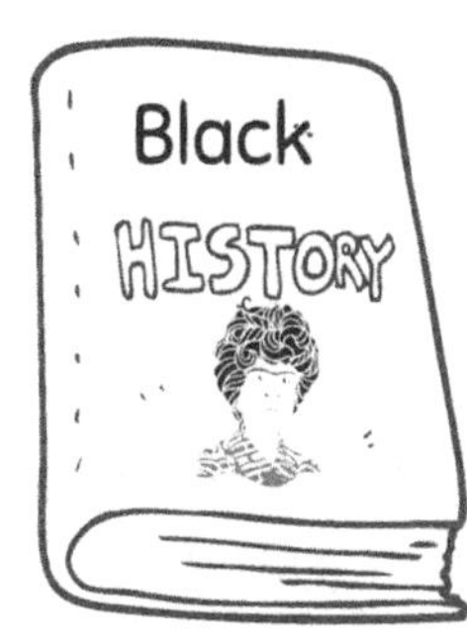

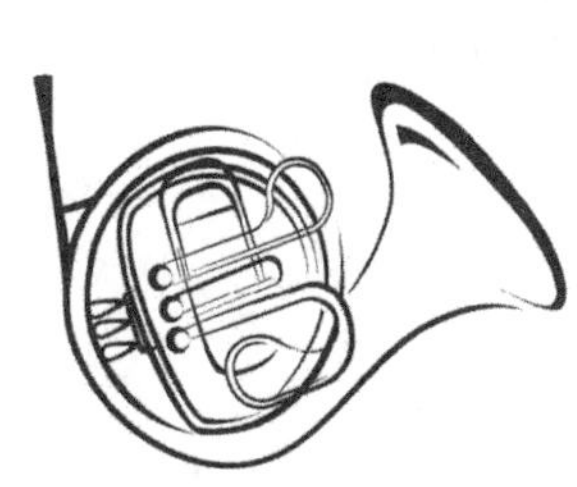

ISBN: 978-1-7370011-2-6

Dedication

I pay homage to my ancestors who paved the way and created an opportunity for me to attend an HBCU. Due to their determination, fight and faith, I now stand as an alumna of the prestigious Howard University.

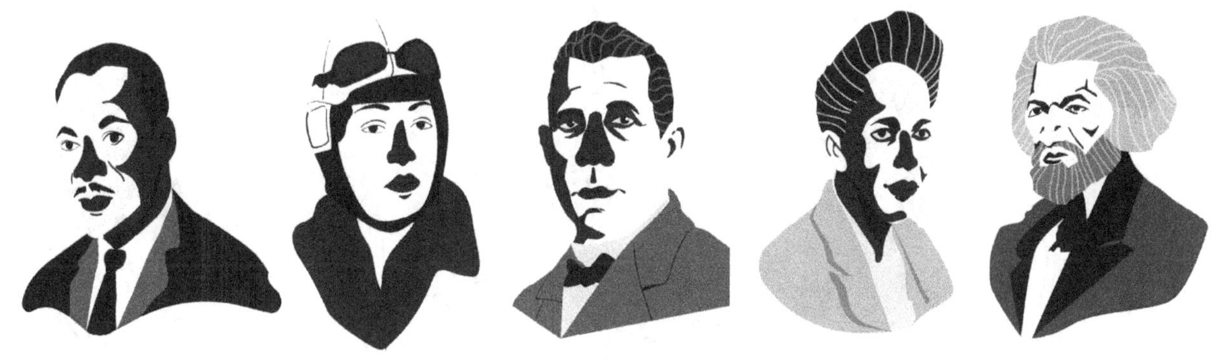

I would like to dedicate this book to my niece, Talore Hill. She represents Black excellence and is a a future HBCU alumna.

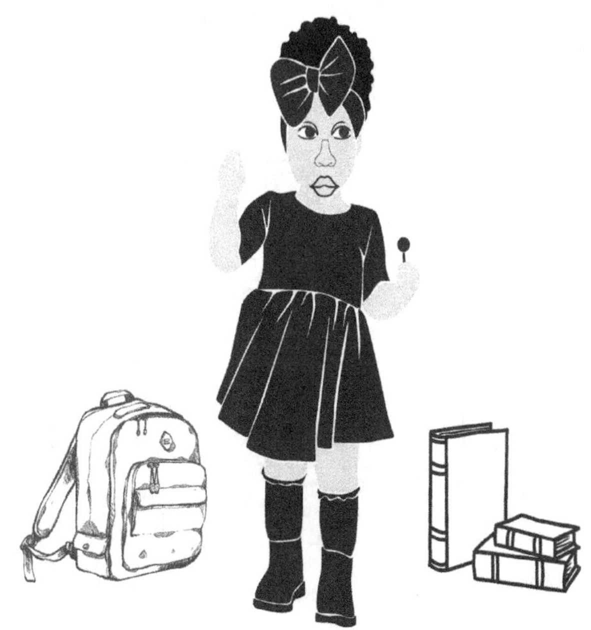

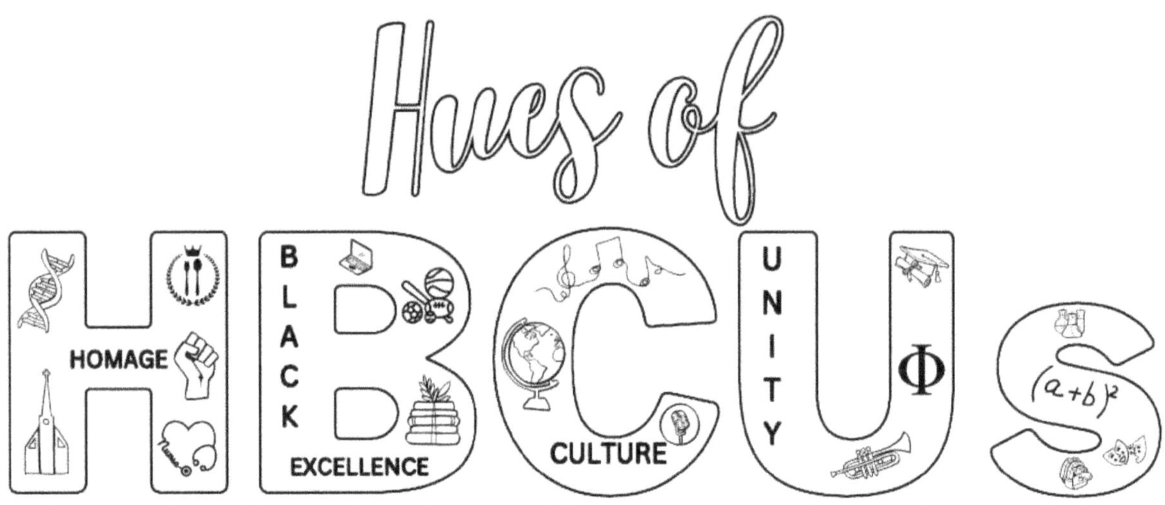

Historically Black Colleges and Universities

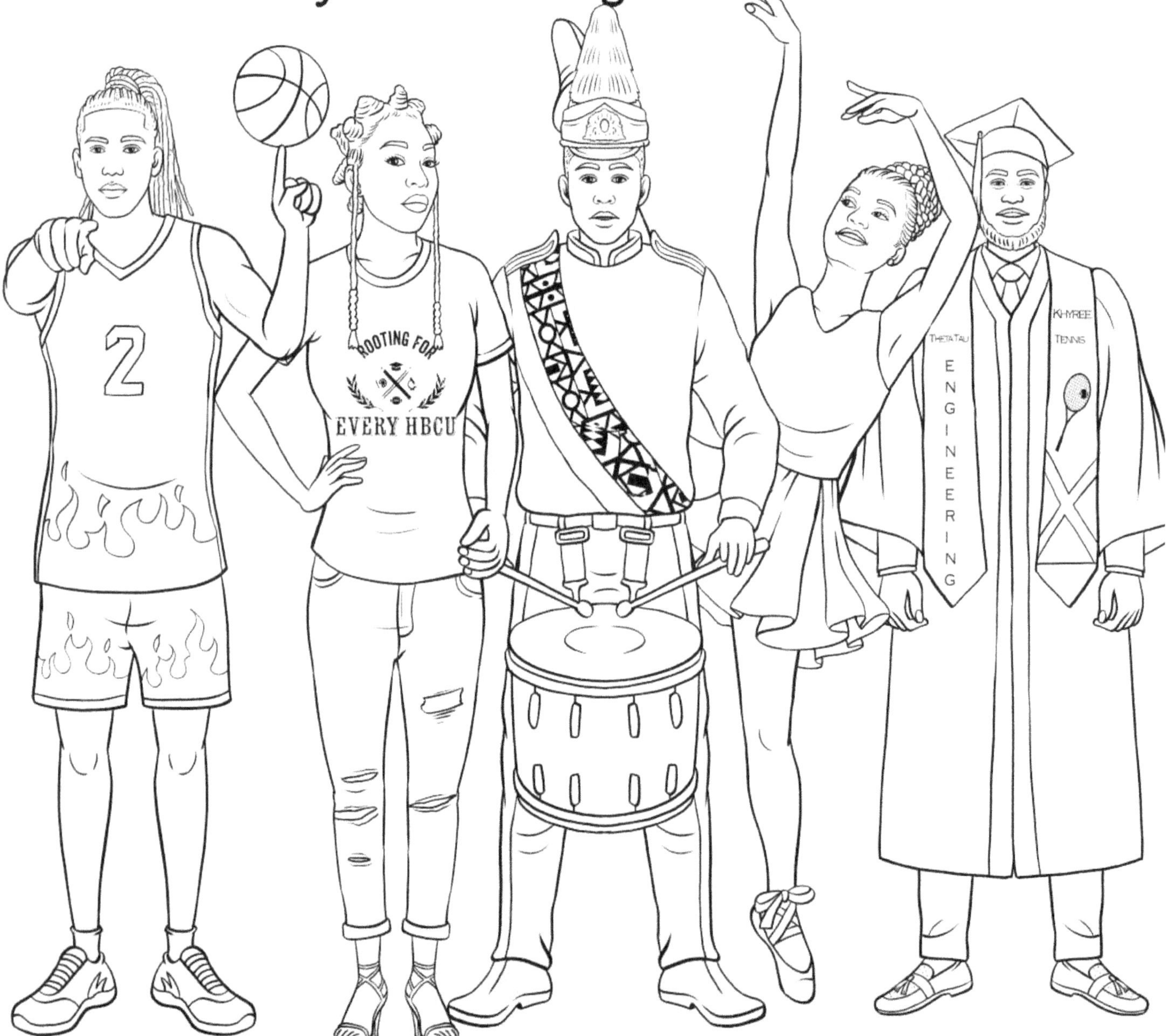

By Tiffany Heard

HBCU Facts Edition

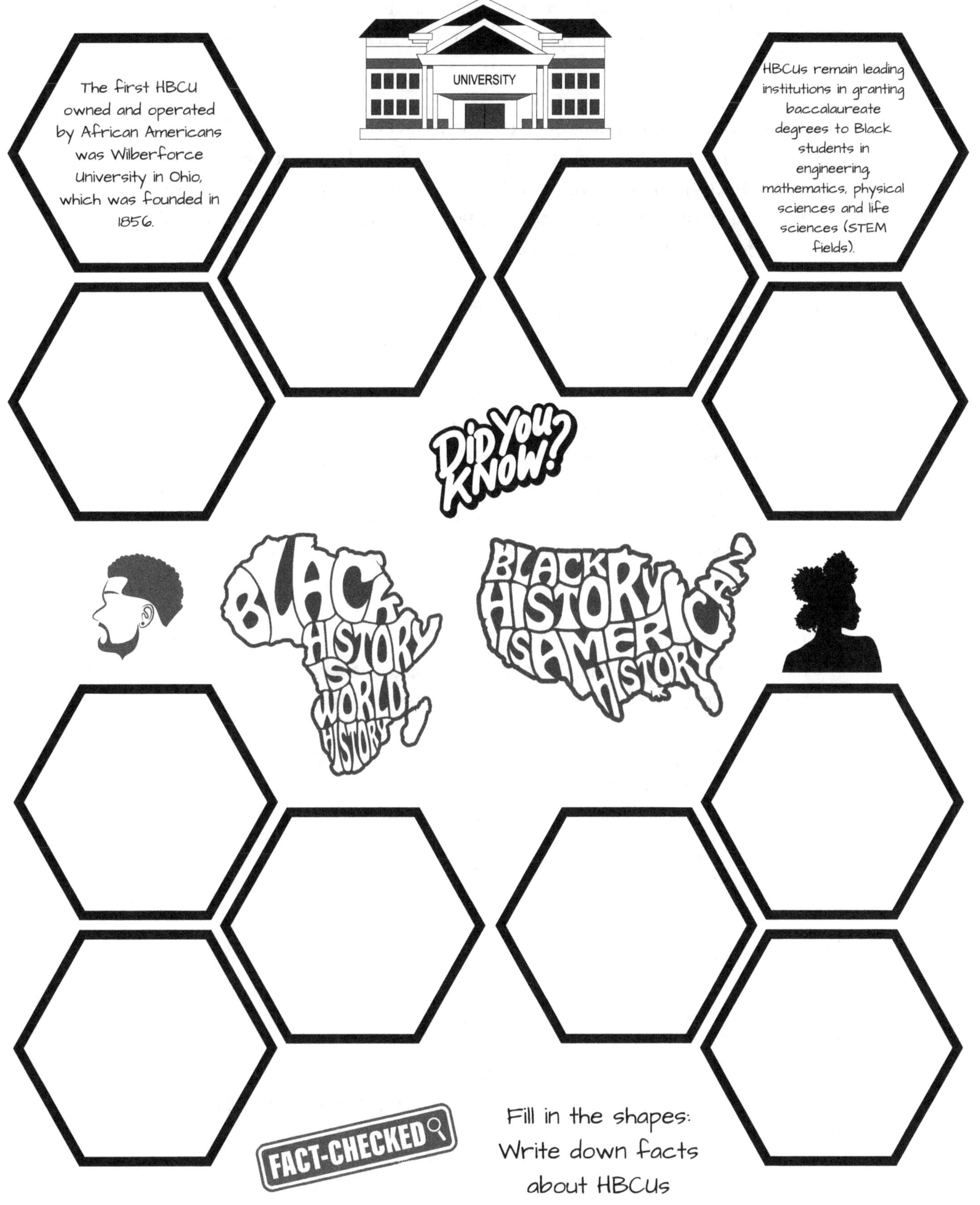

Fill in the shapes: Write down facts about HBCUs

Historically Black College and Universities (HBCUs)

Historically Black Colleges and Universities (HBCUs) are public and private institutions in the US that were established before the Civil Rights Act of 1964. Before the abolishment of slavery in 1865, African Americans were not allowed to learn how to read and write.

Many HBCUs were founded by Black churches, with the help of the American Missionary and Freedman's Bureau, after the Civil Rights War. However, there were several HBCUs founded before the Civil Rights War and they are: Cheyney University of Pennsylvania in 1837, University of the District of Columbia (then known as Miner School for Colored Girls) in 1851, Lincoln University in 1854 and Wilberforce in 1856.

During segregation, southern states prohibited Blacks from attending college. In other areas of the US, Black students were admitted, but the the number of Black students allowed was limited.

In 1862, the federal government issued the Morrill Act. The Morrill Act created land grant colleges that taught agriculture, military tactics and mechanics to the common person. It failed due to the South continuing to discriminate against Black students. However, in 1890, the Second Morrill Act was created and passed. This Act prohibited funding to states that discriminated against Black students. The Second Morrill Act allowed for 19 public Black colleges to be created.

The Higher Education of Act of 1965, defines an HBCU "as a school of higher learning that was accredited and established before 1964 and whose principle mission is to educate African Americans". As a result many many HBCU's were founded.

List the important events that happened in each year	Describe and discuss the following court decisions.
1837	Brown v. the Board of Education (1954)
1851	
1854	Adams v. Richardson (1972)
1856	
1862	
1865	United States v. Fordice (1992)
1890	
1965	

HBCU GEOGRAPHY

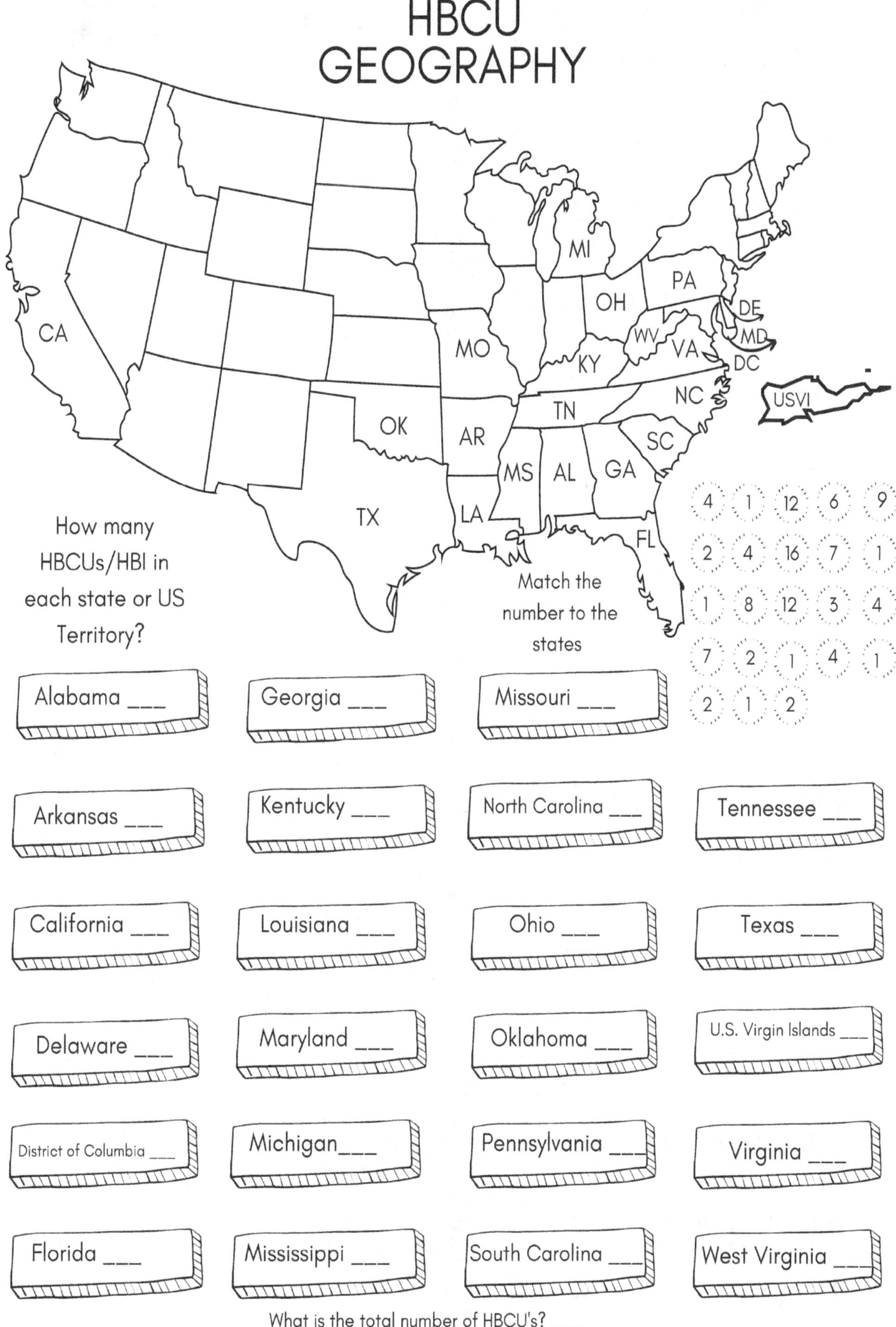

How many HBCUs/HBI in each state or US Territory?

Match the number to the states

Alabama ___

Georgia ___

Missouri ___

Arkansas ___

Kentucky ___

North Carolina ___

Tennessee ___

California ___

Louisiana ___

Ohio ___

Texas ___

Delaware ___

Maryland ___

Oklahoma ___

U.S. Virgin Islands ___

District of Columbia ___

Michigan ___

Pennsylvania ___

Virginia ___

Florida ___

Mississippi ___

South Carolina ___

West Virginia ___

What is the total number of HBCU's? ___

 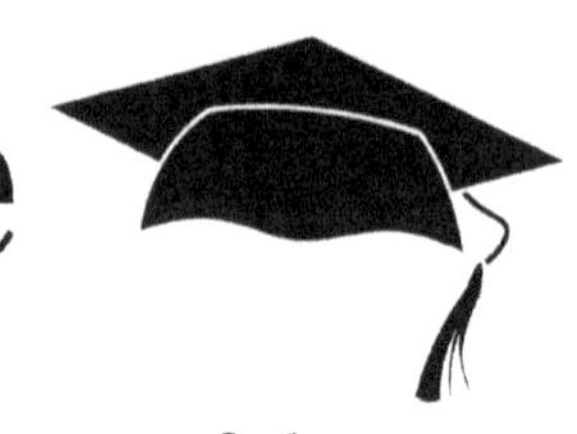

HBCU Timeline

1837 — Cheney University

1851 → University of the District of Colombia

1854 — Lincoln University

1856 → Wilberforce University

1856 — Payne Theological Seminary

1857 → Harris- Stowe State University

1862 — Lemoyne-Owen College

1865 → Bowie State University

1865 — Clark Atlanta University

1865 → Shaw University

1865 — Virginia Union University

1866 → Edwards Water College

1866 — Fisk University

1866 → Lincoln University of Missouri

1866 — Rust College

1867 → Barber Scotia College

1867 — Morehouse College

1867 → Howard University

1867 — Johnson C. Smith University

1867 → Morgan State University

1867 — St. Augustine's University

1867 → Alabama State University

1867 — Fayetteville State University

1867 → Talladega College

1868 — Hampton University

1869 → Clafin University

1869 — Dillard University

1869 → Simmons College

1869 — Tougaloo College

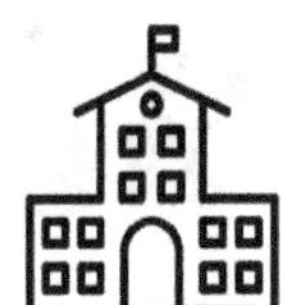 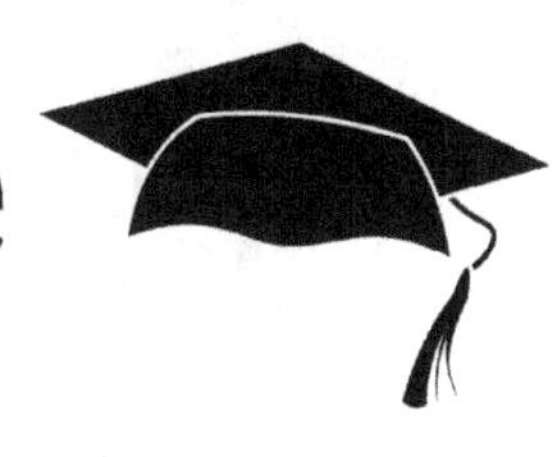

HBCU Timeline

HBCU Timeline

Left	Year		Year	Right
Shorter Collage	1886		1886	Virginia University of Lynchburg
Central State University	1887		1887	Florida A & M University
Savannah State University	1890		1891	Delaware State University
Elizabeth City State University	1891		1891	North Carolina A & T State University
West Virginia State University	1891		1892	Winston-Salem State University
Clinton College	1894		1894	Texas College
Bluefield State College	1895		1895	Fort Valley State University
Oakwood University	1896		1896	South Carolina State University
Langston University	1897		1897	Voorhees College
Miles College	1898		1898	St. Phillip's College
Coppin State University	1900		1901	Grambling State University
Albany State University	1903		1903	Hinds Community College at Utica
Bethune-Cookman University	1904		1908	Morris College
North Carolina Central University	1910		1912	Jarvis Christian College

HBCU Timeline

 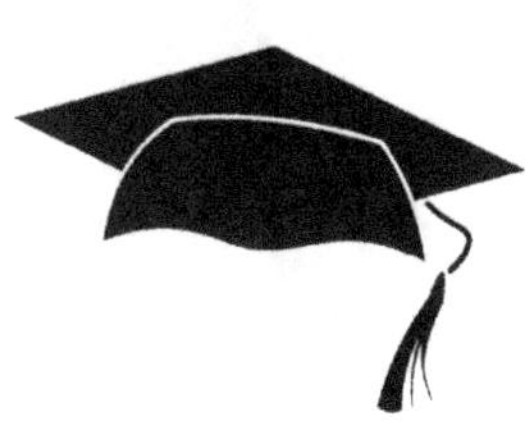

- 1912 — Tennessee State University
- 1915 — Xavier University of Louisiana
- 1924 — American Baptist College
- 1924 — Coahoma Community College
- 1925 — Gadsden State Community College
- 1927 — Bishop State Community College
- 1927 — Texas Southern
- 1947 — Denmark Technical College
- 1935 — Norfolk State University
- 1948 — Southwestern Christian College
- 1949 — Lawson State Community College
- 1950 — Mississippi Valley State University
- 1952 — Shelton State Community College
- 1958 — Interdenominational Theological Center
- 1959 — Southern University at New Orleans
- 1961 — J. F. Drake State Technological College
- 1962 — University of the Virgin Islands
- 1965 — Charles Drew University
- 1967 — Southern University at Shreveport
- 1975 — Morehouse School of Medicine

HBCU JEOPARDY

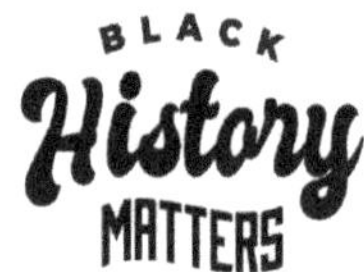   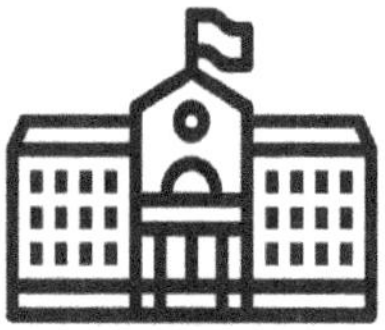 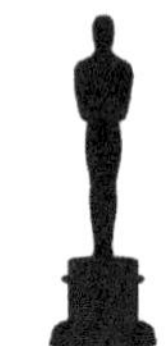

HBCU HISTORY	FRATERNITY SORORITY	MOVIES/ TV SHOWS	HBCU NAMES	FAMOUS PEOPLE
$100 IN 1890, FEDERAL GOV'T GRANTED THIS TO HBCU'S	**$100** IN 1906, FIRST GREEK FRATERNITY FOR AA MEN AT CORNELL UNIVERSITY	**$100** STUDENTS ON A FICTIONAL CAMPUS CALLED HILLMAN COLLEGE	**$100** IN 1837, THE OLDEST HBCU WAS FORMED IN PENNSYLVANIA	**$100** AMERICAN ACTOR AND PLAYWRIGHT WHO STARRED IN BLACK PANTHER
$200 1965, HBCU WAS OFFICIALLY DESIGNATED BY WHICH US DEPARTMENT?	**$200** GREATER SERVICE: GREATER PROGRESS IS THIS SORORITY'S MOTTO	**$200** DEPICTS MARCHING BANDS AND THEIR SIGNIFICANCE AT AN HBCU	**$200** PRIVATE ALL MALE LIBERAL ARTS COLLEGE IN GEORGIA	**$200** POET & PLAYWRIGHT WHO ATTENDED LINCOLN UNIVERSITY
$300 IN 1904, WHO OPENED UP A VOCATIONAL SCHOOL NAMED BETHUNE COOKMAN	**$300** FIRST SORORITY TO CHARTER A CHAPTER IN AFRICA	**$300** STUDENTS AT BLACK MISSION COLLEGE WHO ARE TRYING TO MAKE A IMPACT	**$300** THE ROMAN CATHOLIC CHURCH OPENED KATHARINE & SISTERS OF THE BLESSED SACRAMENT	**$300** ACTRESS WHO ATTENDED SPELMAN AND STARRED ON THE HUXTABLES
$400 THE FIRST HBCU SHAW WAS ESTABLISHED IN WHAT SOUTHERN STATE?	**$400** THIS FRATERNITY IS CONSTITUTIONALLY BOUND TO A SORORITY	**$400** TRUE STORY OF A DEBATE TEAM FROM WILEY COLLEGE	**$400** FOUNDED IN 1966 DUE TO INADEQUATE MEDICAL ACCESS TO WATTS, CA	**$400** GOSPEL SINGER WHO ATTENDED TEXAS SOUTHERN UNIVERSITY
$500 IN 2020, VIRGINIA STATE UNIVERSITY CREATED THIS COURSE	**$500** THIS FRATERNITY HAS A PROGRAM CALLED ISHIELD DESIGNED TO ADDRESS & END ABUSE	**$500** REALITY TV SHOW THAT FOLLOWED STUDENTS AROUND VARIOUS HBCU'S	**$500** IN 1962, THIS COLLEGE WAS CHARTERED ON ST. THOMAS	**$500** RAPPER WHO ATTENDED ALABAMA STATE UNIVERSITY ON A BASKETBALL SCHOLARSHIP

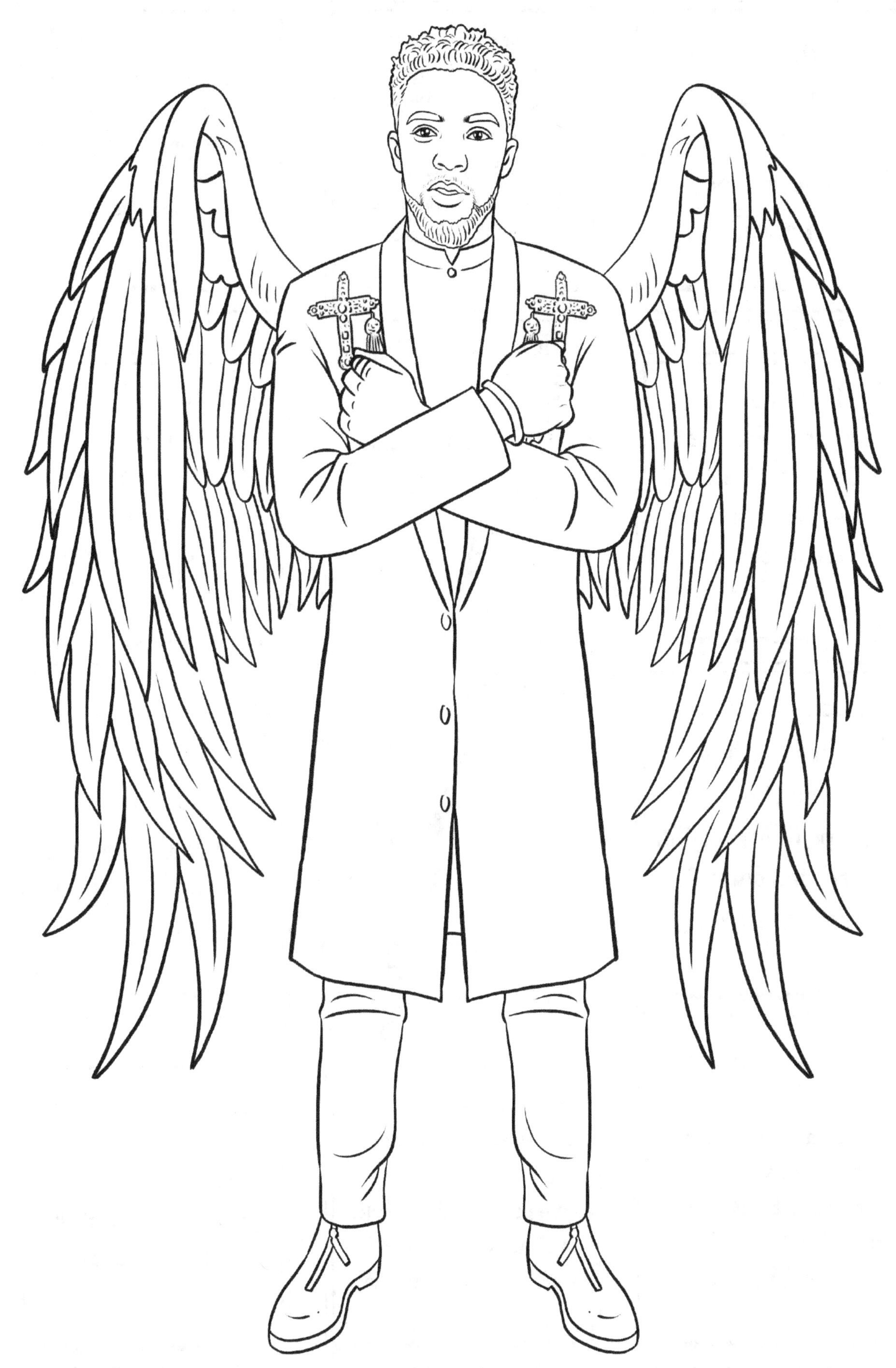

1 AAMU was founded in 1875 by a former slave named

____

2 First choir from an HBCU to be invited to the American Choral Festival in Germany & Alabama Music Educators Association Annual Conference

____

3 You will gain expertise in the areas of engineering, environmental, management, & economic fields of construction projects.

____

"Service is Sovereignty"

A

A   Alabama

1
8
7
5

Agricultural

M   Mechanical

U

University

4 If you have a career in Ecologist, Conservationist, Seed Scientist you have a degree in

____

5 Alumni who won the second season of American Idol and is known for his gospel album "I need an Angel"

____

6 This monthly subscription is in both print and digital form and given to students & alumni.

____

7 The athletic department created a fund to support student athletes

____

8 Freshmen dorm named after a distinguished woman who worked as a professor & residence counselor for AAMU for over 35 years.

____

9 Formed in 1890, they are better known as "Show band of the South" and have performed at events such as the Rose Bowl & Independence Parade

____

10 This minor prepares students in the area of spatial analysis, geospatial technology, and computerized mapping.

____

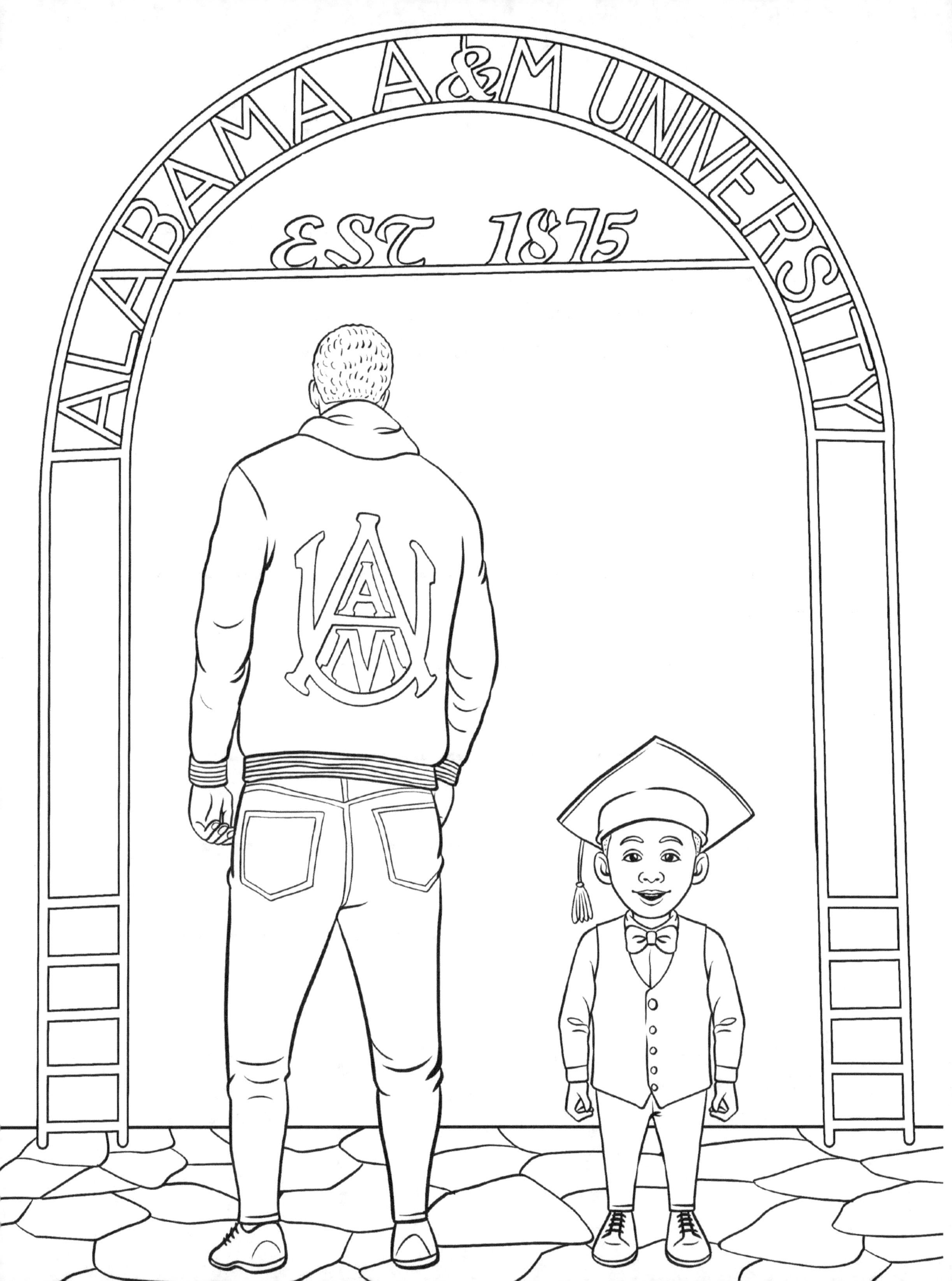

ALABAMA A&M UNIVERSITY
EST 1875

Alabama State University

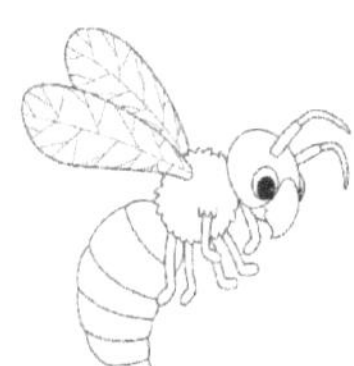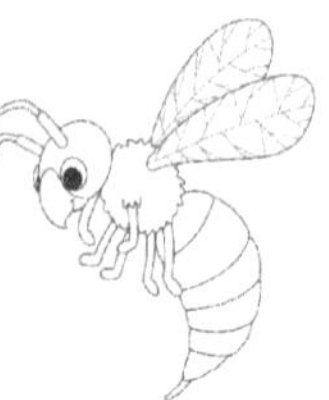

Marion 9: The school was founded by 9 freed slaves whose goal was to build a school for African Americans. ASU was formally known as Lincoln Normal School in Marion, Alabama. In 1887, the school moved to Montgomery, Alabama and evolved from a junior college to a 4 year university.

Directions: Write a letter to the ancestors & answer the following questions below.

Dear

Signed

Name the Alumni: Comedian, TV host, actor & Radio Personality

Name the Plus Size dance team

Which major studies Musculoskeletal Abnormalities?

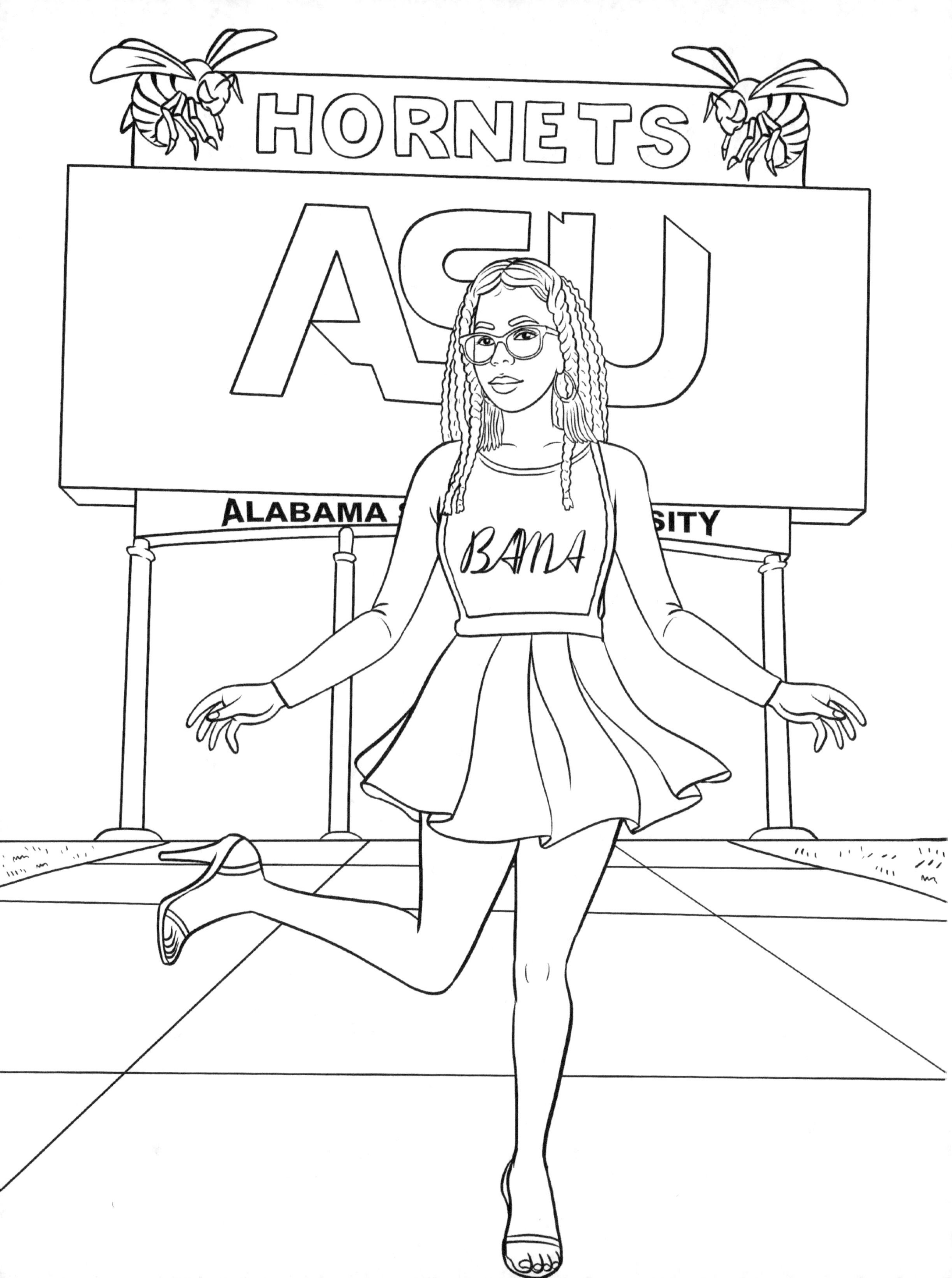

HORNETS
ASU
ALABAMA STATE UNIVERSITY
BAMA

Albany State University

1903

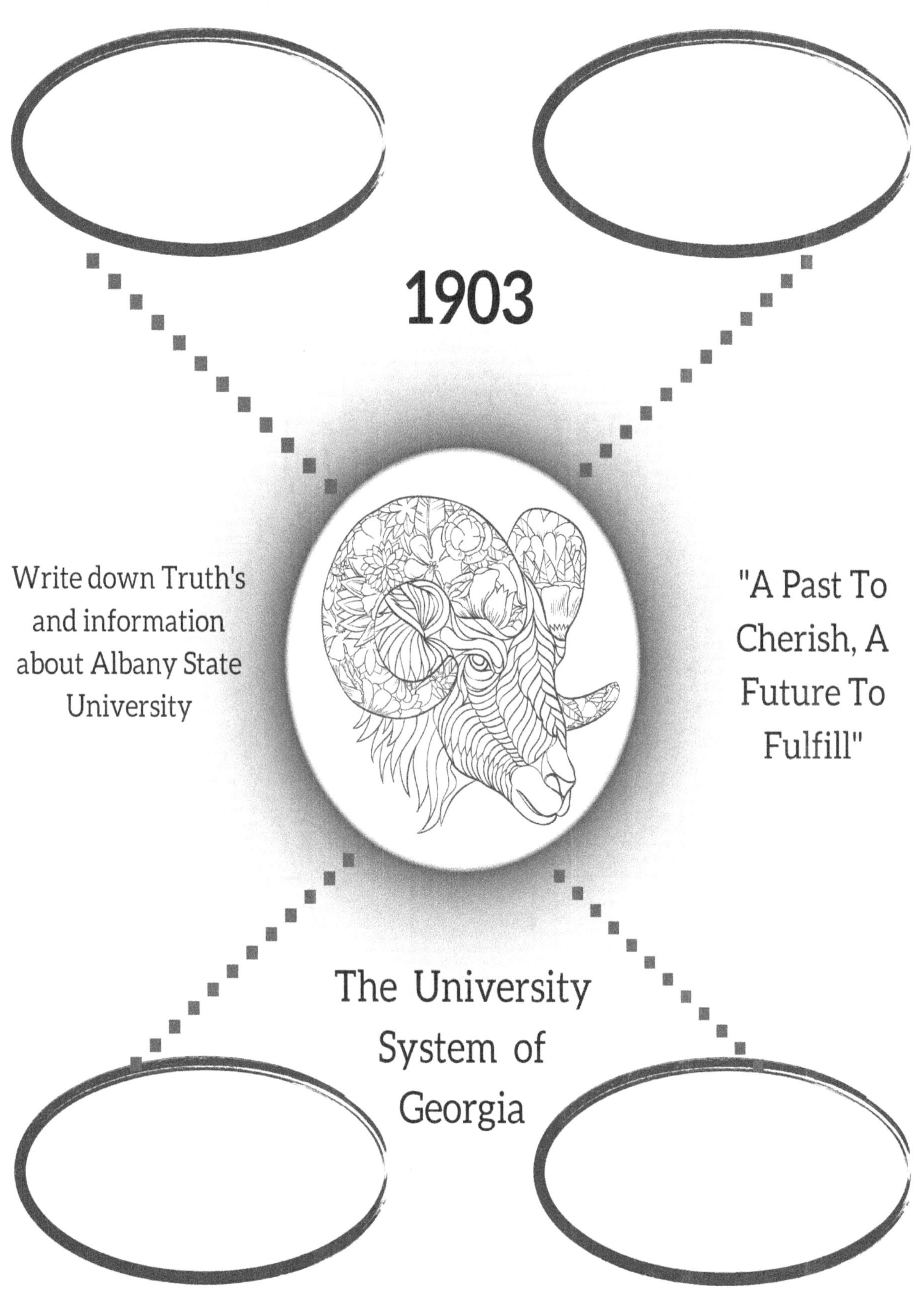

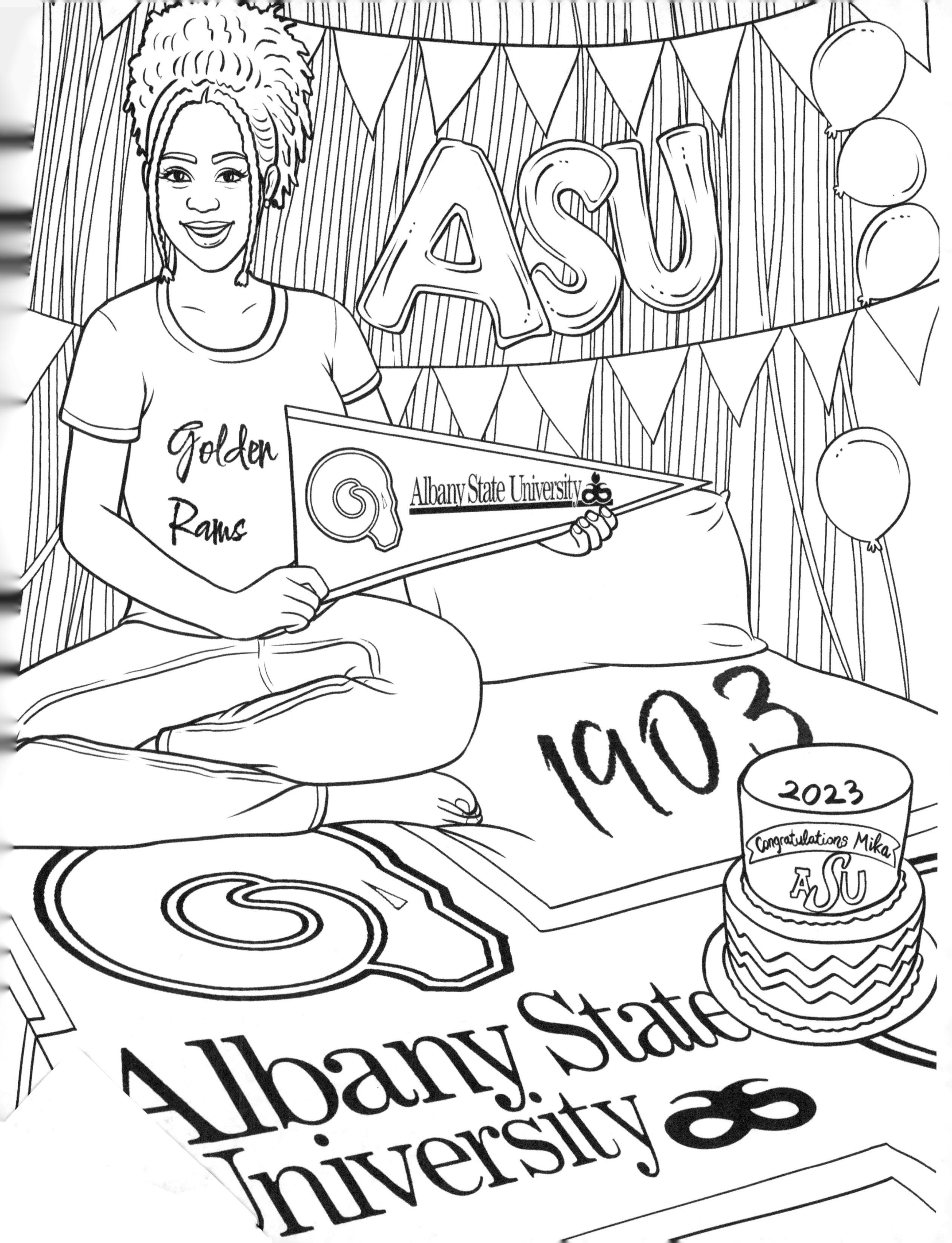

ASU
Golden Rams
Albany State University
1903
2023
Congratulations Mika
ASU
Albany State University

Alcorn State University

MRAEERVHILS

FEARSRM

REEARMEDVSG

EHLAYEALX

ONGNACTICU

ISUNSBES

NREEITCARO

NTMEYODI

NESEMBLE

LIAYRITM

RYMAOGNO

IMCSU

TWEDRSRLA

SUCEAUSNBAEBTS

First president of Alcorn & 1st African American to be sworn in by the US Congress in 1870.

Socially Disadvantaged ____________ and Ranchers Policy Research Center

American Civil Rights Activist in Mississippi

Writer & Author of *Roots* and *The Autobiography of Malcolm X*

The baccalaureate program provides studies in the area of financial services.

The Women's ____________ Center assists entrepreneurs and owners at various stages of development.

This major curriculum prepares students to teach or coach & learns how the body reacts to disease and exercise.

The marching band has played in arenas around the world including performing for President Carter.

The Jazz ____________ was created to allow performance exposure to African American related music.

________ Science: Students will be able to expand both leadership skills & character through Army ROTC.

Masters of Science in Agriculture. The ______ program prepares students to address issues associated with crop production.

This degree will allow students to become efficient ______ educators through the theory of application.

OBGYN and founder of 50 Shades of Pink Foundation

__________ __________ Prevention Program is designed to decrease the problems related to alcohol, tobacco & other drugs use and abuse.

Alcorn State University Motto

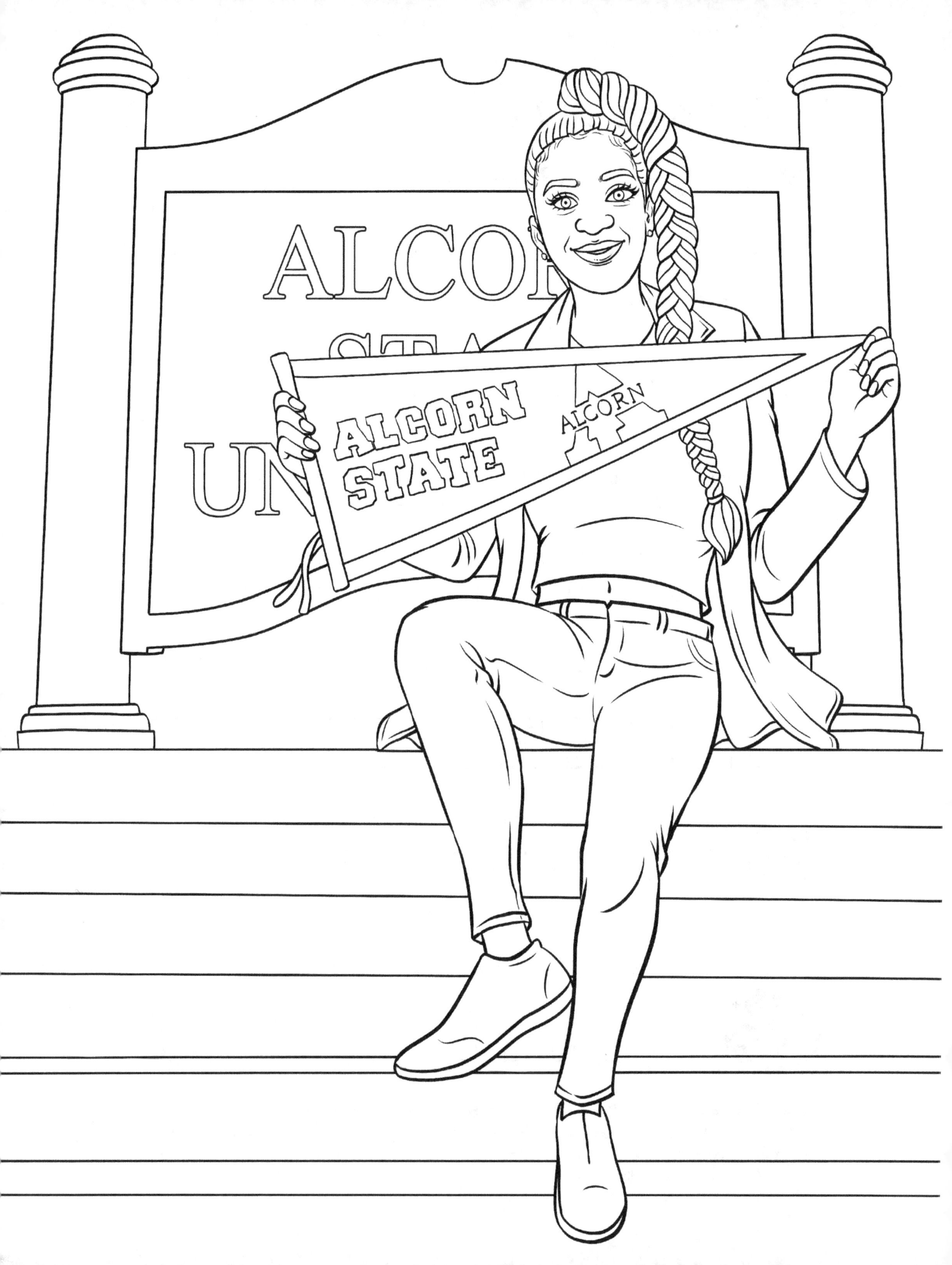

ALCORN
STATE
UNI
ALCORN
STATE
ALCORN

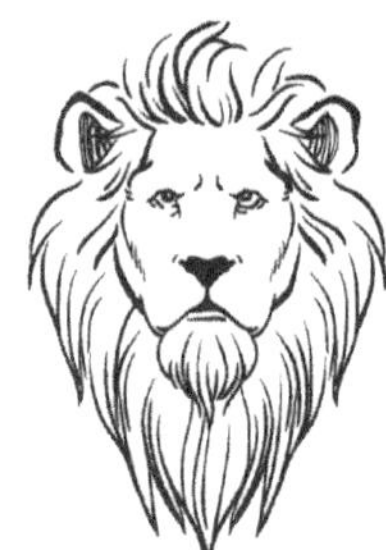

University of Arkansas
At Pine Bluff

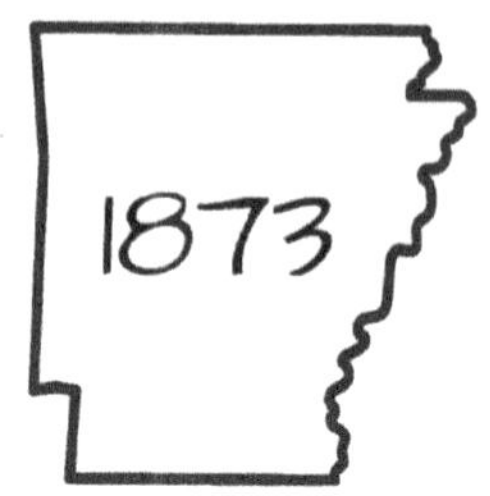

Decode the messages to find interesting facts about University of Arkansas at Pine Bluff.

The department only offers M.S. & PHD in _________ &
fisheries in Arkansas.

A _ _ _ _ _ _ C _ _ _ L _ _ _ E

University _______ and Cultural Center houses the Keepers of the Spirit: The
L.A. Davis Historical Collection which showcases the history of the College.

_ _ _ _ S _ _ _ M

Find out about the latest event in the student run newspaper.

_ _ _ _ _ _ _ _ N _ _ _ _ _ _ _ _ R

_______ Norful graduated with a Bachelors degree in
History & is now a Grammy award winning gospel singer.

_ _ _ _ _ _ K _ _ _ _

The ____Academy prepares students for a global scientific workforce.

_ _ _ _ M

UAPB was founded in 1873 in Pine Bluff Arkansas. It is the state's oldest HBCU and part of the land grant act of 1890. The aquaculture and fisheries supports Arkansas $165 million baitfish industry. UAPB offers the only undergraduate degree in regulatory science which prepares students for careers with the US Department of Agriculture. One of their goals is to increase STEM graduates to work in STEM disciplines.

**B
E
N
E
D
I
C
T**

Directions: Use the words from below to complete the sentences

South Carolina	Big House	Benedict College
Bathsheba Benedict	Preachers	Band of Distinction
Freed Slaves	Rev. John J. Starks	Dr. Rosyln Clark Artis

Benedict is located in Columbia, _____ _____

In 1870, Benedict College was founded by a white women named _____

The school was founded for newly _____ _____ of African descent by northern religious mission societies.

Classes were first held in the _____ _____ aka formers masters mansion.

On November 2, 1894 Benedict Institute was changed to _____ _____

In 1891, _____ earned his bachelor's degree from the college, in 1930 he became the first Black president of the school.

In June 2017, _____ was appointed as the 14th and first female president.

The school was intended for _____ and Teachers. It included subjects such as: grammar, reading, writing, math and religion.

Benedicts Marching Tigers are known as the " _____ _____ _____ "

**C
O
L
L
E
G
E**

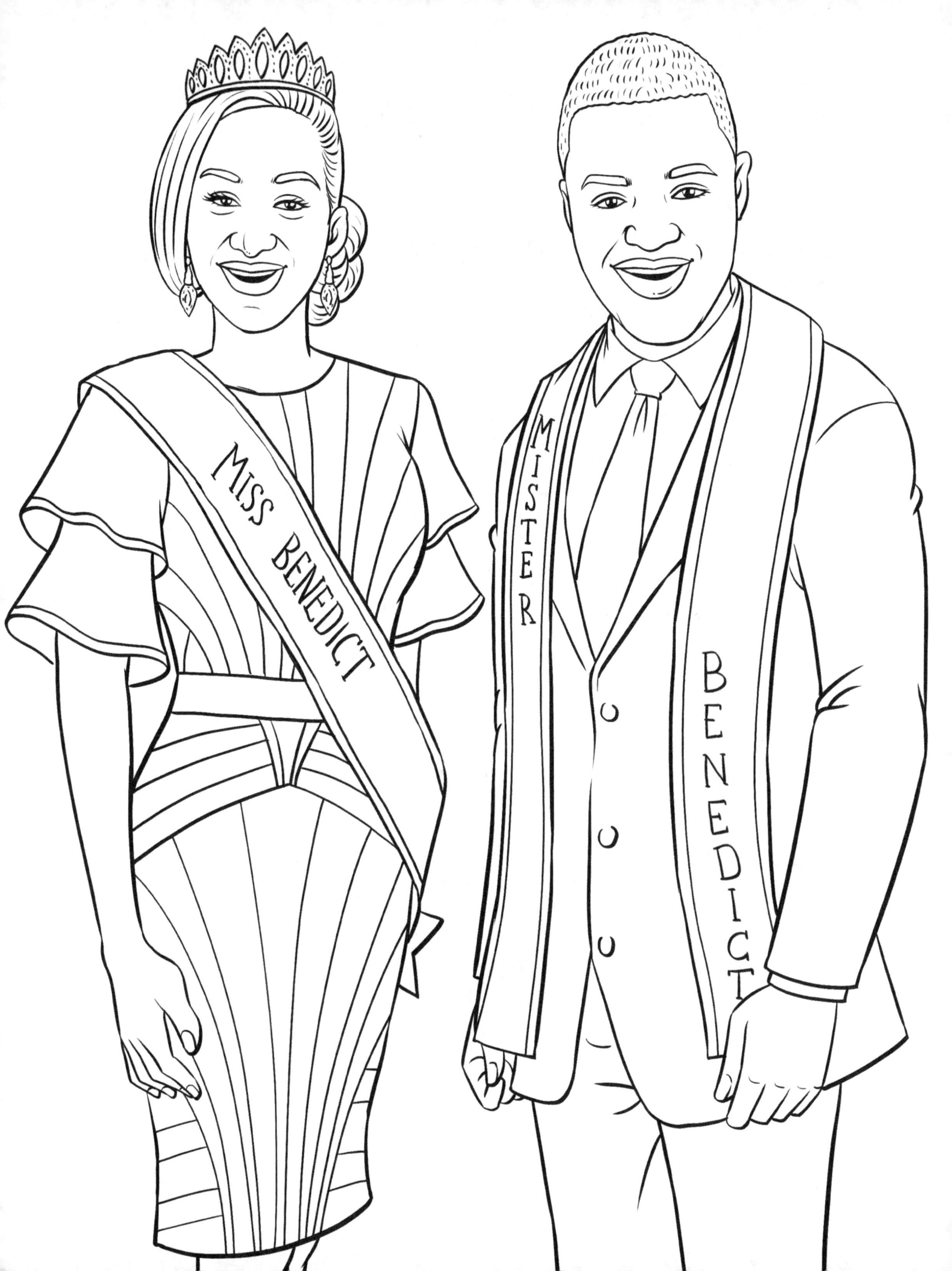

MISS BENEDICT
MISTER
BENEDICT

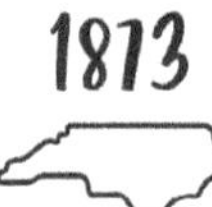

1873

Bennett College

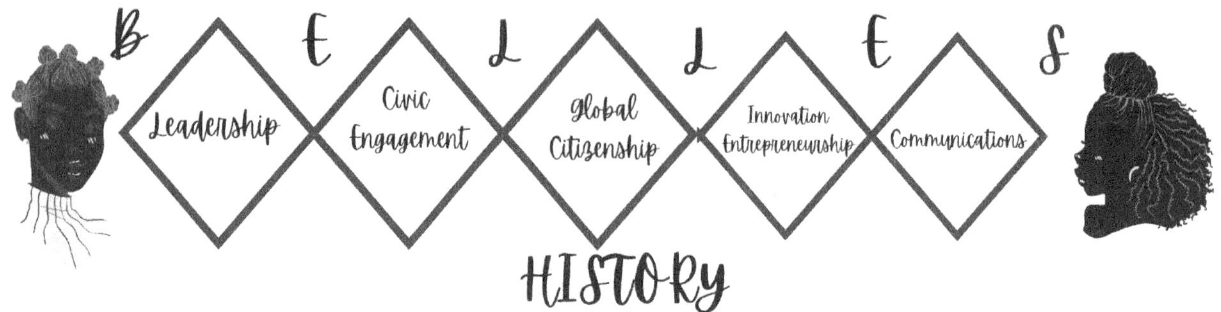

HISTORY

In 1873, Bennett College was started in the basement of a Methodist Episcopal Church. It initially began with both men and woman who studied elementary and secondary classes. Within 5 years, a group of freed slaves purchased what is now the present day school. In 1926, Bennet College became an all women's school with the help of the Women's Home Missionary Society & Board of Education Church.

Create a Mini

Name of Business :

Business Plan

Describe your Business: Is it a product or service

What is your 5 year plan and income projection?

Did you know?

Bennett College has the Women's Business Center of Greensboro

Who is your Target audience? .

Competitive Analysis: Identify 5 competitors

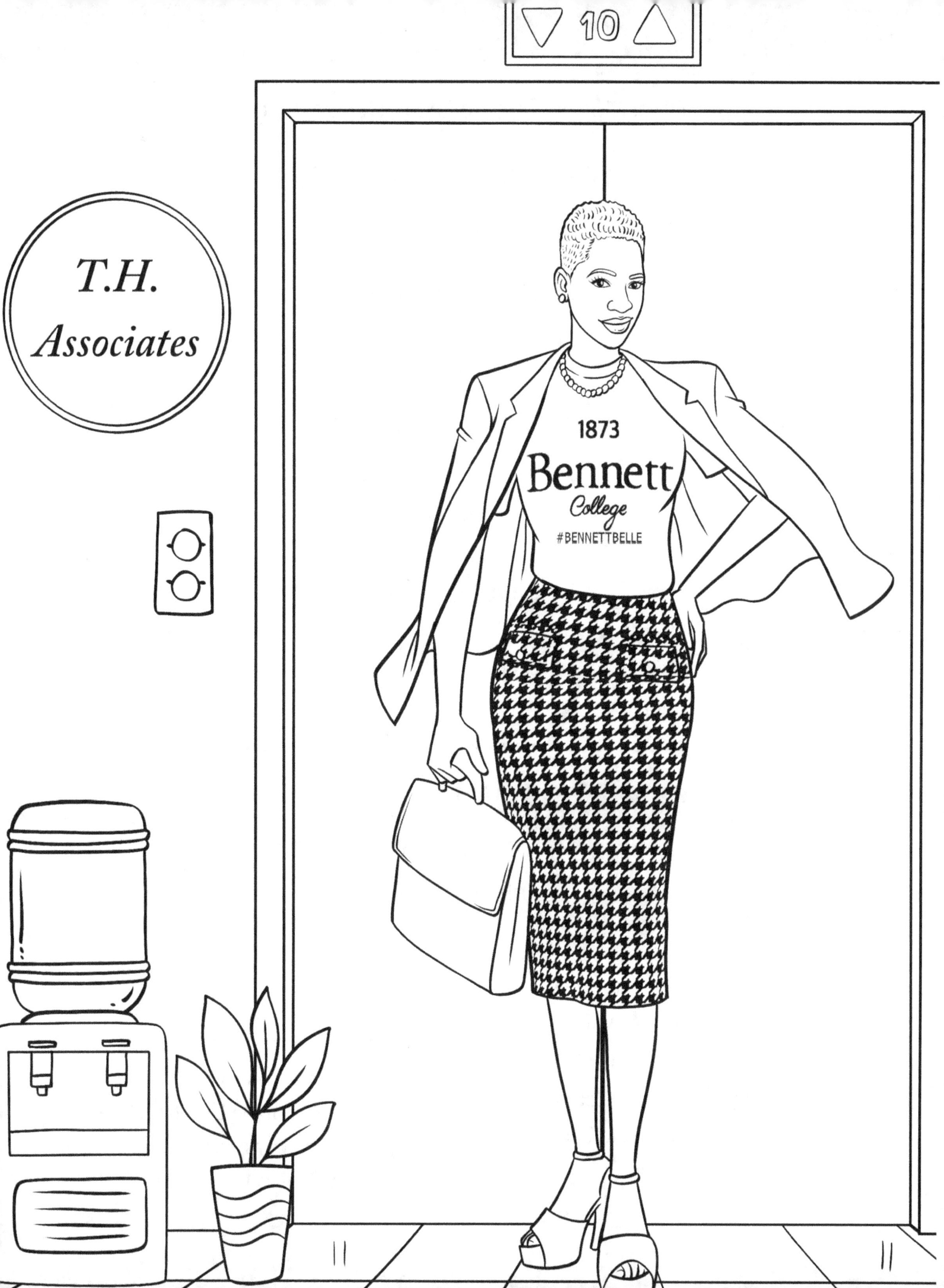

10
T.H.
Associates
1873
Bennett
College
#BENNETTBELLE

Fantasy or Reality

Write F or R under each phrase

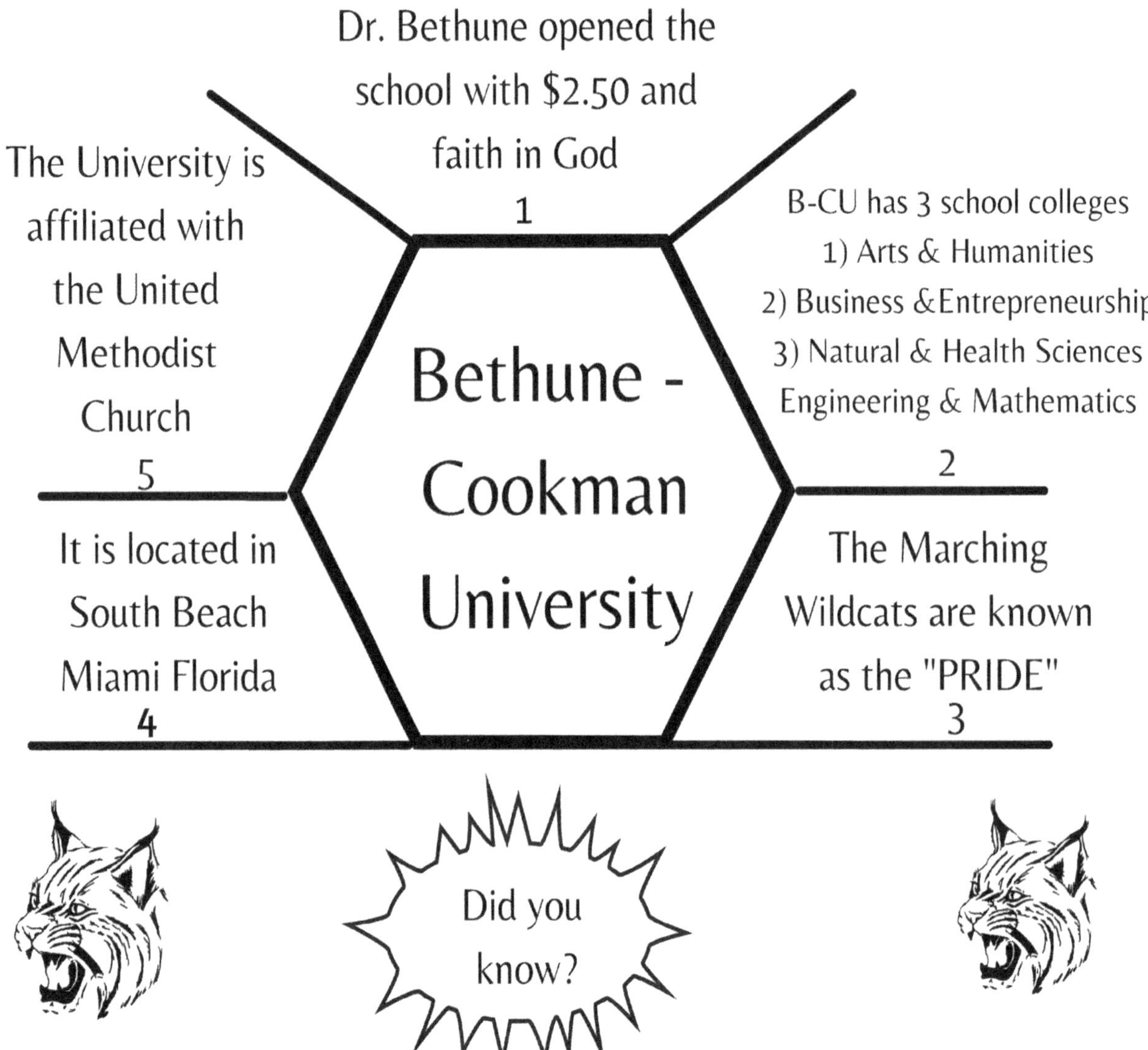

On October 3, 1904 Mary McLeod Bethune opened the Daytona Literary and Industrial Training Schools for Negro Girls, now known as Bethune Cookman University.

Ms. Bethune played a role in the Civil Rights Movement. She founded the National Council of Negro Women, Mary McLeod Hospital & Training Schools for Nurses, Co founder of the United College Negro Fund and was an advisor to Presidents Roosevelt & Truman.

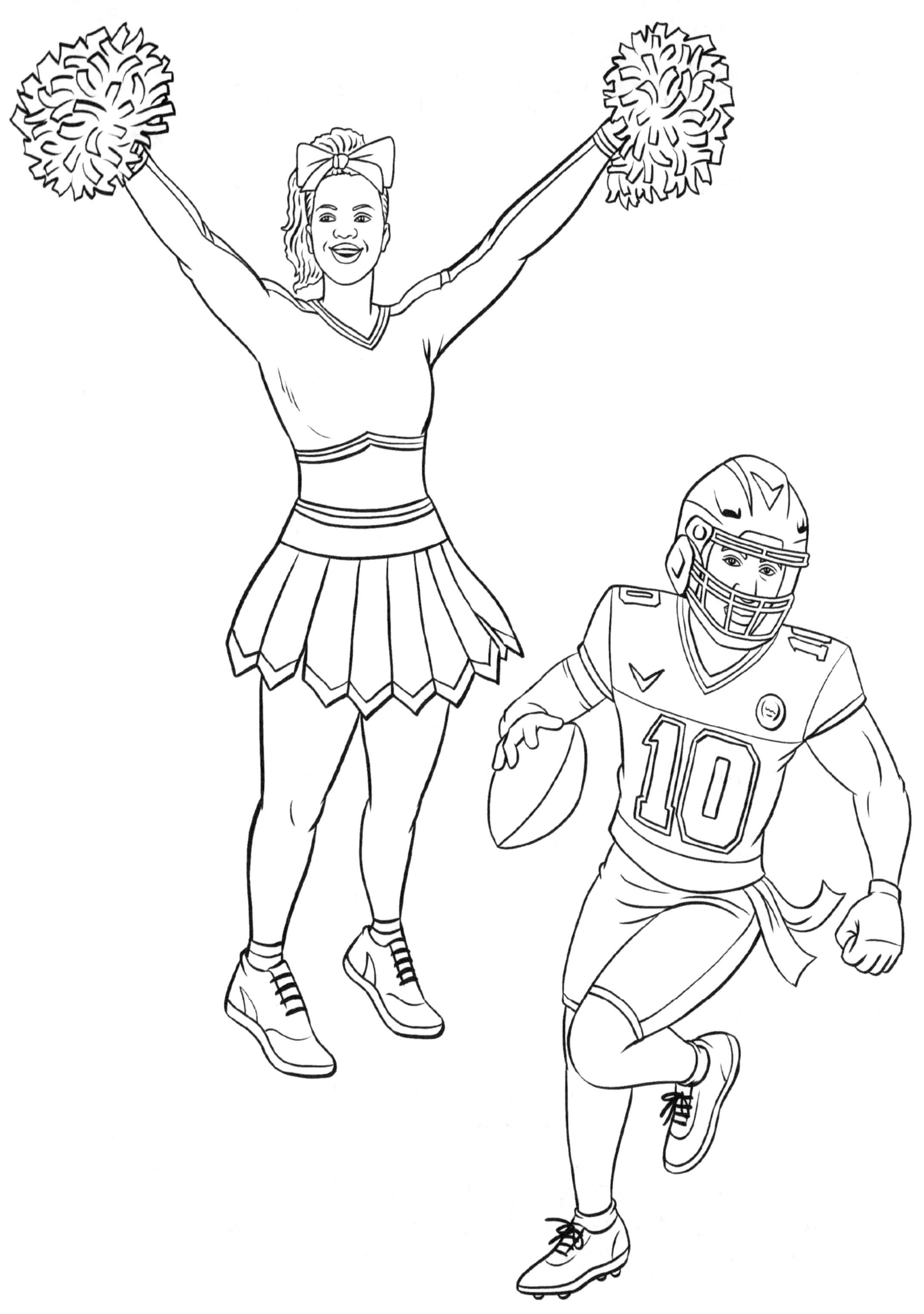

"Aye Aye Bowie" # Bowie State University 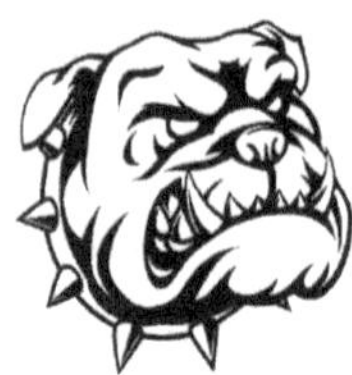

Directions: Match the word to the corresponding History Facts

1 Maryland

A First historically Black public university

2 Social Work

B In 1988, Bowie State College becomes

3 Michelle Obama

C In 1995, Bowie won an 11 year $27 million award

4 Master of Education

D She was the first elected female president in 2017

5 Beatrice Pitts Payne

E Bowie has a military resource center and known as

6 Dr. Aminta H. Breaux

F In 1929, the Alma Mater song was written and published by

7 Charlotte B. Robinson

G Oldest living alumna: In 1928 she graduated Bowie Normal School

8 Bowie State University

H In May 2013, this previous first lady was the commencement speaker

9 Military Friendly School

I In 1969, this program began with 600 students & continues to thrive

10 National Science Foundation/NASA

J First graduate program was offered under president Samuel Myers

New Beginnings

In 1864, 46 men of various backgrounds established The Baltimore Association for the Moral and Educational Improvement of the Colored People. The goal was to provide schools for those who were recently emancipated from slavery. On January 9, 1865, the first Baltimore school was opened. Many years and several locations later, it is now knows as Bowie State University .

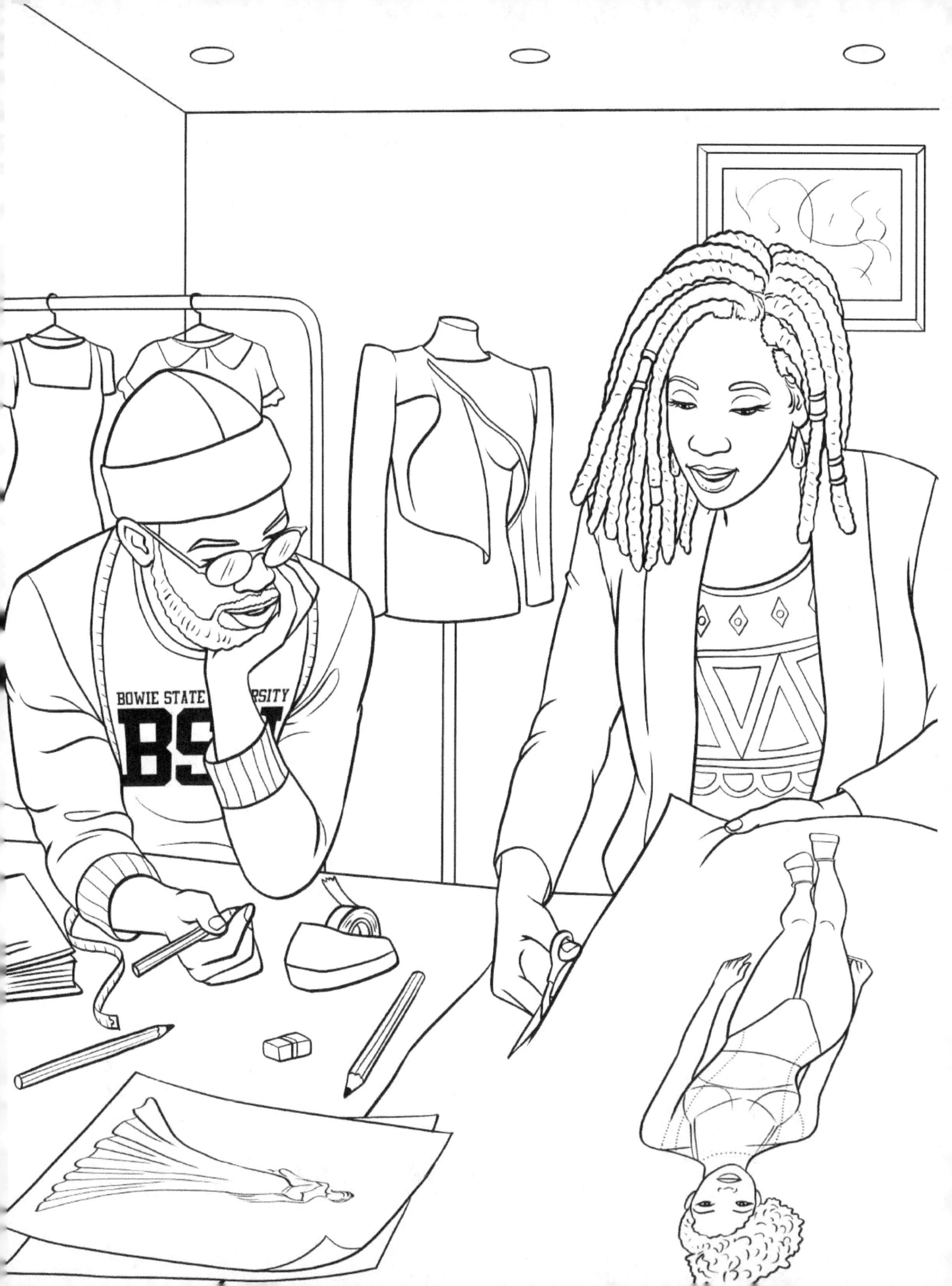

BOWIE STATE UNIVERSITY
BSU

Central State University

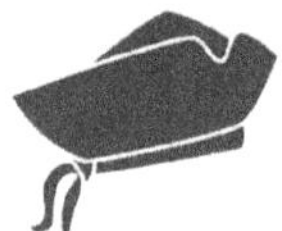 Lets explore the **CSU** campus using our 5 senses. 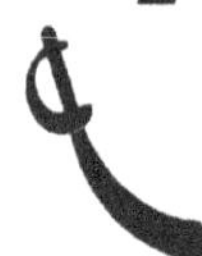

5 things you can 👁 SEE

____

____

____

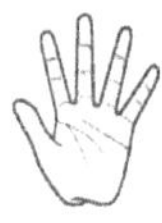 McPherson Memorial Stadium
____

4 things you can HEAR

Invicible Marching Marauders

____

____

3 things you can ✋ FEEL

....

....

....

2 things you can 👃 SMELL

....

....

1 thing you can 👅 TASTE

Engaging Communities and Transforming Lives!

1887

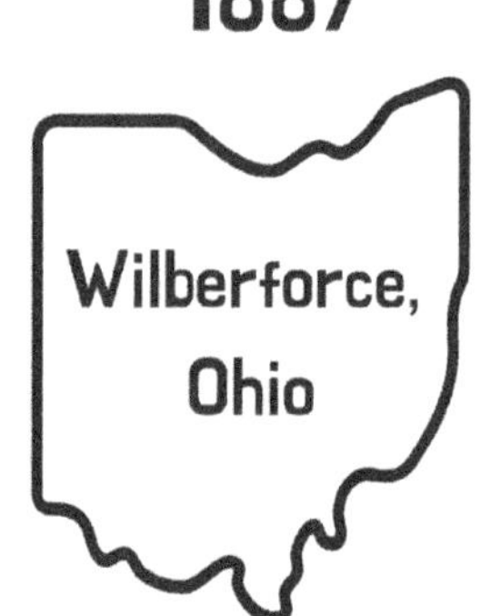

Wilberforce, Ohio

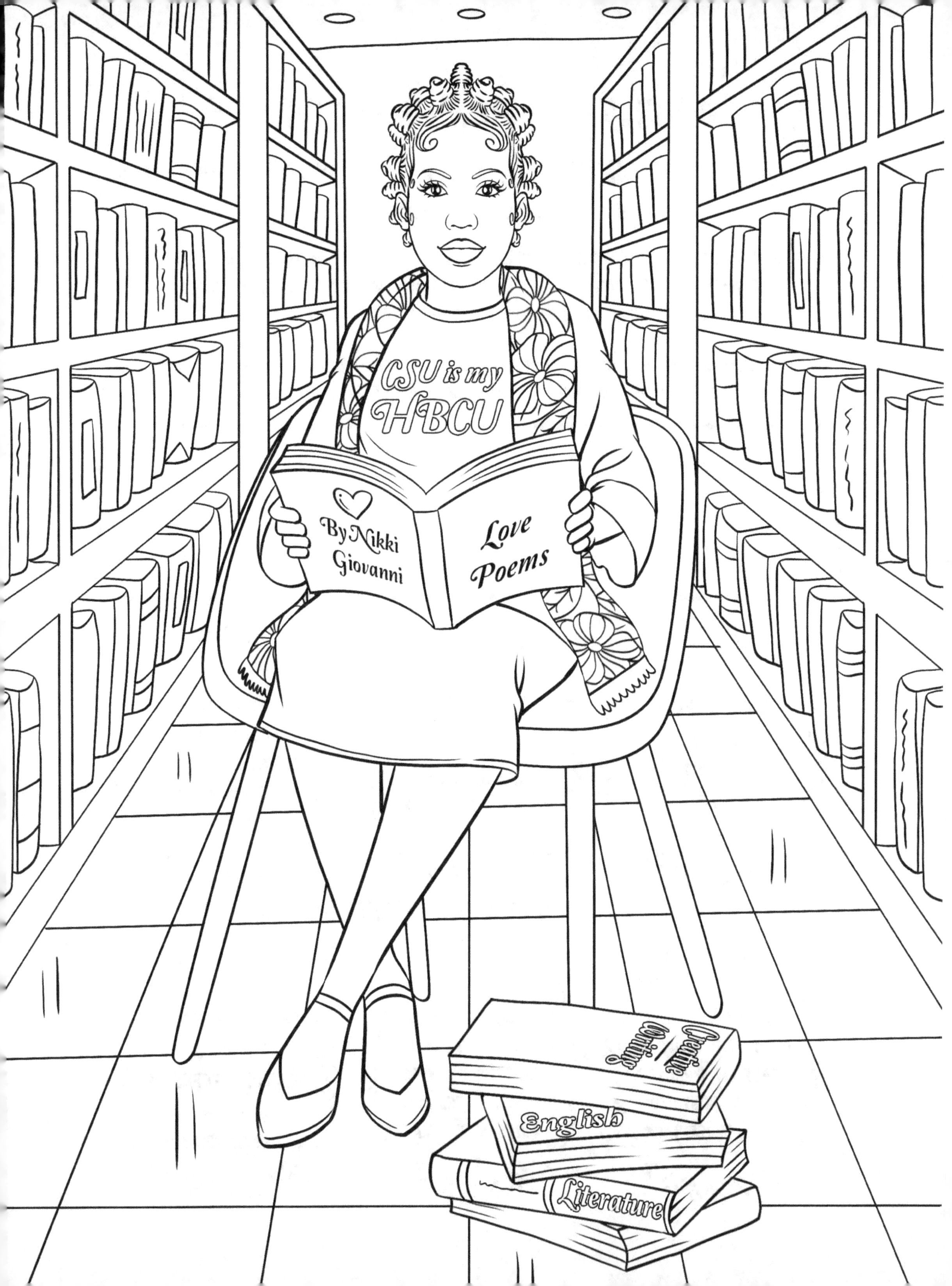

CSU is my HBCU
By Nikki Giovanni
Love Poems
Creative Writing
English
Literature

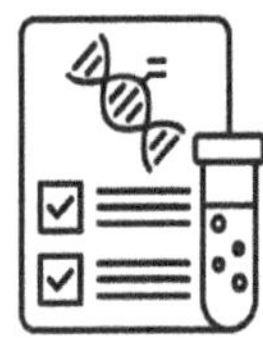
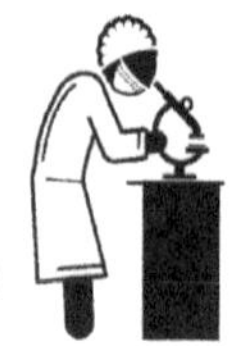

CHARLES R. DREW UNIVERSITY OF
COMPTON MEDICINE AND SCIENCE CALIFORNIA

HISTORICALLY BLACK GRADUATE INSTITUTION

CDU IS DEDICATED TO CULTIVATING EMERGING HEALTH LEADERS THAT ARE FOCUSED ON HEALTH EQUITY AND SOCIAL JUSTICE. HEALTH DISPARITIES SUCH AS DIABETES, CANCER, HIV/AIDS AND CARDIOMETABOLIC IS THE FOCAL POINT OF EDUCATION & TRAINING.

SCENARIO: YOU ARE A GRADUATE STUDENT. CHOOSE A HEALTH DISPARITY TOPIC & DISCUSS WHY YOUR COMMUNITY WOULD BENEFIT FROM FURTHER RESEARCH

BORN: JUNE 3, 1904 IN WASHINGTON, D.C

AT FREEDMAN HOSPITAL HE WAS A SURGERY INSTRUCTOR & ASSISTANT SURGEON

DR. DREW EARNED A DOCTORATE OF SCIENCE IN SURGERY AT COLUMBIA UNIVERSITY

BRIEF FACTS ABOUT DR. CHARLES R. DREW

COMPLETED A THESIS ON "BANKED BLOOD" & APPOINTED DIRECTOR OF THE FIRST RED CROSS BLOOD BANK

BECAME THE MEDICAL DIRECTOR OF BLOOD FOR BRITAIN PROJECT WHERE THEY COLLECTED 14,500 PINTS OF PLASMA

FROM 1942-1950, HE SERVED AS A MEDICINE PROFESSOR AT HOWARD UNIVERSITY

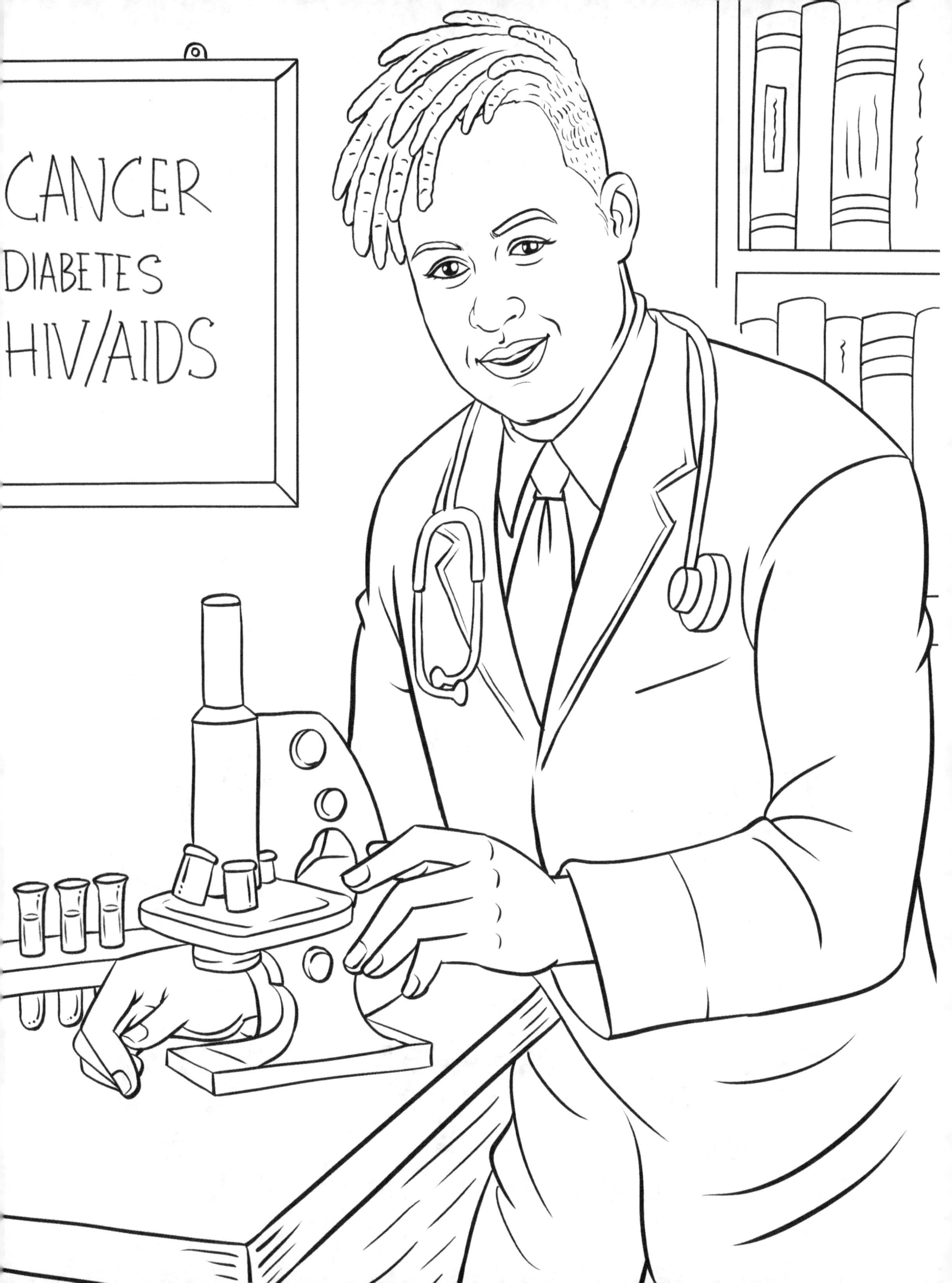

CANCER
DIABETES
HIV/AIDS

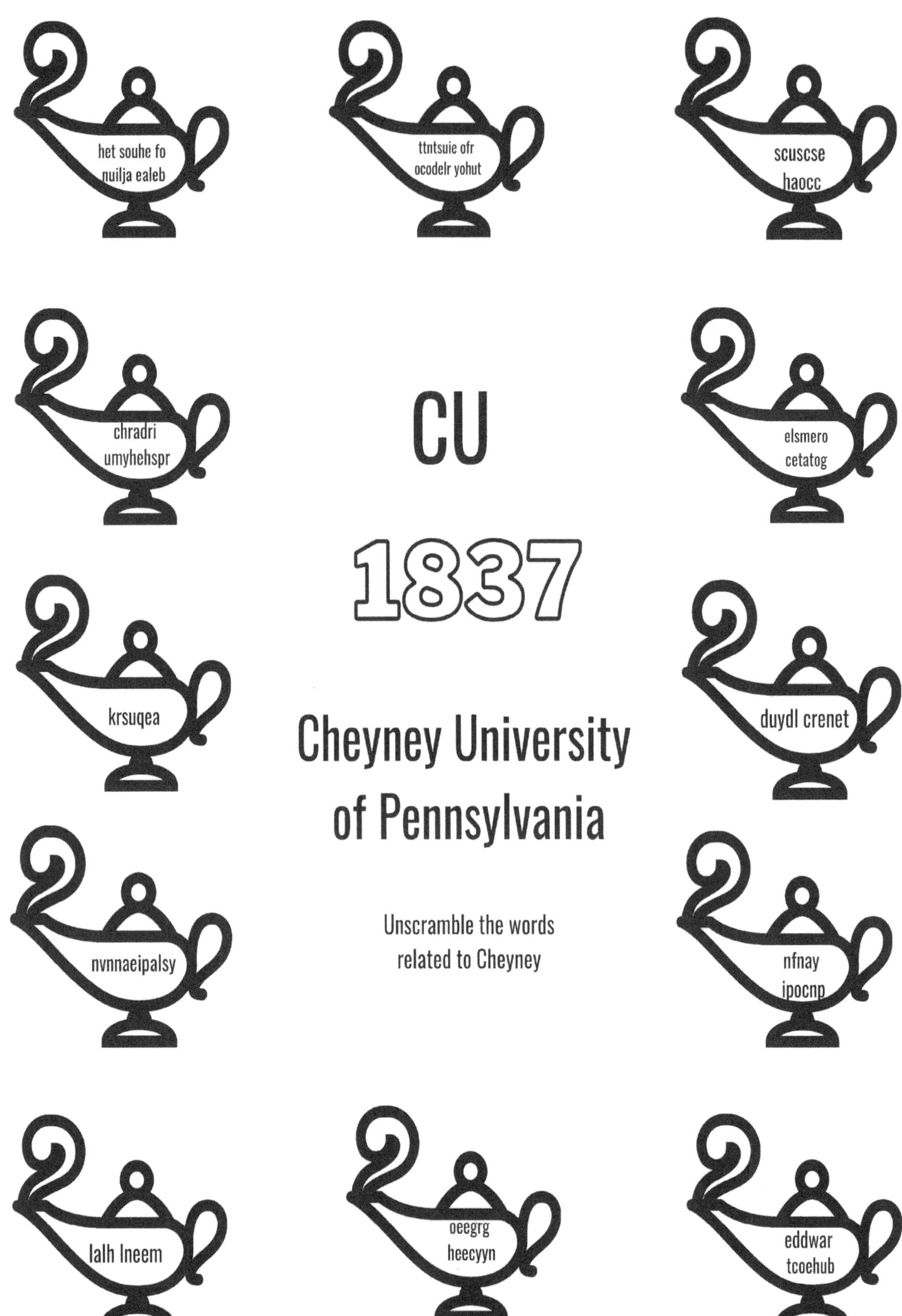

Cheney University is the nations oldest HBCU

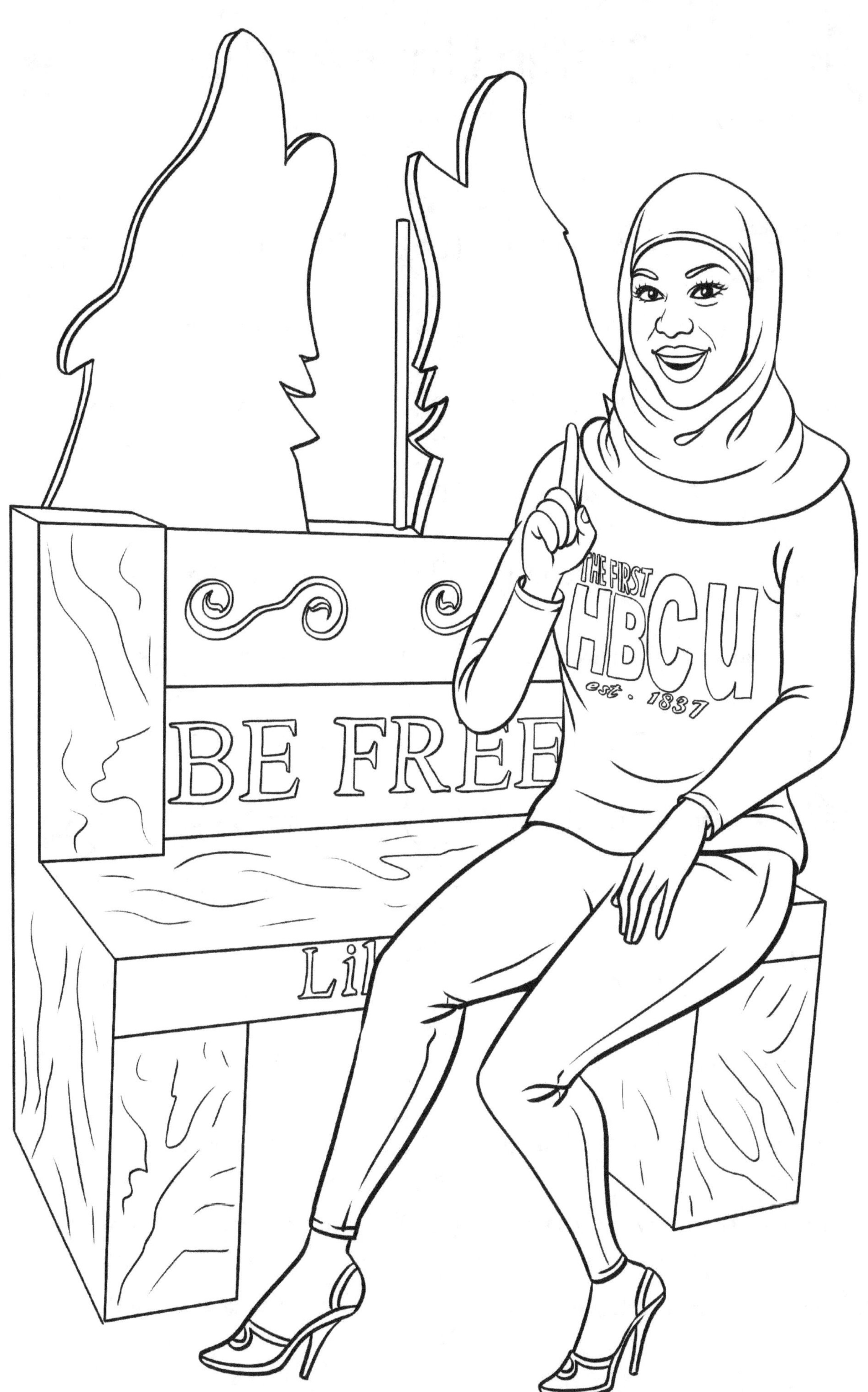
BE FREE
THE FIRST
HBCU
est. 1837
Lil

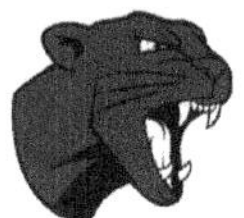 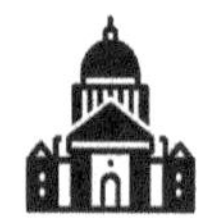

Claflin University

In 1869, Claflin University was founded in South Carolina and was known to accept every one regardless of race.

This

That

Asbury Hall	OR	High Rise
Internships	OR	Cooperative Education
Jazz Ensemble	OR	Lyric Theater
Faculty Exchange	OR	Study Abroad
Studio Art	OR	Philosophy & Religion
Business Administration	OR	Marketing
Trio Program	OR	Student Freedom Initiative
Panther Track & Field	OR	Panther Softball
Bioinformatics	OR	RN to BSN in Nursing
Sport Management	OR	Middle Level of Education
Community Service & Research	OR	Nurture & Fellowship
MS Biotechnology: Climate Change	OR	MS in Criminal Justice
Research related to removing Chromium-6	OR	Use Water Bottle Filtration System
Research Initiative for Scientific Enhancement	OR	Upward Bound Math & Science

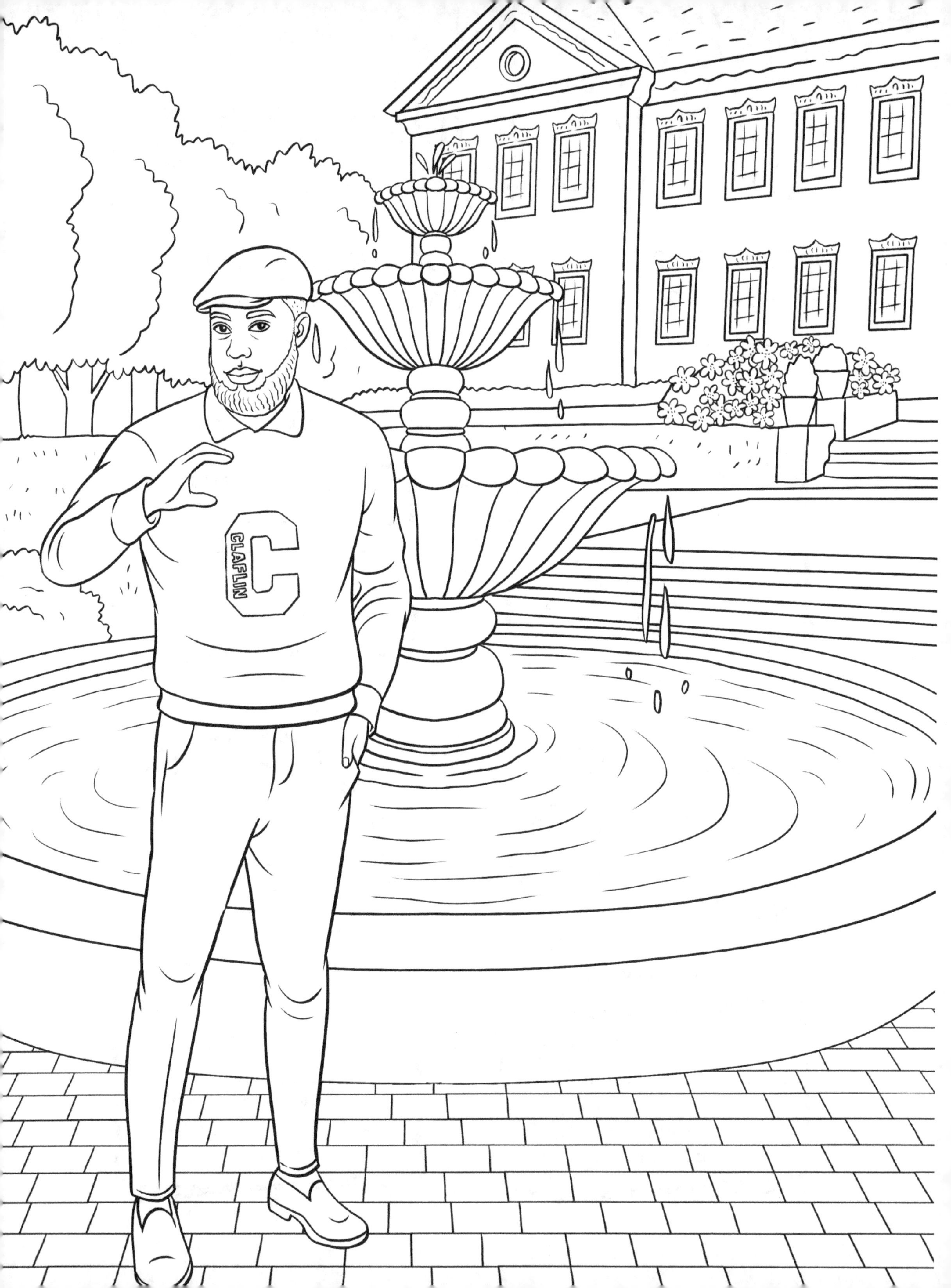

CLAFLIN

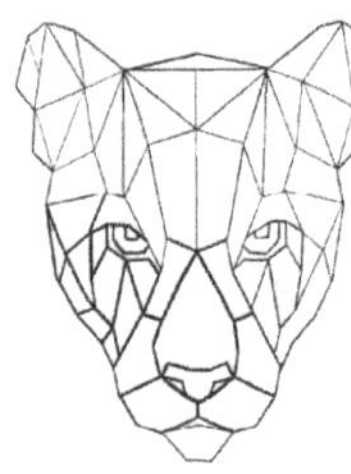# Clark Atlanta University 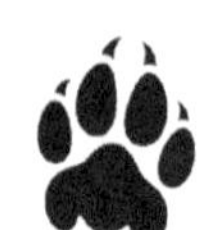

"I'll Find a Way or Make One"

A- 26	E- 22	I- 18	M- 14	Q- 10	U- 6	Y- 2
B- 25	F- 21	J- 17	N- 13	R- 9	V- 5	Z- 1
C- 24	G- 20	K- 16	O- 12	S- 8	W- 4	
D- 23	H- 19	L- 15	P- 11	T- 7	X- 3	

The words are related to Clark Atlanta. Decode the words below using the letters above.

24　26　13　24　22　9

— — — — — —

Center for _____ Research and Therapeutic Development focus on training scientist

11　26　13　7　　19　22　9

— — — —　— — —

24　12　13　8　12　9　7　18　6　14

— — — — — — — — — —

The Atlanta University Center ______ is comprised of 4 HBCUs

25　26　13　23

— — — —

14
___
18
___
20
___
19
___
7
___
2
___

26　21　9　18　24　26　13　26

— — — — — — — —

The only _______ Women's Study in the World

14
___
26
___
9
___
24
___
19
___
18
___
13
___
20
___

23　6　　25　12　18　8

— — — — — — —

Founding Faculty in the School of Social Worker W.E.B _____

22　3　11　22　9　18　26　13　24　22

— — — — — — — — — —

As a CAU freshman, you will learn about the culture, community, traditions & legacy.

14　22　7　19　　12　23　18　8　7

— — — — — — — — —

Clark Atlanta values religion & spirituality. They are closely related to the United _______ Church

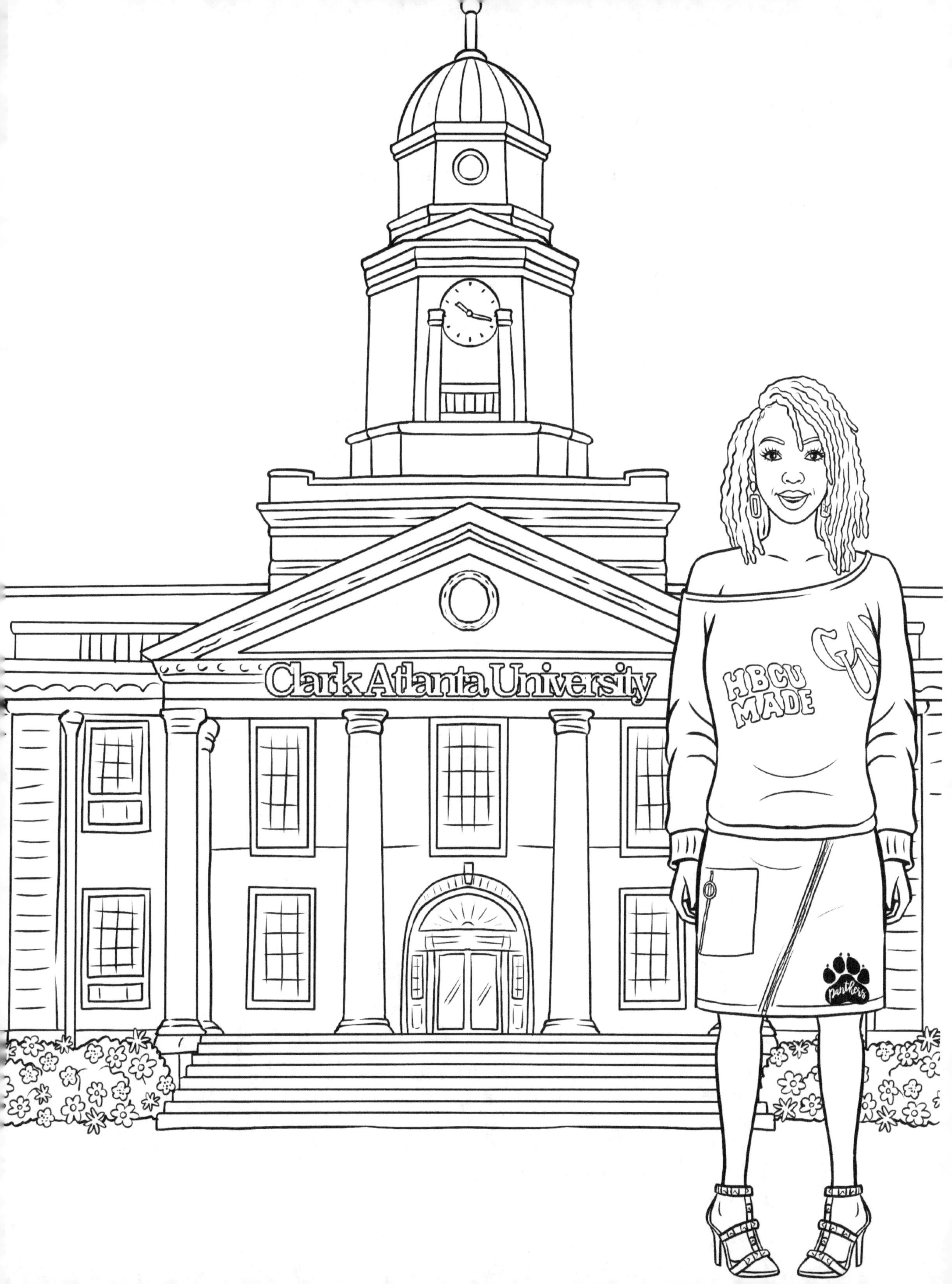

Clark Atlanta University
HBCU MADE
CAU
Panthers

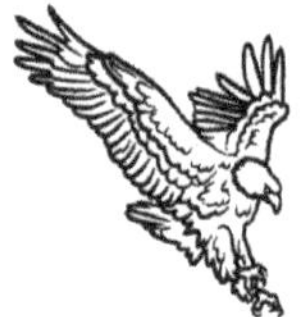# Coppin State University

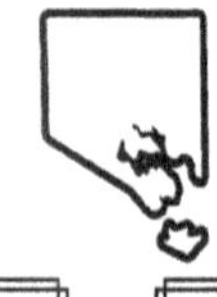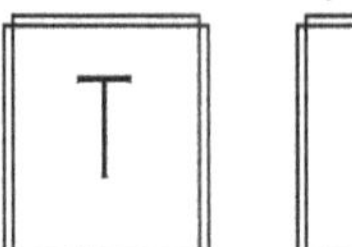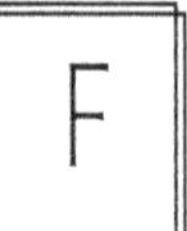

Circle True or False next to each statement below.

1. You cannot receive a certificate in Forensic Investigations.

T   F

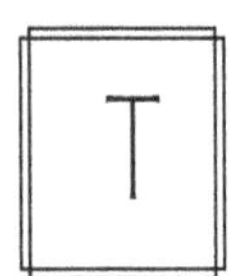   T   F   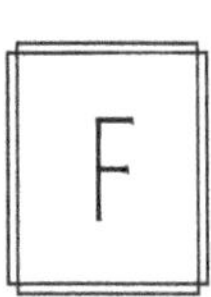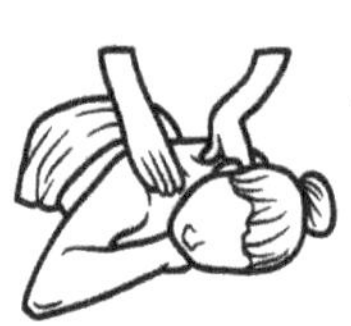

2. Wellness program offers Massage Tuesdays and Cooking Demonstrations.

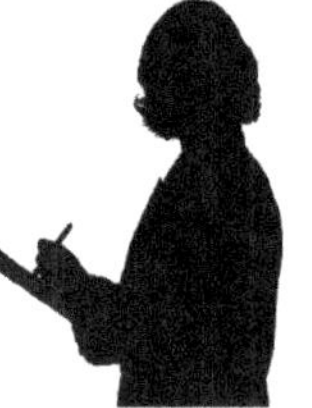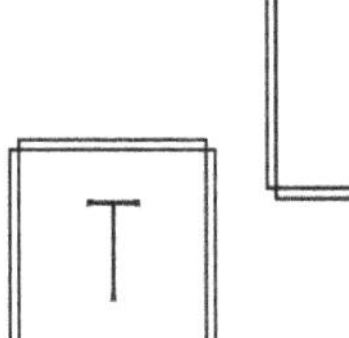

T   F

3. Coppin University is named after Fanny Jackson Coppin, a trailblazer in teacher education.

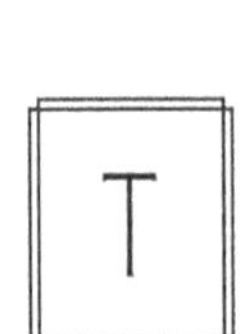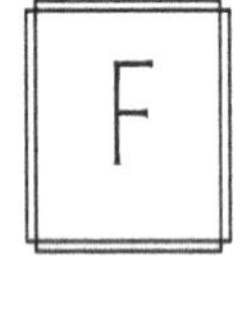   T   F   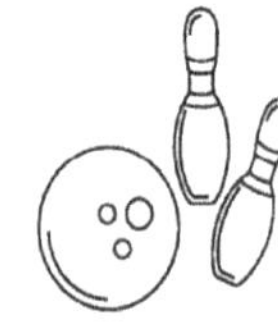

4. Men's sport teams include Tennis & Basketball: Women's sports teams include Bowling & Volleyball.

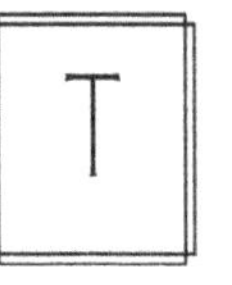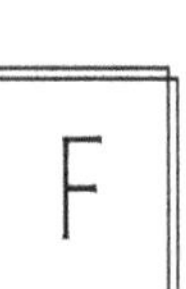

T   F

5. If you major in Entertainment Management for Music, you must complete an internship & a Marketing Research class.

T   F

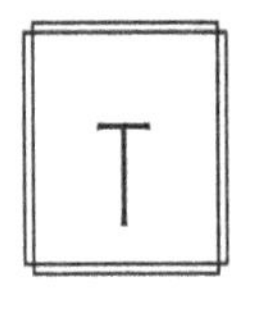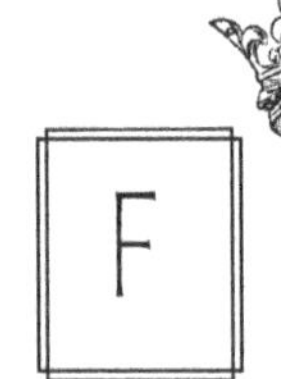

T   F

6. The Coppin Pageant began in 1944 and the royal court serve as ambassadors and represent the student body.

7. As a graduate student, you can graduate with an M.S. in Addiction Counseling and or M.S. in Polymer and Material Sciences.

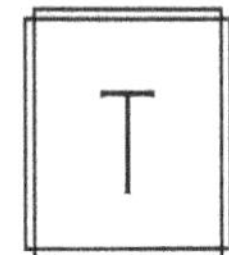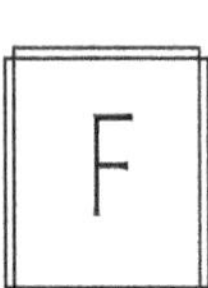

T   F

F

T

8. The Hawk is the school mascot and the school color blue represents loyalty & responsibility and gold stands for seeking attention.

9. Sponsored Scholarships include: Alumni Association, Dance program, Theater Arts, Presidential, India-Intercontinental, Merit & Presidential.

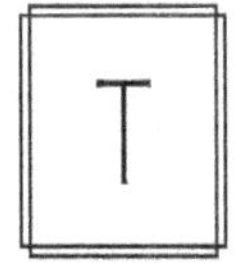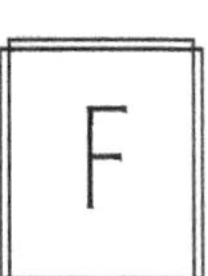

T   F

T   F

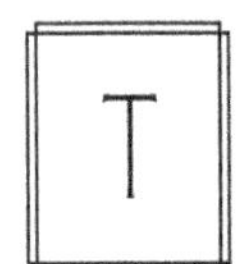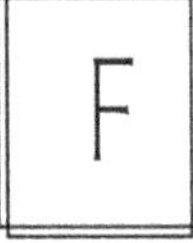

10. The Ophthalmic Research Laboratory is currently exploring "oxygen free radicals, pathogenesis of ocular diseases" with a focus on the retina.

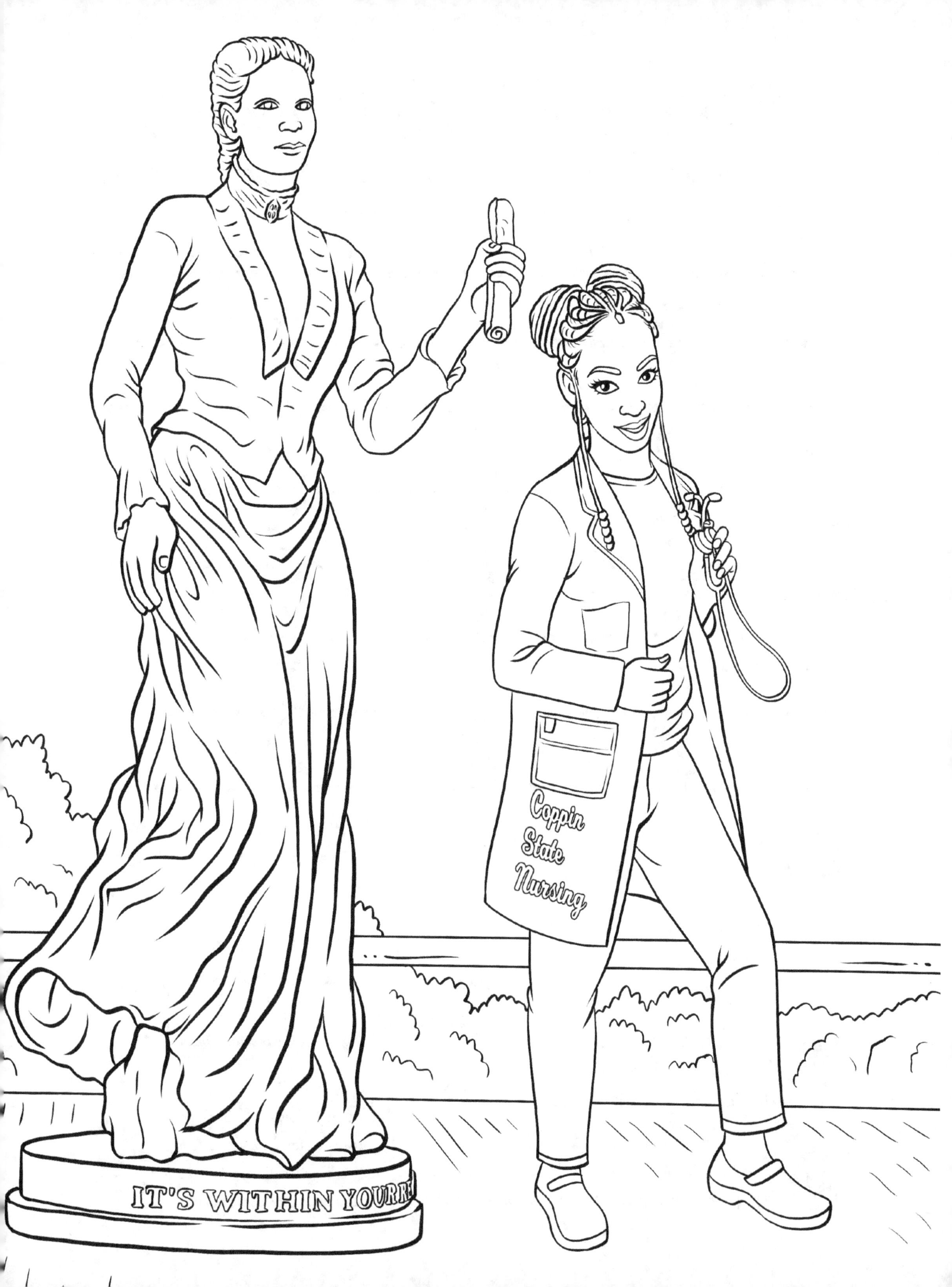

Coppin State Nursing
IT'S WITHIN YOUR RE

Delaware State University

Find that major, complete the grid below to learn more about various degrees

Major	Course	Degree	Professional Career
Animal & Poultry Science	Livestock Production	Agriculture, BS	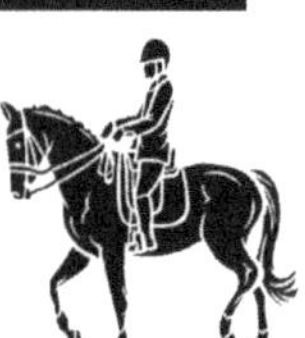 Farm Management
	Modern Laser Spectroscopic		
		Aviation, BS	
			University Professor
Public Health			
			Fashion Merchandising

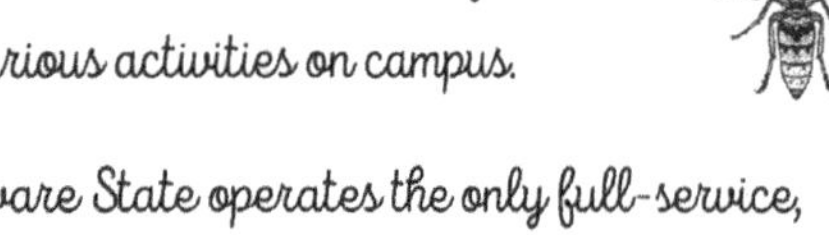

1891

The school was established on May 15, 1891 and known as Delaware College for Colored Students

Only HBCU with a collegiate Equestrian program

DSU is located in Dover, Delaware but also has campuses in Wilmington & Georgetown

The DSU steel orchestra focuses on traditional calypso of Trinidad & the greater Caribbean region

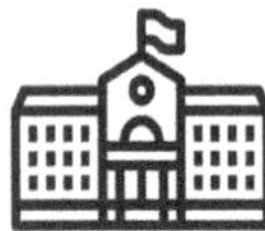

Muslim Fellowship goal is to empower the Muslim community through various activities on campus.

Delaware State operates the only full-service, university-based flight school in the mid-Atlantic area. It prepares students for a career in the aviation industry.

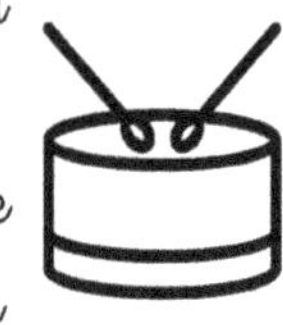

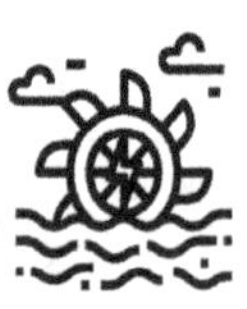

Research: Delaware EPSCoR goal is to understand how we sustain water, energy & natural resources in vulnerable coastal locations.

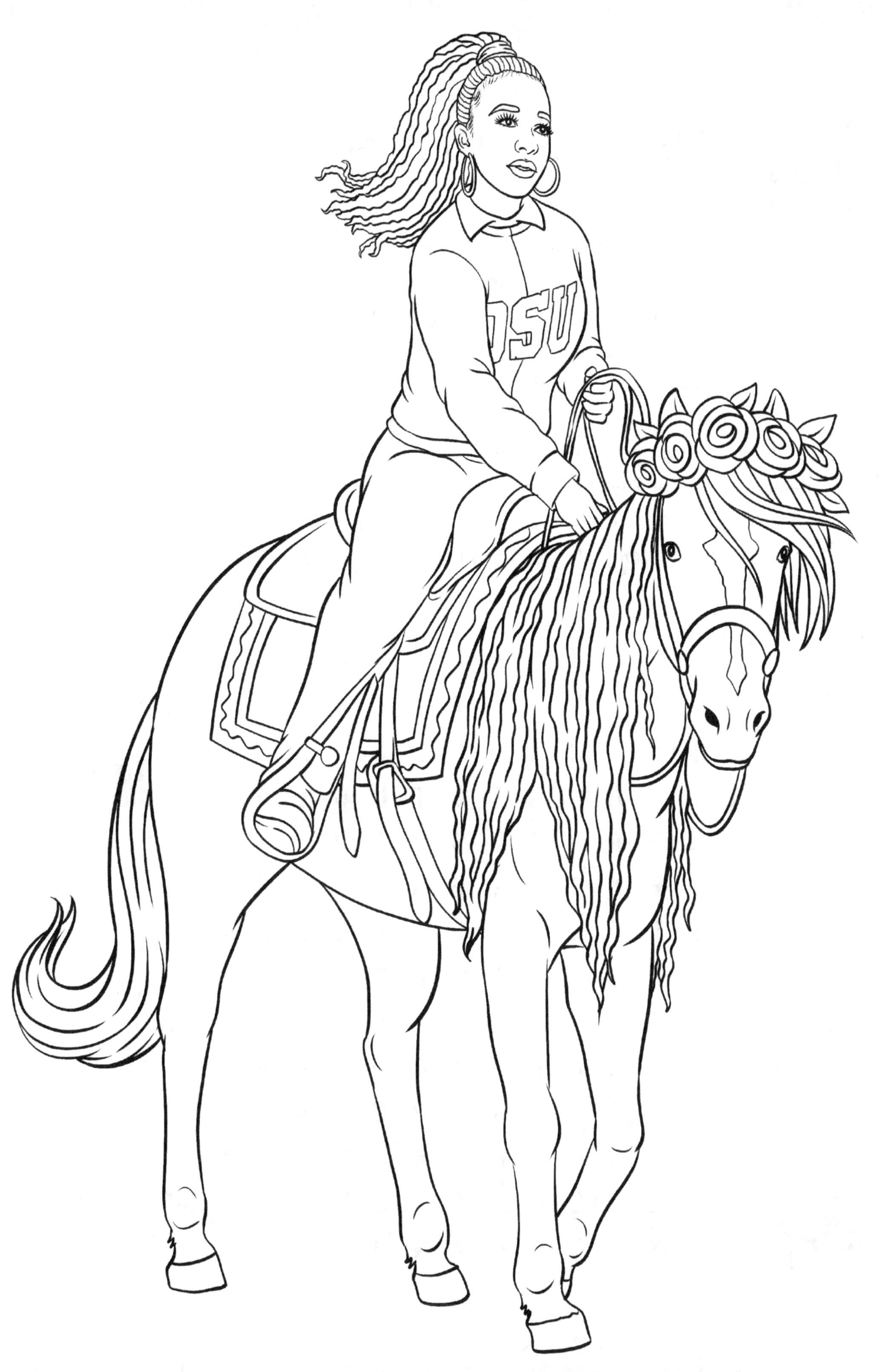

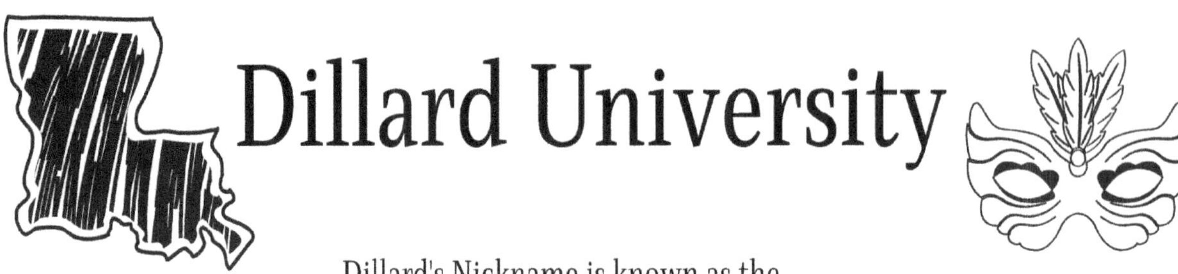

Dillard University

Dillard's Nickname is known as the ___

Dillard University is located in New Orleans, ___

First HBCU in Louisiana to offer a bachelor degree in ___

___ Program was created to research African American Material Culture

___ Honor Society known for high academic honor in the area of Psychology

He is known as the "Hip Hop Prez" and increased financial gains for the university

___Access is a textbook program that allows student to receive a reduced material cost

Cafeteria, post office, Student Government office & lounge can be found in ___ Hall

___ Scholarship is for student athletes and is named after a previous globetrotter member

___ Chapel is formed to promote spiritual growth & bring the religious community together

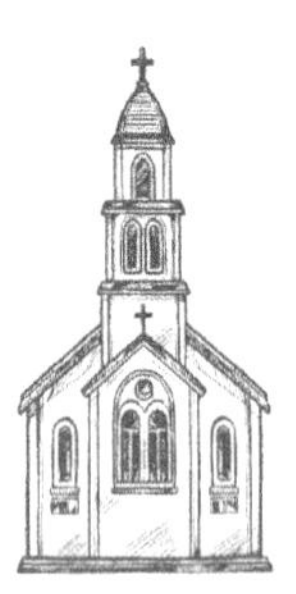

Follett
Kearny
Psi Chi
Louisiana
Kimbrough

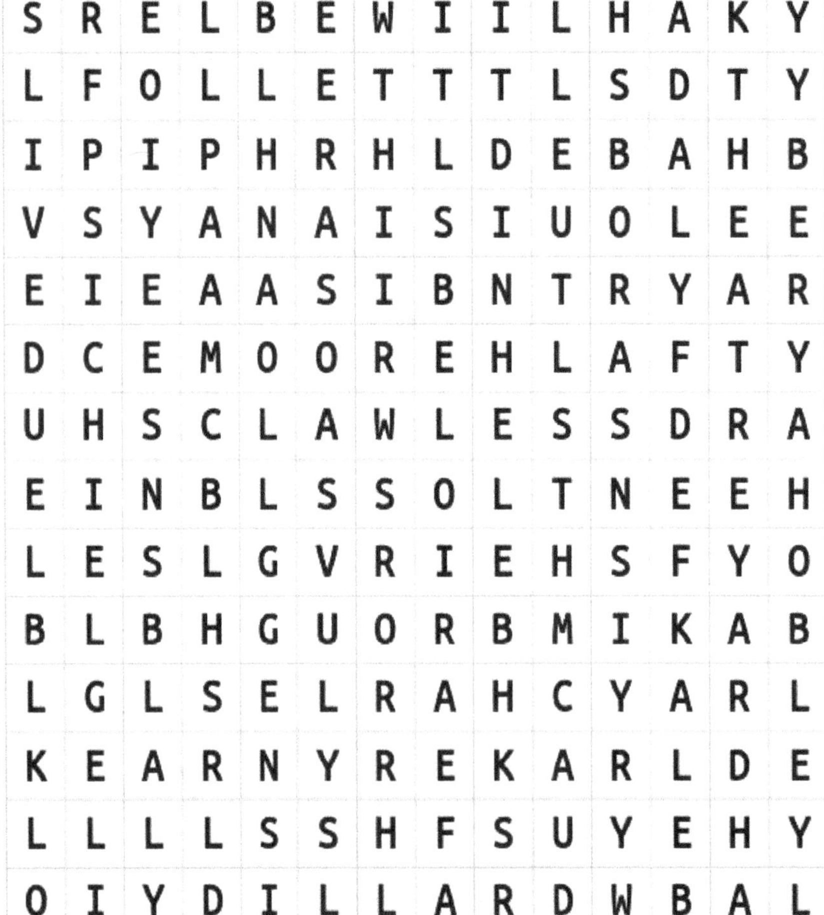

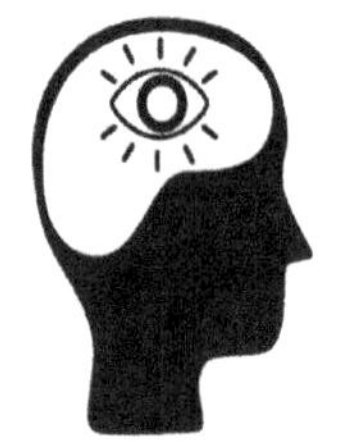

Hobley
Theatre
Lawless
Bleu Devils
Ray Charles

S	R	E	L	B	E	W	I	I	L	H	A	K	Y
L	F	O	L	L	E	T	T	T	L	S	D	T	Y
I	P	I	P	H	R	H	L	D	E	B	A	H	B
V	S	Y	A	N	A	I	S	I	U	O	L	E	E
E	I	E	A	A	S	I	B	N	T	R	Y	A	R
D	C	E	M	O	O	R	E	H	L	A	F	T	Y
U	H	S	C	L	A	W	L	E	S	S	D	R	A
E	I	N	B	L	S	S	O	L	T	N	E	E	H
L	E	S	L	G	V	R	I	E	H	S	F	Y	O
B	L	B	H	G	U	O	R	B	M	I	K	A	B
L	G	L	S	E	L	R	A	H	C	Y	A	R	L
K	E	A	R	N	Y	R	E	K	A	R	L	D	E
L	L	L	L	S	S	H	F	S	U	Y	E	H	Y
O	I	Y	D	I	L	L	A	R	D	W	B	A	L

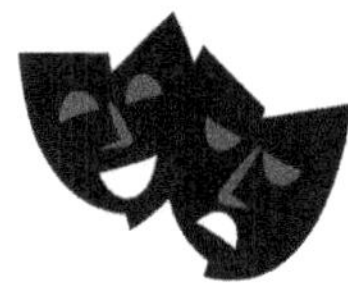

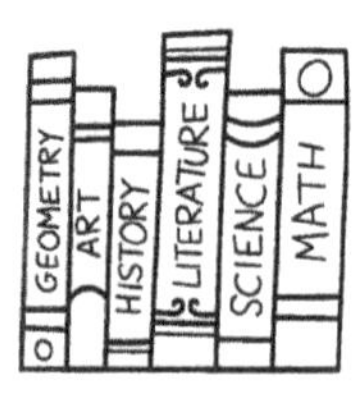

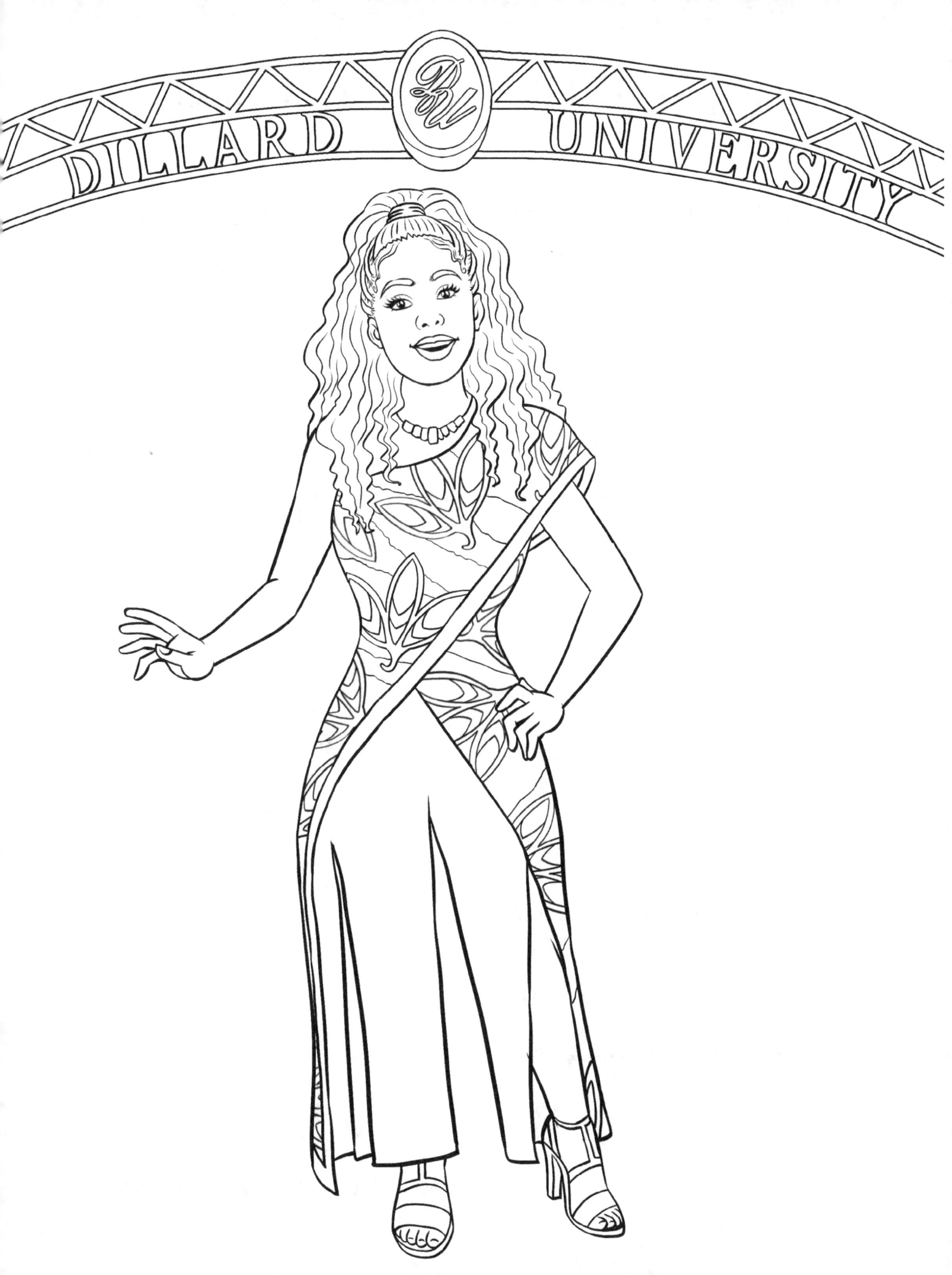

DILLARD UNIVERSITY

University of the District of Columbia

In 1851, Myrtilla _______founded the Normal School For Colored Girls. Federal _____College, ____________ Technical Institute, ___ Teachers college were unified to form present day University of the District of __________. It is the only _______university in the city.

Name the 7 UDC academic schools & programs:

1.
2.
3.
4.
5.
6.
7.

How many words can you make from University of DC related to HBCU's

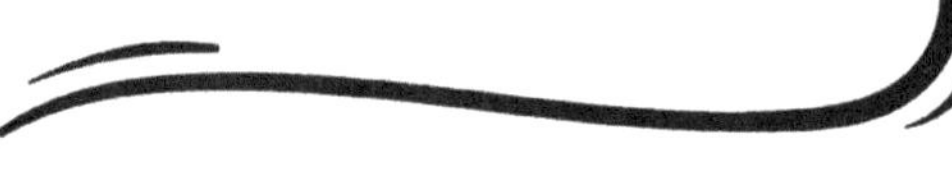

The flagship campus is located in Van Ness Campus NW. Name the other 3 locations

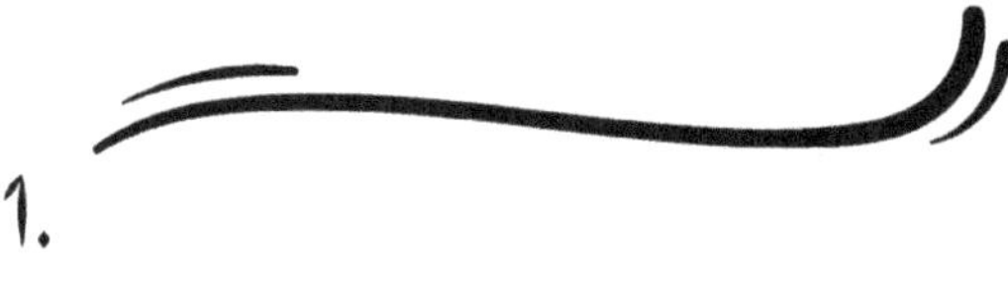

1.
2.
3.

"Aspire, Accomplish, Take on the Word"

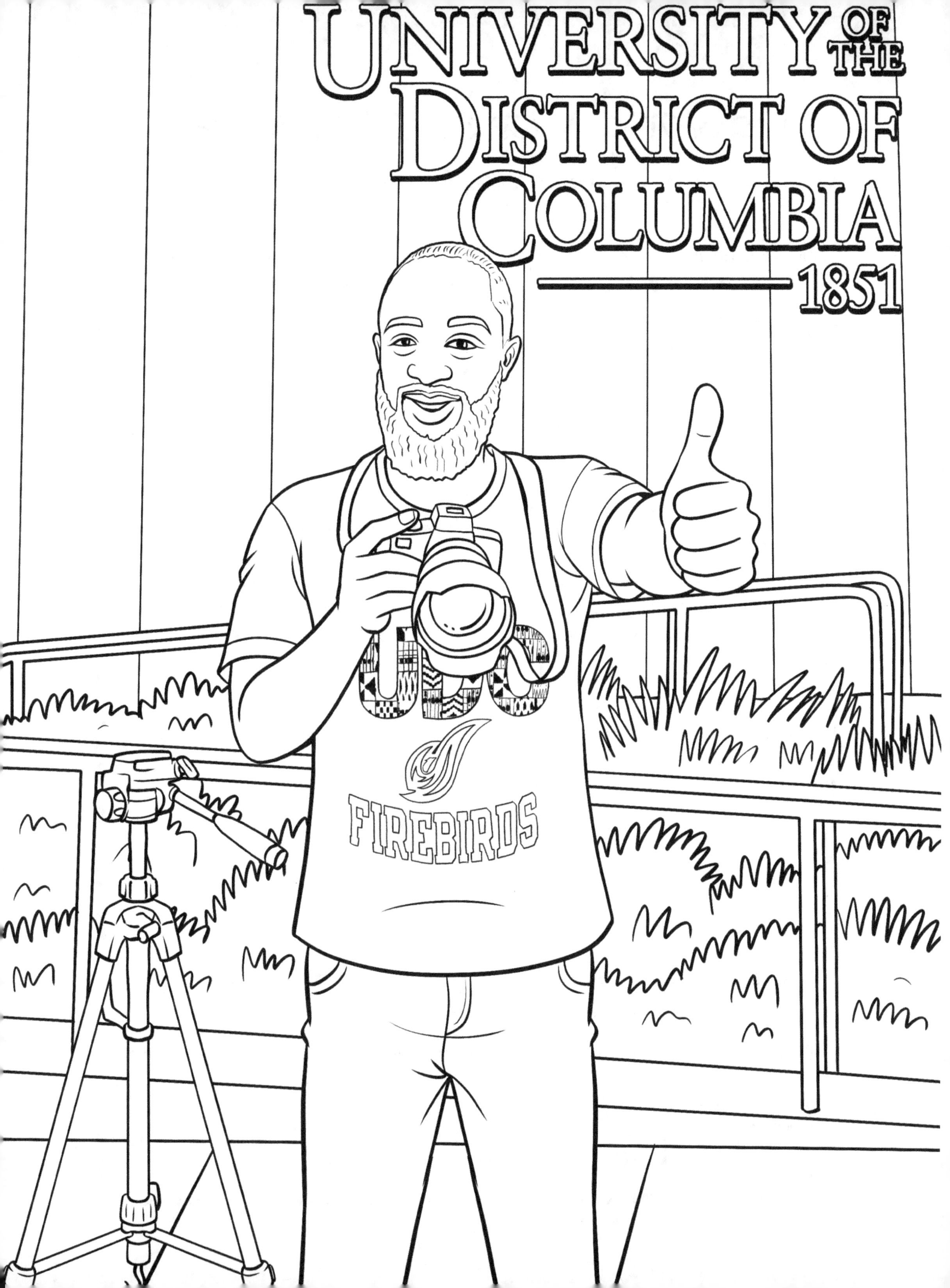

UNIVERSITY OF THE
DISTRICT OF
COLUMBIA
1851
UDC
FIREBIRDS

Edward Waters University
"Emerging Eminence"

Where is Edward Waters located?
A. Miami, Florida
B. Jacksonville, Florida
C. Gainesville, Florida

In 1866, it was founded by members of
A. Church of God in Christ
B. National Baptist Convention
C. African Methodist Episcopal Church

Historic Facilities:
What is the importance of Centennial Hall

Tigers & Lady Tiger. Which intercollegiate team are you part of?

Choose a Student, Campus & National Organization to join.

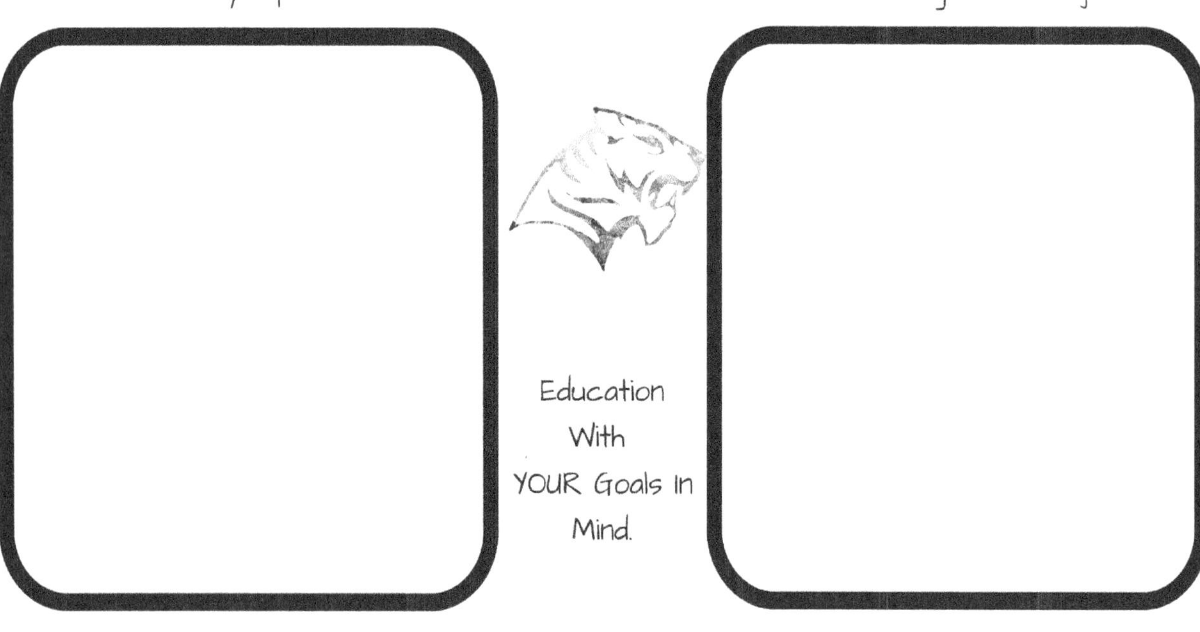

Education With YOUR Goals In Mind.

Fun Fact: EWU Marching Band is known as the Triple Threat Band. The Sight, The Sound, The Fury

If you were given a full ride scholarship, which undergraduate & graduate degree would you choose & why?

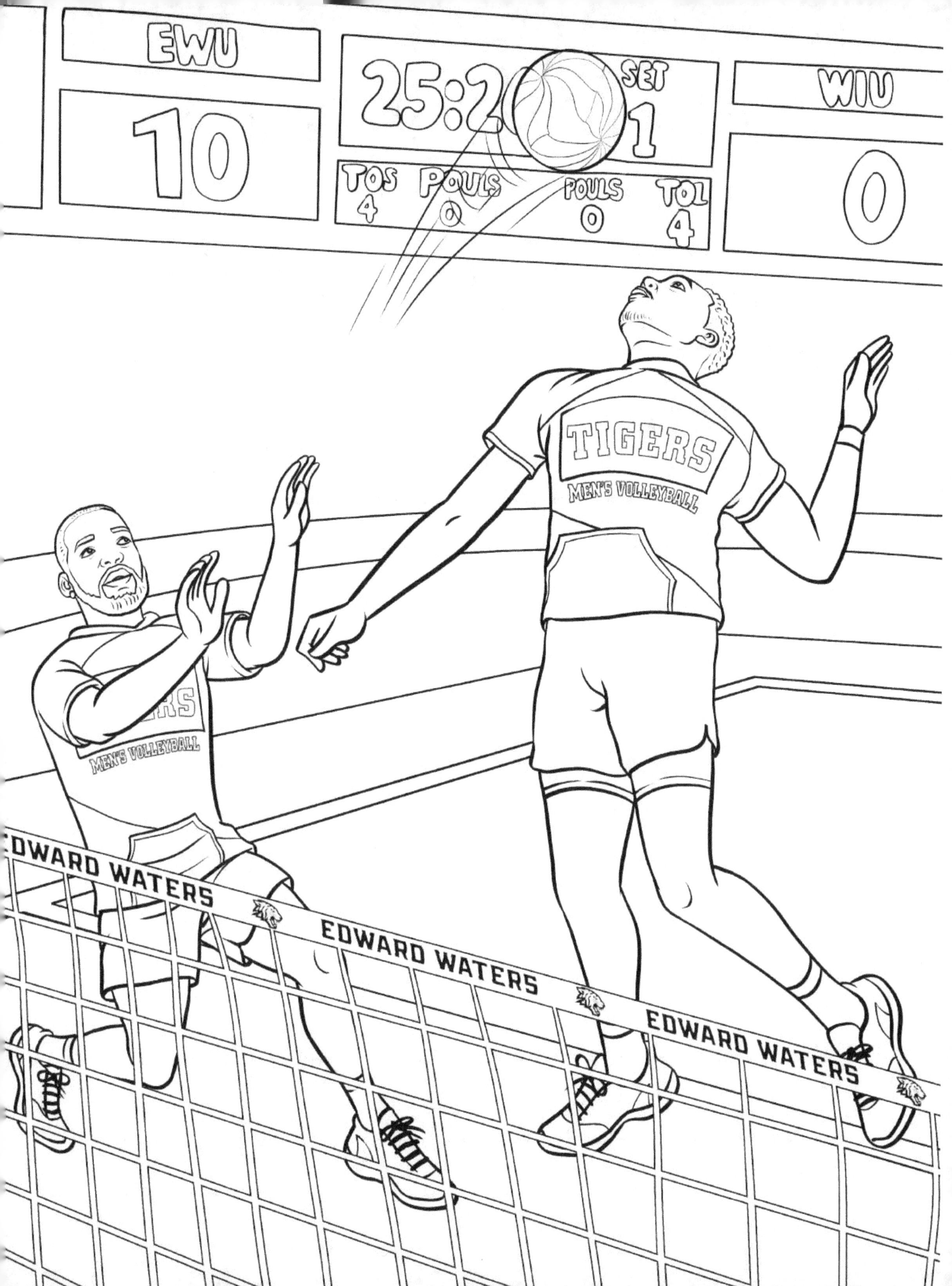

EWU
10
25:2
SET
1
WIU
0
TOS
4
POULS
0
POULS
0
TOL
4
TIGERS
MEN'S VOLLEYBALL
MEN'S VOLLEYBALL
EDWARD WATERS
EDWARD WATERS
EDWARD WATERS

Elizabeth City State University

Solve Each Problem using subtraction, multiplication or division. Fill in the blanks below with the correct answer

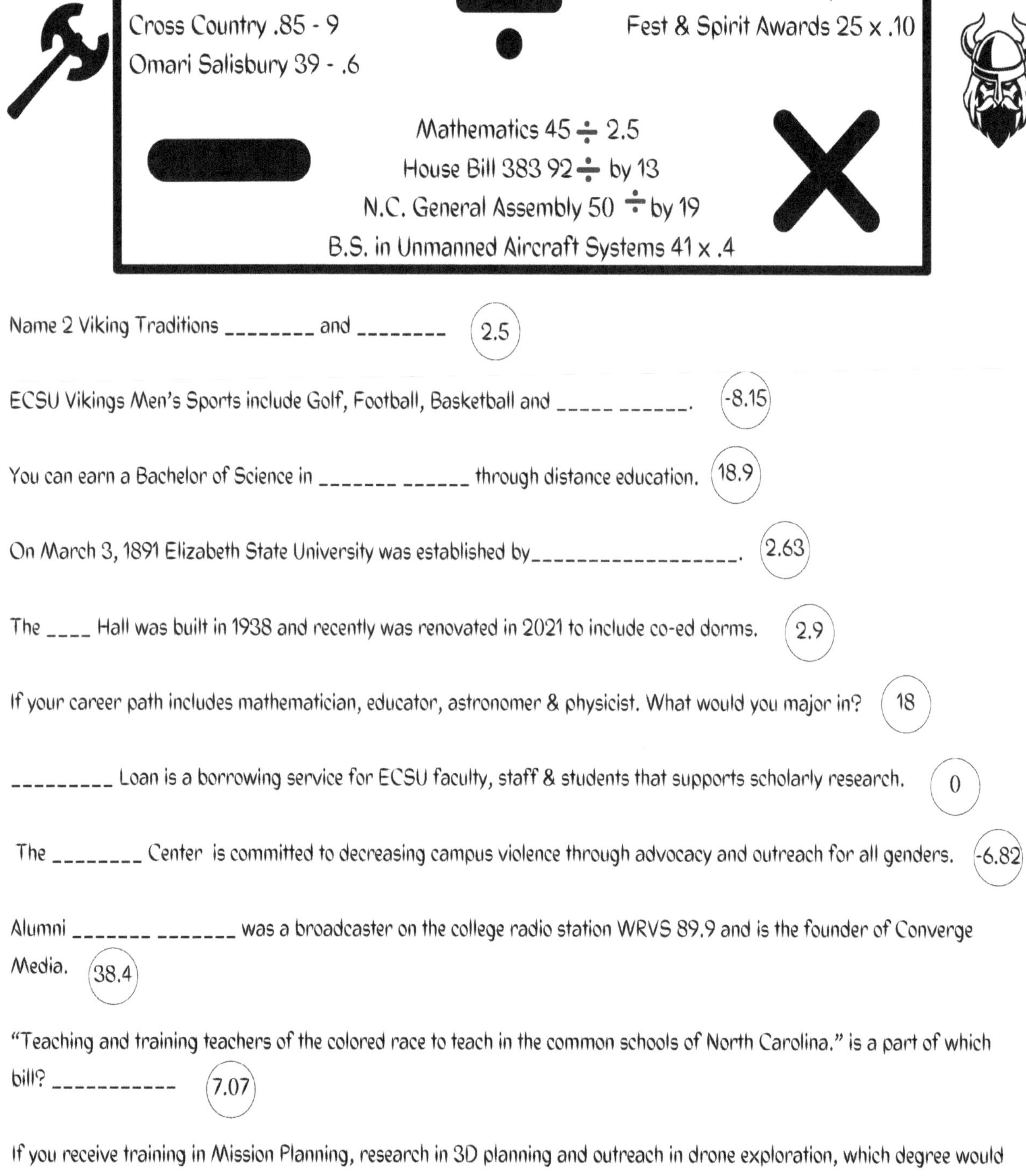

Name 2 Viking Traditions ________ and ________ 2.5

ECSU Vikings Men's Sports include Golf, Football, Basketball and _____ ______. -8.15

You can earn a Bachelor of Science in _______ ______ through distance education. 18.9

On March 3, 1891 Elizabeth State University was established by_________________. 2.63

The ____ Hall was built in 1938 and recently was renovated in 2021 to include co-ed dorms. 2.9

If your career path includes mathematician, educator, astronomer & physicist. What would you major in? 18

_________ Loan is a borrowing service for ECSU faculty, staff & students that supports scholarly research. 0

The ________ Center is committed to decreasing campus violence through advocacy and outreach for all genders. -6.82

Alumni _______ _______ was a broadcaster on the college radio station WRVS 89.9 and is the founder of Converge Media. 38.4

"Teaching and training teachers of the colored race to teach in the common schools of North Carolina." is a part of which bill? __________ 7.07

If you receive training in Mission Planning, research in 3D planning and outreach in drone exploration, which degree would you receive? ____________ 16.4

"To Live is to Learn"

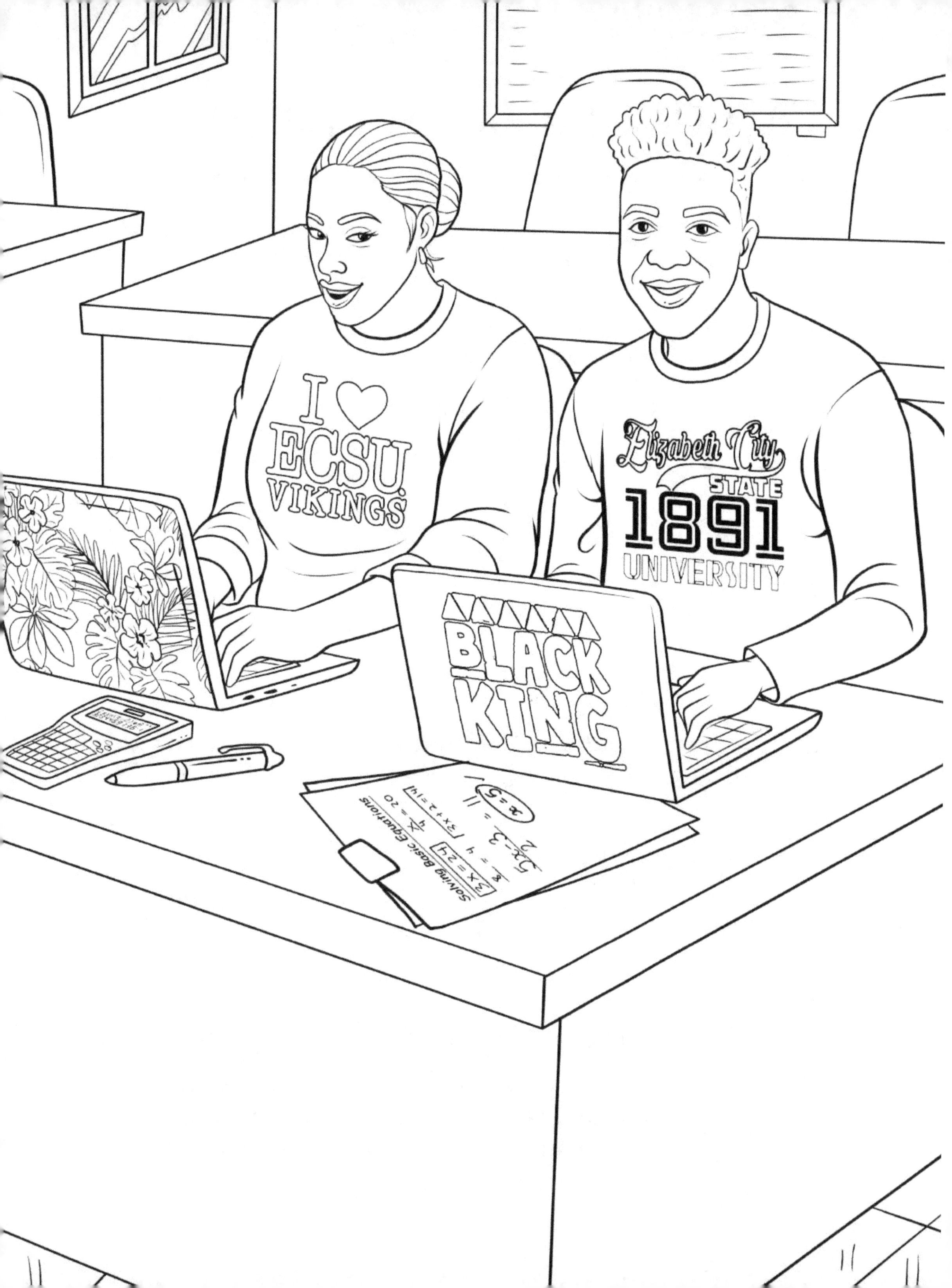

I ♥ ECSU VIKINGS
Elizabeth City
STATE
1891
UNIVERSITY
BLACK KING
Solving Basic Equations

Fayetteville State University

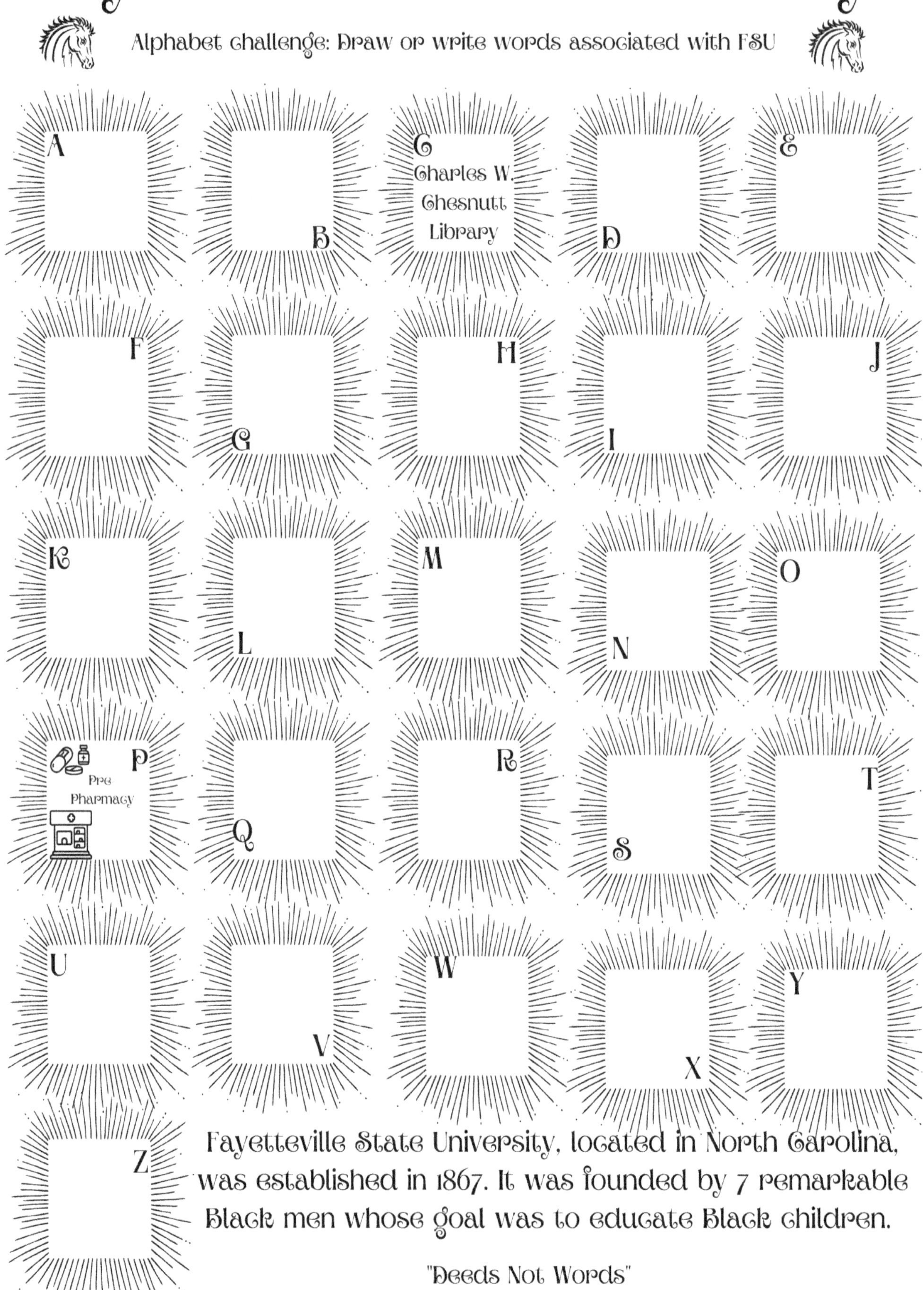

Fayetteville State University, located in North Carolina, was established in 1867. It was founded by 7 remarkable Black men whose goal was to educate Black children.

"Deeds Not Words"

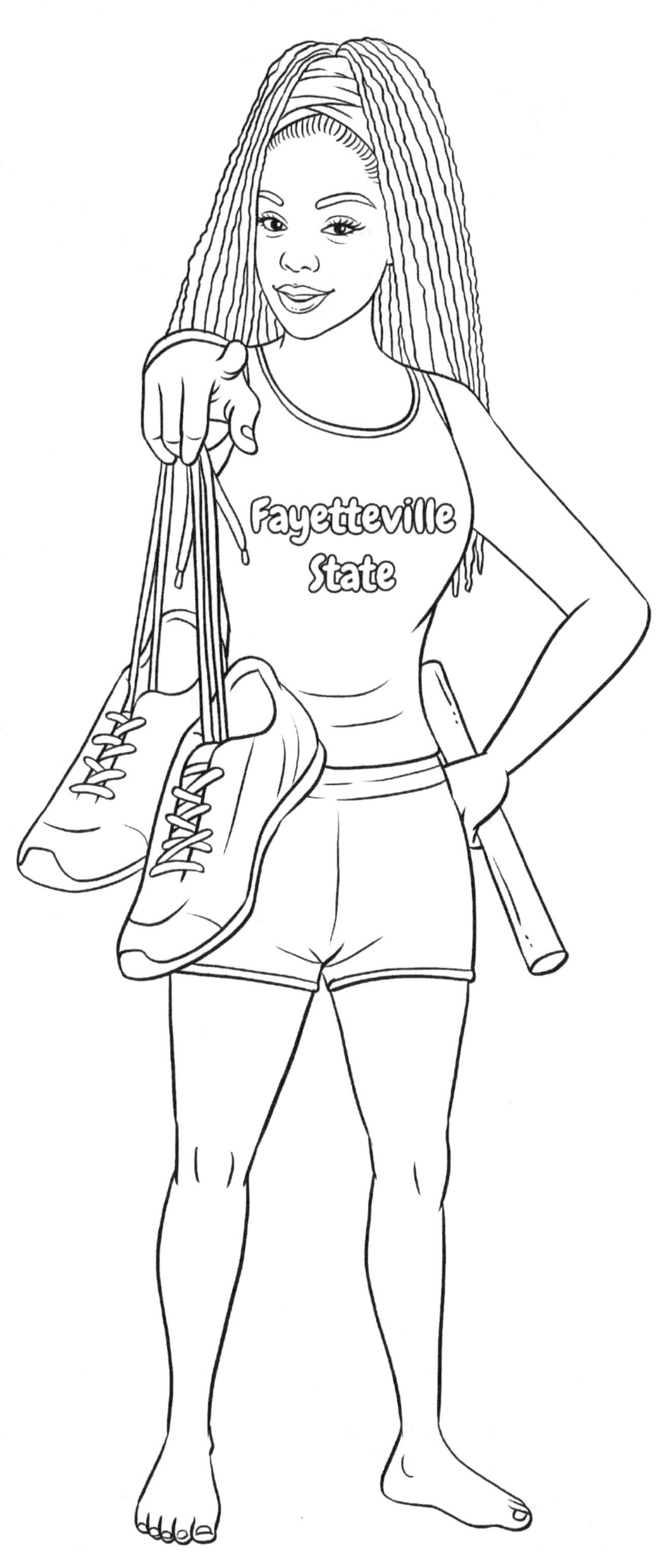

Fayetteville
State

Fisk University

She was an activist, journalist and attended Fisk University.

A) Dorothy Height

B) Mary Church Terrell

C) Ida B. Wells-Barnett

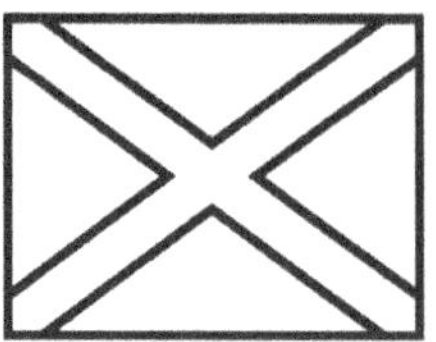

On October 6, 1871, these student left campus to travel the world in hopes to fundraise for the school.

A) Jubilee Singers

B) Canton Spirituals

C) The Soul Stirrers

What year did Mr. Ogden, Reverend Cravath & Reverend Smith establish Fisk School in Nashville?

A) 1885

B) 1865

C) 1855

Bonus Question
Students who are interested in studying cybersecurity, preventing terrorist attacks should major in?

A) Criminal Justice

B) Psychology

c) Homeland Security

If you are from Jamaica, St. Lucia, Barbados, Haiti or Antigua, which student organization would you join?

A) Black Student Union

B) Caribbean Student Association

C) The Memphis Club

Editor of the literary magazine on campus is the author of "Hip Hop speaks to children"

A) Diane Nash

B) Judith Jamison

C) Nikki Giovanni

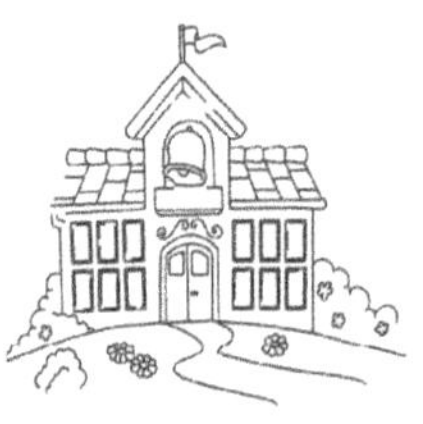

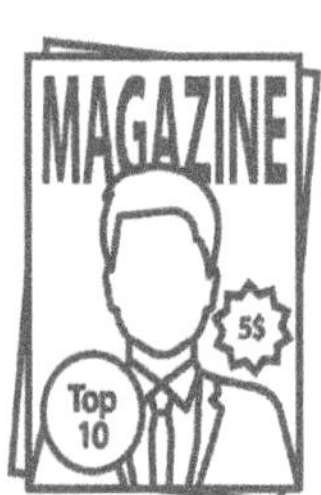

If you complete a degree within 4 years & maintain a 3.0 GPA, join this program & obtain a Master's degree for a reduced tuition.

A) Fisk Master Bonus

B) Fisk Master Incentive

C) Fisk Advanced Honorarium

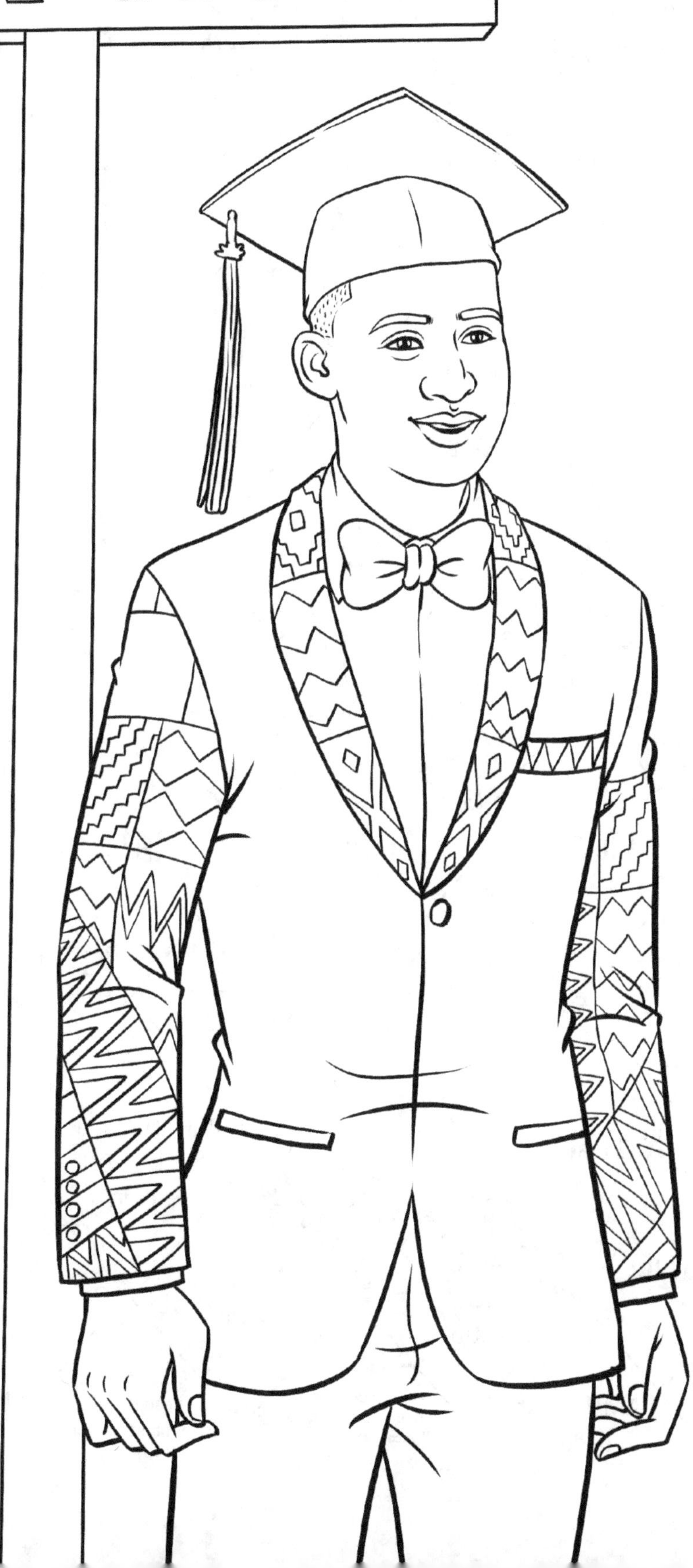
FISK WAY

Florida Agricultural Mechanical University

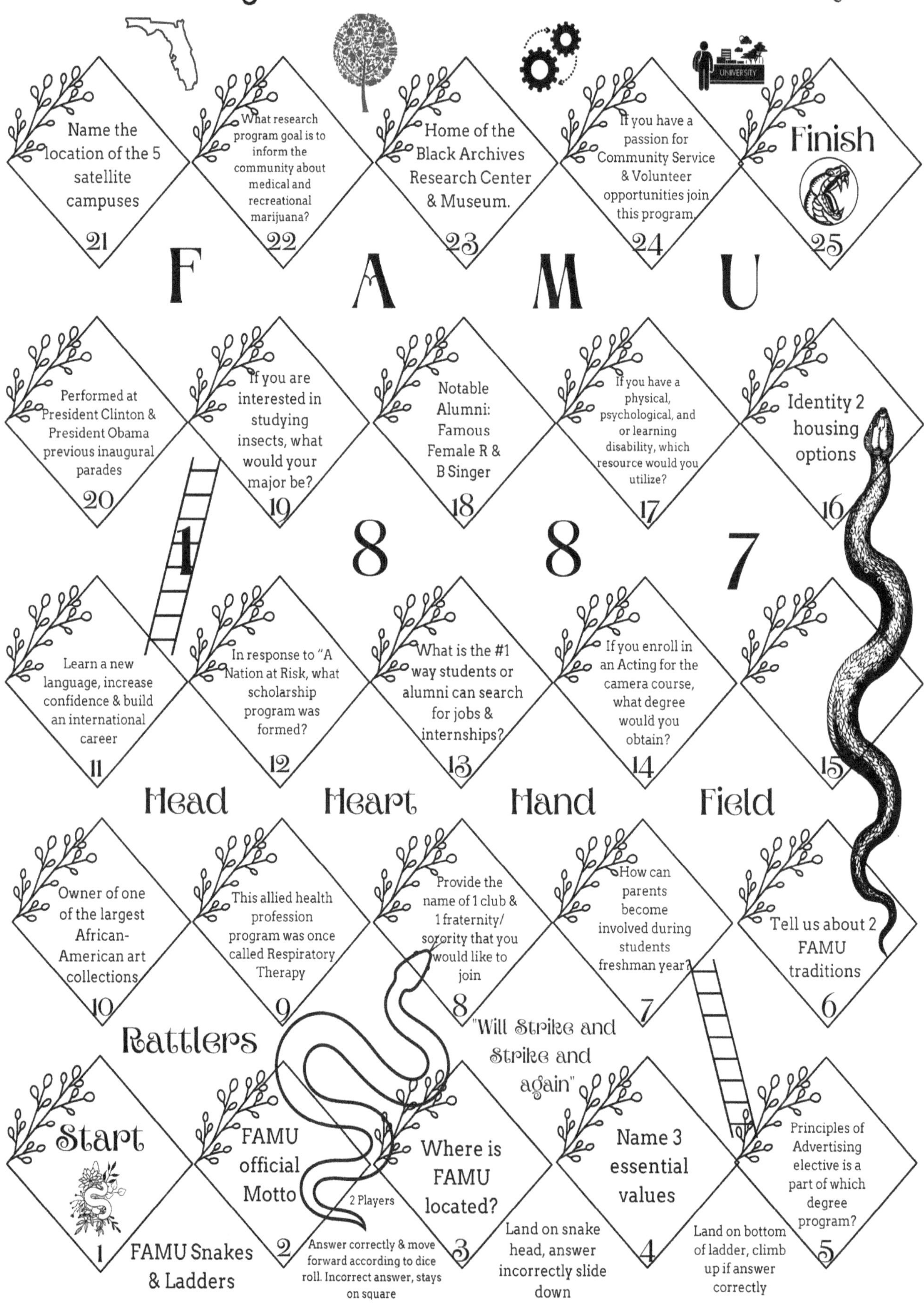

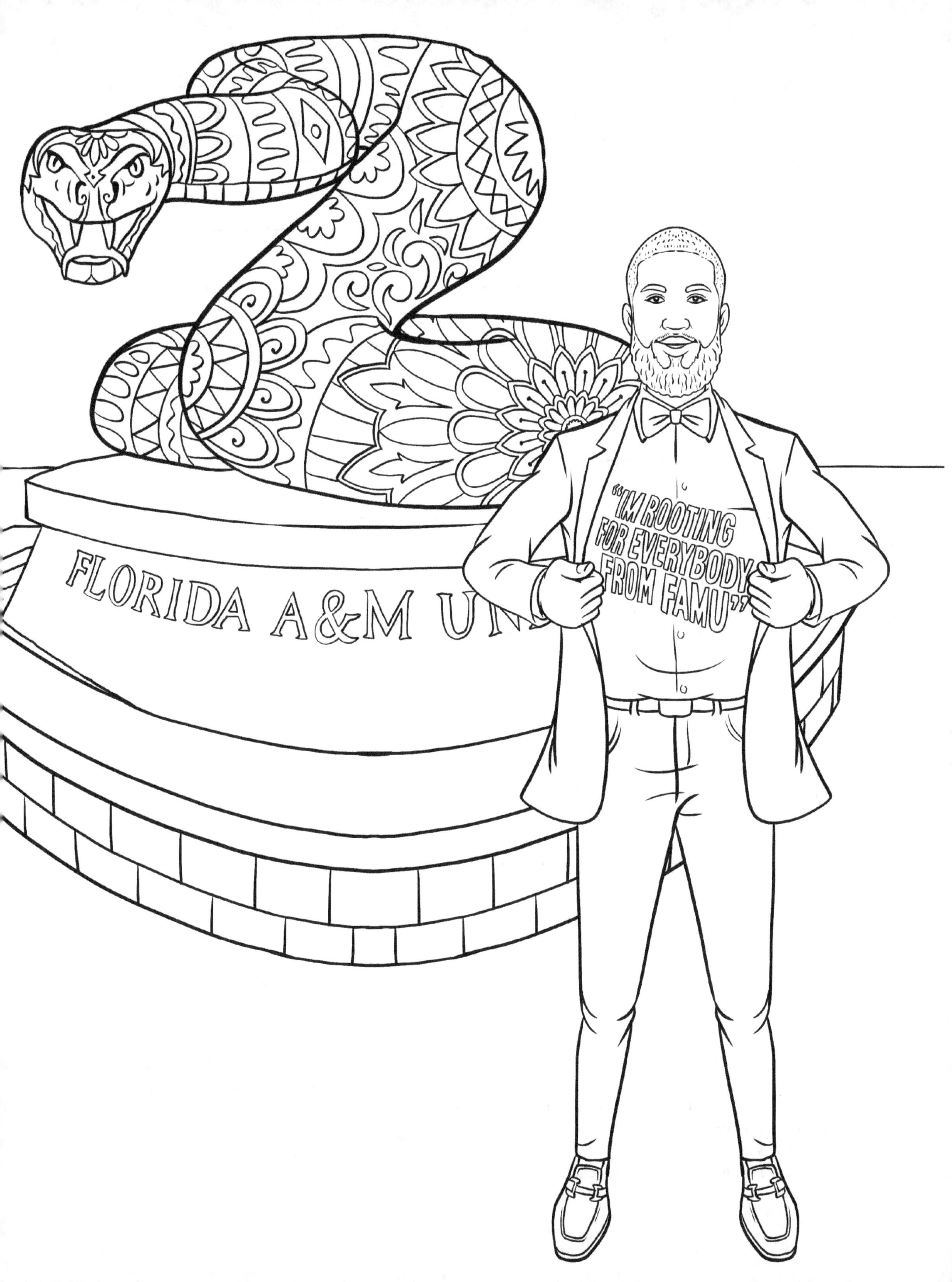

FLORIDA A&M UN...
"I'M ROOTING FOR EVERYBODY FROM FAMU"

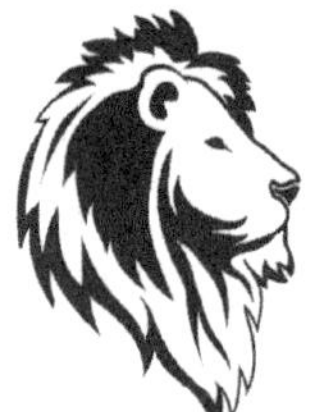

Florida Memorial University

L E A D E R S H I P   C H A R A C T E R   S E R V I C E

Poetry Frame: Write a free verse poem about FMU using the guide lines

Line 1: Year started & name of university

Line 2: Why was the university started

Line 3: Black National Anthem Name. (Author & Music Composer)

Line 4: Civil Rights involvement

Line 5: School of Business: Choose a major & why?

Line 6: School of Education : Which degree would you obtain?

Line 7: School of Arts & Sciences: Which Major would like to know more about

Line 8: Decide which club or organization would you be a part of?

Line 9: Global Education: Where do you want to study abroad ?

Line 10: The Roar. Lion Essence or F.I.E.R.C.E

Line 11: FMU Lion Athletic Sport

Line 12: Mascot. School Colors

Line 13: Motto

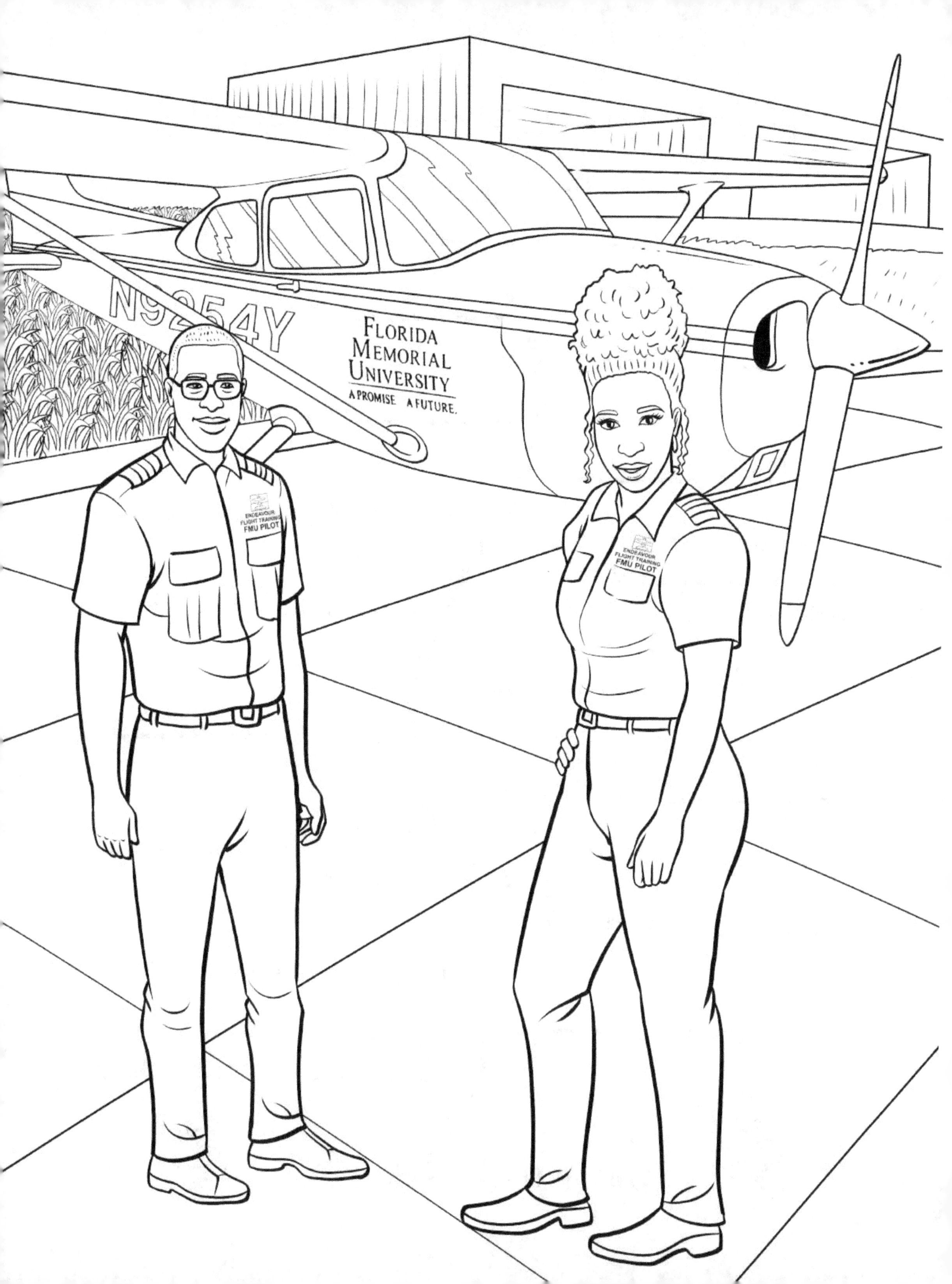

N9254Y
FLORIDA MEMORIAL UNIVERSITY
A PROMISE A FUTURE.
ENDEAVOUR FLIGHT TRAINING
FMU PILOT
ENDEAVOUR FLIGHT TRAINING
FMU PILOT

Fort Valley State University

Finish The Phrase

Warner _________

_________ Church

Computer _________

_________ Leadership

Mr. & Miss _________

_________ Technology

_________ Economics

Environmental _________

_________ Memorial Library

_________ In The _________

John Wesley _________

_________ & Egg Show

The _________

Voices of Faith _________

Army _________ Cadet

_________ Marching Band

"Empower the Possible"

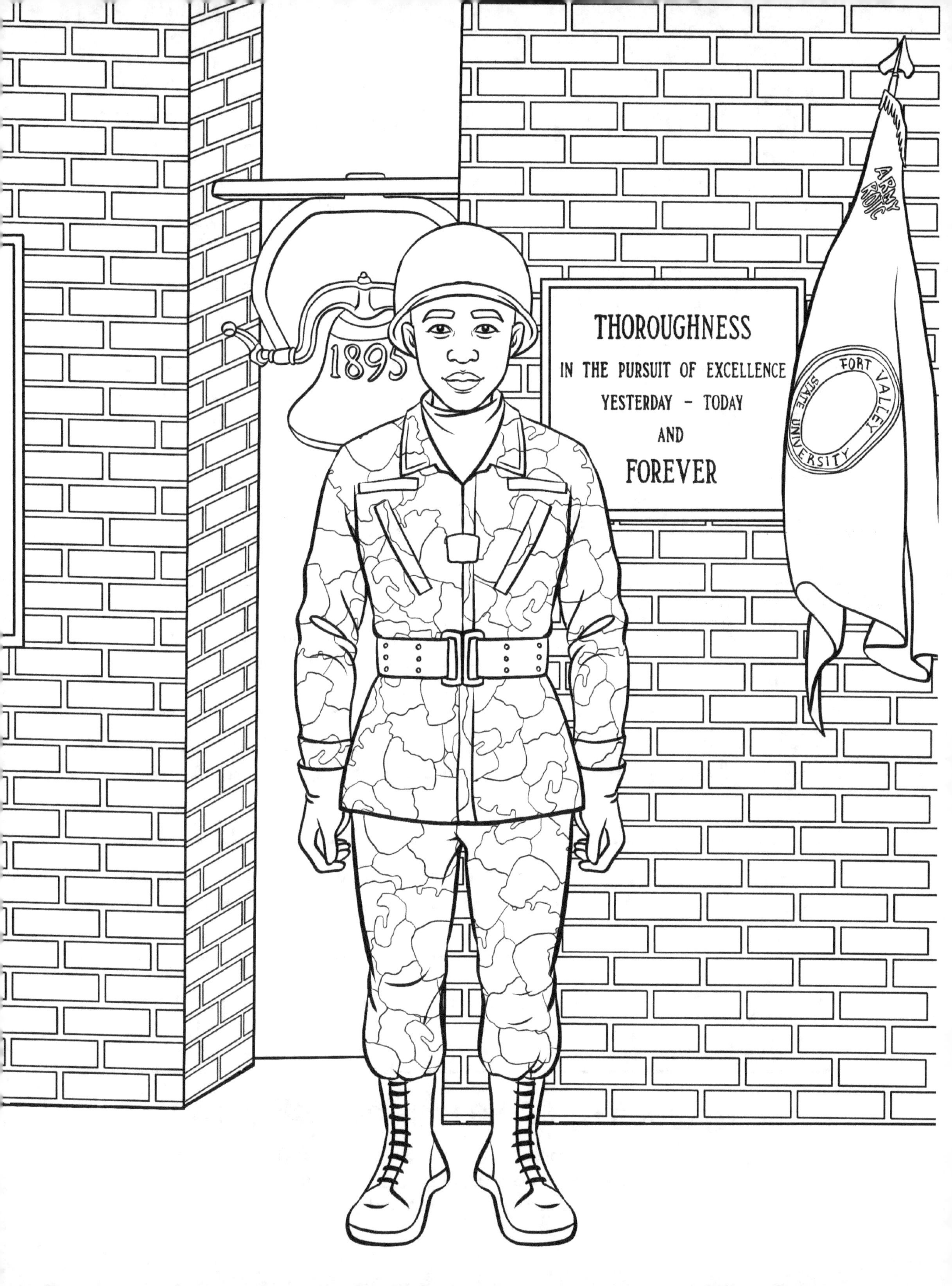

1895
THOROUGHNESS
IN THE PURSUIT OF EXCELLENCE
YESTERDAY - TODAY
AND
FOREVER
FORT VALLEY STATE UNIVERSITY
ARMY ROTC

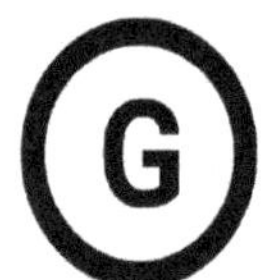 **G**

Grambling State University

In 1901, Grambling University was founded. It transpired as a result of Black farmers in rural North Louisiana wanting to educate their Black children.

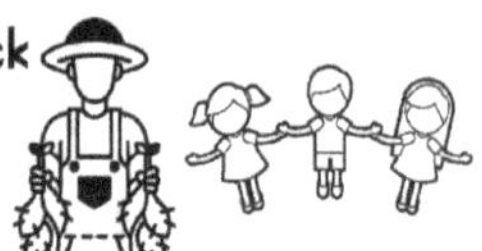

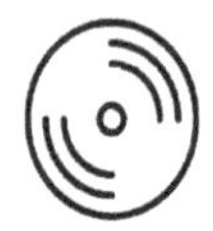

$C = E$ $T = D$

CD   Tie

Located on Grambling Campus is a museum named after famous head coach _ _ _ _ _ G. Robinson.

$B +$ Down $D = R$

This building was a former dormitory & was named after Hallie Q. _ _ _ _ _ who was a Lecturer & Elocutionist.

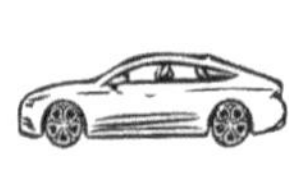 $C = M + C$ 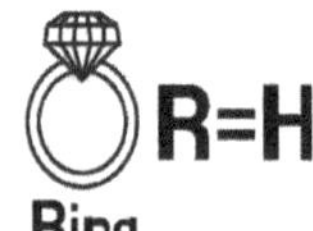 $R = H$

Car   Ring

Known as the "best band in the land" Tiger _ _ _ _ _ _ _ _ Band.

$J +$ 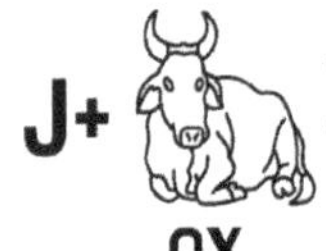 OX $X = H + N$ Sun $U = O$

Foster _ _ _ _ _ _ _ Health Center offer services such as medical care, health counseling, wellness education and assessments.

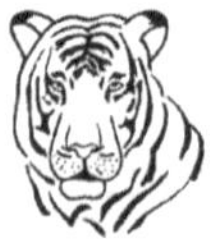 Tiger   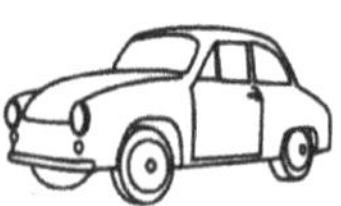 Car $+D$

_ _ _ _ _ 1 _ _ _ _ is important at serves as an ID, meal plan, purchases, event access & more.

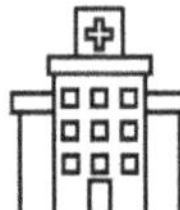 $+I+$ 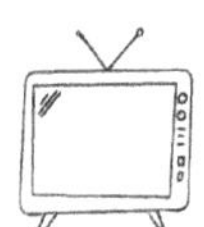 $V = Y$

Obtain a Bachelor of Science Degree in cybersecurity, the goal is to teach students how to keep technology safe.

N +  CALL   A-LL

The athletics department is part of the _ _ _ _ Division I-FCS.

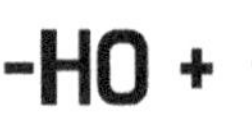 CAB $A = Y + E$ Horse $-HO +$ CD $D = U$ RAT $A = I + Y$

Obtain a Bachelor of Science Degree in _ _ _ _ _ _ _ _ _ _ _ the goal is to teach students how to keep technology safe.

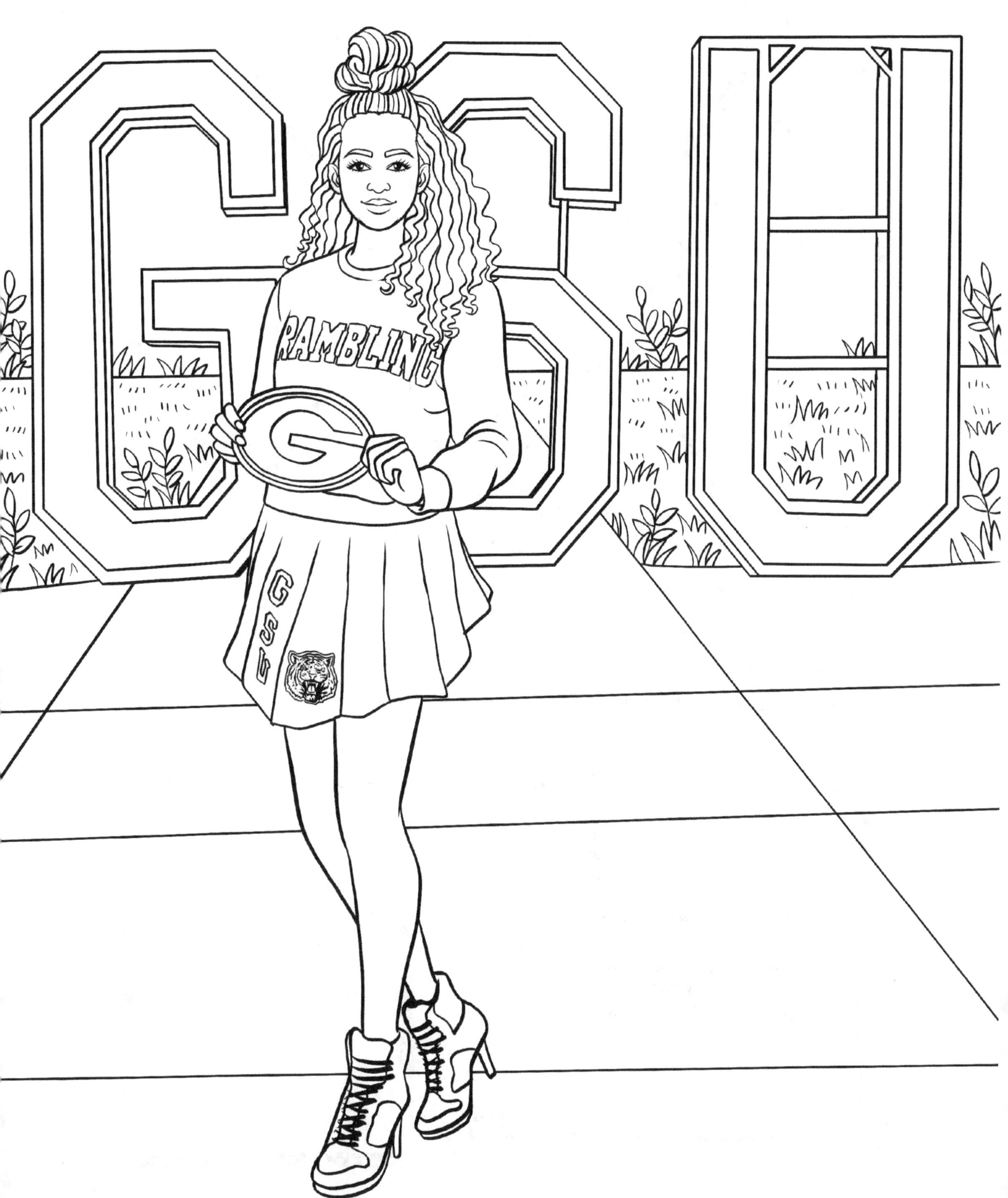

GSU
RAMBLING
G
GSU

Hampton University

On February 11, 1960 Hampton Institute students were the first in Virginia to participate
A) Bus Boycott
B) Lunch Counter Sit-in,
C) Voting Rights

What year was the Hampton Normal & Agriculture Institute founded?
A) 1868
B) 1849
C) 1855

In 1878, Hampton housed these students and began a program that was active for over 40 years.
A) African American
B) Mexican American
C) Native American

"The Standard of Excellence, An Education for Life"

The Alumni Office of Affairs is an integral part of Hampton University. What role would you play ensuring the success of future students as an alumni?

What is the significance of the Emancipation Oak on the campus of Hampton University?

If you were a Hampton Pirate, which athletic team would you join & why?

You are a junior at the School of Liberal Arts and Education, which major and career are you most inspired by?

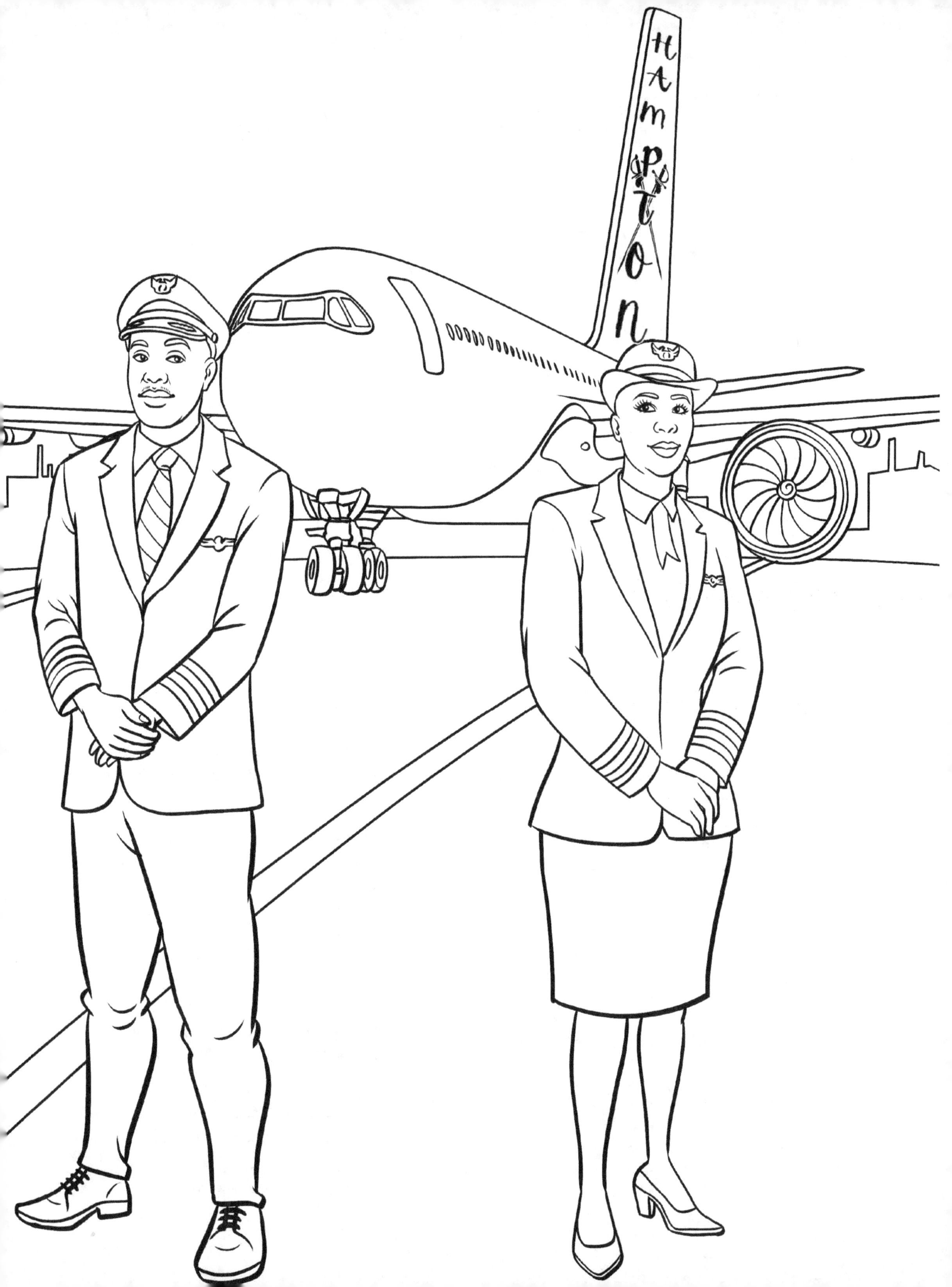

HAmPtOn

Howard University

H U 1867

The Mecca of Black Education

You Know!

Brief History

Howard University was chartered on March 2, 1867 in Washington DC. It was founded by General Oliver Otis Howard. In its first 5 years, it educated over 150,000 freed slaves. Howard played a role in the Civil Rights movement. Students started the "stool-technique" they would sit at stools in local cafeterias that denied African Americans. A student in both Philosophy & Divinity by the name of Kwame Toure, created "Black Power" & worked as a voting activist.

Complete the crossword puzzle related to the Academic School & Colleges

Picture Landmark Scavenger Hunt: Take a photo in front of each location

The Yard
Howard Hall
Burr Gymnasium
Founders Library
Student Health Center
Andrew Rankin Chapel
Ralph J. Bunche Center
Howard University Hospital
Harriet Tubman Quadrangle
Frederick Douglass Memorial Hall

Best HBCU

H _ _ _ _ _ _ _ _

Name 5 publications

1.

2.

3.

4.

5.

What is the commercial radio station?

What is the public television station?

Howard University has produced some of the most brilliant, influential, powerful leaders in the world. Find these prominent alumni.

Amiri Baraka
Ben Ali
Carter Woodson
Cathy Hughes
Debbie Allen
Elijah Cummings
Frances Cress
Jamilah Lemiux
Kamala Harris
Lance Gross
Marlon Wayans

Nick Cannon
Omar Tyree
Pearl Cleage
Phylicia Rashad
Ralph Bunche
Roberta Flack
Sean Combs
Toni Morrison
Vashti Mckenzie
Wayne Frederick
Zora Neale

```
T r u t h v s i r r a H a l a m a K s a
n d S e r v a N k c a l F a t r e b o R
i c e Y Z B j s i B Z Q i F a k m J K I
u O I n r n N L h c e d R X h o P a q a
O e D Q U c q a Q t k n S E C P f m C N
W I P g u r y n p T i C A n n w d i a o
G S w h r L q c R T L M a l D u T l t Q
P e a r l C l e a g e e c n i c P a h F
w h b m o I e G V J S T J k n I Z h y R
n o s d o o w r e t r a C J e o w L H a
e l a e N a r o z b I I t z h n n e u l
i N s s e r C s e c n a r F N u z m g p
x G n G M x l s E H S y b k v Y o i h h
R P h y l i c i a R a s h a d i s u e B
M a r l o n w a y a n s D h e G C x s u
o q i A k c i r e d e r F e n y a w k n
i g O V A s g n i m m u c h a j i l E c
n o s i r r o M i n o T Y e o u H l Z h
n e l l A e i b b e D O m a r T y r e e
a k a r a B i r i m A L Y e K M b A E r
```

Once you find all the words. Copy the unused letters starting in the top left corner into the blanks to reveal the hidden message.

_ _ _ _ _ _   _ _ _ _

_ _ _ _ _ _ _ _ _ _

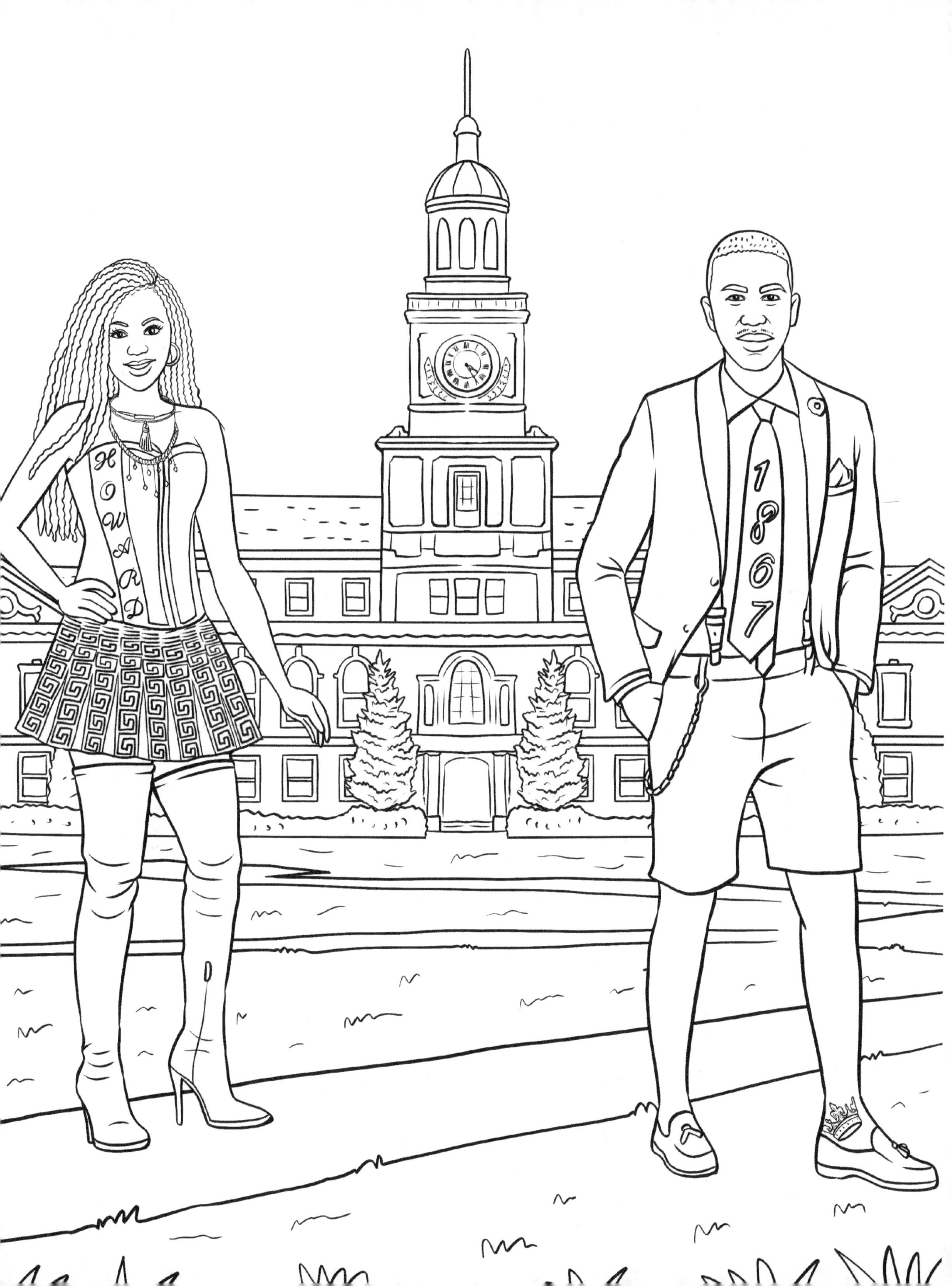

HOWARD
1867

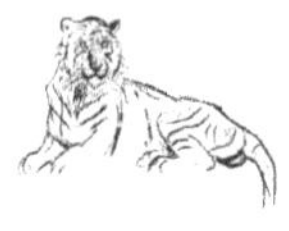

Jackson State University 1877

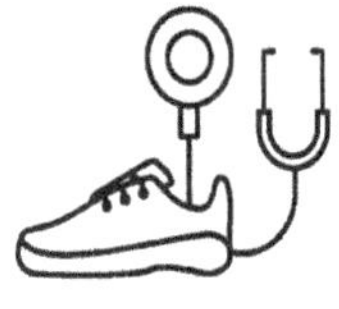

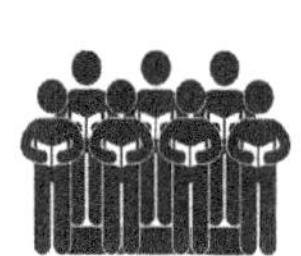

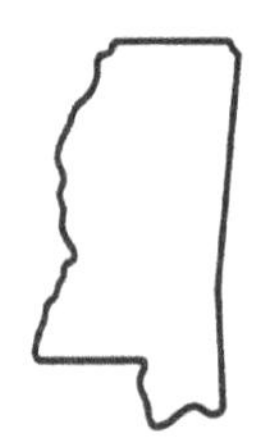

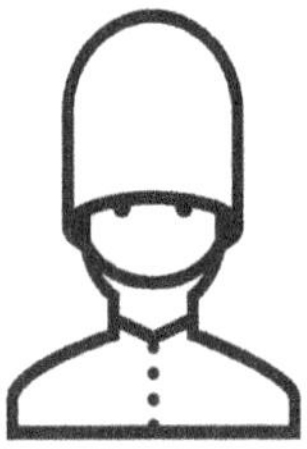

p c z e n g e w b k i u s c s m a
s e l o t b l a v p b s i a o e i
l e r e i a t v p w p j o w c t d
n s t v o t t i x t m s b s i e e
c v u t a p s s q k h s u h a o m
n s y l e s a m n l t i d u l r s
j s i m i s p t o o z m b s w o t
f o d s h h j l r o s y e j o l r
n v s t i g e r s a b k w w r o o
c i v i l r i g h t s c c y k g p
m s l a g n e b e u l b i a z y s
a c c o u n t i n g a l b n j i h
y c i l o p h t l a e h e r o g s
j a z z s t u d i e s w m t x s k
e c a p s o r e a l l a h r e y a
s d g t u a u r b a n d e s i g n
r i o h c s s a m z b u h c k t v

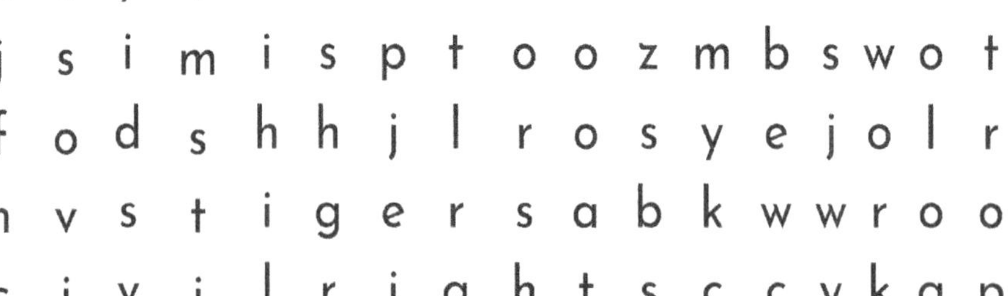

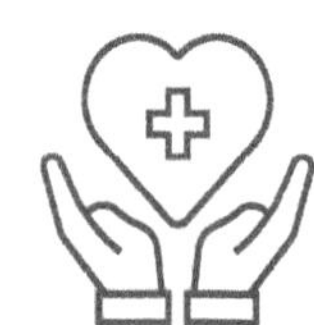

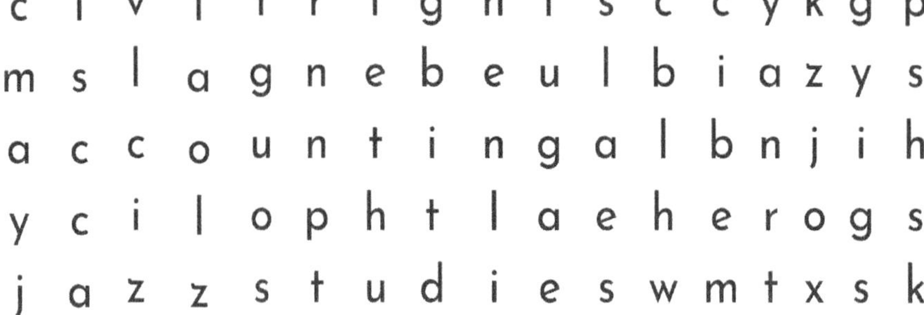

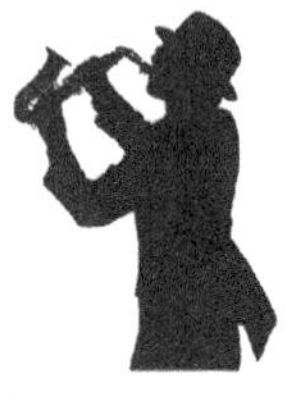

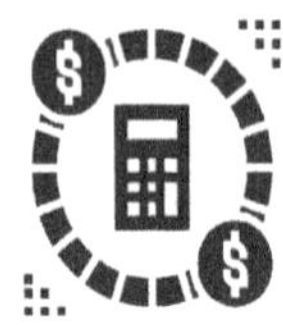

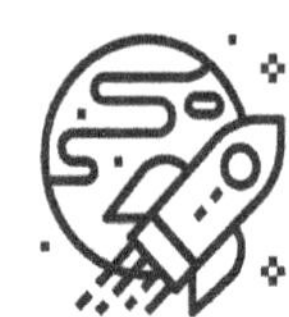

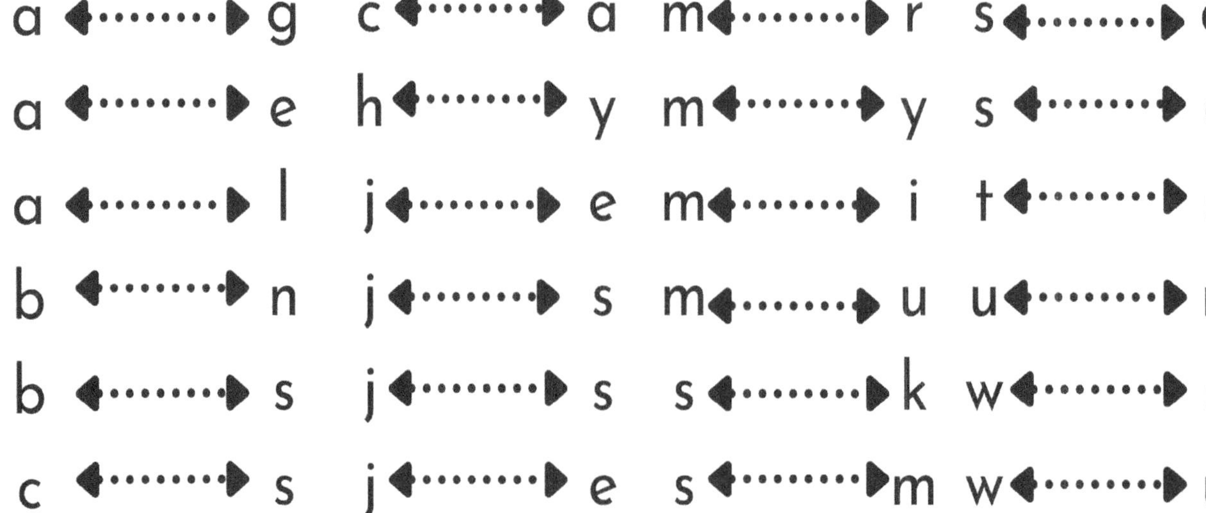

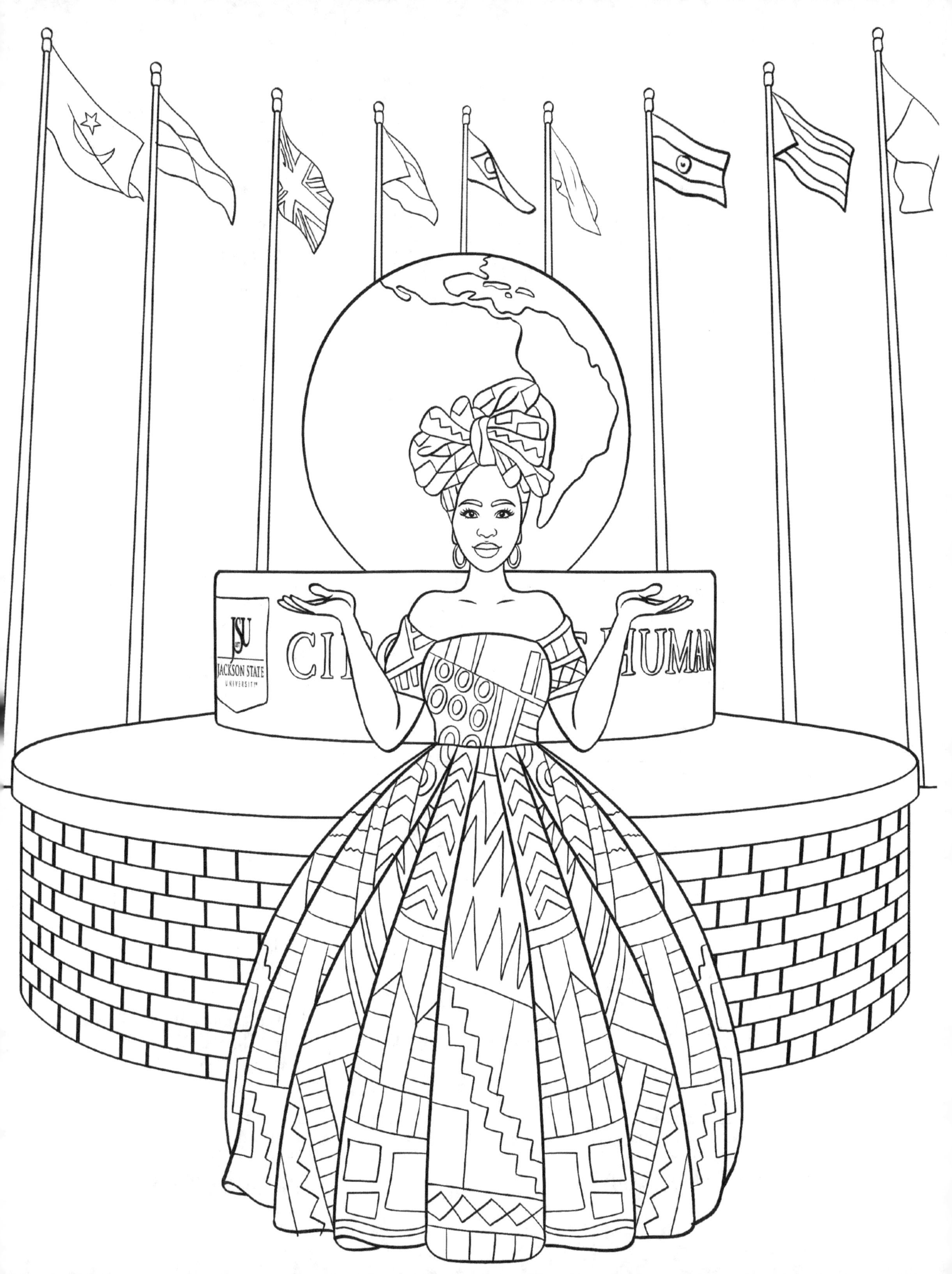

JSU
JACKSON STATE
UNIVERSITY
CITY OF HUMAN

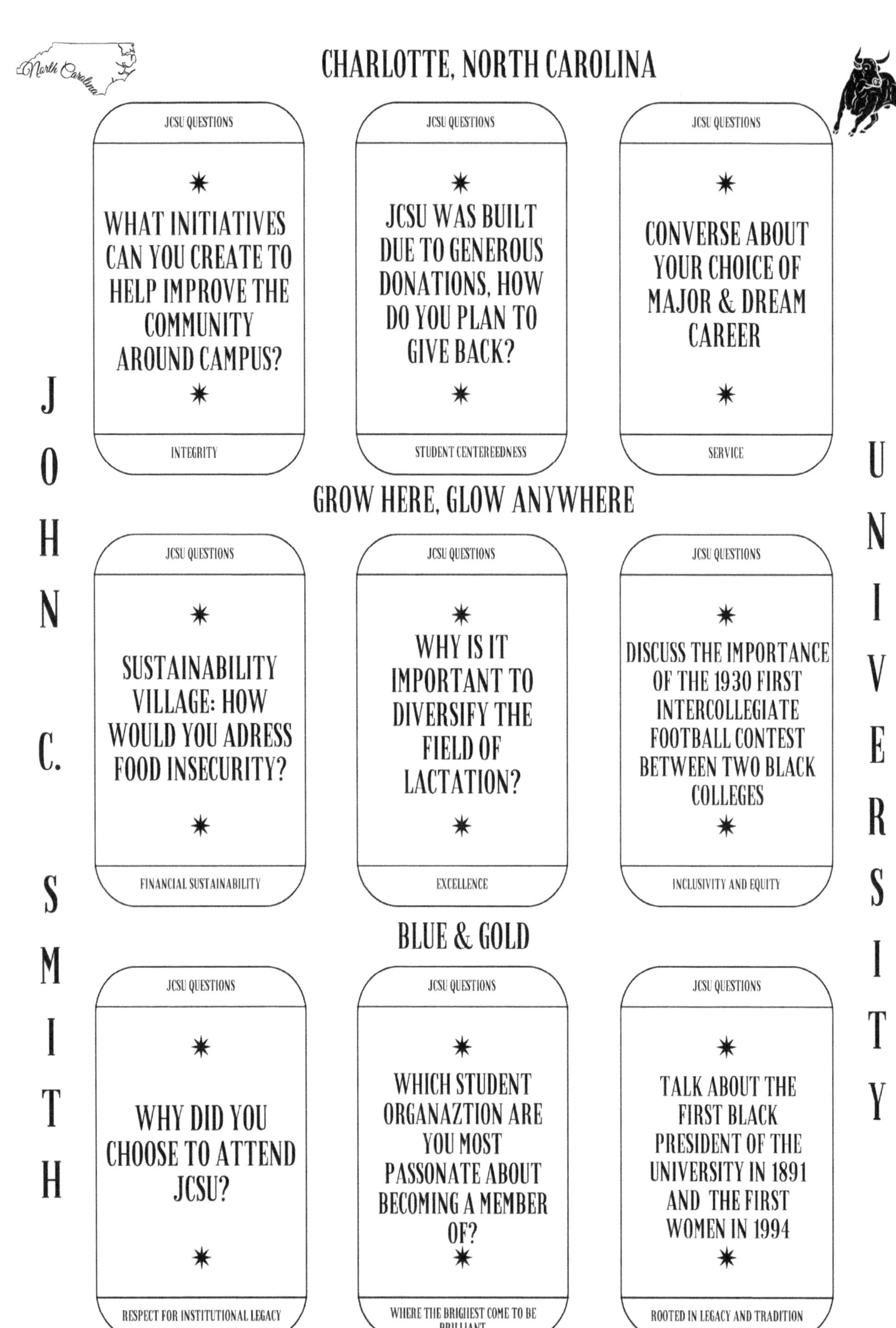
JCSU QUESTIONS

WHAT INITIATIVES CAN YOU CREATE TO HELP IMPROVE THE COMMUNITY AROUND CAMPUS?

INTEGRITY

JCSU QUESTIONS

JCSU WAS BUILT DUE TO GENEROUS DONATIONS, HOW DO YOU PLAN TO GIVE BACK?

STUDENT CENTEREEDNESS

JCSU QUESTIONS

CONVERSE ABOUT YOUR CHOICE OF MAJOR & DREAM CAREER

SERVICE

GROW HERE, GLOW ANYWHERE

JCSU QUESTIONS

SUSTAINABILITY VILLAGE: HOW WOULD YOU ADRESS FOOD INSECURITY?

FINANCIAL SUSTAINABILITY

JCSU QUESTIONS

WHY IS IT IMPORTANT TO DIVERSIFY THE FIELD OF LACTATION?

EXCELLENCE

JCSU QUESTIONS

DISCUSS THE IMPORTANCE OF THE 1930 FIRST INTERCOLLEGIATE FOOTBALL CONTEST BETWEEN TWO BLACK COLLEGES

INCLUSIVITY AND EQUITY

BLUE & GOLD

JCSU QUESTIONS

WHY DID YOU CHOOSE TO ATTEND JCSU?

RESPECT FOR INSTITUTIONAL LEGACY

JCSU QUESTIONS

WHICH STUDENT ORGANAZTION ARE YOU MOST PASSONATE ABOUT BECOMING A MEMBER OF?

WHERE THE BRIGHEST COME TO BE BRILLIANT

JCSU QUESTIONS

TALK ABOUT THE FIRST BLACK PRESIDENT OF THE UNIVERSITY IN 1891 AND THE FIRST WOMEN IN 1994

ROOTED IN LEGACY AND TRADITION

JOHN C. SMITH

UNIVERSITY

CONVERSATION QUESTIONS

1867

THE GOLDEN BULLS

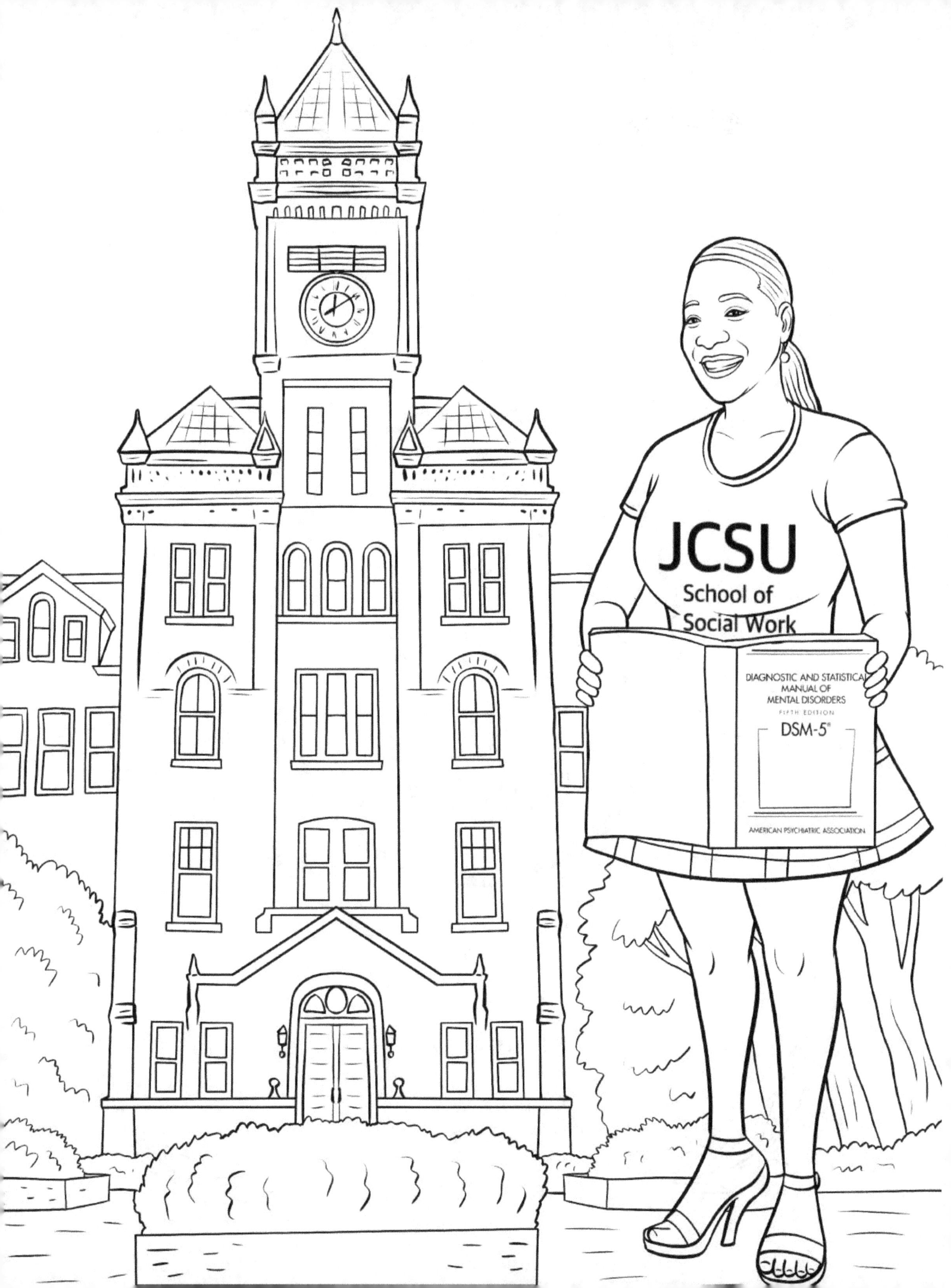

JCSU
School of
Social Work
DIAGNOSTIC AND STATISTICAL
MANUAL OF
MENTAL DISORDERS
FIFTH EDITION
DSM-5
AMERICAN PSYCHIATRIC ASSOCIATION

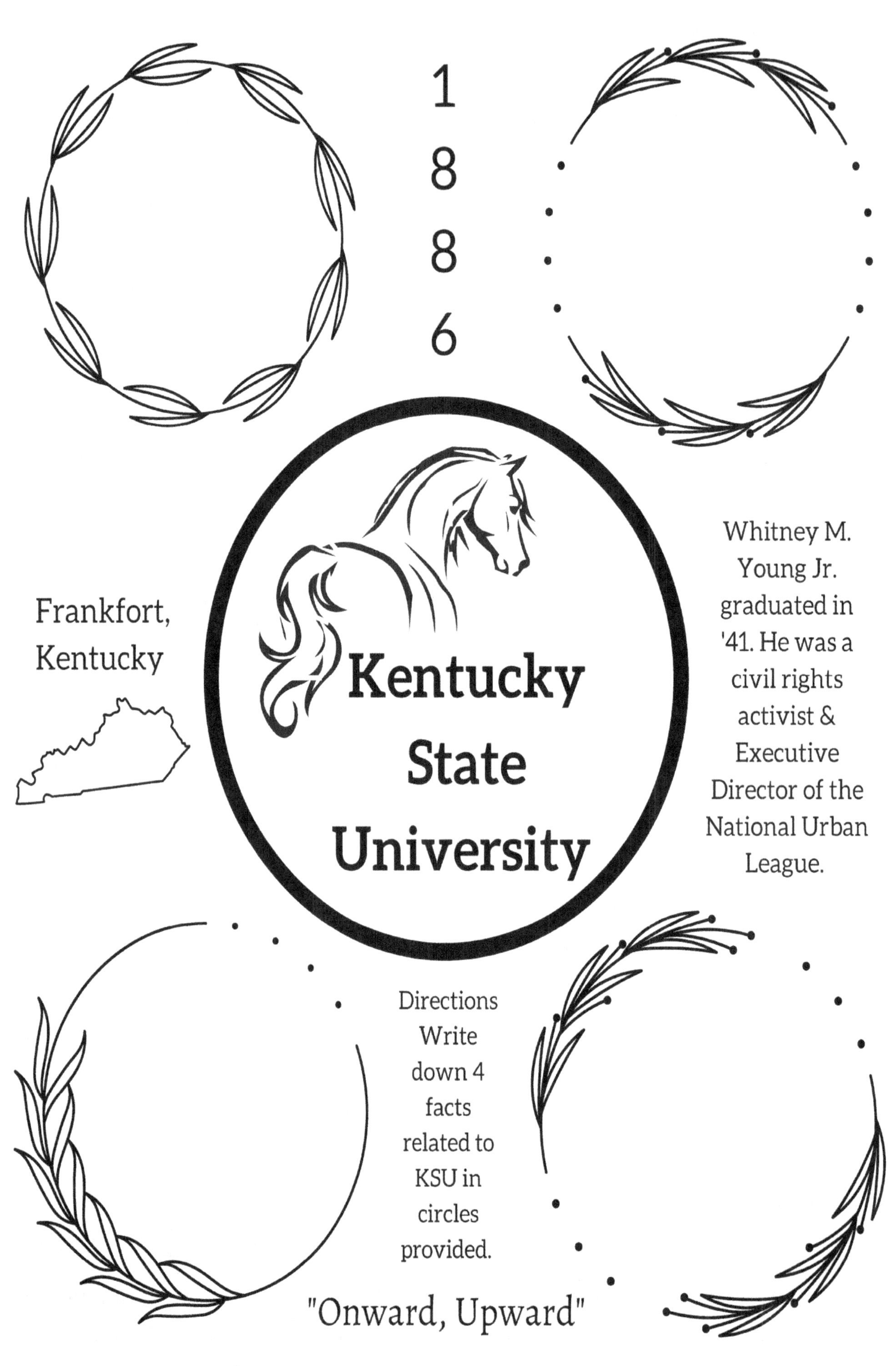

1886
Frankfort, Kentucky
Kentucky State University
Whitney M. Young Jr. graduated in '41. He was a civil rights activist & Executive Director of the National Urban League.
Directions
Write down 4 facts related to KSU in circles provided.
"Onward, Upward"

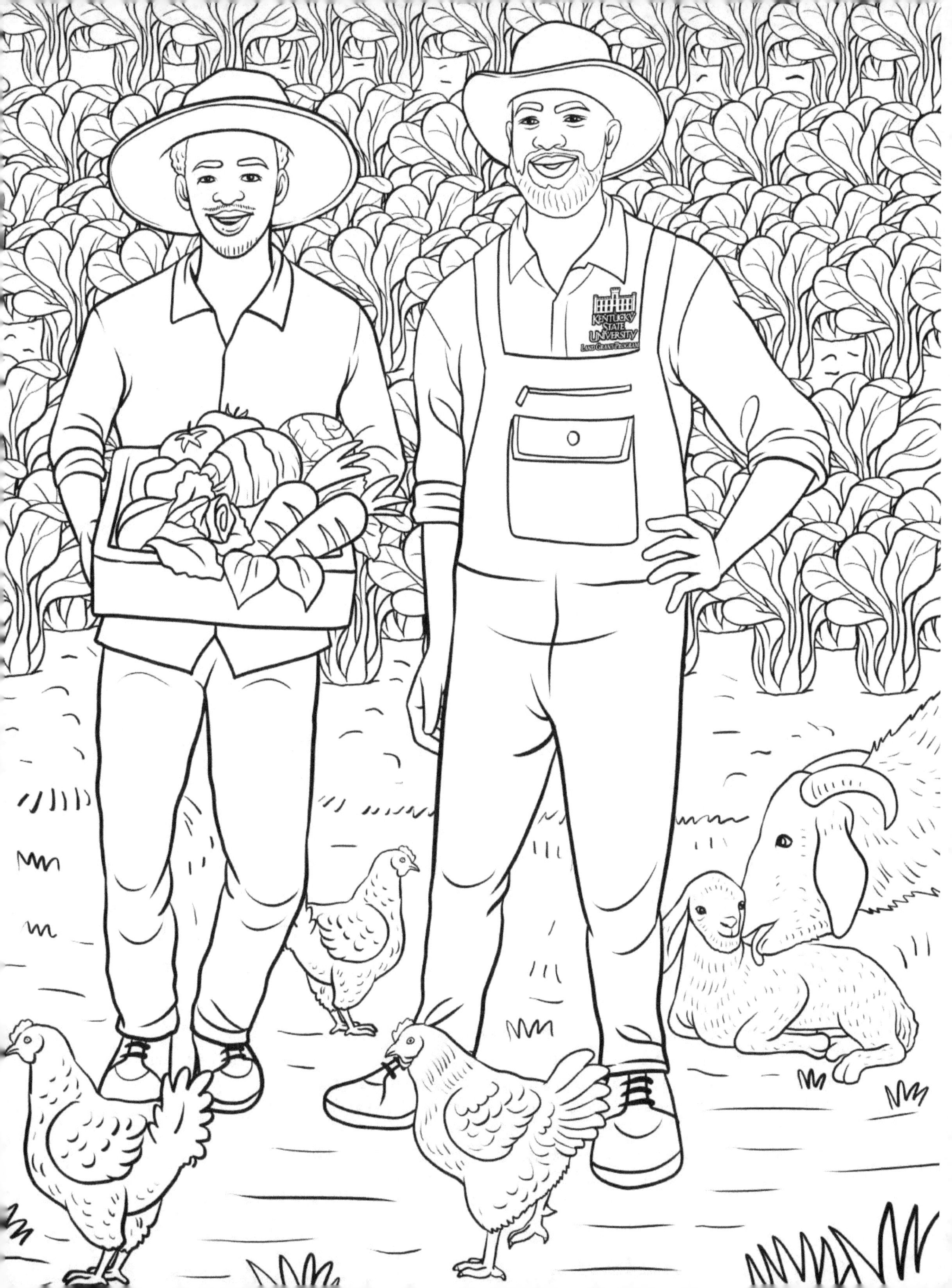

Down

1. On the Langston Tulsa campus, you can earn a Masters of Education in ______

3. What state is Langston University located in?

6. The broadcast journalism department students have the opportunity to write for this newspaper.

7. This camp is provided to acclimate new students to college life by touring the campus & meeting peers.

9. This scholarship is provided to eligible incoming freshmen and covers tuition, room & book stipend.

10. The only HBCU in Oklahoma.

12. The band is known as the Marching ____

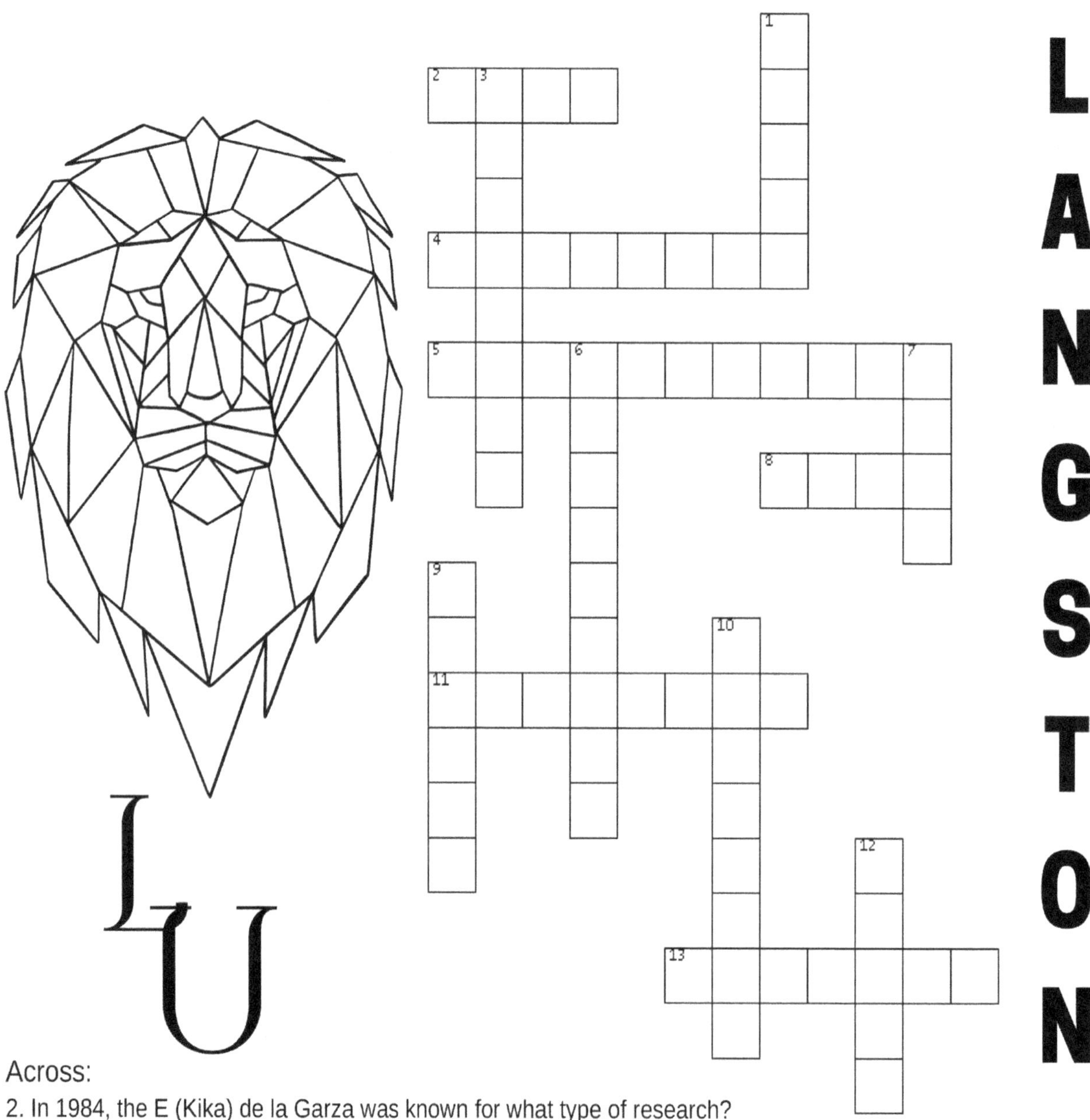

Across:

2. In 1984, the E (Kika) de la Garza was known for what type of research?

4. Which president had this philosophy, "serve the people of the state at the point of their greatest need."

5. Langston University was filmed on this popular reality TV show on BET network

8. Thanks to the Higher Emergency Relief Fund, Langston was able to wipe out 4.6 million in balances for students enrolled in a "pandemic semester" to ______

11. In 2001, the weekend college in Oklahoma City offered a Bachelors in which studies?

13. In 1890, the university was founded on a land grant through which Act?

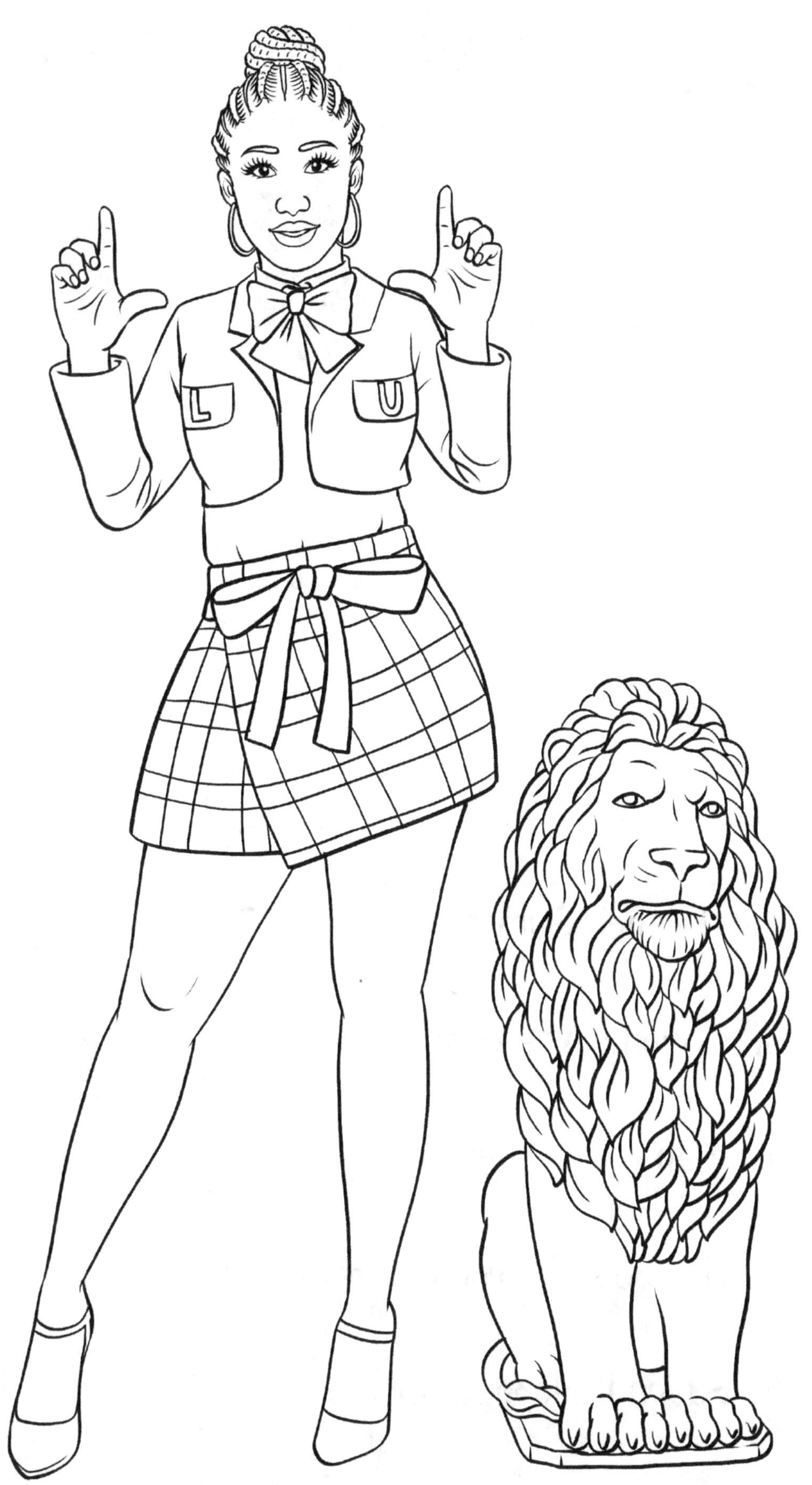

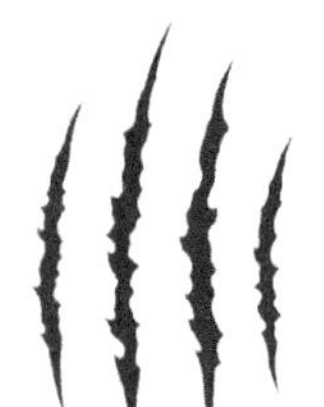

Lincoln University

Learn, Liberate, Lead

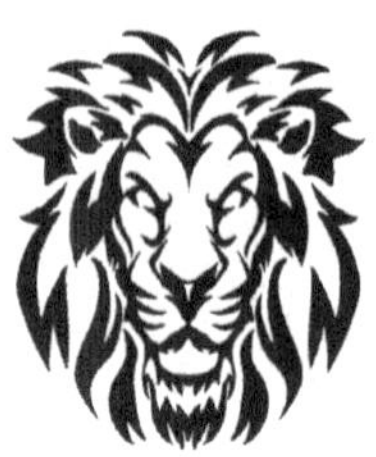

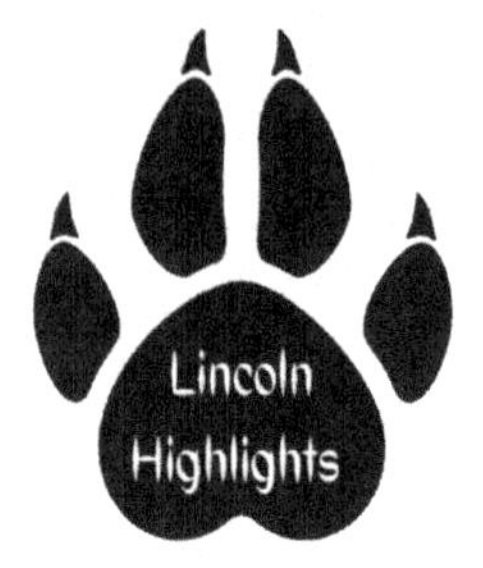

Lincoln University is the first degree granting HBCU in the country

Approximately 20% of African American physicians & 10% of attorneys graduated from Lincoln.

What major are you most passionate about?

Enhance your experience by choosing 3 clubs to join.

Alumni Spotlight

1. Brenda Allen

2. Francis Summer

3. Kwame Nkrumah

4. Langston Hughes

5. Thurgood Marshall

6. Saara Kuugongelwa

Match the Alumni, year degree earned and career.

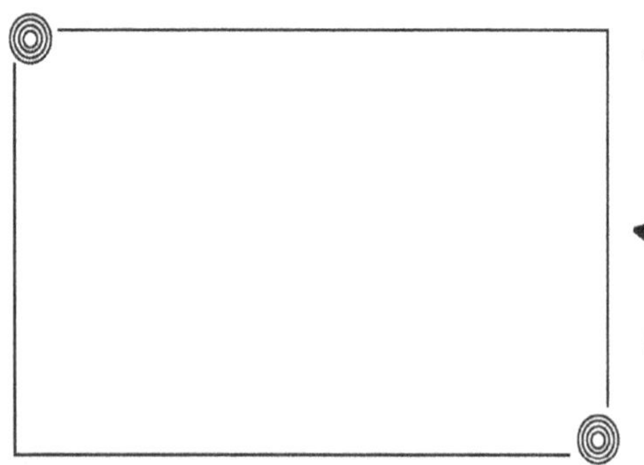

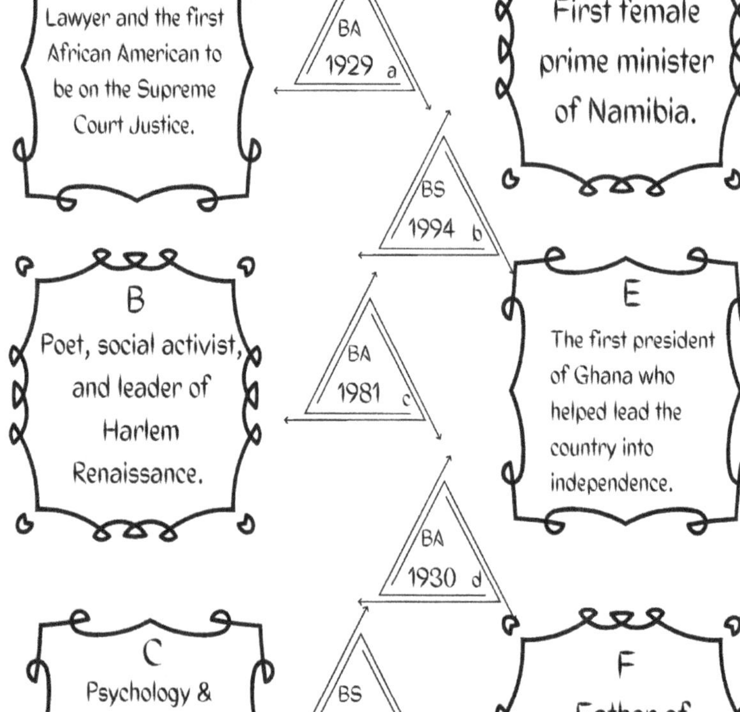

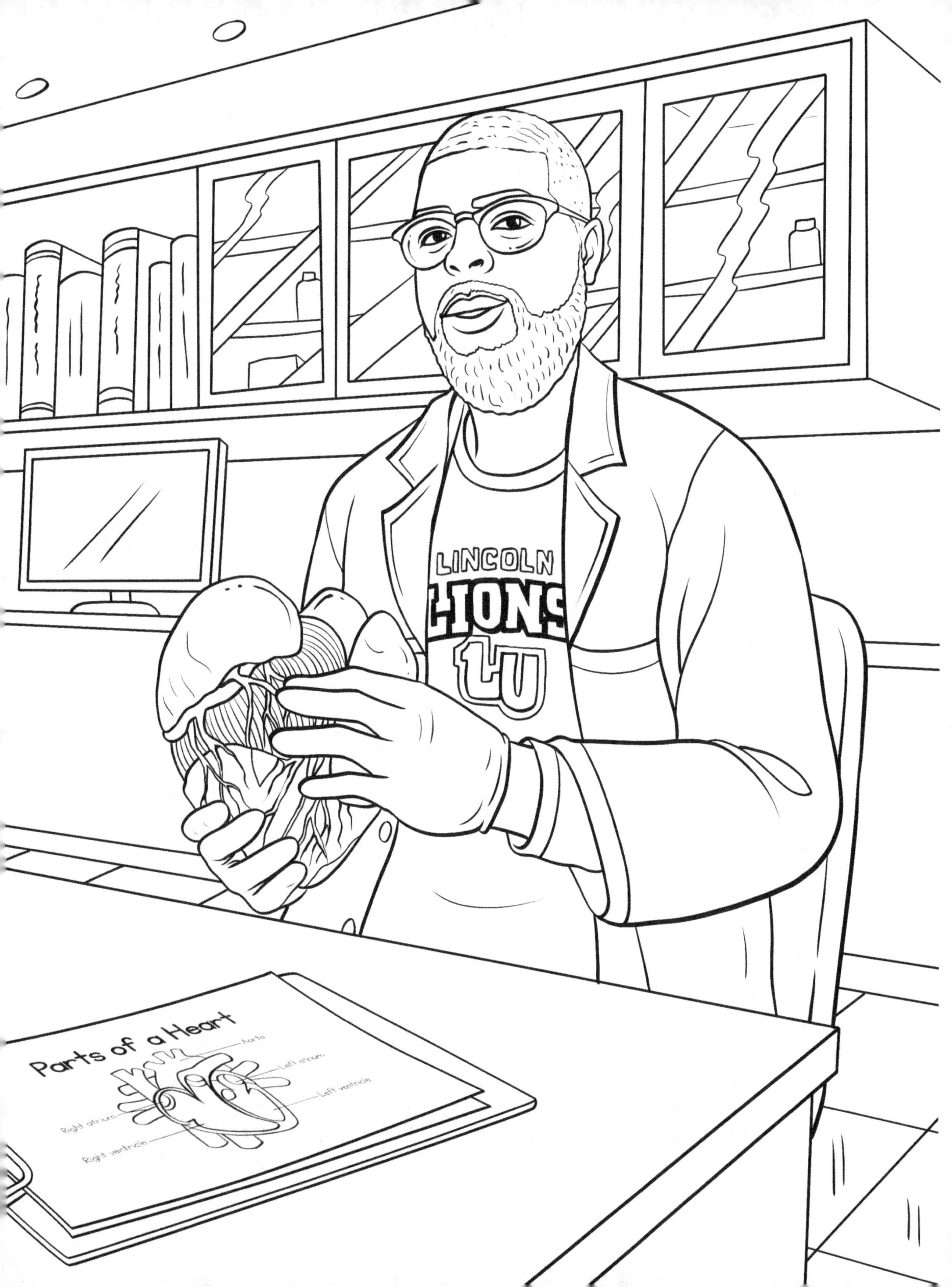
LINCOLN
LIONS
LU
Parts of a Heart
Aorta
Left atrium
Left ventricle
Right atrium
Right ventricle

University of Maryland Eastern Shore

Deeds, not Words

Accounting
Aerospace
Agribusiness
Animal poultry
Art Education
Aviation
Biochemistry
Chemistry

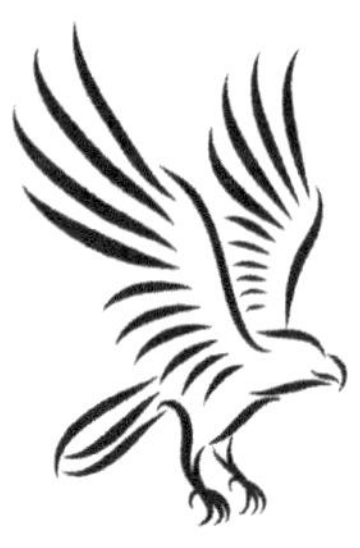

Criminal Justice
Cybersecurity
Dietetics
Digital Media
Finance
Fisheries Science
Golf Management
Hospitality

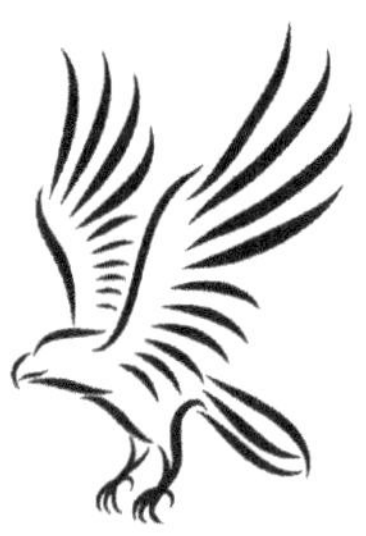

Marine Ecology
Marketing
Pharmaceutical
Rural Health
Sequential Arts
Special Education
Toxicology
Urban Forestry

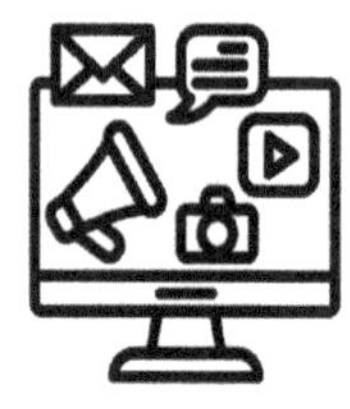

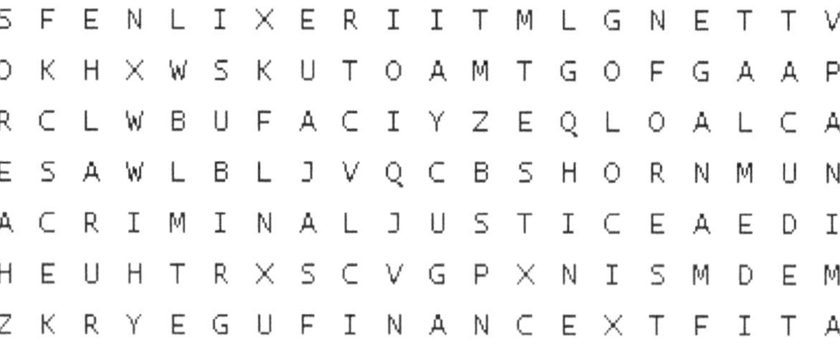
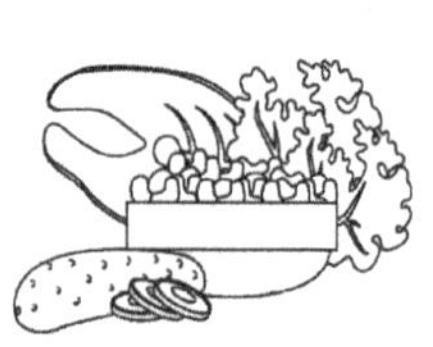
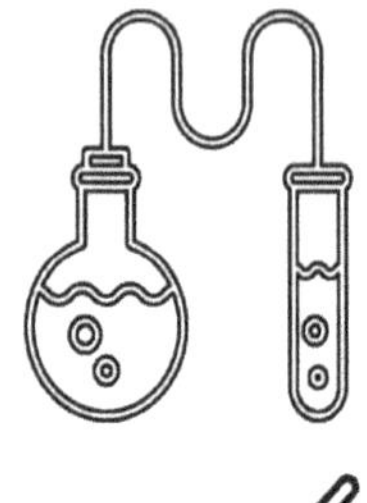
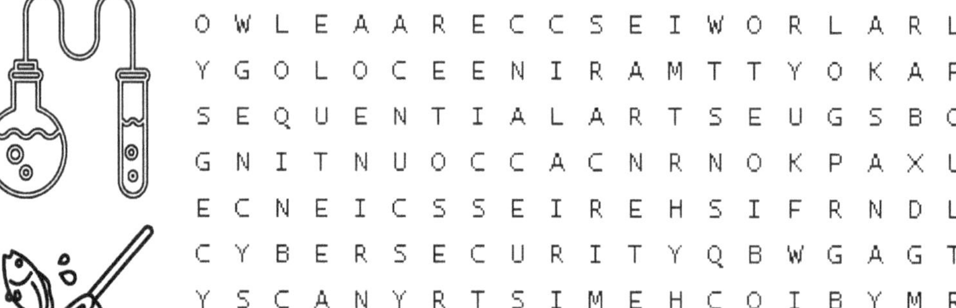
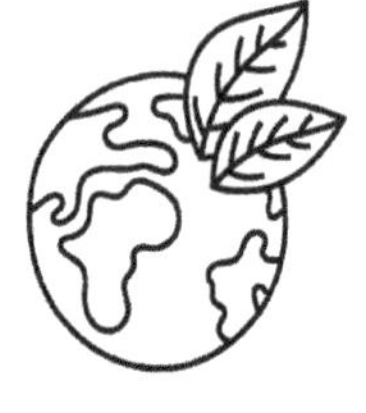
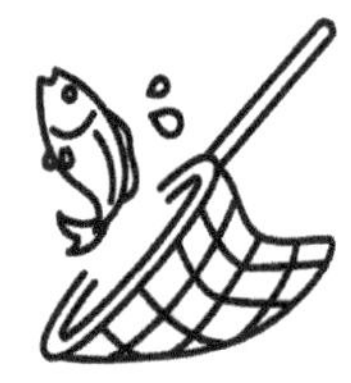
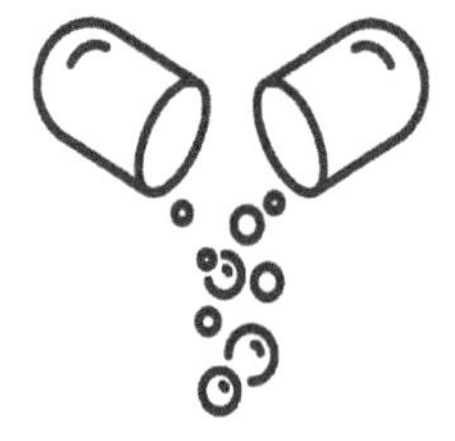

```
E J H D D S Y A E W Y X Q H H U T D K N
C H T W I S T R T A S C O C N R N I N M
A X L H H E J M T X R S N O Y B E G O L
P D A P W N T M C S P R I J Y A M I I K
S F E N L I X E R I I T M L G N E T T V
O K H X W S K U T O A M T G O F G A A P
R C L W B U F A C I Y Z E Q L O A L C A
E S A W L B L J V Q C B S H O R N M U N
A C R I M I N A L J U S T I C E A E D I
H E U H T R X S C V G P X N I S M D E M
Z K R Y E G U F I N A N C E X T F I T A
O W L E A A R E C C S E I W O R L A R L
Y G O L O C E E N I R A M T T Y O K A P
S E Q U E N T I A L A R T S E U G S B O
G N I T N U O C C A C N R N O K P A X U
E C N E I C S S E I R E H S I F R N D L
C Y B E R S E C U R I T Y Q B W G A G T
Y S C A N Y R T S I M E H C O I B Y M R
L A C I T U E C A M R A H P U R M I Q Y
S P E C I A L E D U C A T I O N R J I A
```

University of Maryland Eastern Shore is a public land grant research university located in Princess Anne, Maryland. The doors opened on September 13, 1886 under the auspice of Delaware Conference of Methodist Episcopal Church. Benjamin and Portia Bird welcomed the first 9 students. After multiple name changes, it eventually became UMES on 1970.

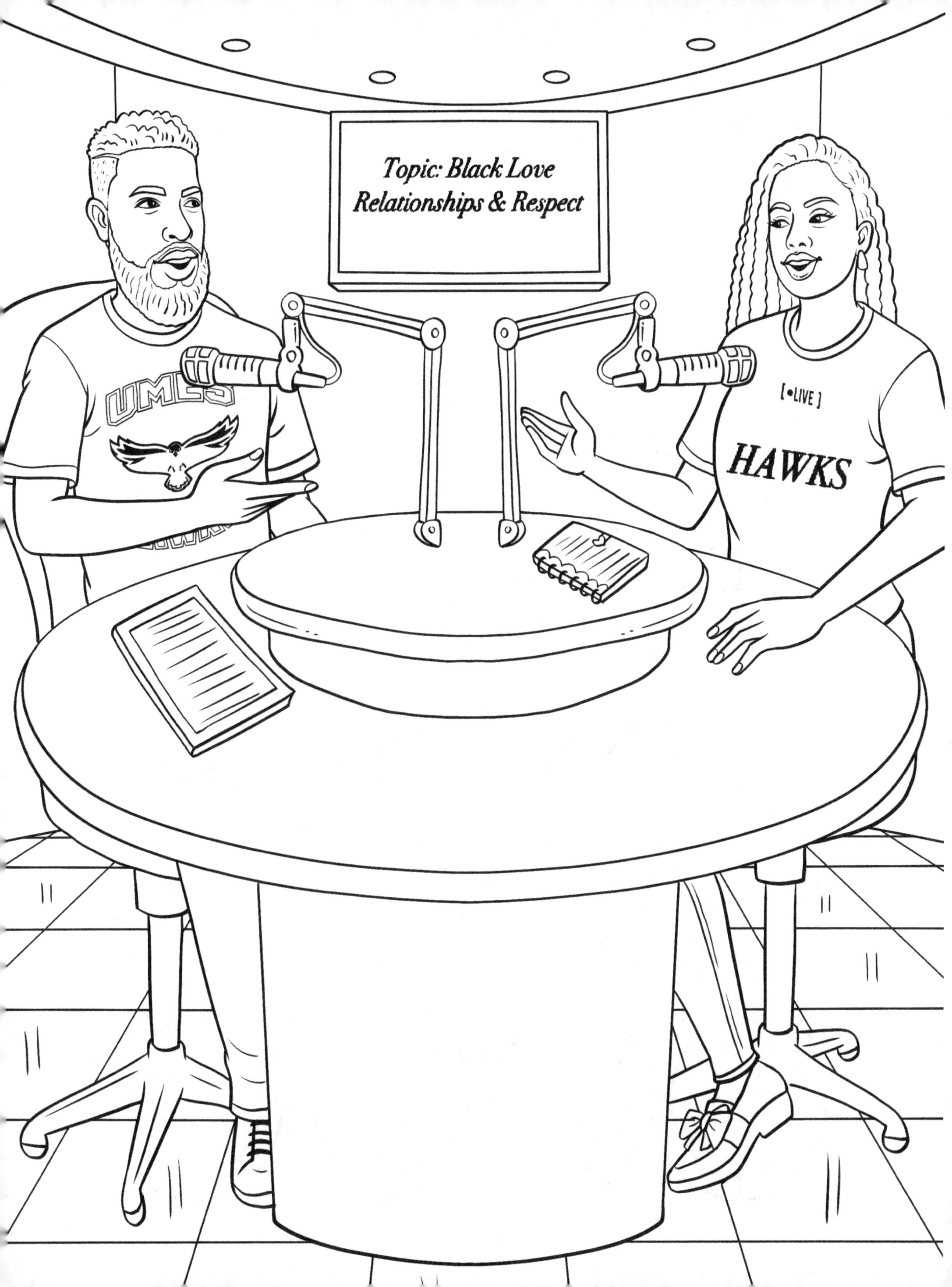

Topic: Black Love
Relationships & Respect
UMES
LIVE
HAWKS

Meharry Medical College

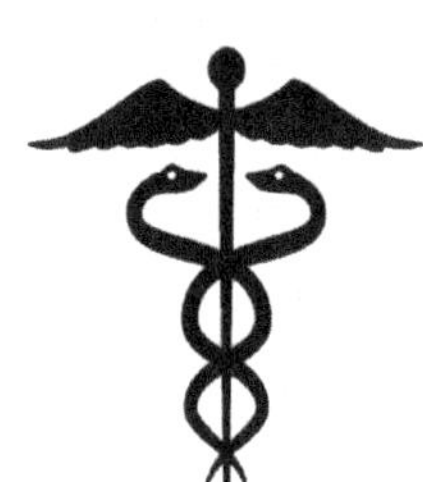
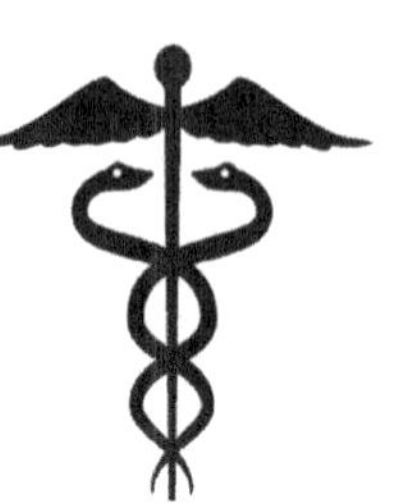

2 Players. Each person will provide the correct answer for each phrase or question. If correct shade in with a color of choice. 1st one to get 4 in a row wins the game.

Where is Meharry located?

Campus guide known as the "storyteller"

Name the Irish immigrant Salt Trader

An annual event when students discovery where they will be placed for residency.

Name the Clinical Sciences Surgery department

Center to maintain physical health

The first founding president from 1876-1921

Which Masters degree uses computer science & statistical concepts?

Clinic in Nashville General Hospital

Registered students must have or purchase this insurance

Research in women's health care

What year was Meharry chartered?

1893, First female graduate to receive a medical degree

Student organization that wants to end racial discrimination medicare care

What project is used to modify risk for chronic diseases?

Notable Alumni: President of the Republic of Malawi

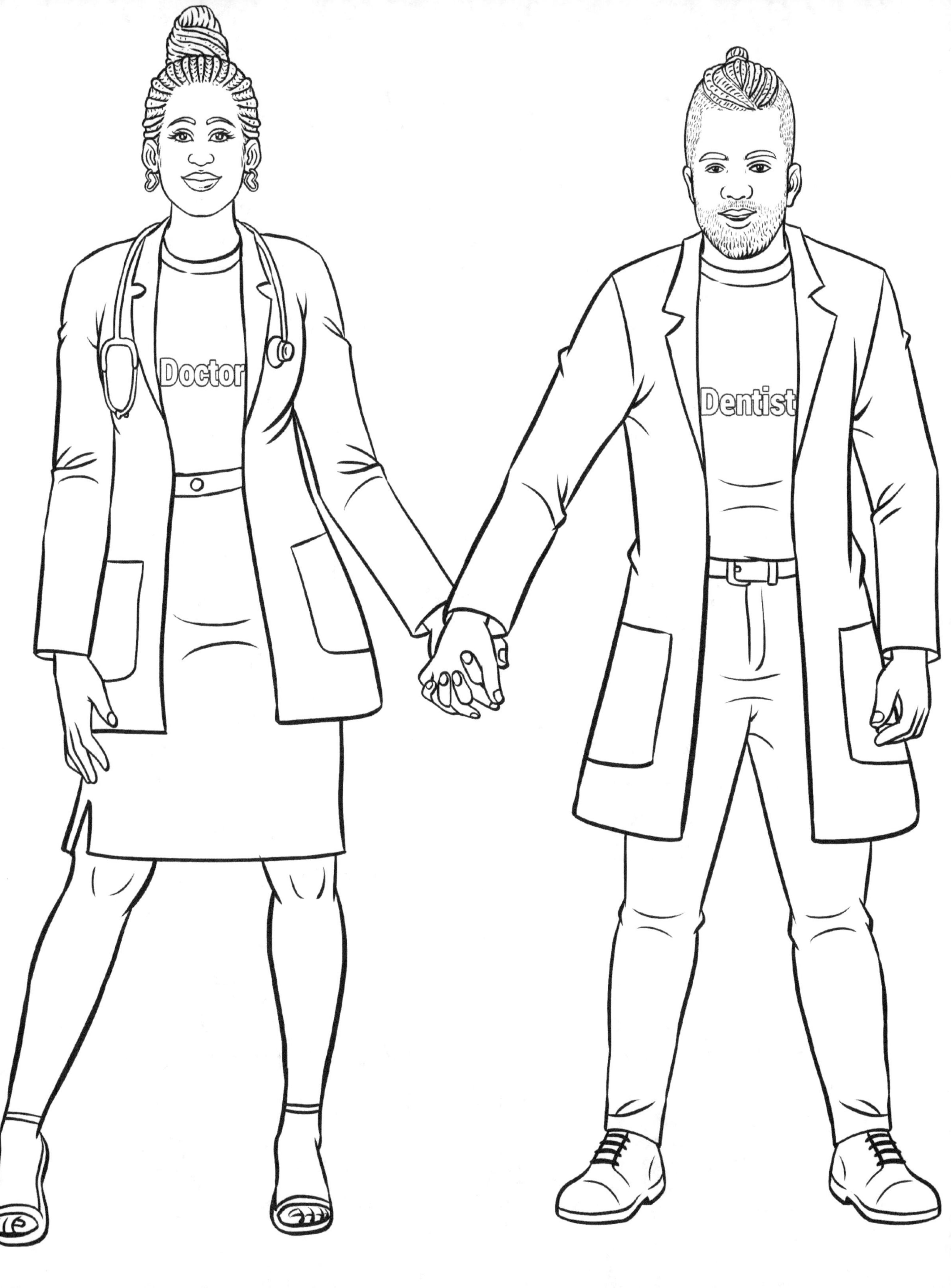

Doctor
Dentist

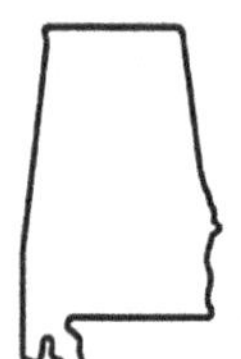

Miles College

Miles College is a private HBCU located in Fairfield, Alabama. Founded in 1898, they are associated with the Christian Methodist Episcopal Church and the United Negro College Fund. Miles College has played a huge role in the Civil Rights Movement. They continue to innovate in areas of STEM, entrepreneurship, leadership and so much more.

Karaoke Edition. Directions: 1) Choose a word from the list 2) take 2 minutes to create a song/rap involving the word. 3) Ready, Set, Perform

Black Lives Matter

Accounting

Bears

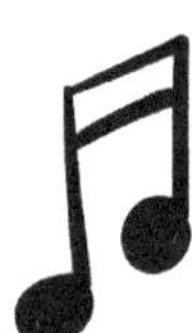

Alabama

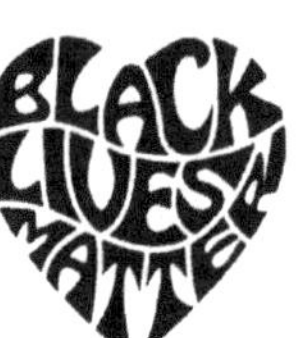

Milean

Cross Country

Early Childhood Education

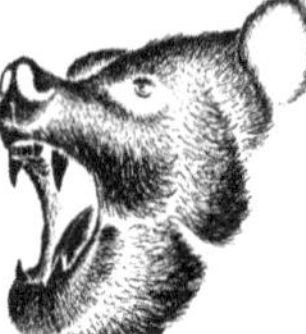

Coding

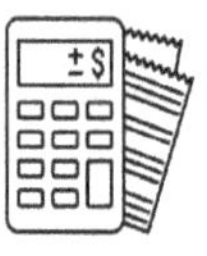

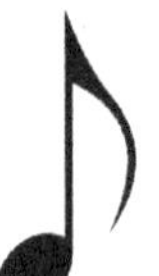

History

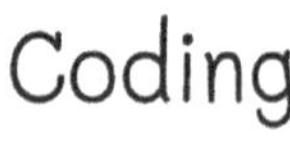

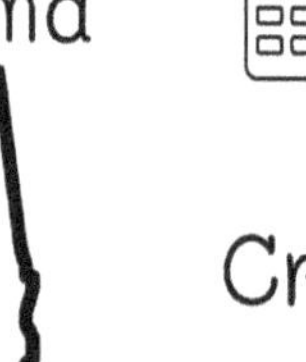

Pre-Law

Chemistry

Intelligence Community

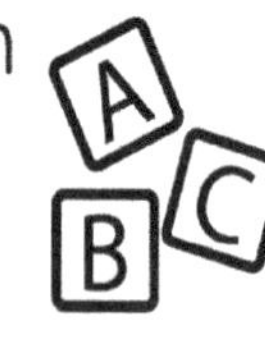

Miles College

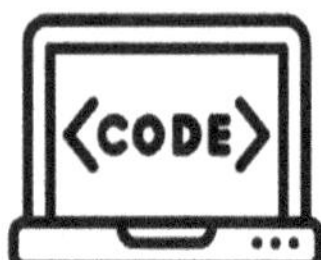

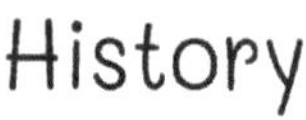

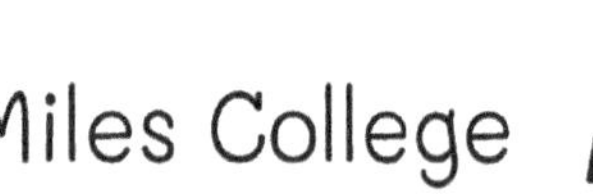

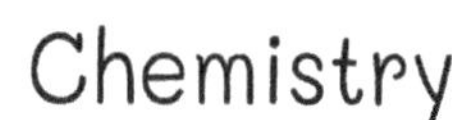

Social Work

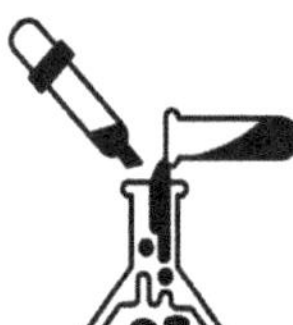

Purple Marching Machine

Golden Voices

Social & Economic Justice

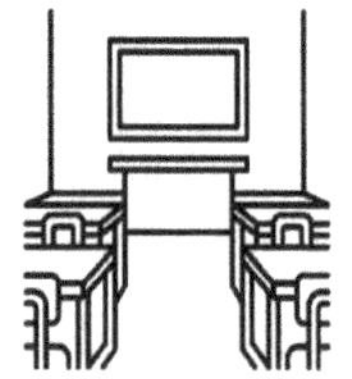

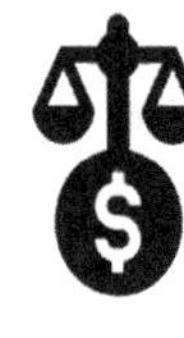

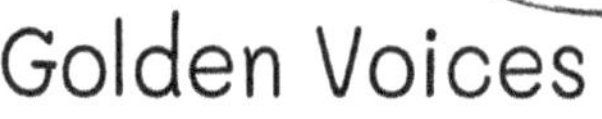

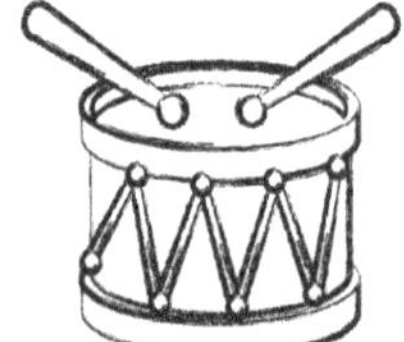

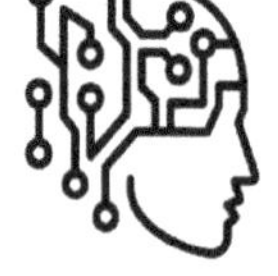

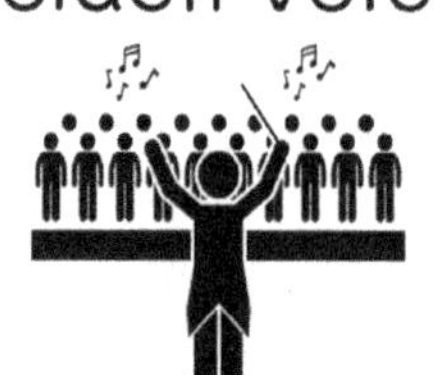

Graphic Design

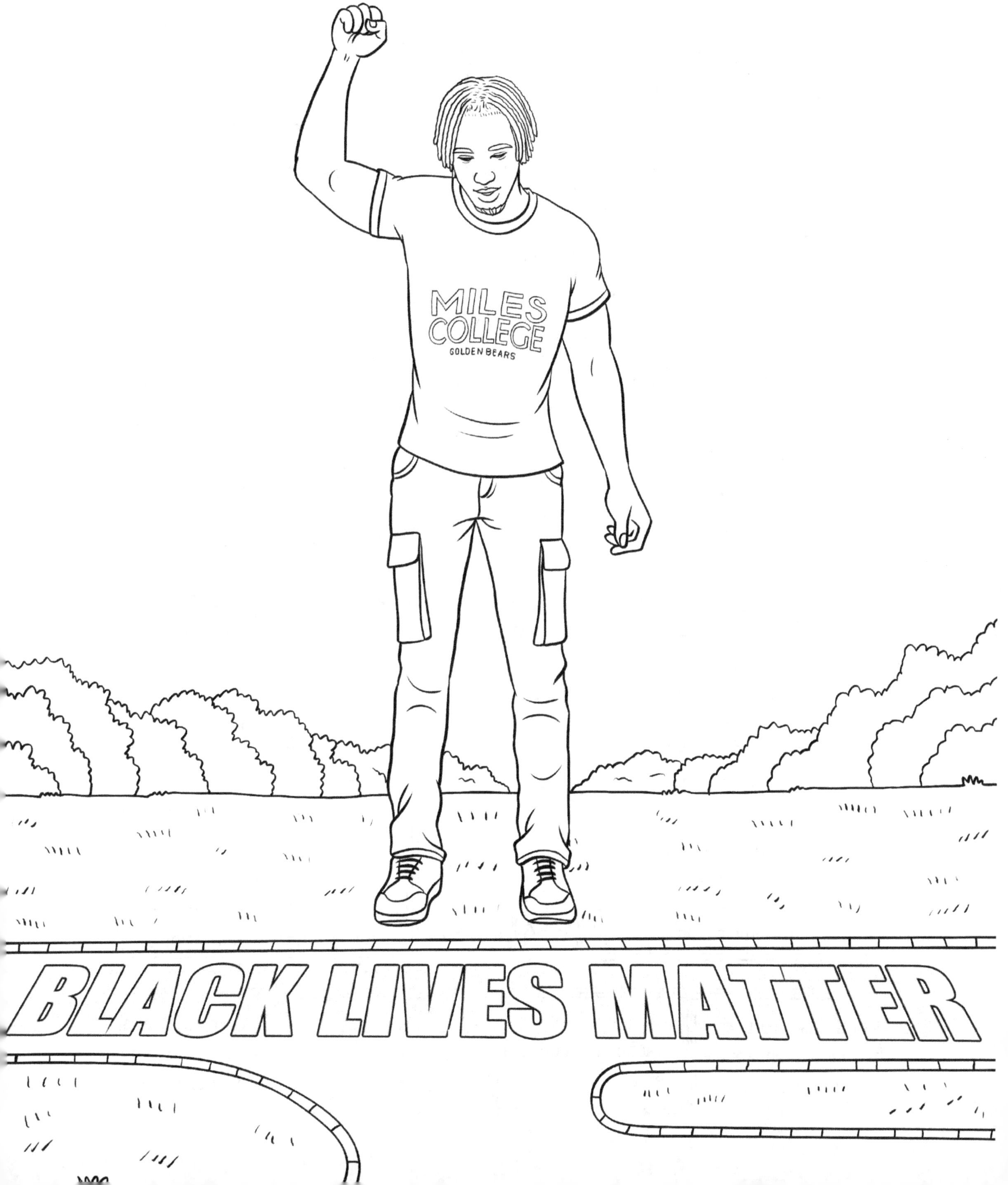

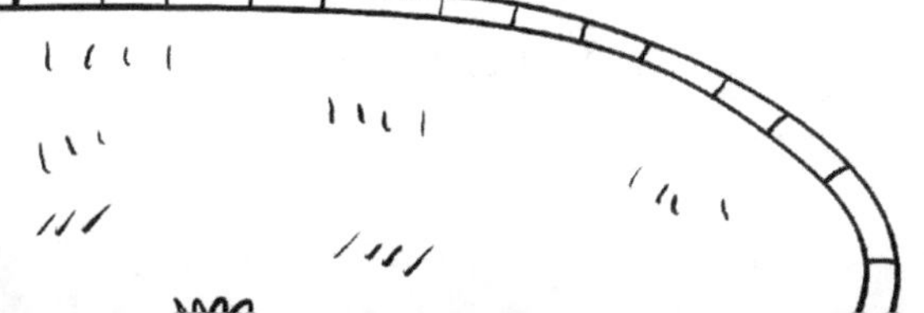

MILES
COLLEGE
GOLDEN BEARS
BLACK LIVES MATTER

MARTIN LUTHER KING JR . AT MOREHOUSE COLLEGE

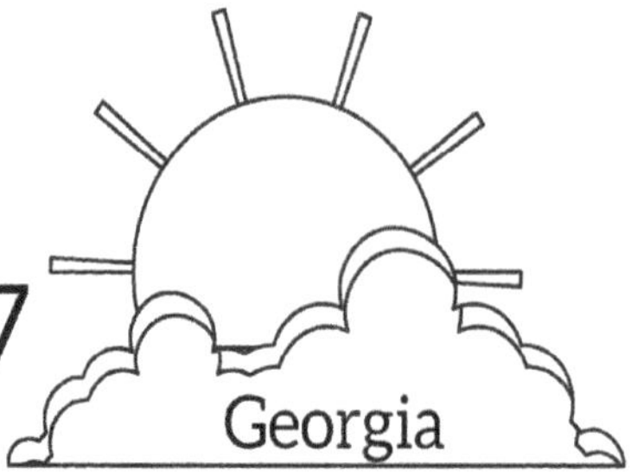

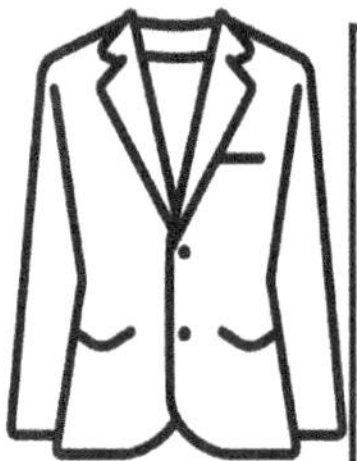

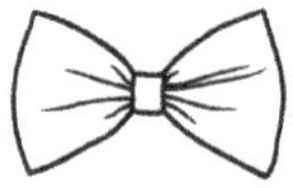

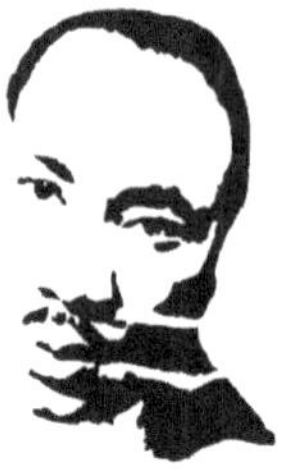

Match the statement to the correct year

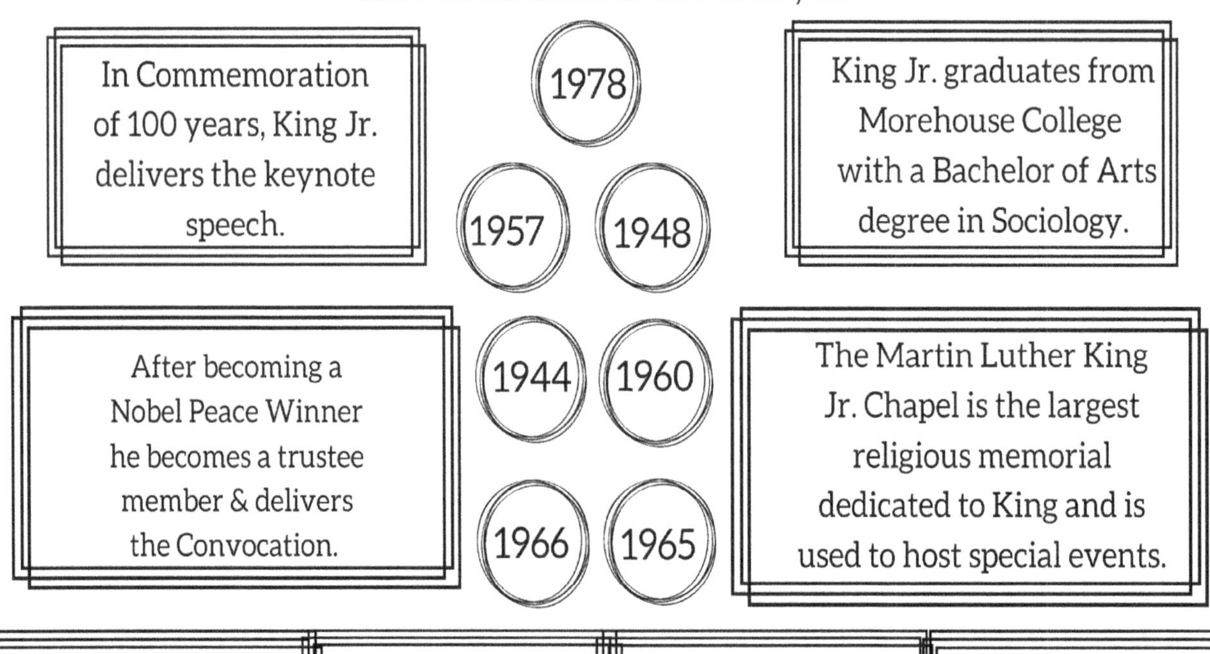

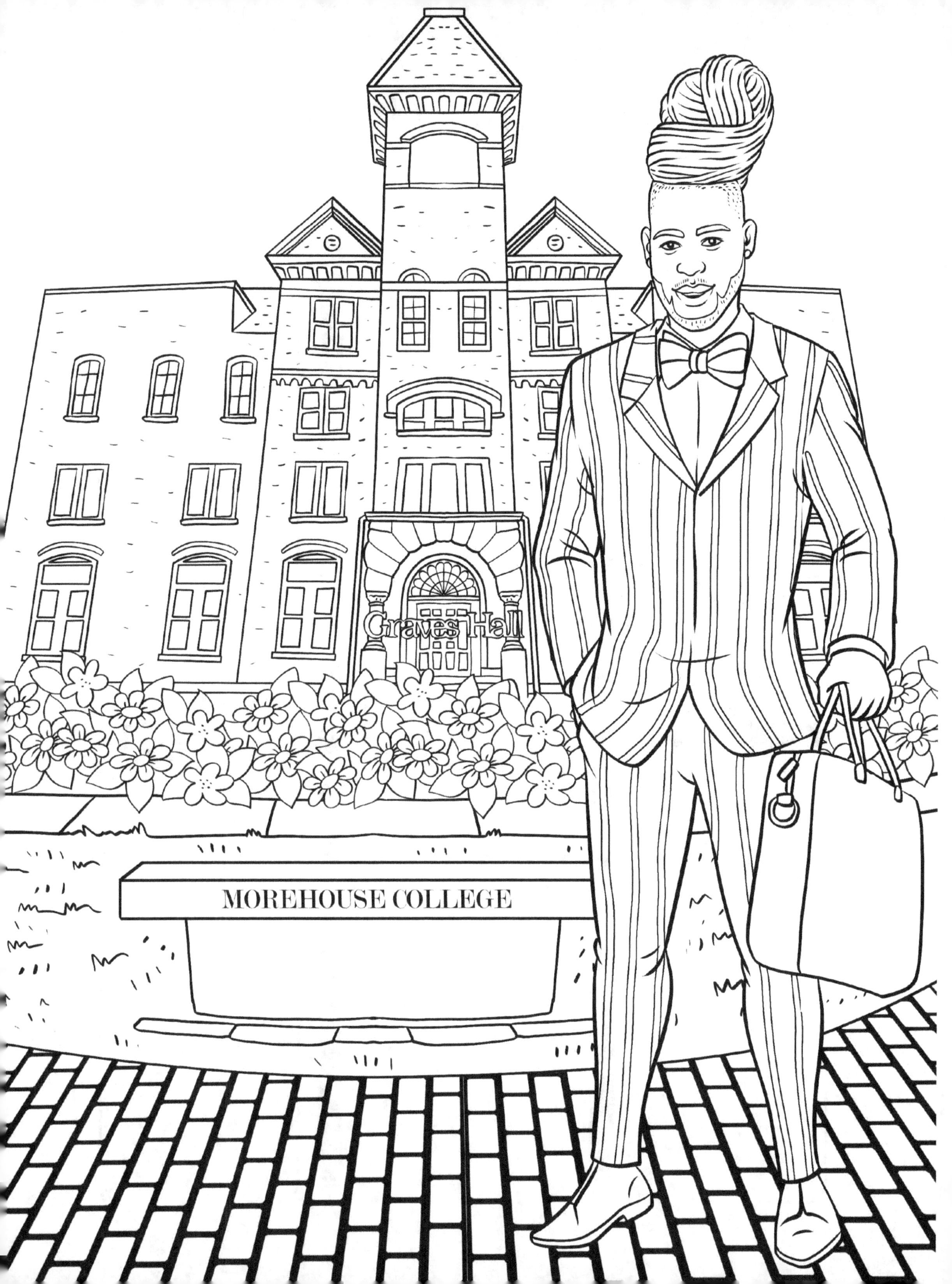

Graves Hall
MOREHOUSE COLLEGE

Morgan State University

Create a pamphlet for new incoming students

Provide 3 Historical Facts

“ ”

Draw Holmes Hall

Tell us about the Men's Track & Field Team

“ ”

You are receiving a Masters Degree in International Studies, what type of career may you have?

“ ”

Baltimore

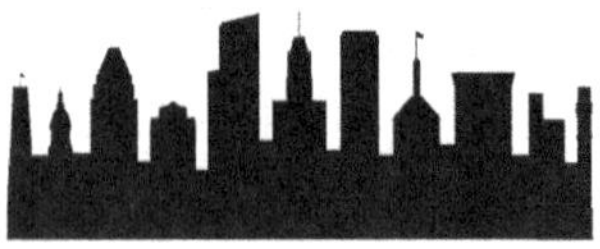

Maryland

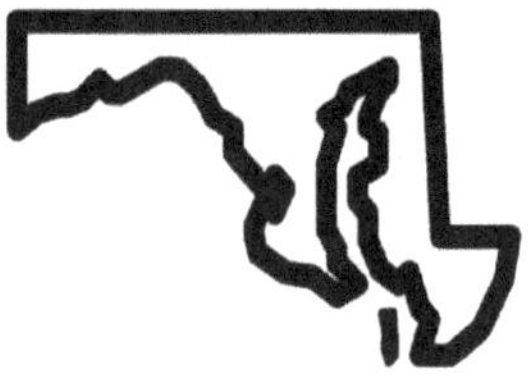

Choose an undergraduate major and describe 1 course you would take

“ ”

You are a journalism student on WEA 88.9 FM What is your favorite program & why?

“ ”

Sketch a Bear

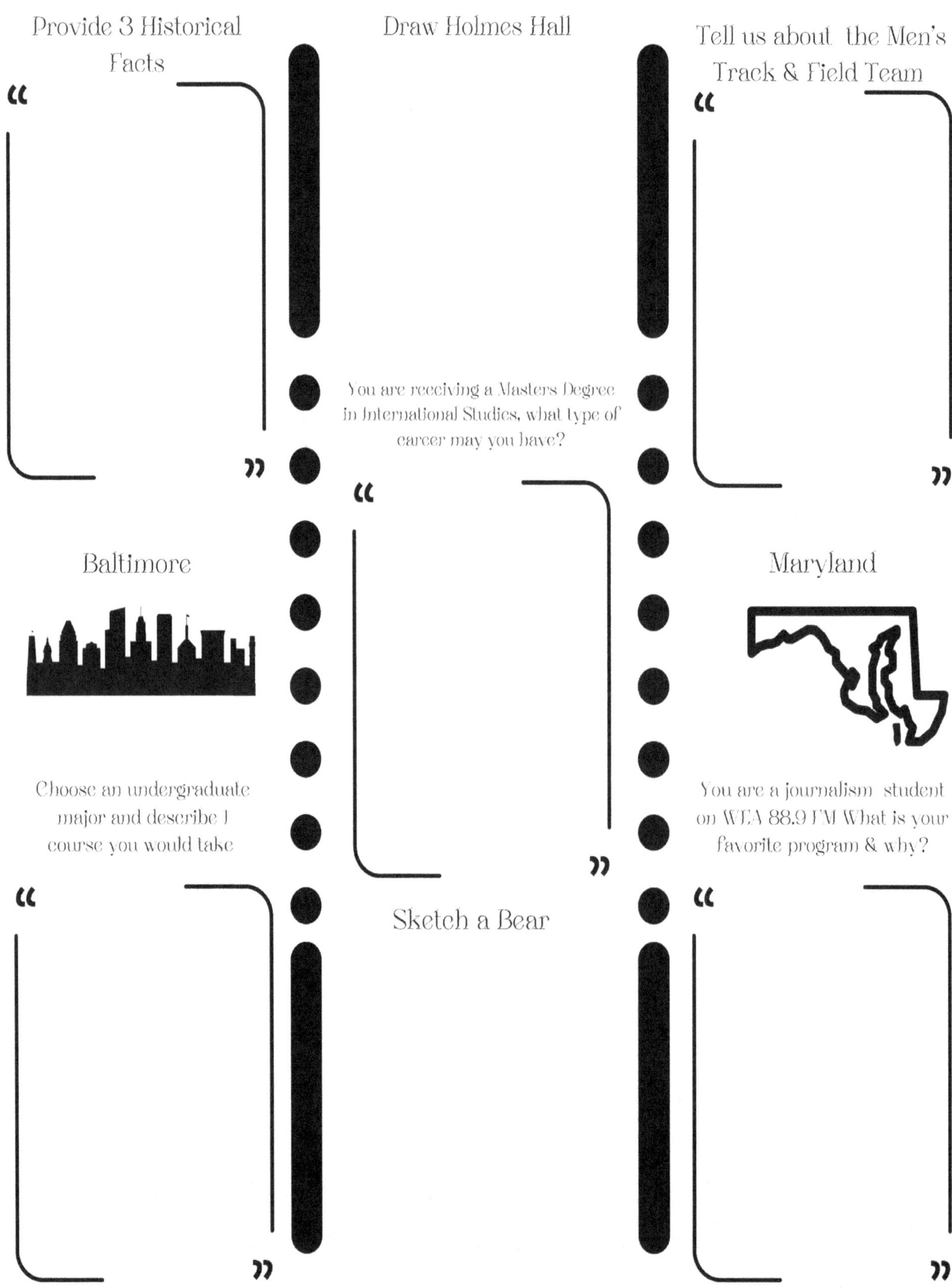

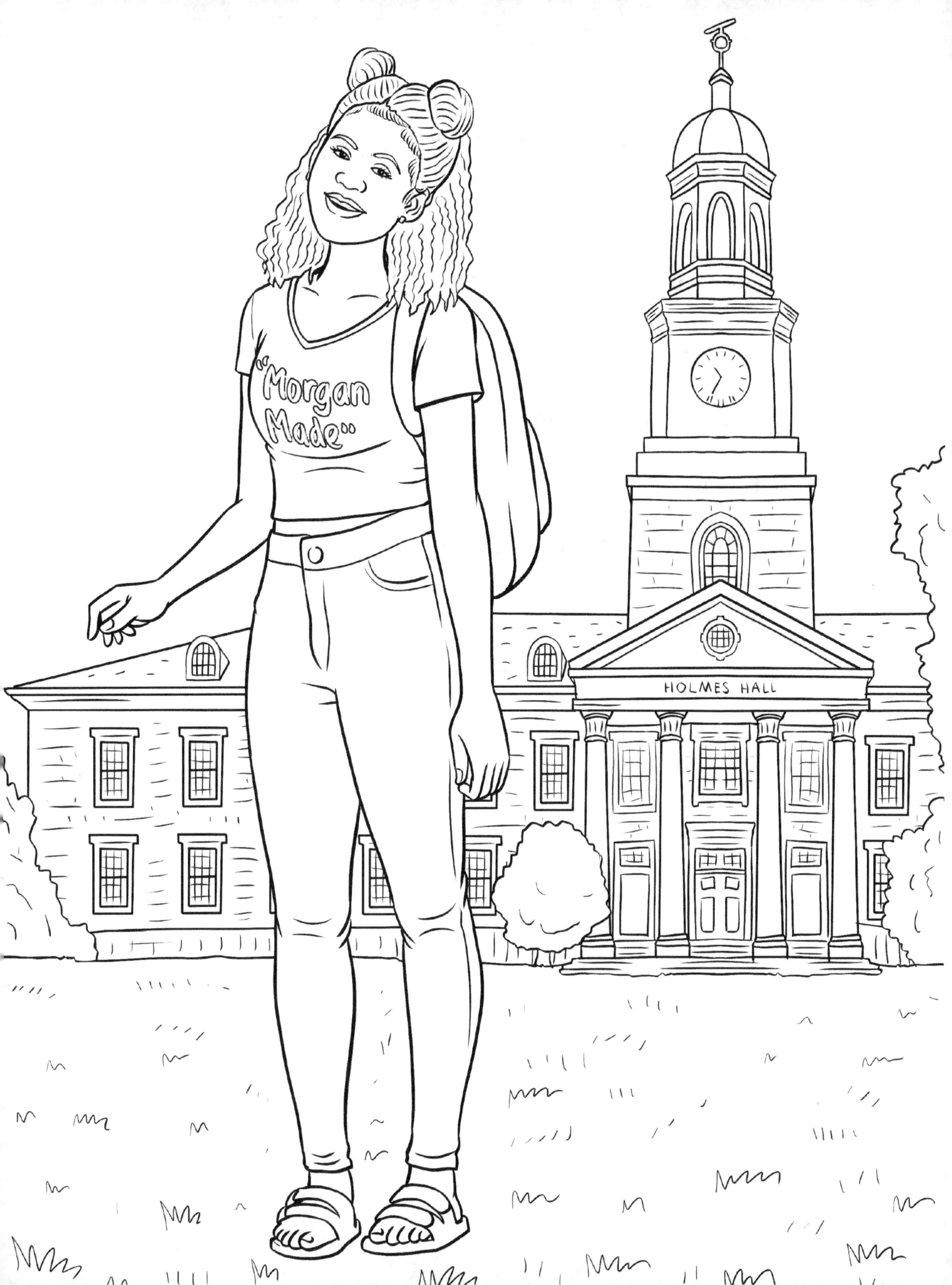

"Morgan Made"
HOLMES HALL

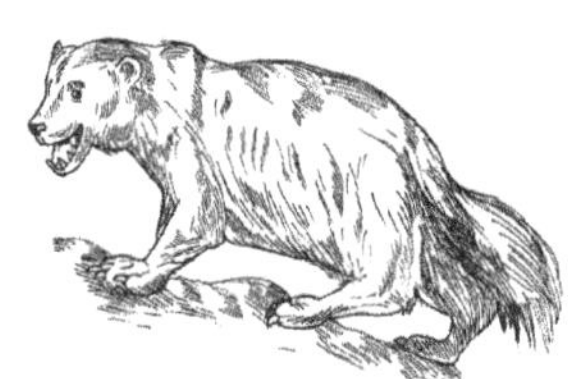 # Morris Brown College 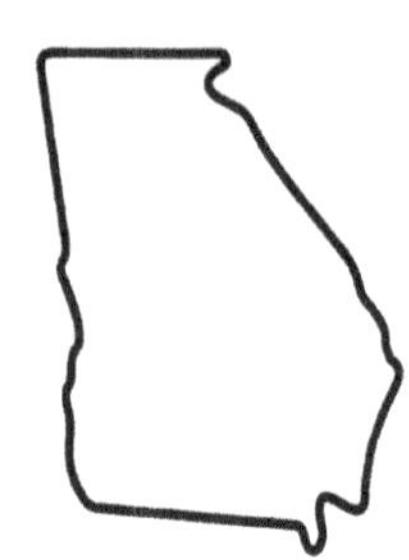

Provide 7 additional interesting facts about Morris Brown

1. In 1881, Morris Brown is the first HBCU in Georgia to be founded by Black People.

2. OutKast released "Morris Brown" song which features the Marching Wolverines band.

3. The movie "Drumline" was partially filmed at the college.

4.

5.

6.

7.

8.

9.

10.

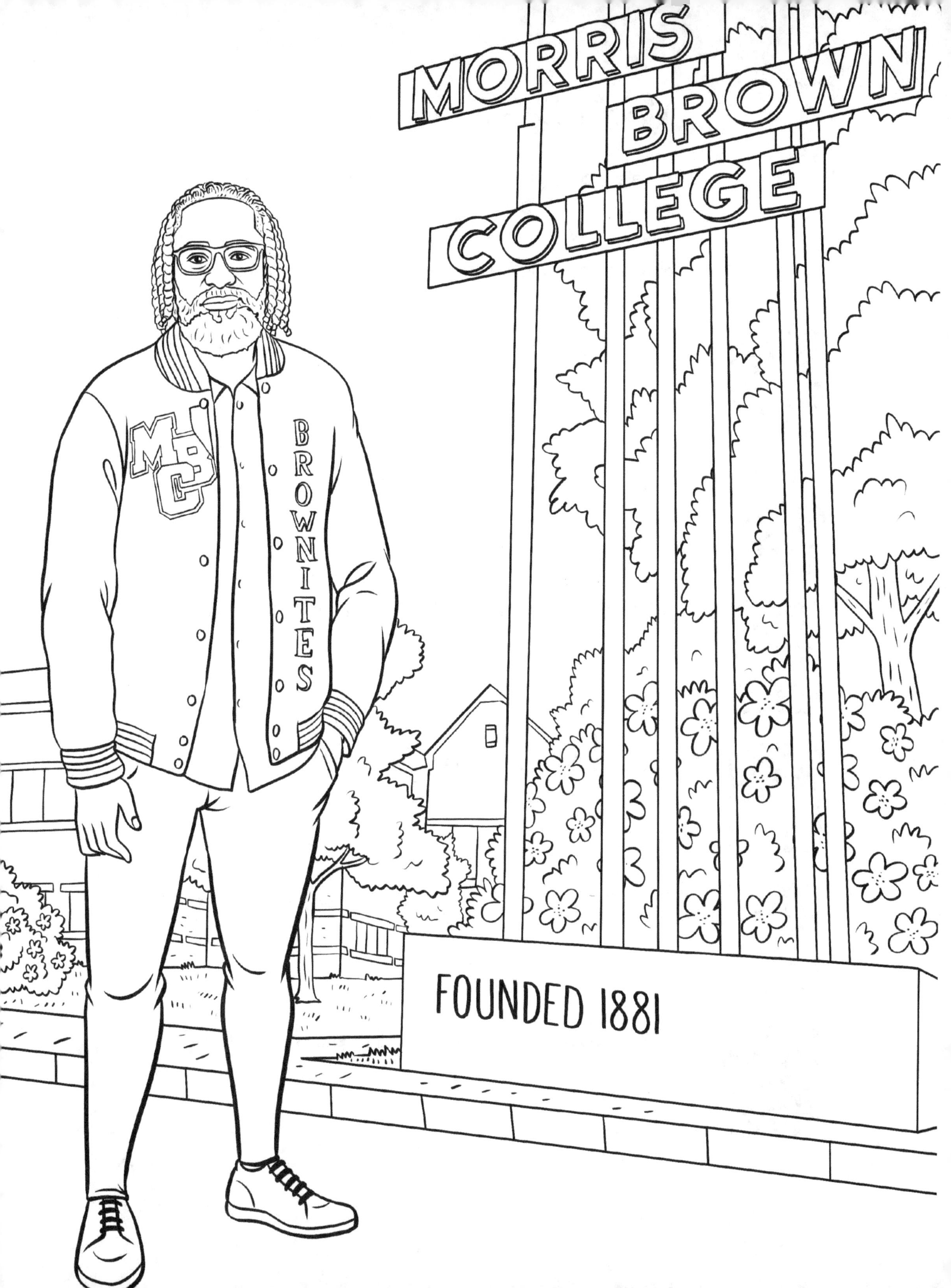

MORRIS
BROWN
COLLEGE
MBC
BROWNITES
FOUNDED 1881

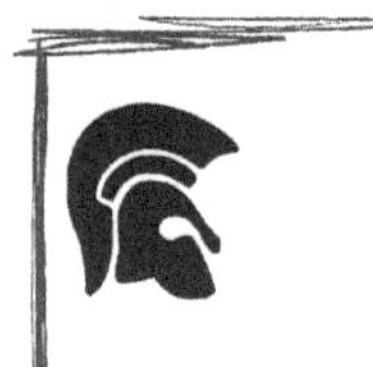

Norfolk State University

Materials: Dice 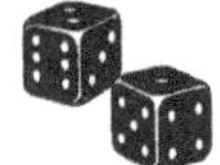 Objective: Find more information about the Spartans

Activity: Roll dice based on the number rolled and respond to the prompt.

Identify 1 Historical Fact about Norfolk

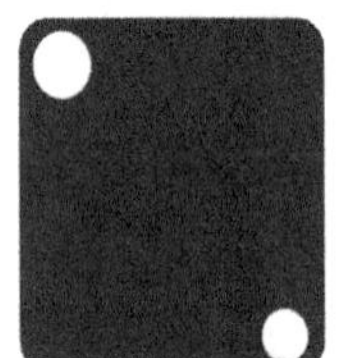

Name 2 scholarships that you can apply to study abroad

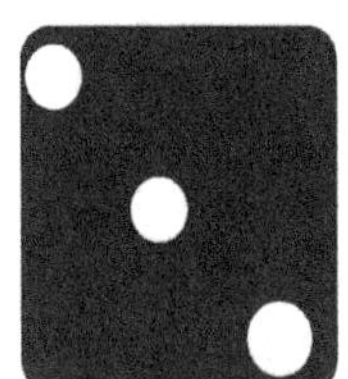

Name 3 organizations that you would like to join on campus

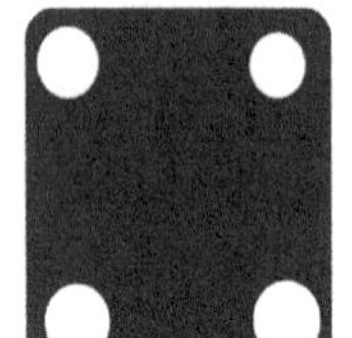

Name 2 Mental Health Resources & 2 Workshops

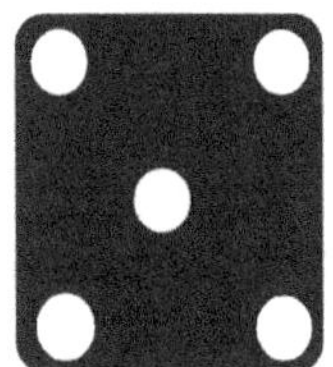

Write down 2 Bachelor, 2 Masters & 1 Doctoral Degree Program

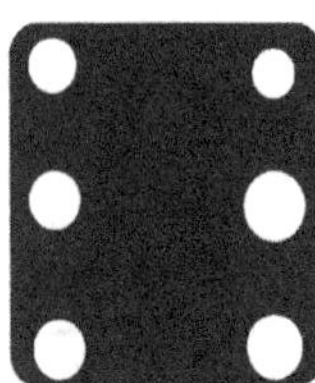

Provide 6 reasons why you should attend Norfolk University

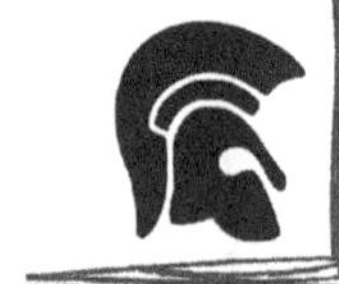

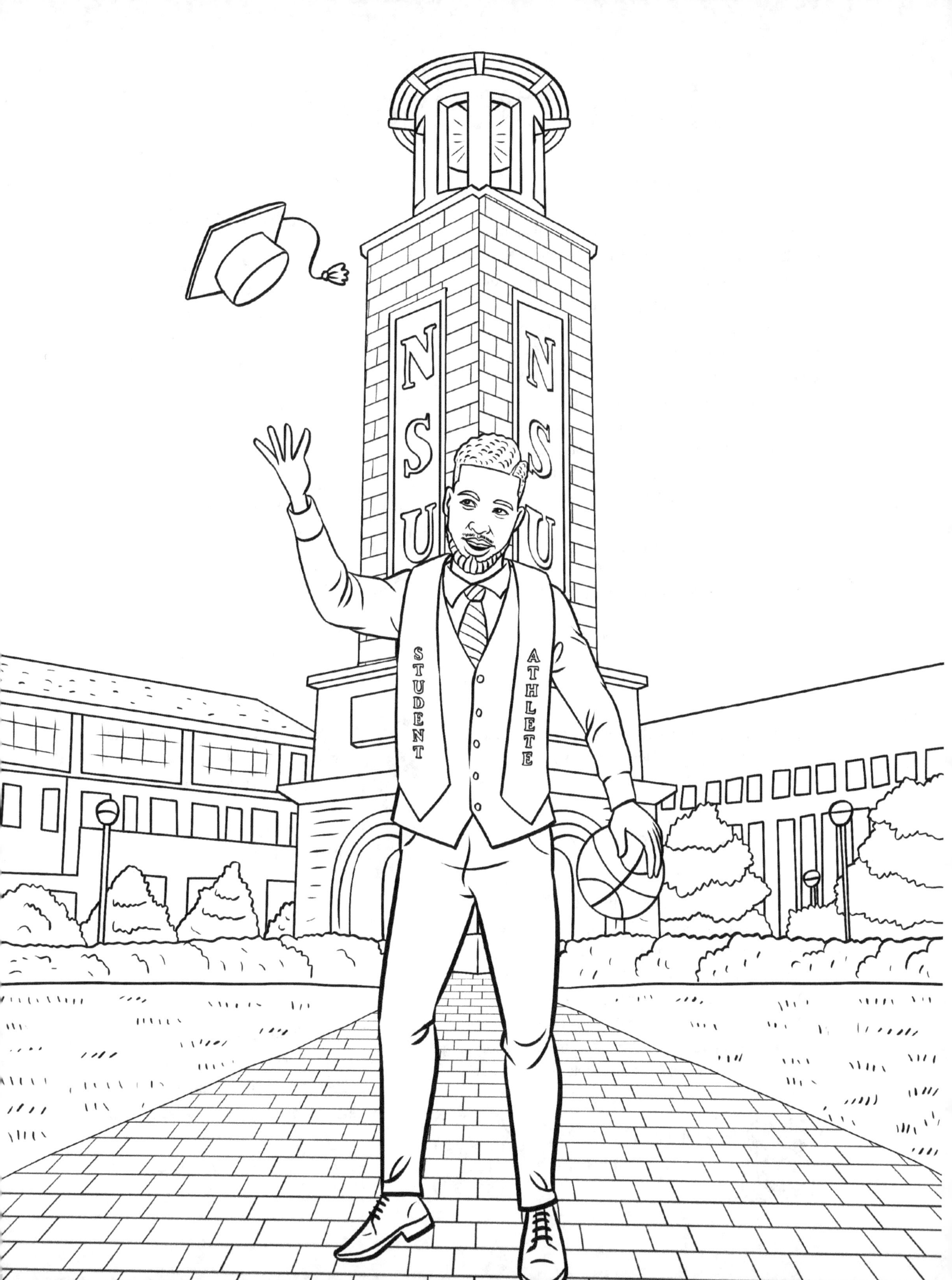

N
S
U
N
S
U
STUDENT
ATHLETE

North Carolina A&T 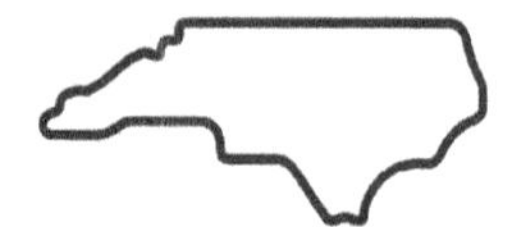

A & T Four

On February 1, 1960, 4 Freshman students Ezell Blair Jr. (now Jibreel Khazan), Franklin McCain, Joseph McNeil and David Richmond made history. They courageously walked to downtown Greensboro. As a silent protest to end segregation, they boldly sat at a white only counter in F.W. Woolworths store. Located in front of Dudley Hall is the February One Monument a bronze statue to show recognition for their bravery. In Aggie Village, they also have residence halls named after the 4: Richmond Hall, McCain Hall, Blair Hall and McNeil Hall. In addition, NC A&T now offers a February One scholarship program for selected students.

Questions & Answers

What occurred on February 1, 1960?

What is the importance of A&T 4?

What is the name of the Statue located in front of Dudley Hall?

Would you have been fearless enough to participate in segregated lunch counter?

Truth about North Carolina A&T

- Largest HBCU in the U.S.A
- Human Lactation Consultant Certificate is offered
- Only University to offer a Bachelor of Science in Geomatics
- The University Farm has horticulture products & livestock
- Masters of Sciences in Mental Health Counseling is offered
- #1 Producer of Black Engineers to pursue a doctorate degree
- #1 Producer of degrees conferred to African Americans in N.C
- Earn a PHD in agricultural and environmental sciences program
- The University Gallery holds a large collection of A.A. History in N.C.

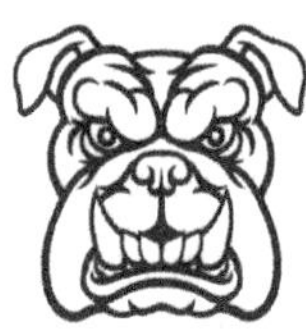

Who was the 2012 commencement speaker?

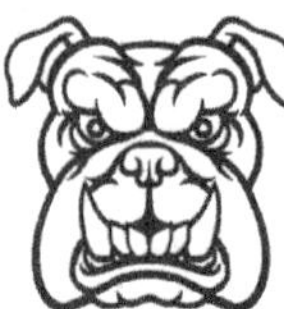

Influential Leaders

In 1971, Ronald McNair graduated with a Bachelor of Science degree in Engineering in Physics. He went onto be selected in the NASA astronaut program and was the 2nd African American to fly in space.

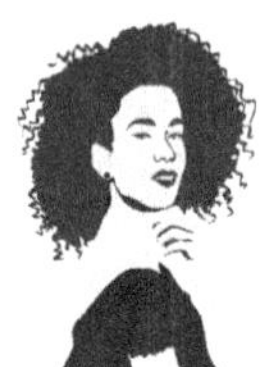

Janice Bryant Howroyd earned a scholarship and graduated with a Bachelor's degree in English and a Doctorate in Humanities. She is the founder and CEO of The Act One Group. She is known as being the first A.A. women to build a billion dollar company.

Reverend Jessie Jackson was an athlete, student body president and active in the Civil Rights Movement. He graduated with a Bachelors of Science in Sociology. He started and operated Organization PUSH. Reverend Jackson became involved in politics and was a candidate for presidency.

Secret Code

Use the alphabet secret code: Acronym for "Achieving Great Goals in Everything – Producing Renowned Individuals Dedicated to Excellence."

1 7 7 9 5   16 18 9 4 5

_ _ _ _ _   _ _ _ _ _

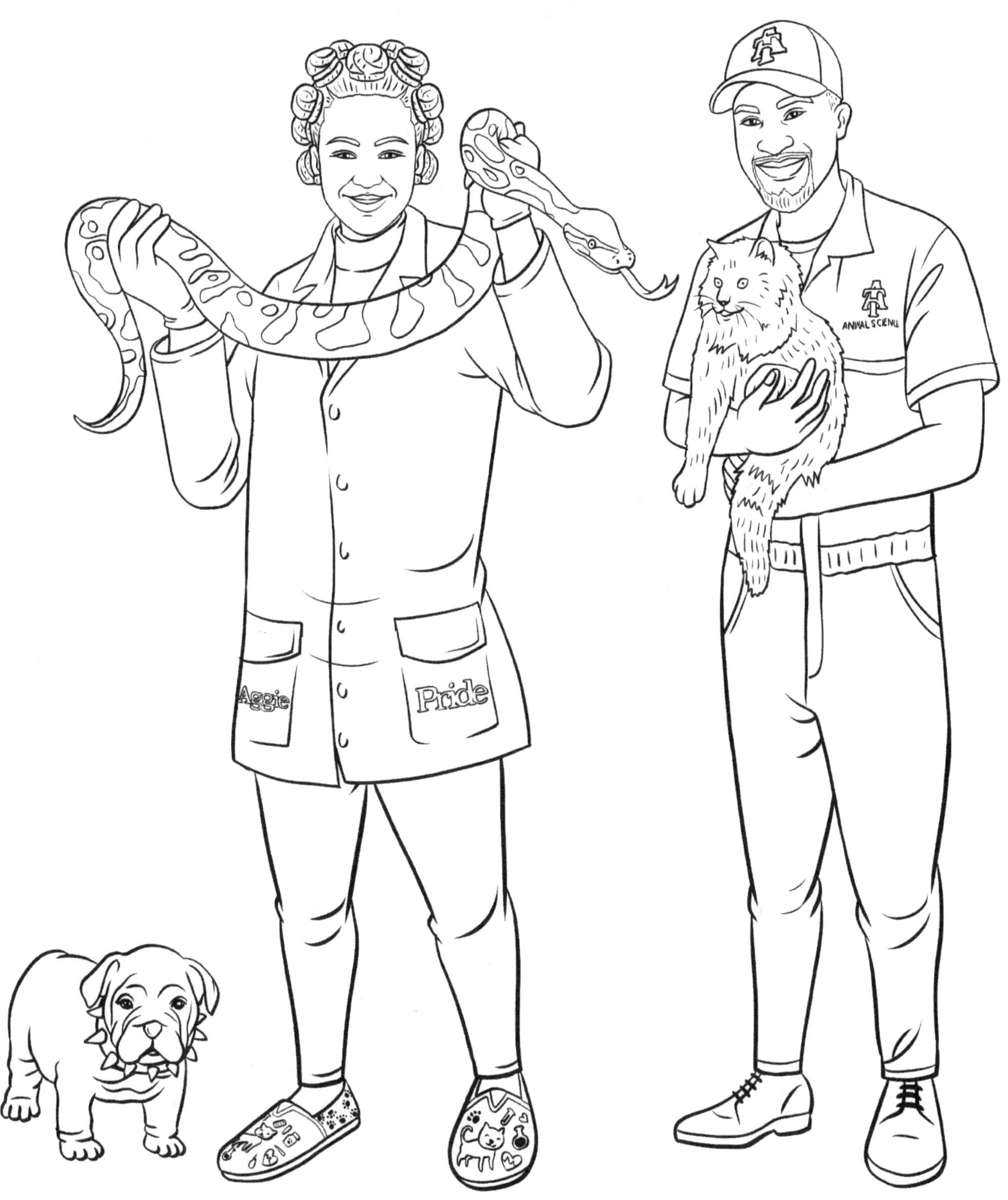

Aggie
Pride
ANIMAL SCIENCE

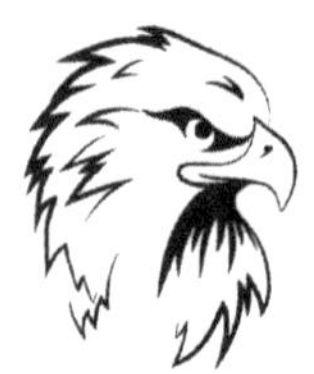 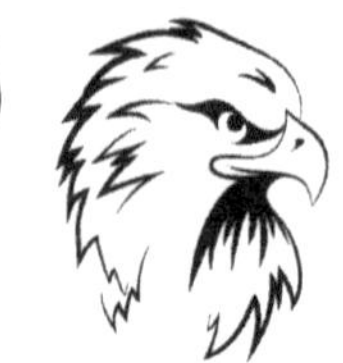

North Carolina Central University

"Truth and Service"

Please answer the questions below

In 1910, James Shepard founded the private National Religious Training School and Chautauqu, now known as NCCU. As you can imagine he faced many difficulties along the way. If you had the opportunity to have a business lunch with him, what would you ask him?

NCCU School of Law created a research initiative called The Social Justice and Racial Equity Institute to address systematic racism. Identify systems and structures that are in place that highlight ways African Americans are disadvantaged. Provide solutions to combat these issues.

Bringing the world to you and taking you to see the world! - Office of International Affairs- NCCU offers the opportunity to study abroad in over 50 countries. If you could learn anywhere in the world, where would you go and why?

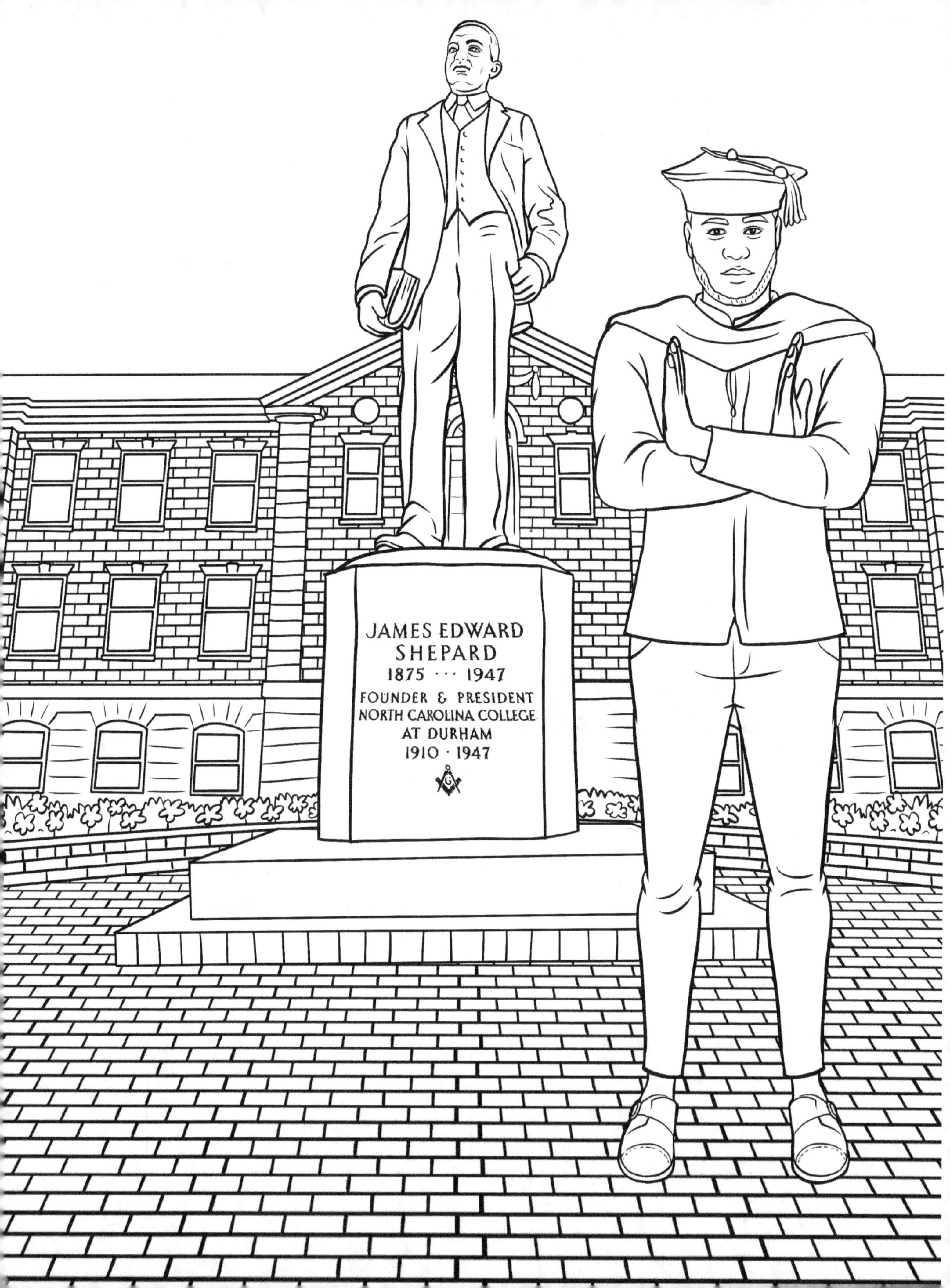

JAMES EDWARD
SHEPARD
1875 · · · 1947
FOUNDER & PRESIDENT
NORTH CAROLINA COLLEGE
AT DURHAM
1910 · 1947

OAKWOOD UNIVERSITY

ALL THE LATEST BREAKING NEWS FROM OAKWOOD

HISTORY & HIGHLIGHTS

E
N
T
E
R

D
E
P
A
R
T

Picture: Oakwood Farms Market

MOST MEMORABLE MOMENT

T
O

L
E
A
R
N

OAKWOOD UNIVERSITY CHURCH

T
O

S
E
R
V
E

Academic Experience: Which major & why?

OAKWOOD CHOIRS

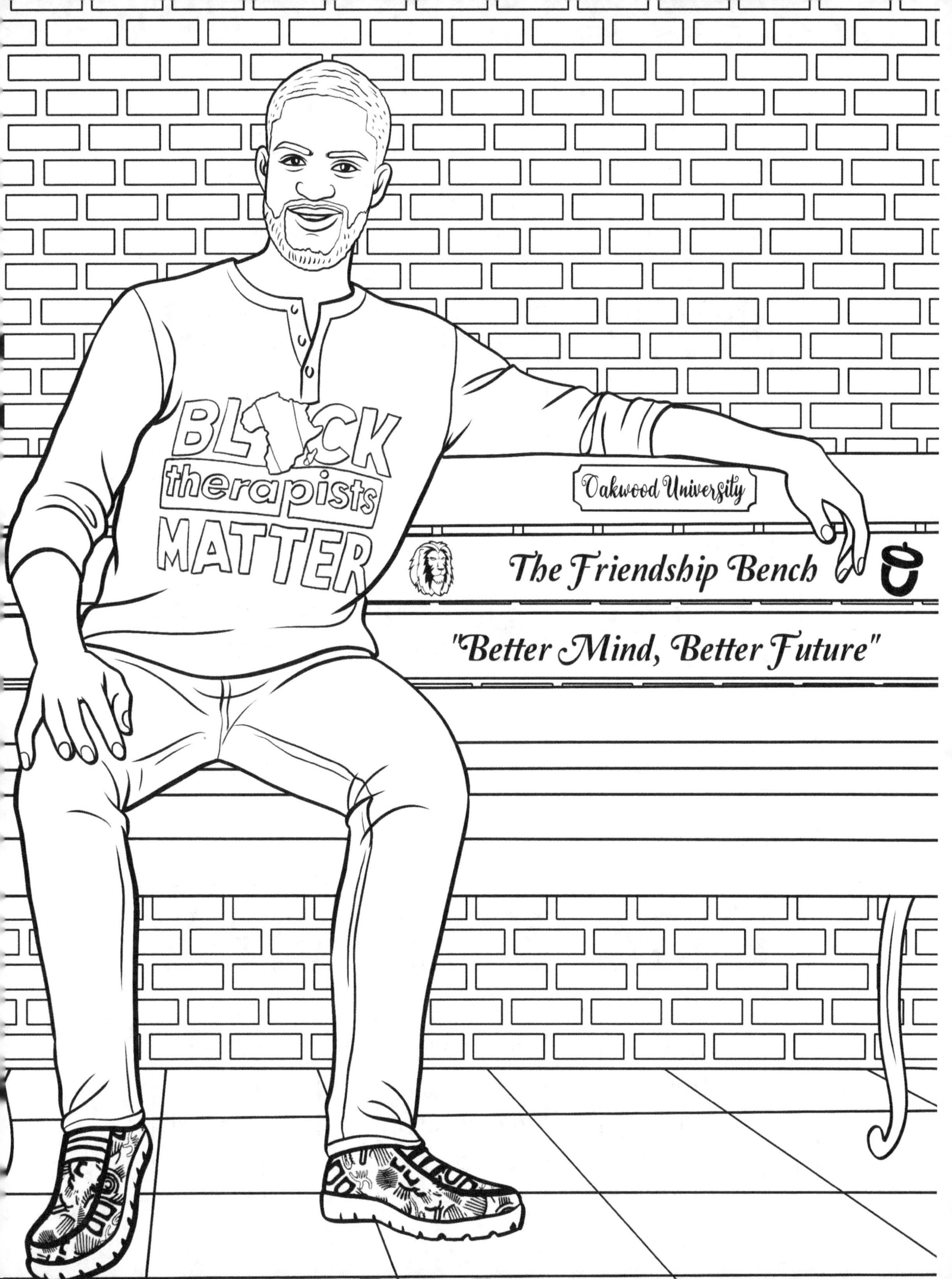
BLACK
therapists
MATTER
Oakwood University
The Friendship Bench
"Better Mind, Better Future"

PAINE COLLEGE

The words are related to Paine College. Have your partner guess the word at the top of each box written in White. Remember you cannot say the words written in Black when describing the word or you lose a point. 30 seconds on the clock. Now switch partners.

TABOO EDITION

GROUP ACTIVITY

AUGUSTA

Golf
Maine
Georgia
Richmon
James Brown

SOCIOLOGY

Behavior
Psychology
Criminology
Anthropology
Social Science

DR. CHERYL EVANS JONES

Dean
Faculty
Academic
President
Accreditation

UNITED METHODIST

Church
Episcopal
Founders
Christianity
Denomination

LIONS

Cat
Tiger
Animal
Mascot
Cougar

WESLEY FELLOWSHIP

Ministry
Revivals
Religion
Missions
Organization

HOLY SPIRIT

God
Son
Truth
Father
Comforter

BUSINESS ADMINISTRATION

Marketing
Accounting
Information
International
Management

HEAL COMPLEX

Gym
Athletics
Volley Ball
Basket Ball
Games

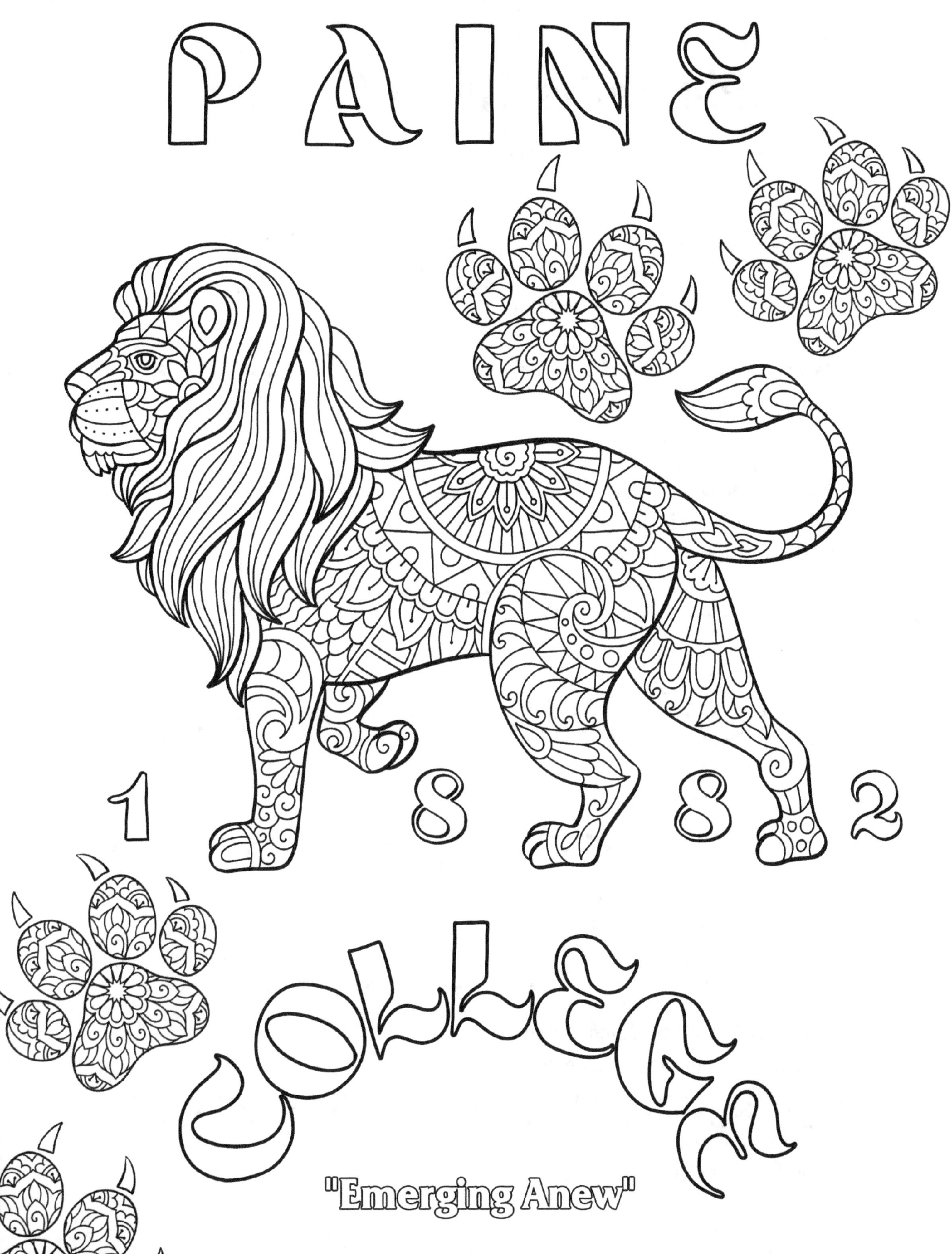

PAINE
1 8 8 2
COLLEGE
"Emerging Anew"

Philander Smith College

"Think Justice"

Internet Scavenger Hunt

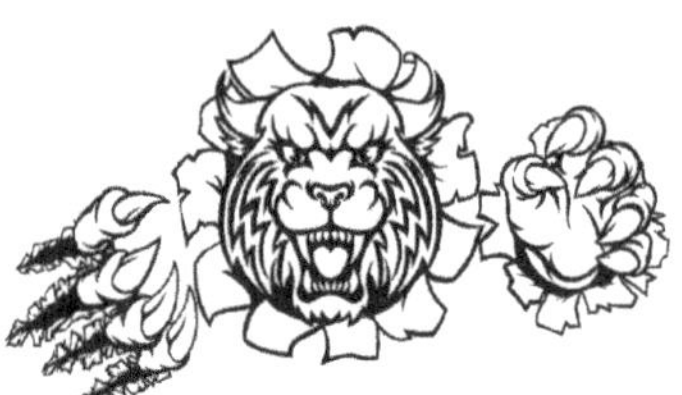

Using the website below, answer
the following questions.
URL: Philander.edu

Moving Philander Forward:
Name 2 Initiaves

Which Majors are in the
Division of Social Sciences?

What is the mission
of the Panther Pantry?

What scholarships are
available to students?

Provide a brief synopsis of your
favorite athletic news article.

Discuss a distinguished Alumni & mention
there contributions to the community.

Name the oldest
Black Methodist Church

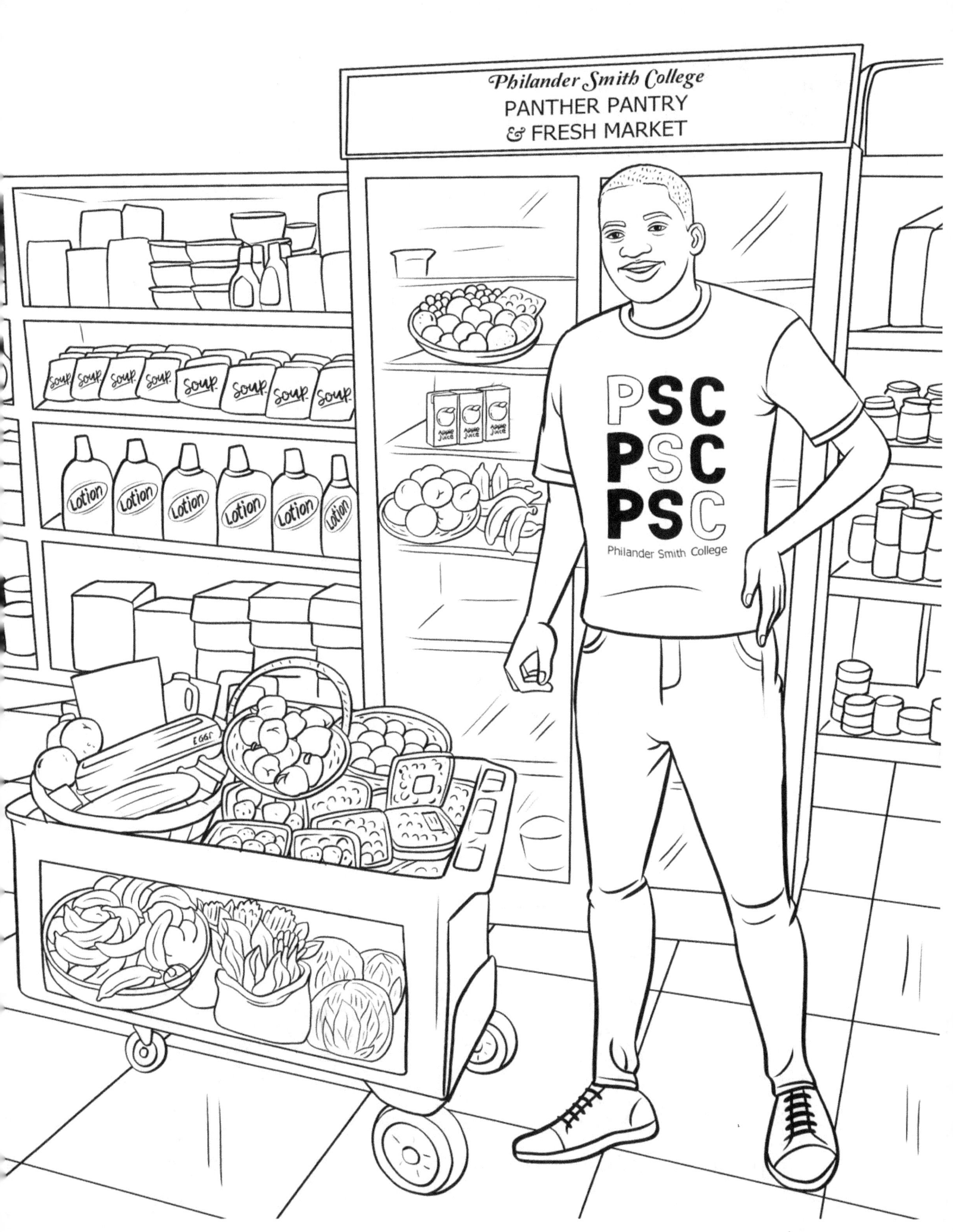

Philander Smith College
PANTHER PANTRY
& FRESH MARKET
Soup
Lotion
PSC
PSC
PSC
Philander Smith College

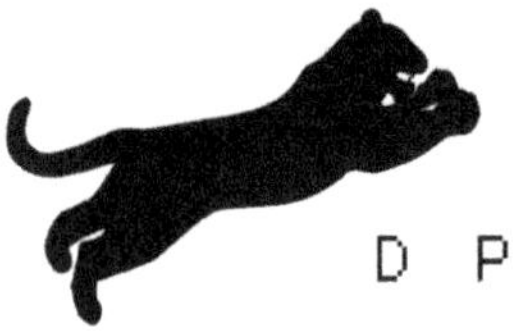

P R A I R I E

V I E W A&M

```
D P D R A U I R I E E V T E M S I Y
E E W N M P R O R D U J L R E E C M
D E G A A S P A R L C A O U T X D E
U A V X C L H T A P D I V T S O E D
P P O E E S B N C Y O R T C P F L A
E Z G R L T D A P K U N L E U K P C
T J N A B G T A R T X L I T X C B A
V H E O R A N Z H D Z Y R I V A N L
Z M E A D T S S U F N G Y H Y L S A
R A N H H Q I R F I N A N C E B E C
V T F E I M E K E D N G S R N B V I
Q E R J M L E K A H S D N A H T B D
F S F O T H L Y J M T K F X V J R E
J H N V B M R O T S G N I H C R A M
L S I F Y R A R B I L N A M E L O C
L O O W E I V E I R I A R P S S I M
J U V E N I L E J U S T I C E L U R
K Z T Z E D H H D Z W E K E H Z U V
```

Directions: Find words. Copy the unused letters starting in the top left corner into the blanks to reveal the hidden message.

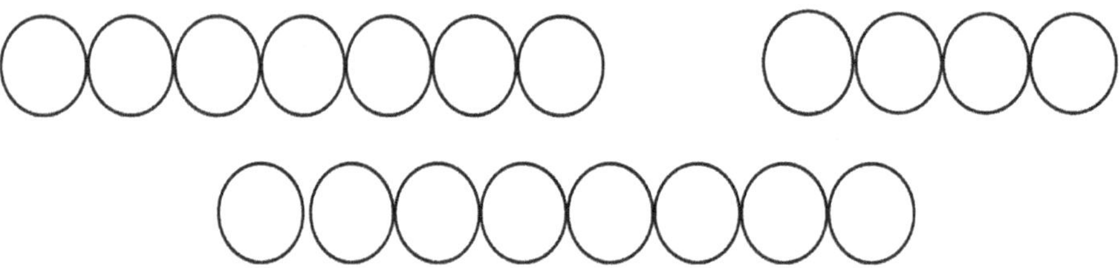

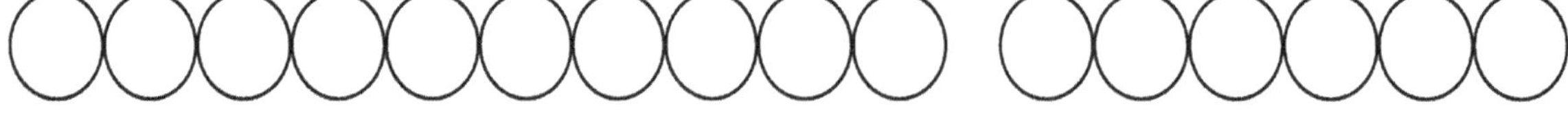

Architecture
Finance
Lady Panthers
Meal Share
Panthers Abroad
Sandra Bland
TEXGED

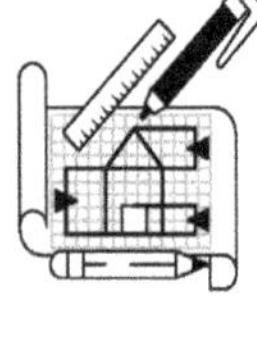

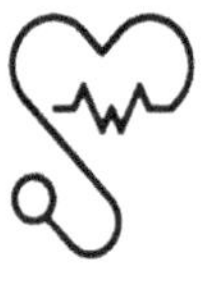

Black Foxes
Hand Shake
Land Grant
Medical Academy
PVAMU
STEM
The Hill

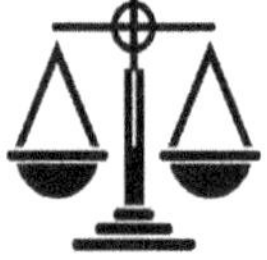

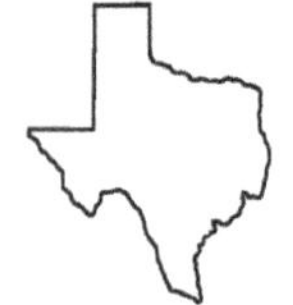

Coleman Library
Juvenile Justice
Marching Storm
Miss Prairie View
Ruth Simmons
Texas
TJCPC

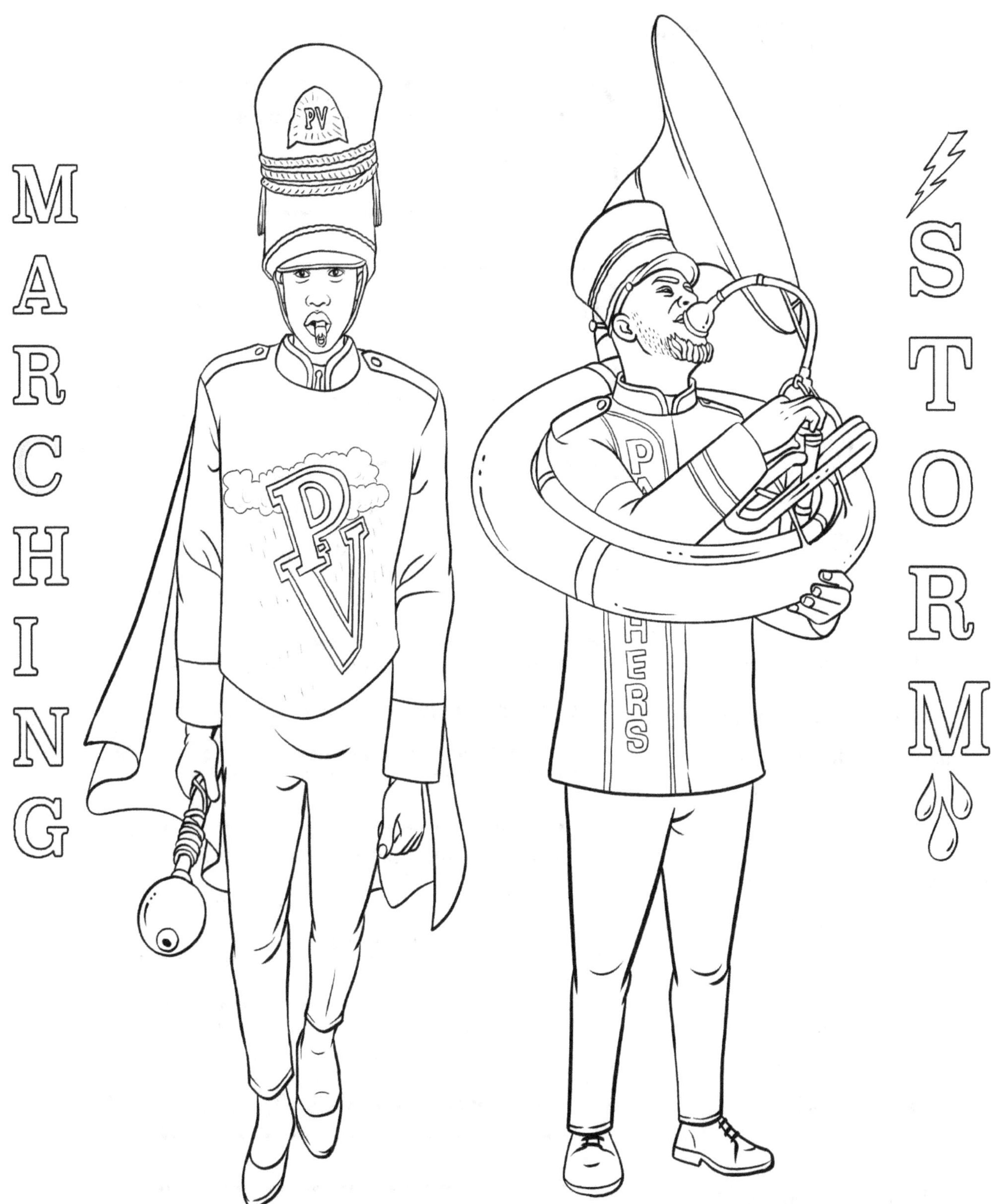

MARCHING
PV
P V
PANTHERS
STORM

Savannah State University

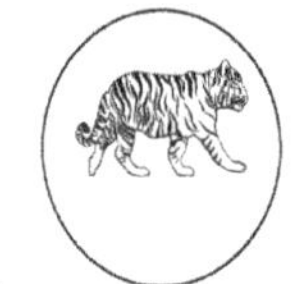
Savannah State University *@ savstate*

Home

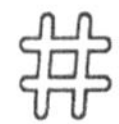
Explore

Notifications

Messages

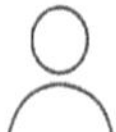
Profile

More

What's Happening?

- Powerhouse of the South marched to the beat of their own drum at Homecoming

- Help is not a bad 4 letter word. Counseling services are available

- Explore Savannah this weekend. Meet at Forsyth Park

Directions: Write down who tweeted each quote. What is their twitter handle?

I am the first HBCU in Georgia and and the first in the beautiful coastal landscape

I am the proud alumni of the class of 1902, and I became the president in 1921

Extra Extra Read all about it, I bring you the latest tea from one student to another

I will be earning my tiger stripes as I travel across the world while giving back to an international community

Feet apart, arms just right, swing just right and you might hit something. Thanks for honoring me with Spirit of Sport Award

We educate you by making you think, and allow Jazz, Neo Soul, Latin, Blues and Indian tunes vibrate through your body

The ecosystem is my oyster, and the "university by the sea" is where I learn about the diversity of the underworld

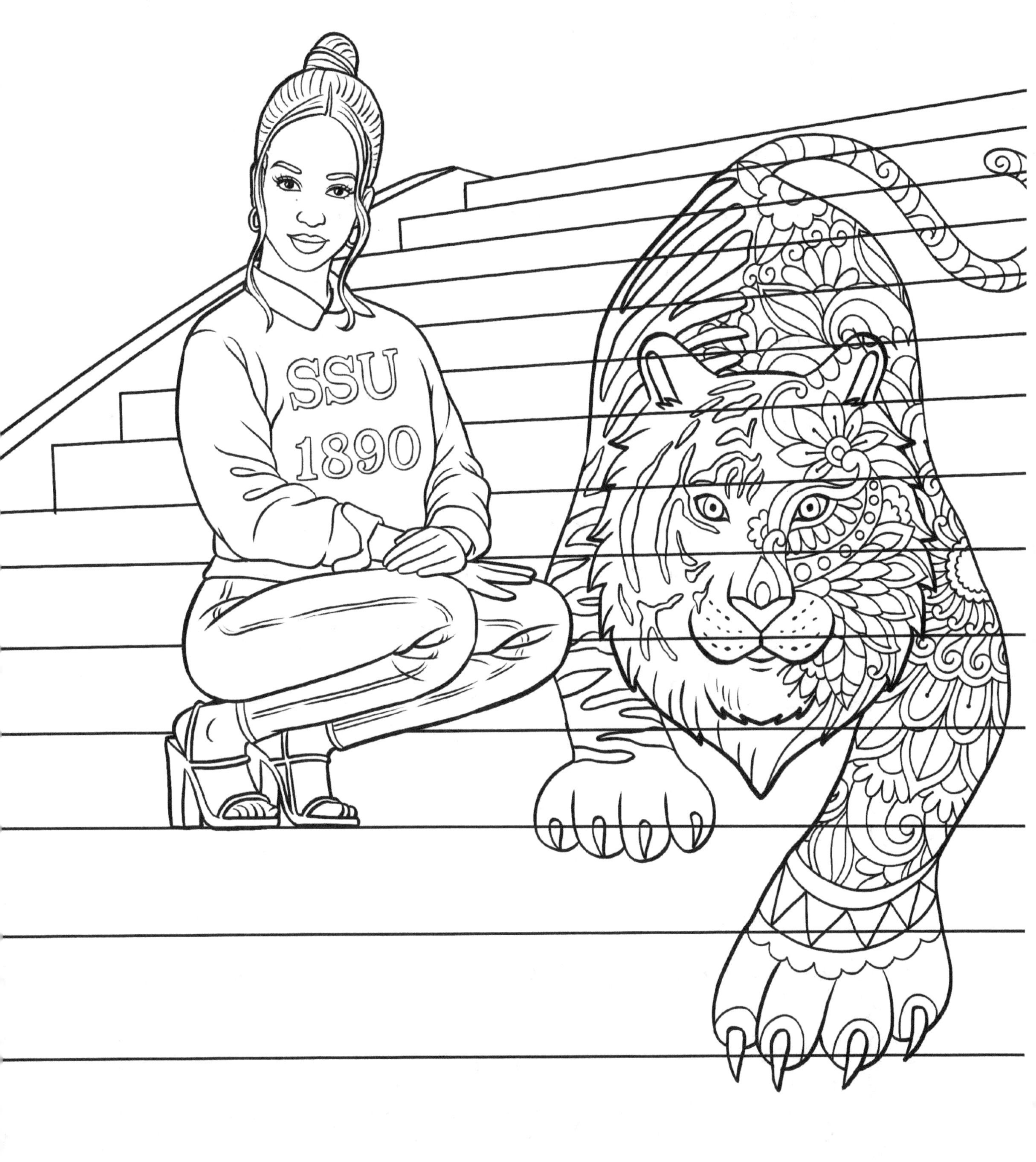
SSU
1890

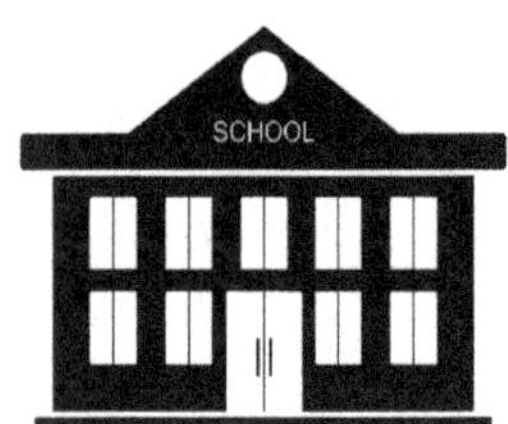

Selma University

"Making the vision clear to runners" Inspired by Habakkuk 2:2

Write Factual (F) or Deceptive (D) for each statement below

Selma University offers both general and ministerial degrees. ___

You can receive a Bachelor of Arts in Bible and Pastoral Ministry. ___

Selma University was founded in 1878 to train preachers and teachers. ___

Students are not part of the Student Government Association & do not have voting privileges. ___

The Christian Service Program objective is to have students involved in every aspect of ministry. ___

It is both a tradition & requirement for students to attend chapel/convocation every Wednesday. ___

Explain the Significance/Relevance of the names to Selma University Below.

Henrietta M. Gibbs

Reverend Fred Shuttlesworth

William H. McAlpine

Mattie Moss Clark

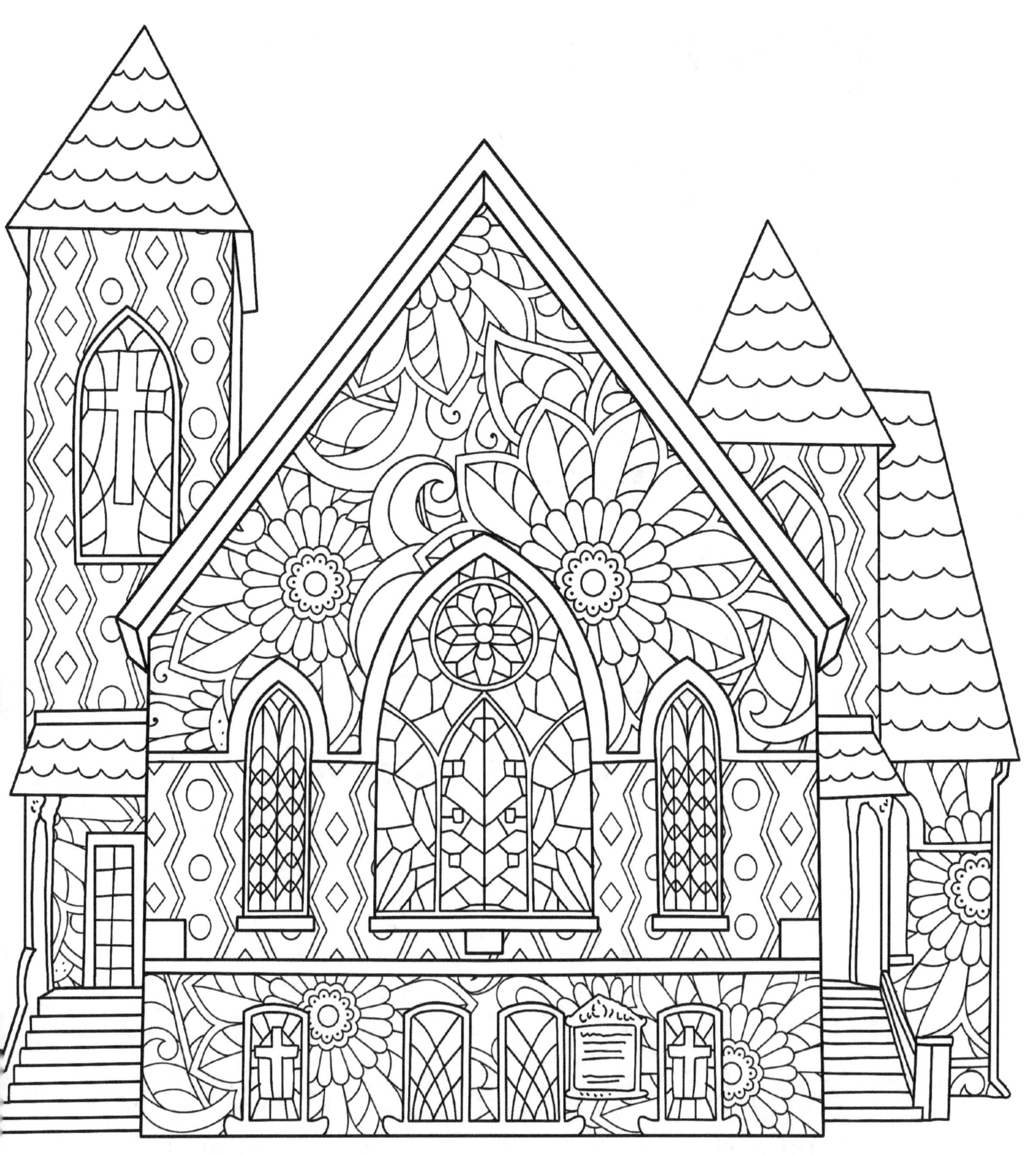

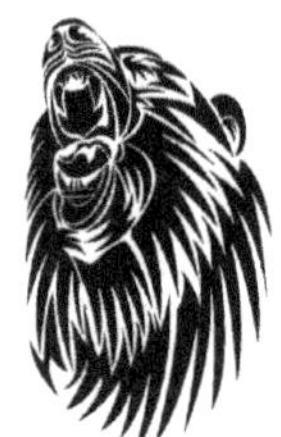 # Shaw University 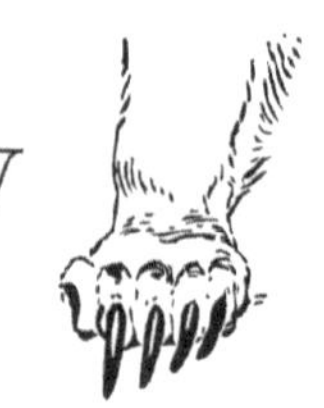

Shaw University was established in 1865 is located in Raleigh, North Carolina. It is the oldest HBCU in the southern states.

This committee was established on campus in 1960	Name a famous notable alumni	This degree prepares students for ministerial ordination or full time ministry
What major would allow you to become a lyricist, composer, music teacher, band and choral director?	The first HBCU that allowed who to attend?	Student run non-profit organization that empowers people to speak about mental health
What is the name of the famous marching band?	Discuss a University Tradition	This center offers discussion, lectures, workshops, & advocacy work to discuss issues of race, health, violence, racism & social inequities

"For Christ & Humanity"

Motto

Directions: Shaw University Tic Tac Toe. Choose S or U. If you guess the correct answer put an S or U. First one to gets 3 in a row is the winner

Hail, Dear old Shaw U

Alma Mater

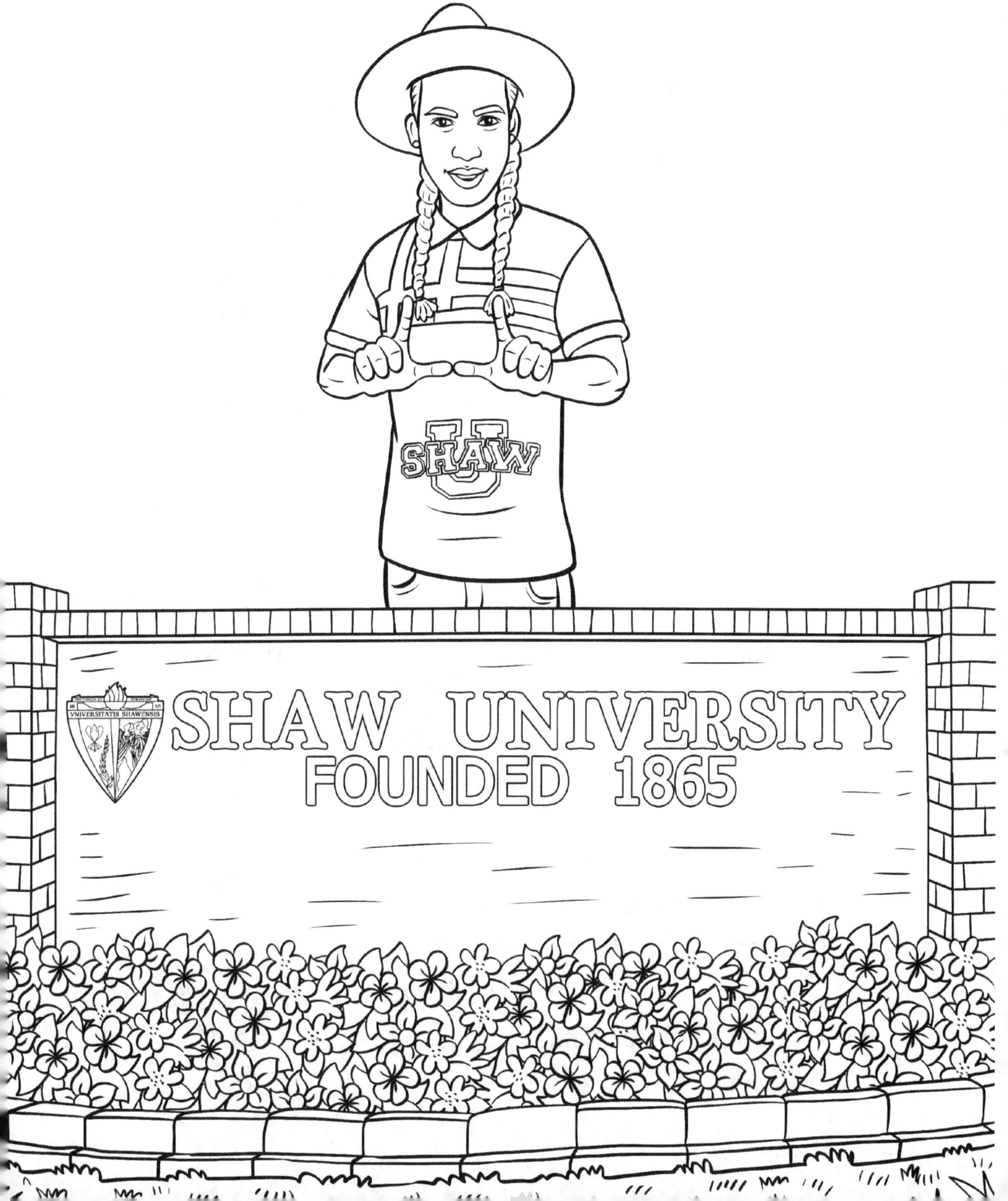

SHAW
U
VNIVERSITATIS SHAWENSIS
SHAW UNIVERSITY
FOUNDED 1865

Simmons College of Kentucky

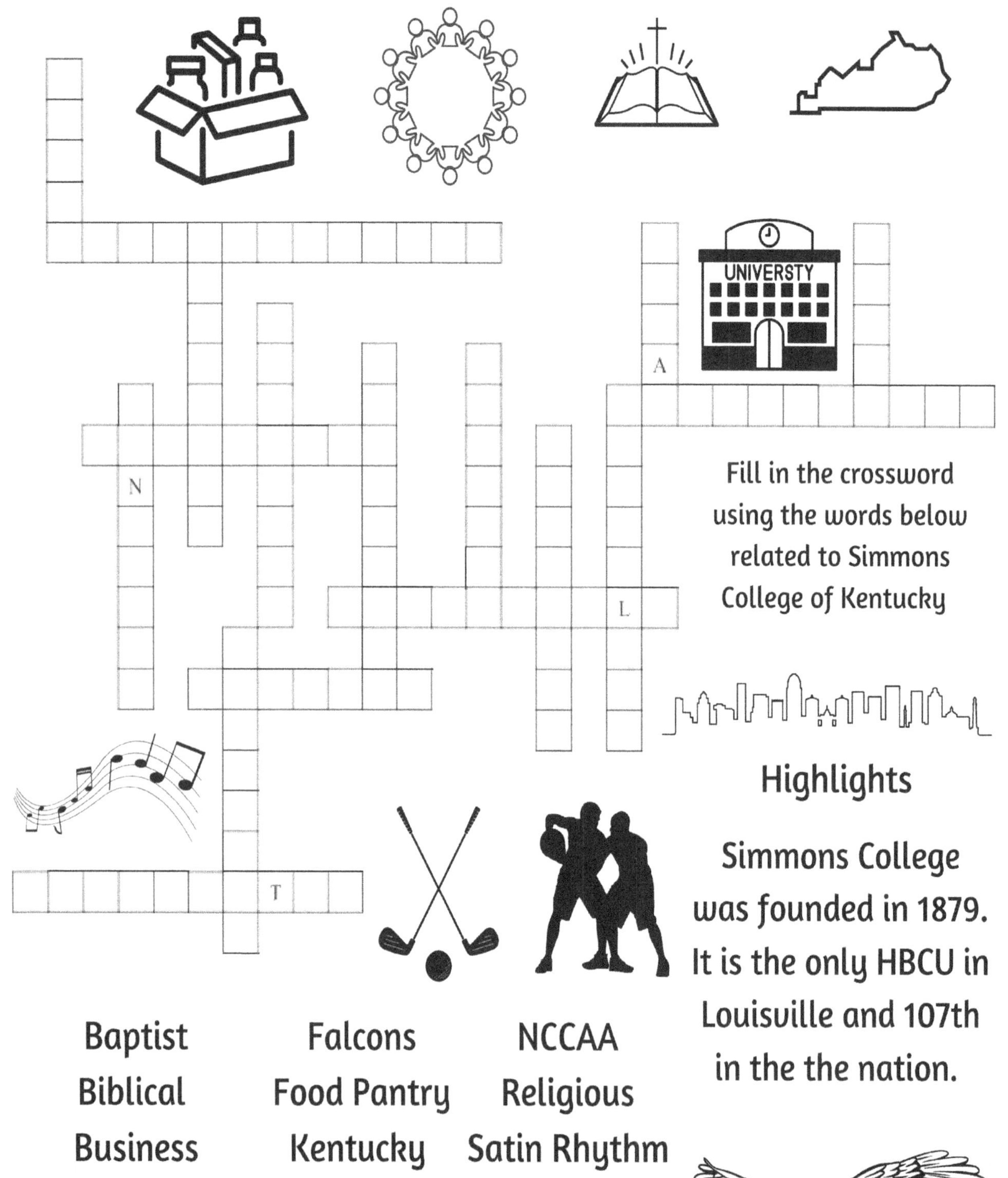

Fill in the crossword using the words below related to Simmons College of Kentucky

Highlights

Simmons College was founded in 1879. It is the only HBCU in Louisville and 107th in the the nation.

Baptist
Biblical
Business
Cosby
Cross Cultural
Dr. Simmons

Falcons
Food Pantry
Kentucky
Louisville
Marching
Music

NCCAA
Religious
Satin Rhythm
Sociology
Spalding

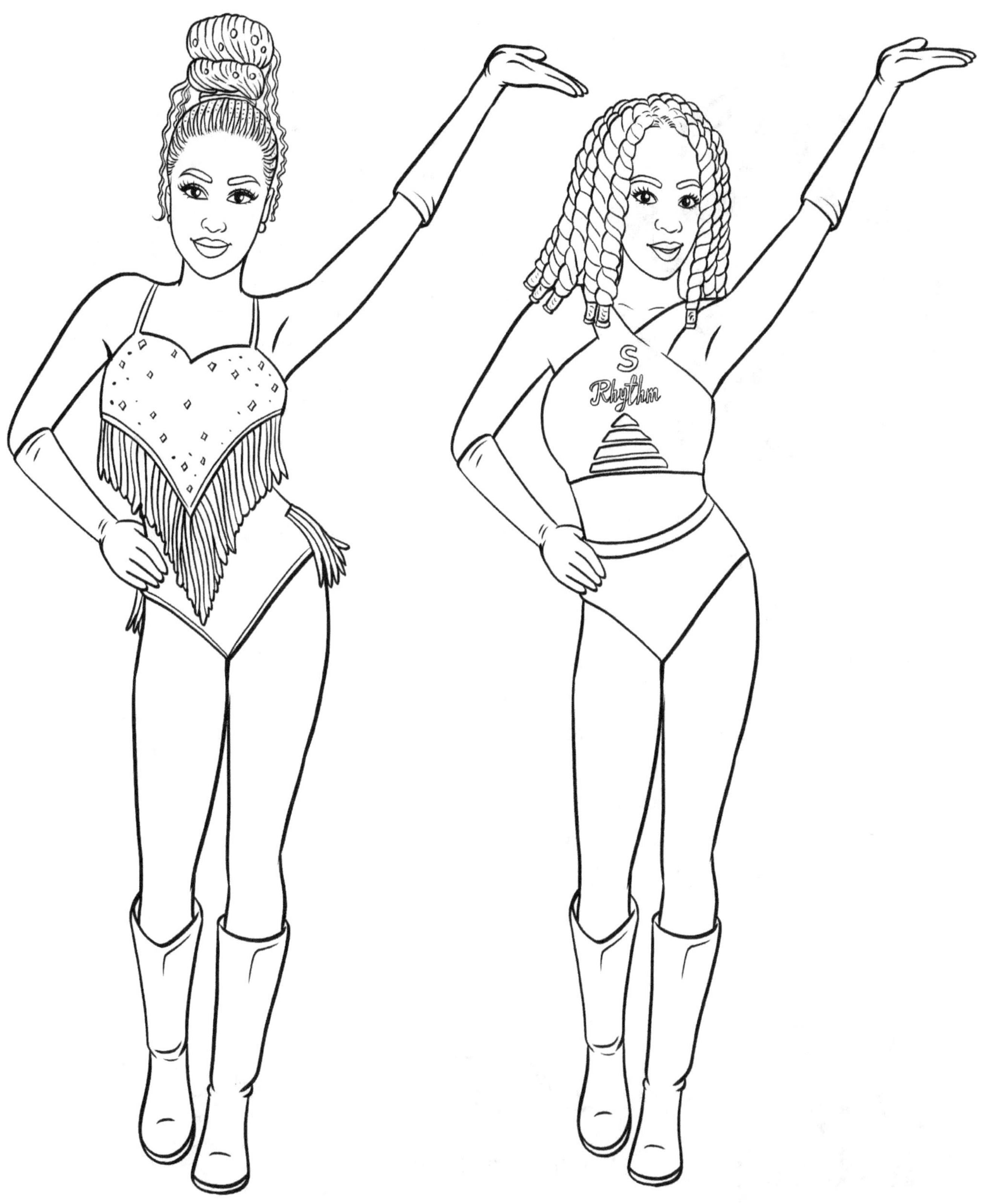
S
Rhythm

South Carolina State University
Scoop on SCSU

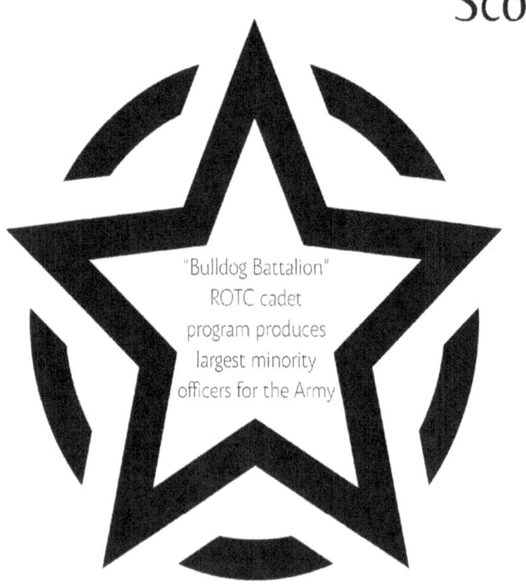

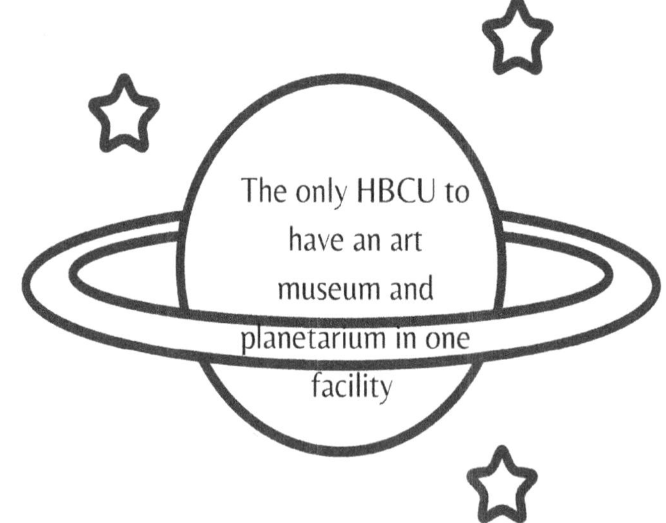

In 1896, South Carolina State University was founded as a public college for Black youth. It is land grant institution which made it difficult to provide agricultural & mechanical training. Despite great difficulties during the great depression, WWII & Civil Rights movement the university survived and continue to make great strides in the world. SCSU offers degrees in the areas of arts, business, humanities, natural sciences, mathematics, engineering, agribusiness, drama, fashion merchandise & so much more.

<u>Write 3 additional unique facts about SCSU</u>

1.

2.

3.

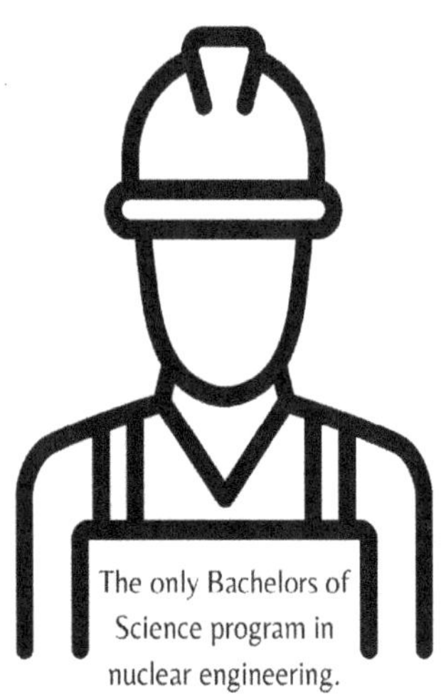

1896
Knowledge, Duty, Honor

In the 1950's & 60's students participated in Civil Rights demonstrations.

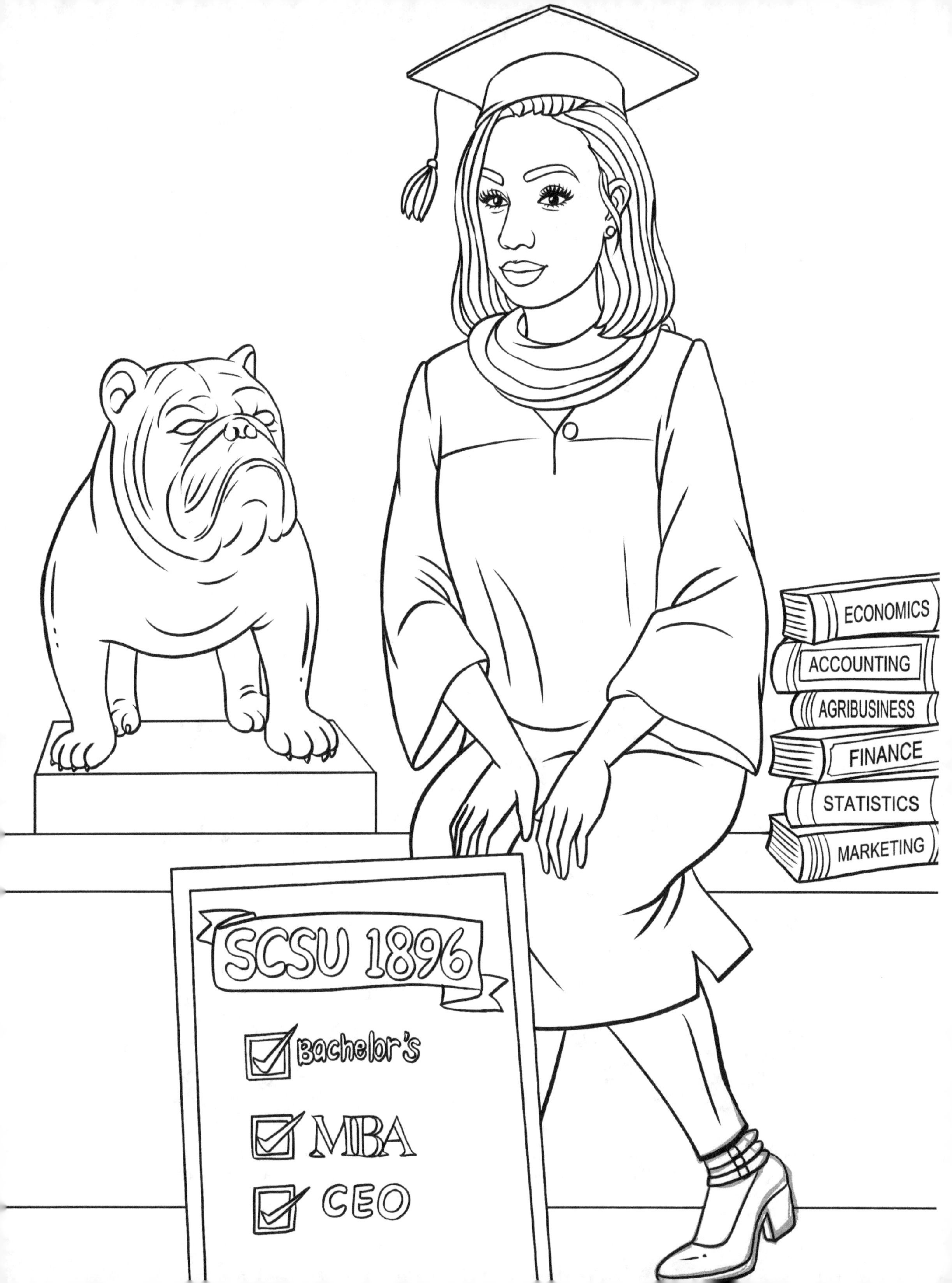

ECONOMICS
ACCOUNTING
AGRIBUSINESS
FINANCE
STATISTICS
MARKETING
SCSU 1896
Bachelor's
MBA
CEO

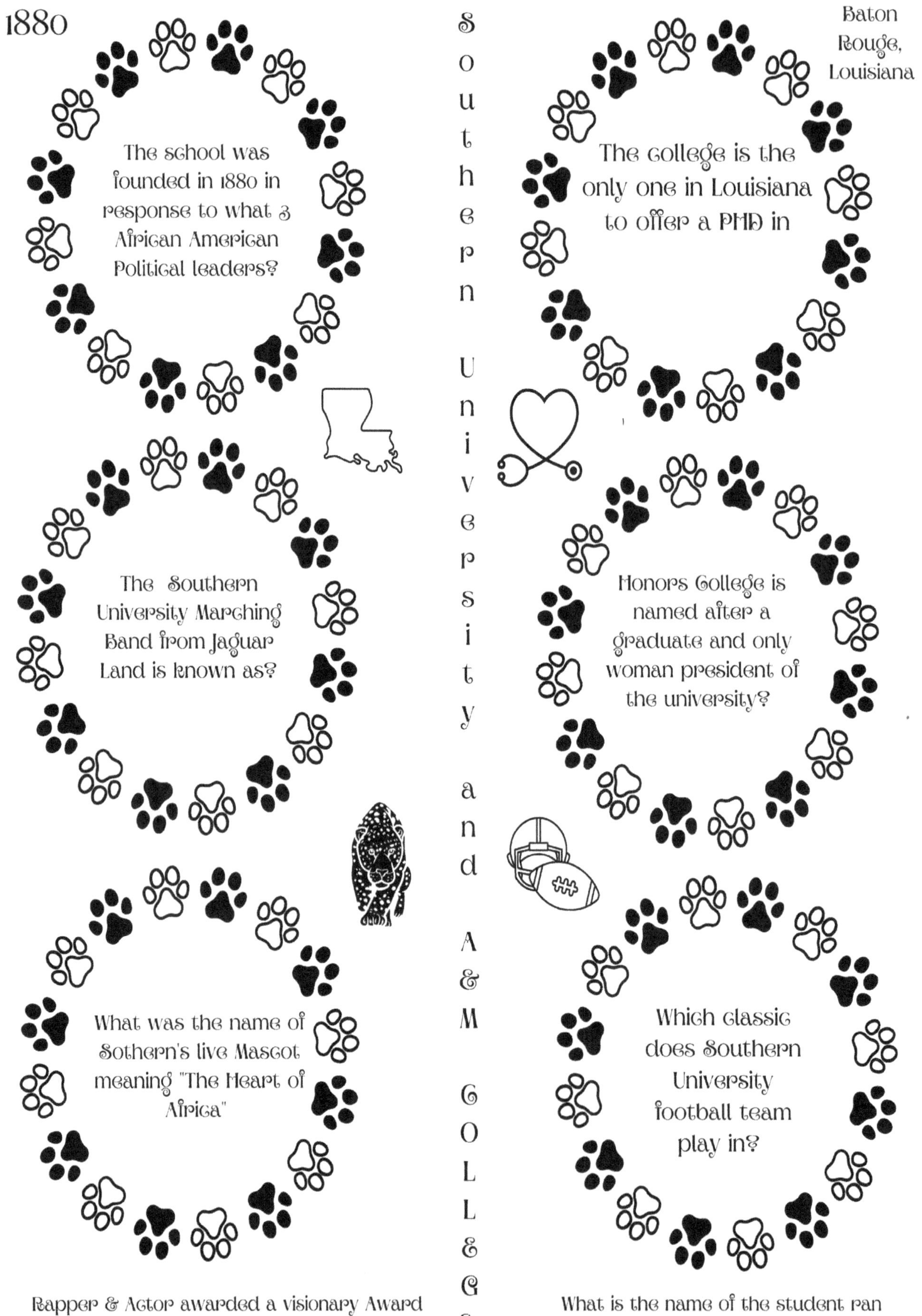

1880

Baton Rouge, Louisiana

Southern University and A&M COLLEGE

The school was founded in 1880 in response to what 3 African American Political leaders?

The college is the only one in Louisiana to offer a PHD in

The Southern University Marching Band from Jaguar Land is known as?

Honors College is named after a graduate and only woman president of the university?

What was the name of Sothern's live Mascot meaning "The Heart of Africa"

Which classic does Southern University football team play in?

Rapper & Actor awarded a visionary Award fir his work during Hurricane Katrina.

What is the name of the student ran newspaper called?

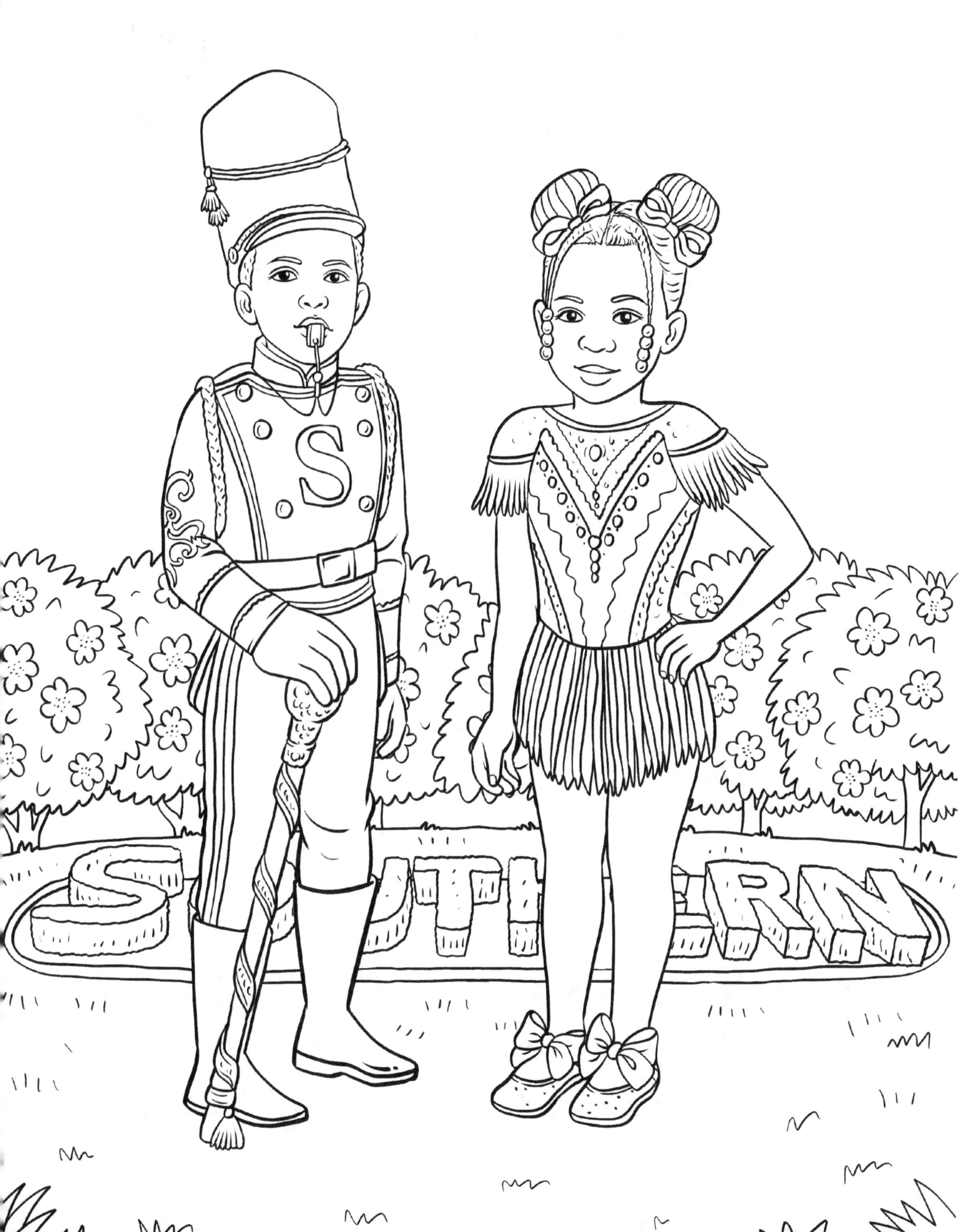

S
SUTHERN

Spelman Bingo
1881

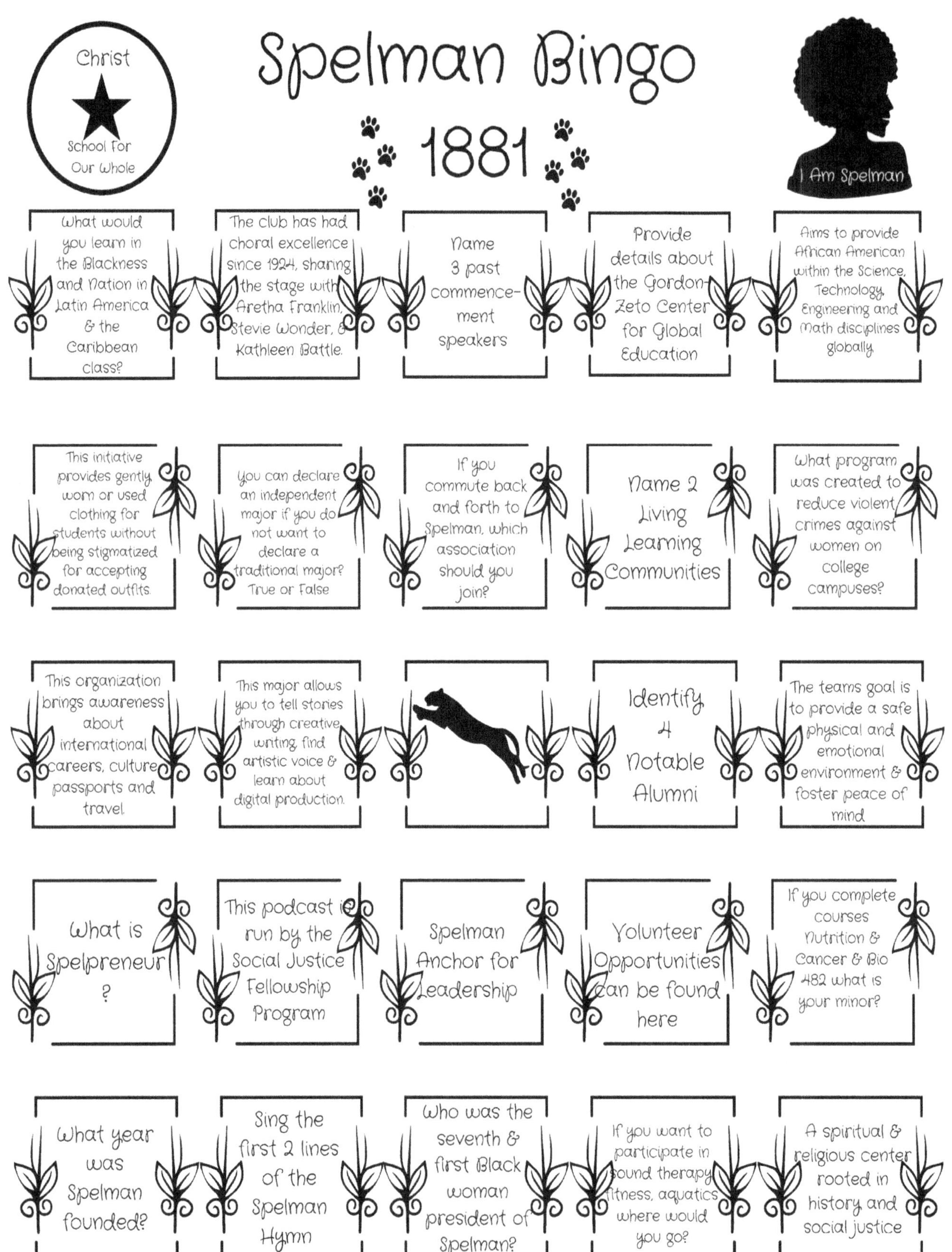

What would you learn in the Blackness and Nation in Latin America & the Caribbean class?	The club has had choral excellence since 1924, sharing the stage with Aretha Franklin, Stevie Wonder, & Kathleen Battle.	Name 3 past commencement speakers	Provide details about the Gordon-Zeto Center for Global Education	Aims to provide African American within the Science, Technology, Engineering and Math disciplines globally
This initiative provides gently worn or used clothing for students without being stigmatized for accepting donated outfits.	You can declare an independent major if you do not want to declare a traditional major? True or False	If you commute back and forth to Spelman, which association should you join?	Name 2 Living Learning Communities	What program was created to reduce violent crimes against women on college campuses?
This organization brings awareness about international careers, culture passports and travel.	This major allows you to tell stories through creative writing, find artistic voice & learn about digital production.		Identify 4 Notable Alumni	The teams goal is to provide a safe physical and emotional environment & foster peace of mind
What is Spelpreneur ?	This podcast is run by the Social Justice Fellowship Program	Spelman Anchor for Leadership	Volunteer Opportunities can be found here	If you complete courses Nutrition & Cancer & Bio 482 what is your minor?
What year was Spelman founded?	Sing the first 2 lines of the Spelman Hymn	Who was the seventh & first Black woman president of Spelman?	If you want to participate in sound therapy, fitness, aquatics where would you go?	A spiritual & religious center rooted in history and social justice

"A Choice to Change the World"

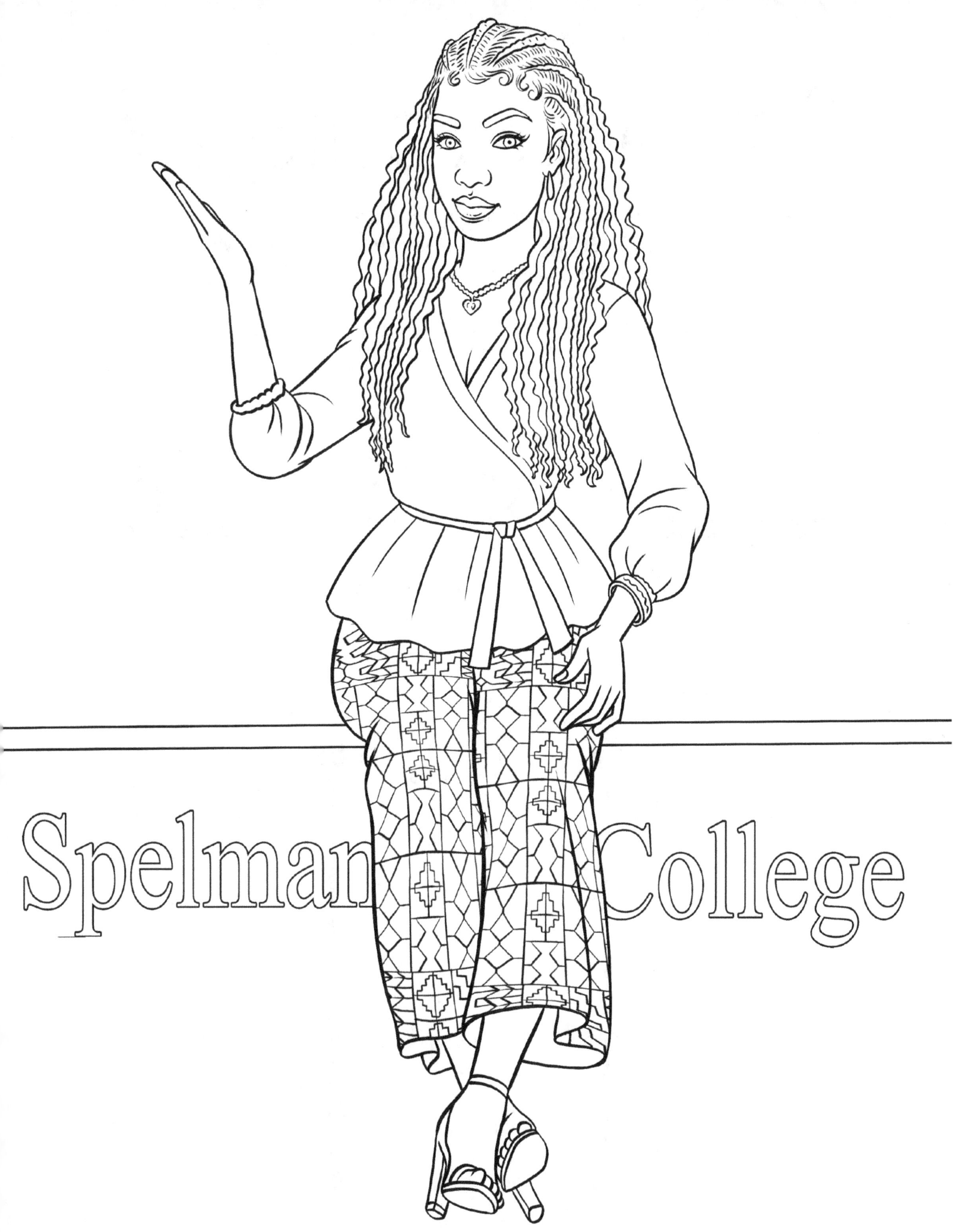

Spelman College

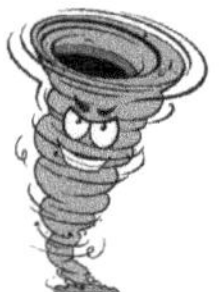 # Talladega College 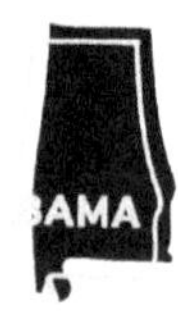

Talladega College is the oldest private historically Black college in Alabama. It was founded on November 20, 1865 by 3 former slaves: Ambrose Headen, William Savery and Thomas Tarrant, who met a convention with new freedman in Mobile, Alabama.

Fallen Puzzle Directions: The letters from each cell are below the puzzle.
Try to rebuild the original message by choosing the letters for each cell.
Clue: Message is part of the commitment from the convention.

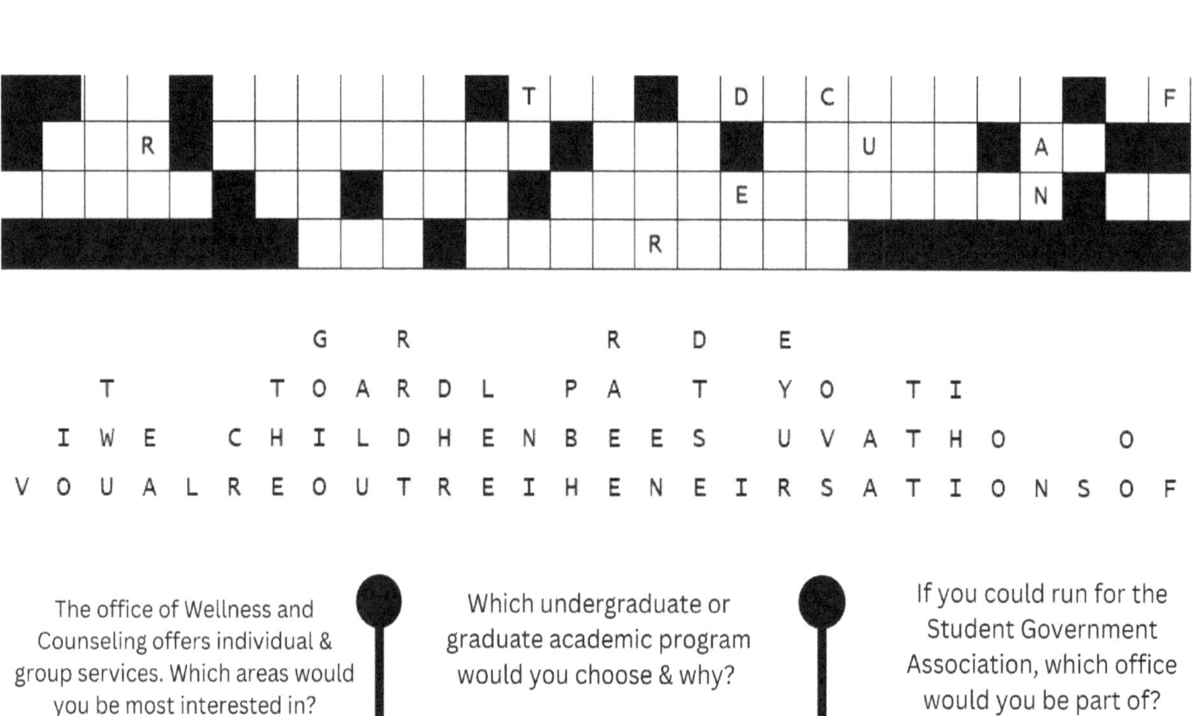

The office of Wellness and Counseling offers individual & group services. Which areas would you be most interested in?

Which undergraduate or graduate academic program would you choose & why?

If you could run for the Student Government Association, which office would you be part of?

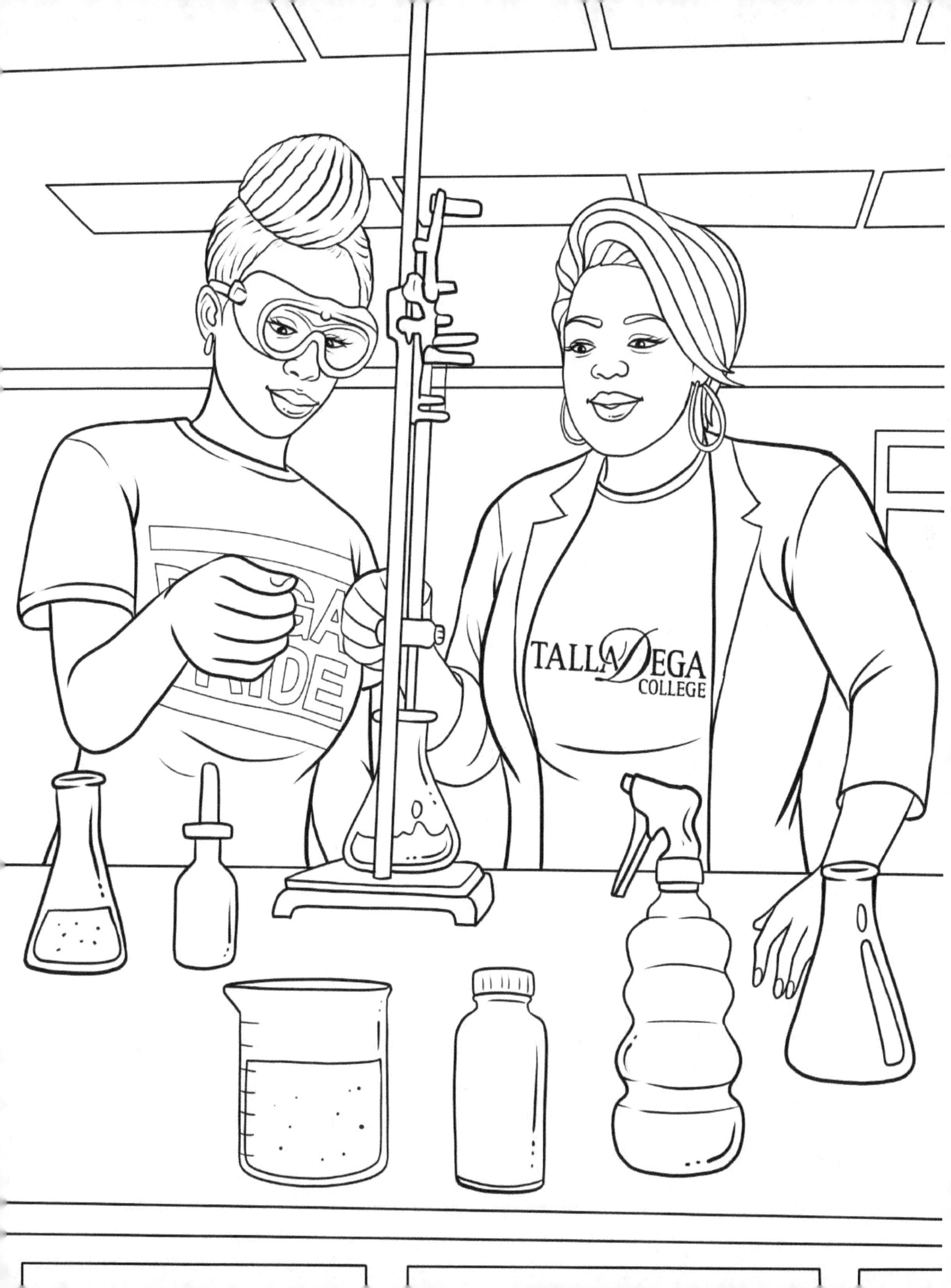

GA
PRIDE
TALLADEGA
COLLEGE

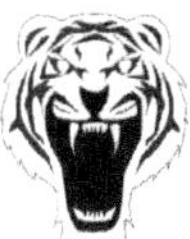

Tennessee State University

Which research facility would you rather study in: Biological Sciences and Chemistry (Tissue Culture) or College of Education (Racial Trauma & Mental Health Disparities)?

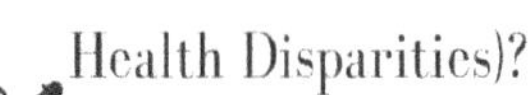
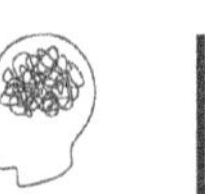

Would you rather be a member of the radio station WTST Blaze or The Meter aka student newspaper?

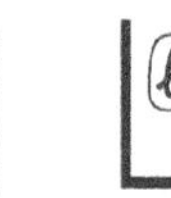

When visiting the University Counseling Center would you rather participate in individual therapy for crisis issues or group counseling for alcohol and substance use?

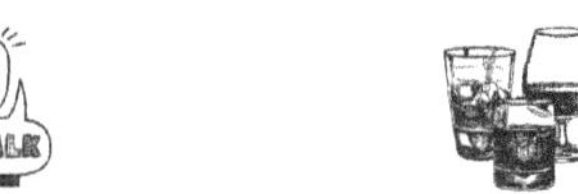

Would you rather become student government President or be part of the royal team Miss/Mister Tennessee State University?

Would you rather take a non credit educational course in continuing education or explore a degree in weekend and evening college?

Would you rather earn a bachelor's degree in Urban Policy and Planning or International Business?

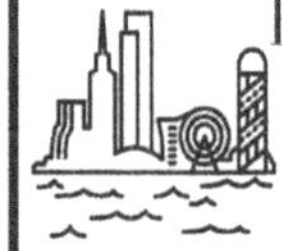
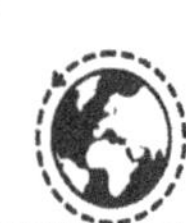

Would you rather study Aviation Flight or Supply Chain Management?

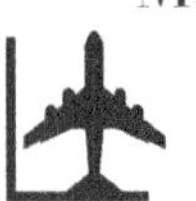
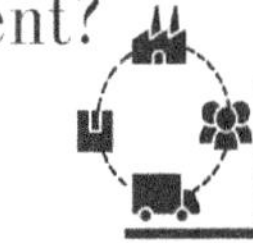

Would you rather stay in Ford Residential Complex apartments or Harriet Hodgkin's Hale Hall dorms?

Would you rather earn a M.S. in Agricultural Science concentrating on Biotechnology or M.S. in Environmental Science concentration in Natural Resources?

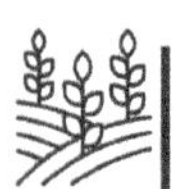

Would you rather be in the Aristocrat of Bands or the Sophisticated Ladies?

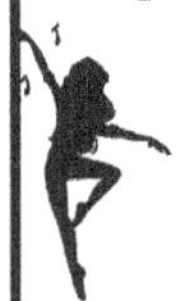
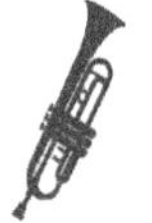

Would you rather obtain an Associates degree in Nursing or Dental Hygiene?

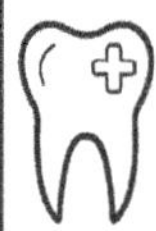
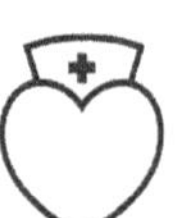

Would you rather be Oprah Winfrey a TV/Radio show host, actress, & author or Wilma Rudolph an Olympic Medalist & Hall of Famer for the year?

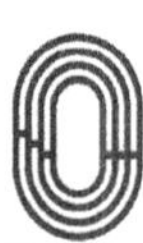

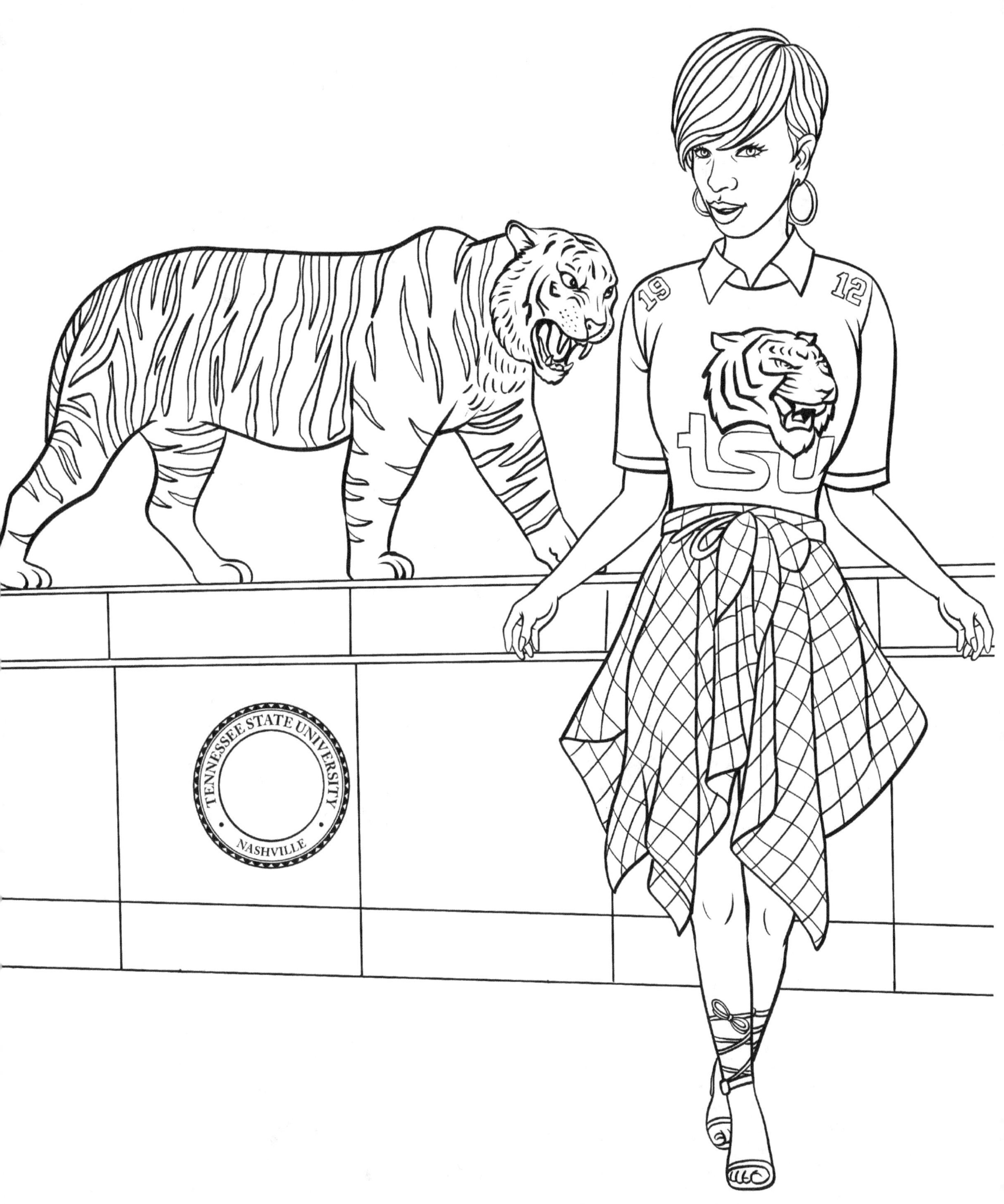

19
12
TSU
TENNESSEE STATE UNIVERSITY
NASHVILLE

Texas Southern University

Motto: "Excellence in Achievement"

Values: Creative, Efficient, Engagement, Excellence, Inclusive, Student Centered, Collaborative

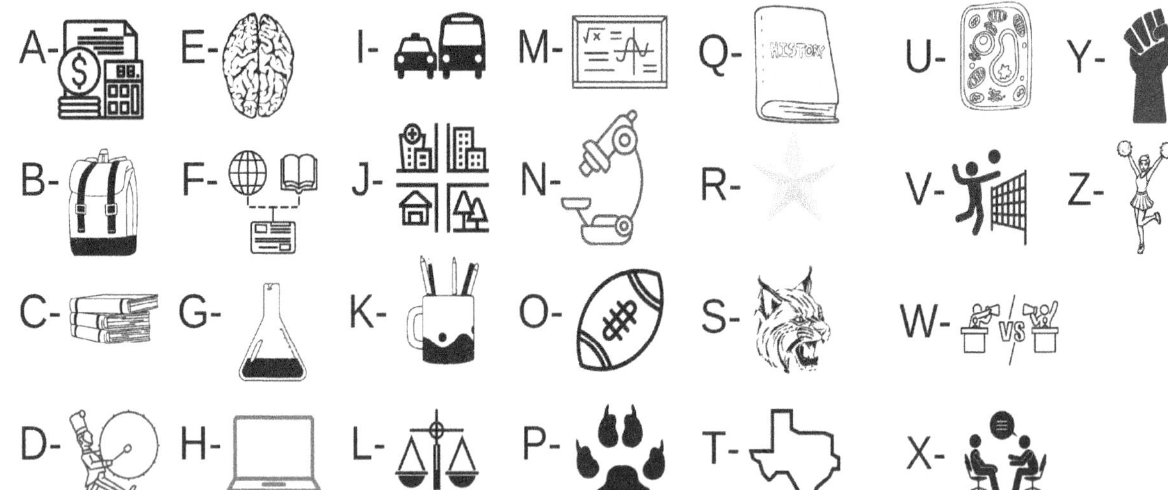

The words below are related to Texas Southern University. Decode them below using the pictures above.

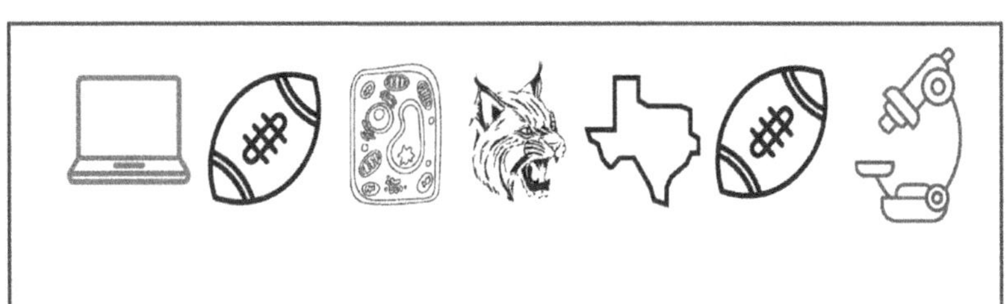

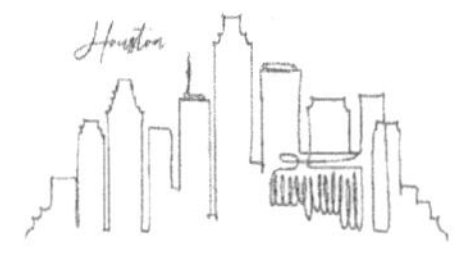

Where is Texas Southern University Located?

____

Center for Excellence in "Urban ______" Research center focuses on community & schools.

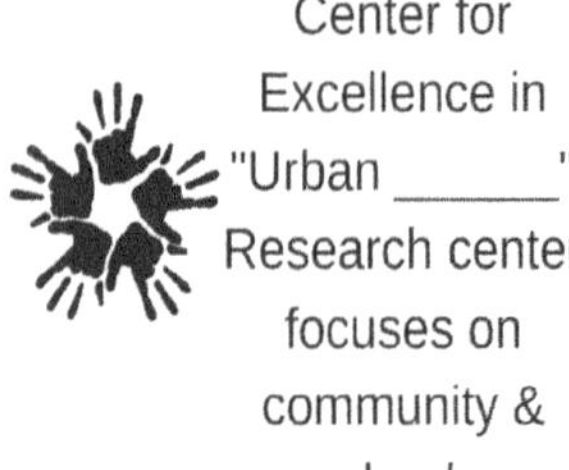

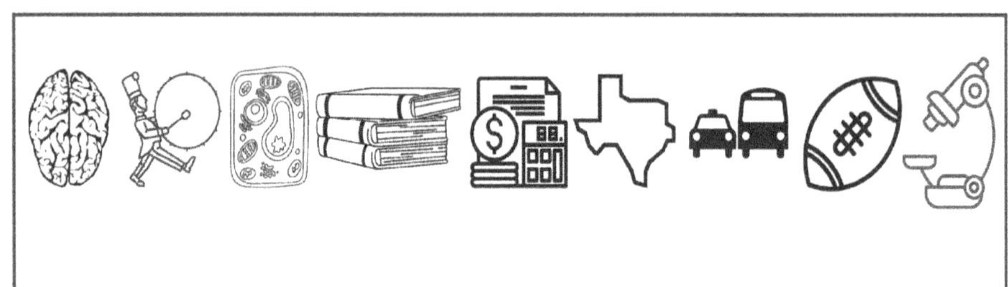

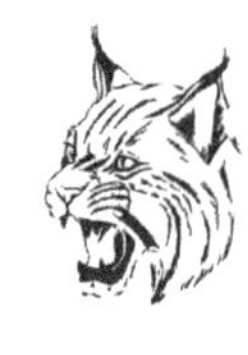  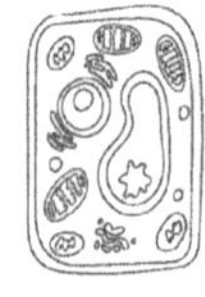 

Famous Marching Band: "Ocean of ______"

Notable Alumni: Rapper & Singer

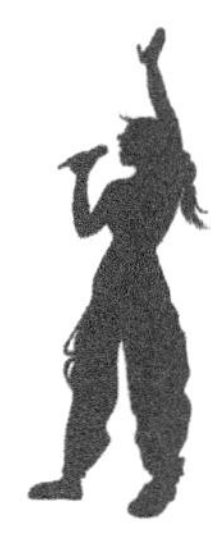

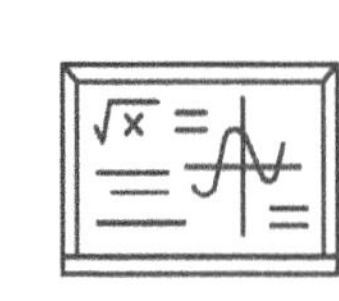 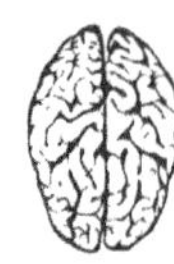 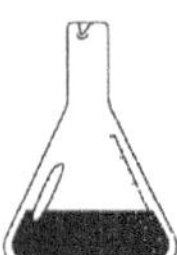 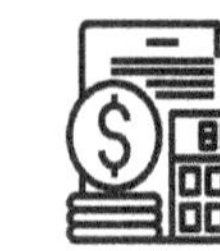 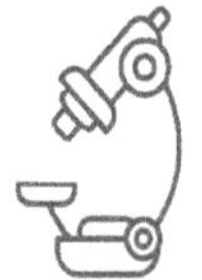

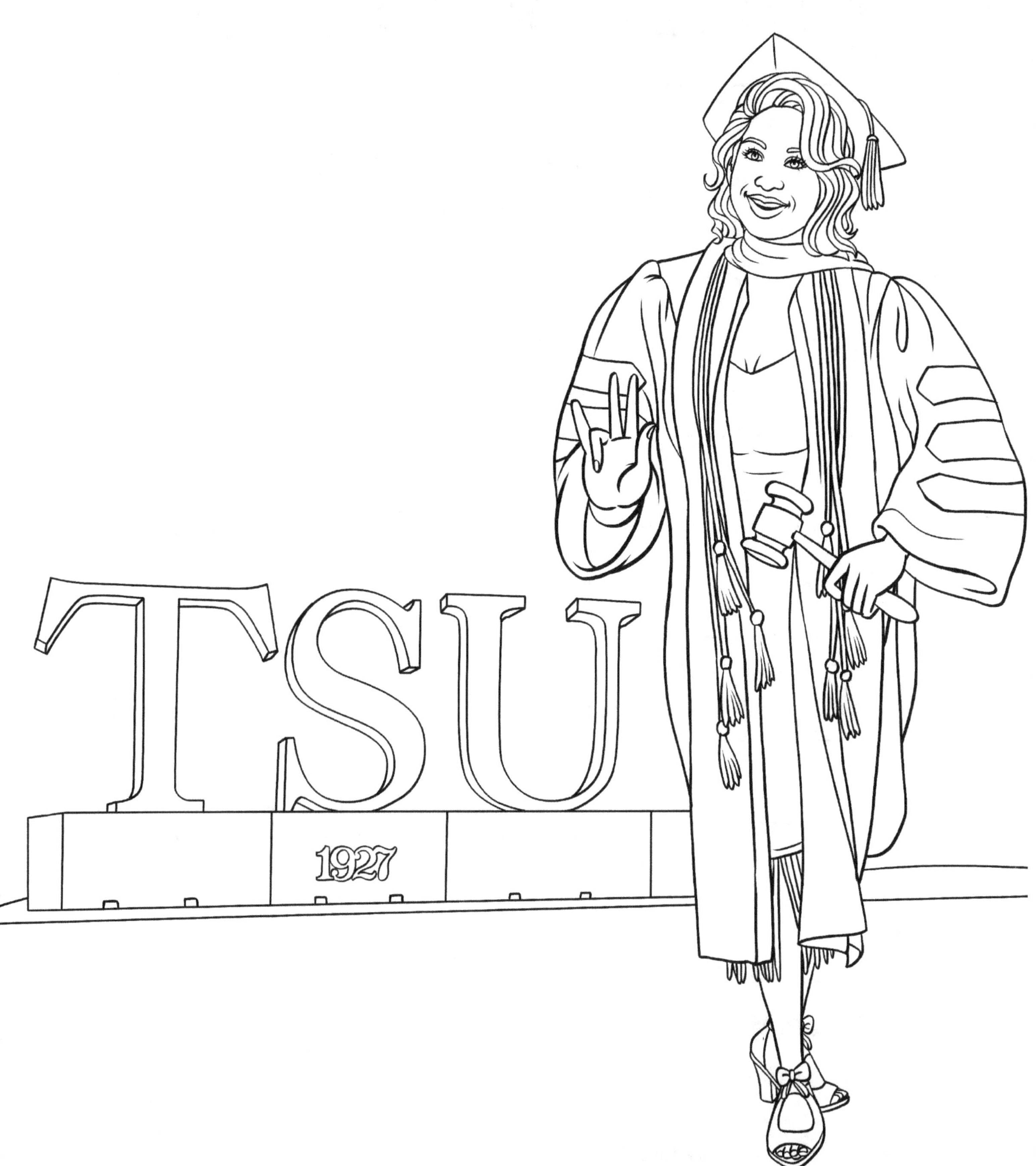

TSU
1927

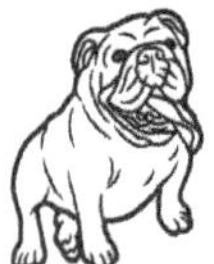 # TOUGALOO COLLEGE 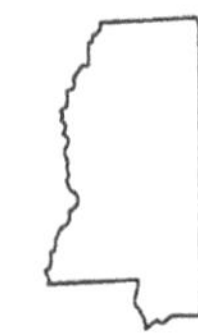

Tougaloo College is located in ________________

What year was the College founded? ________________

Who founded Tougaloo? ________________

Which movement did they spearhead ________________

What began in 1963? ________________

What museum did the college establish? ________________

Create a portrait that will be placed in the famous Art Collection

Describe the Tougaloo Nine

My top 3 favorite majors

1. ________________

2. ________________

3. ________________

Expound on the Civil Rights Library & Archives

"Where History Meets the Future"

Which special programs would you be most interested in?

____

____

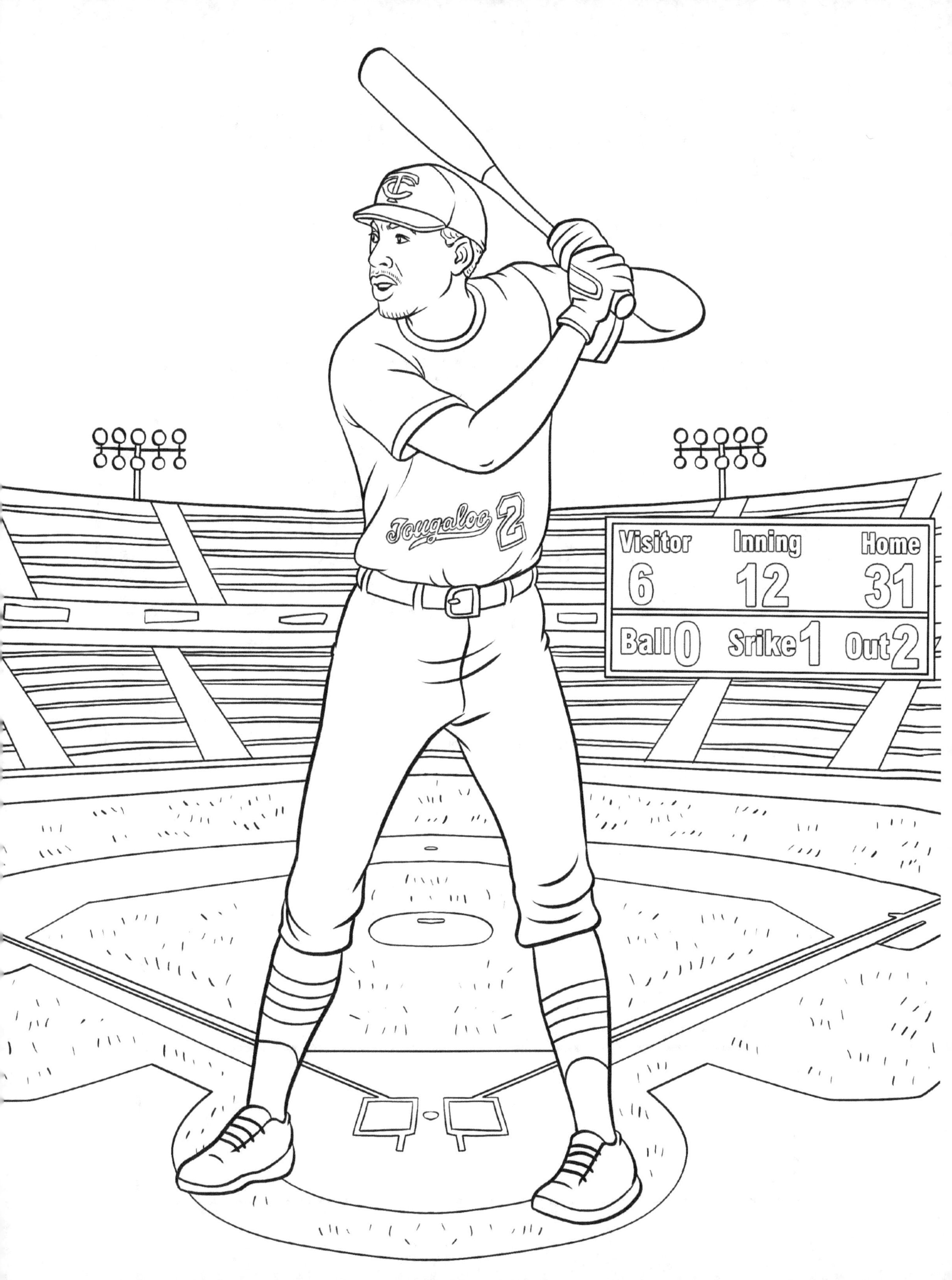

Jougaloc 2
Visitor
6
Inning
12
Home
31
Ball 0
Srike 1
Out 2

Tuskegee University

Provide details about the Tuskegee Airmen & the pivotal role they played in the institute history.

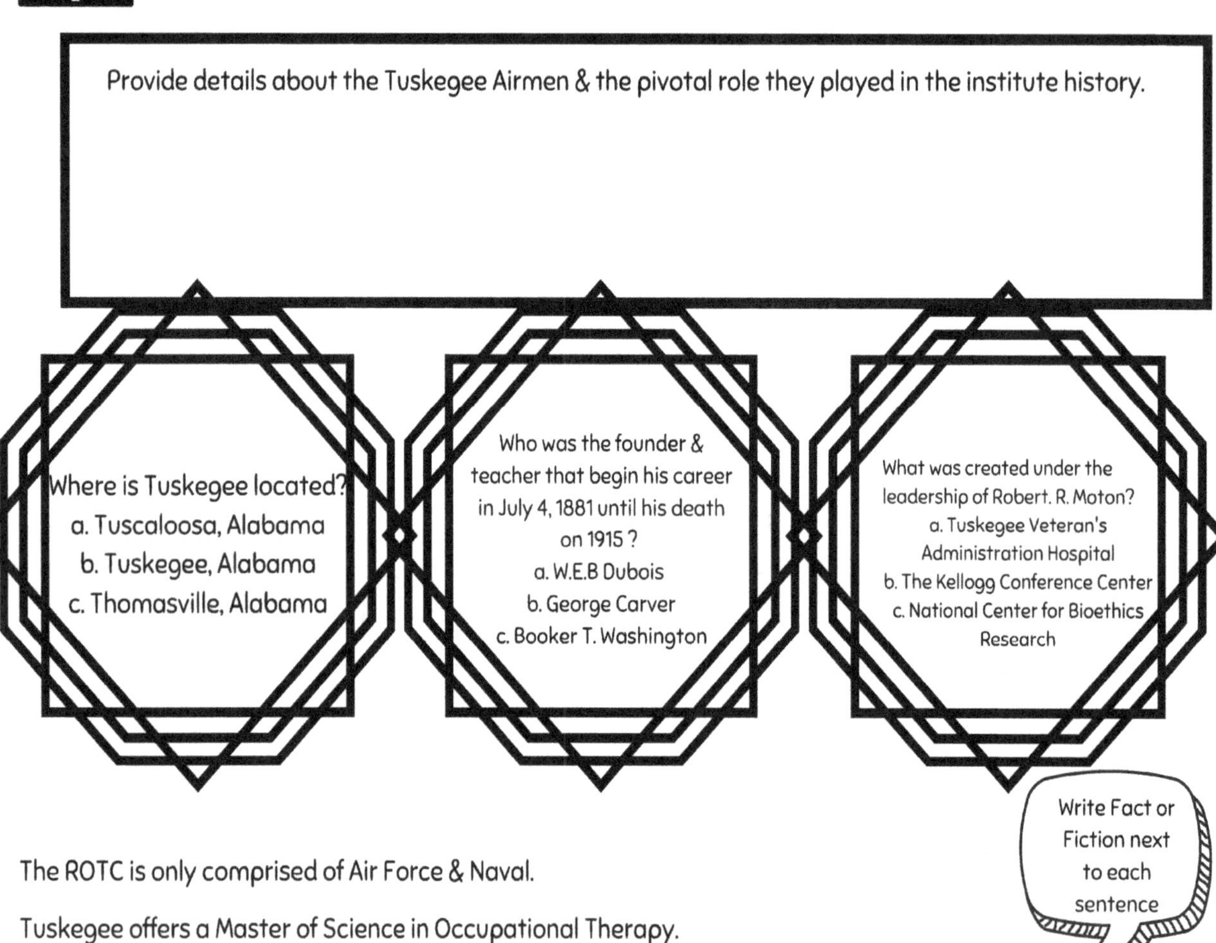

The ROTC is only comprised of Air Force & Naval.

Tuskegee offers a Master of Science in Occupational Therapy.

You can complete a Bachelor of Architecture, once you complete the pre program.

College of Veterinary Medicine is the only veterinary professional program located at an HBCU.

A minor in Social Work will allow for a service learning component to gain experience in the field.

TU Global offices collaborate with Jamaica University of West Indies Nitrogen fixation in cowpeas.

As a public health major, During Jr. Year 2nd Semester you would not be taking Life Cycle Nutrition.

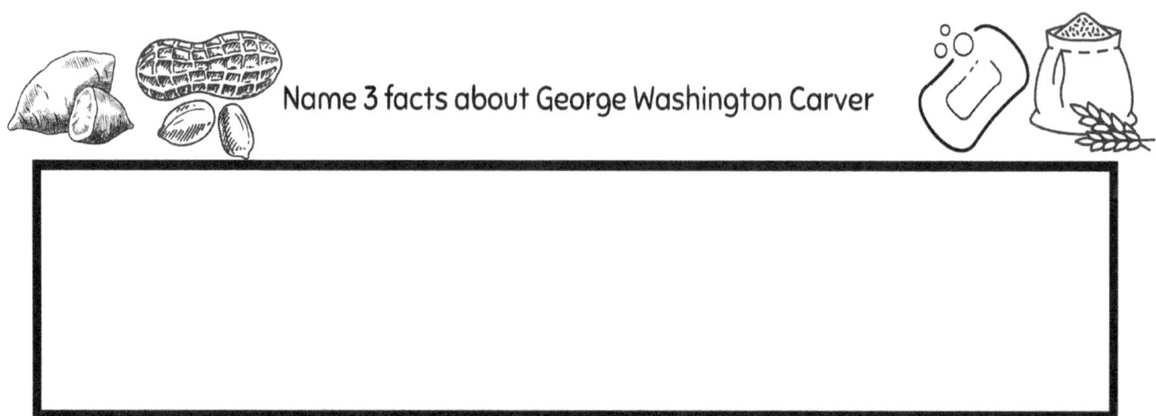

Name 3 facts about George Washington Carver

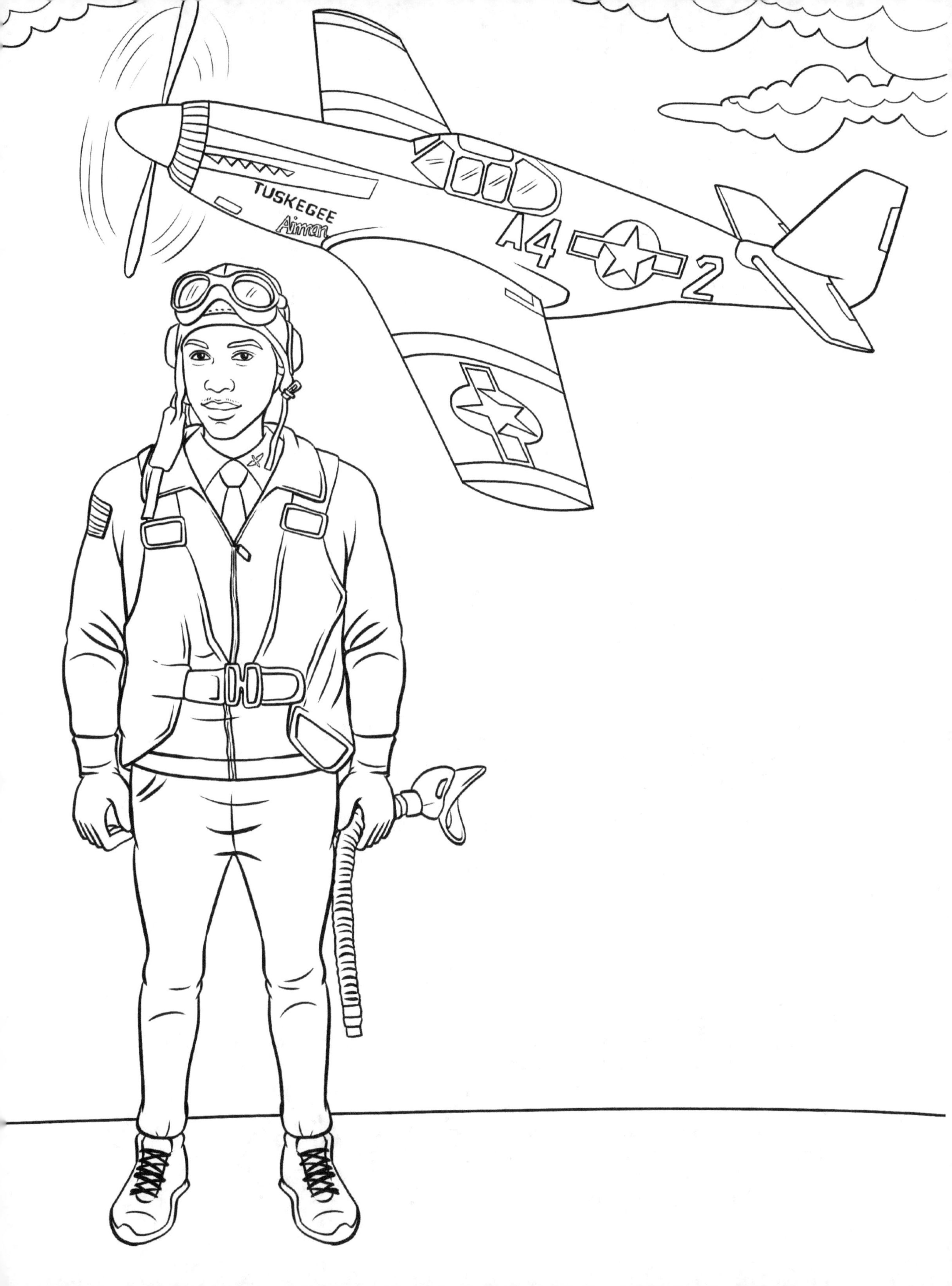

TUSKEGEE
Airman
A4
2

Board Game

Start

When was UVI founded?

Where are the 2 UVI campuses located?

The Program's goal is to reduce drug use & prevent HIV infection among college students

Two Studios; One United Message

Sing a line from Alma Mater by the Sea

If you have a Bachelor of Science in Marine Biology, name a class that you would take?

UVI students can participate in the National Student Exchange as a freshman? T or F

University of the Virgin Islands

1962

What year did UVI become an HBCU?

This international refereed journal has a Caribbean Focus.

What is the NCAA College Basketball Tournament called?

USVI and BVI are in collaboration for which exchange program?

If you are an aspiring school counselor, what would you get a degree in?

Which scholarship is available to students given by the UVI scholarship committee?

What island is the Academic Center located on?

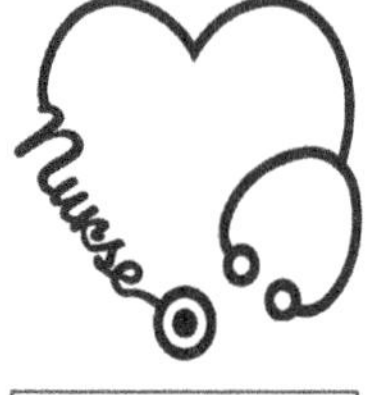

Answer correctly move 2 steps forward

Answer correctly, opponent will take 3 steps backward

What are the 4 roles of the executive branch of the Student Government Association?

If you take Maternal Newborn Nursing, what degree might you receive?

Notable Alumni: UVI's first ever Rhode Scholar & cabinet minister of St. Kitts & Nevis

What does ECS stand for?

What is UVI's Mascot?

This club features aerobic equipment such as weights, stair master, treadmills & exercise bikes.

"Historically American. Uniquely Caribbean. Globally Interactive."

Incorrect Answer move 3 steps backward

If you want to be a federal patrol, police officer, customs agent, marshal, or corrections officer. What would you major in?

Name an organization that you would like to join?

If you wanted to join the Virgin Island Parade & fete, what committee would you join?

If you take Creative Assessment (CLIC 814) What PHD degree would you obtain?

What role would you play if you served as a good role ambassador for the UVI?

How many dorm halls on St. Thomas/St. Croix?

Does the UVI offer a Senior Citizen Education Program for residents 60 and older? Y or N

Finish

Directions: Each player will take turns to see who can correct the guest answer. If you answer correctly move forward unless otherwise stated if not stay in same square. Player who reaches the finish square is the winner.

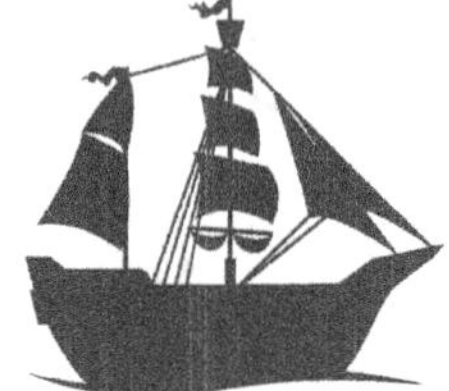

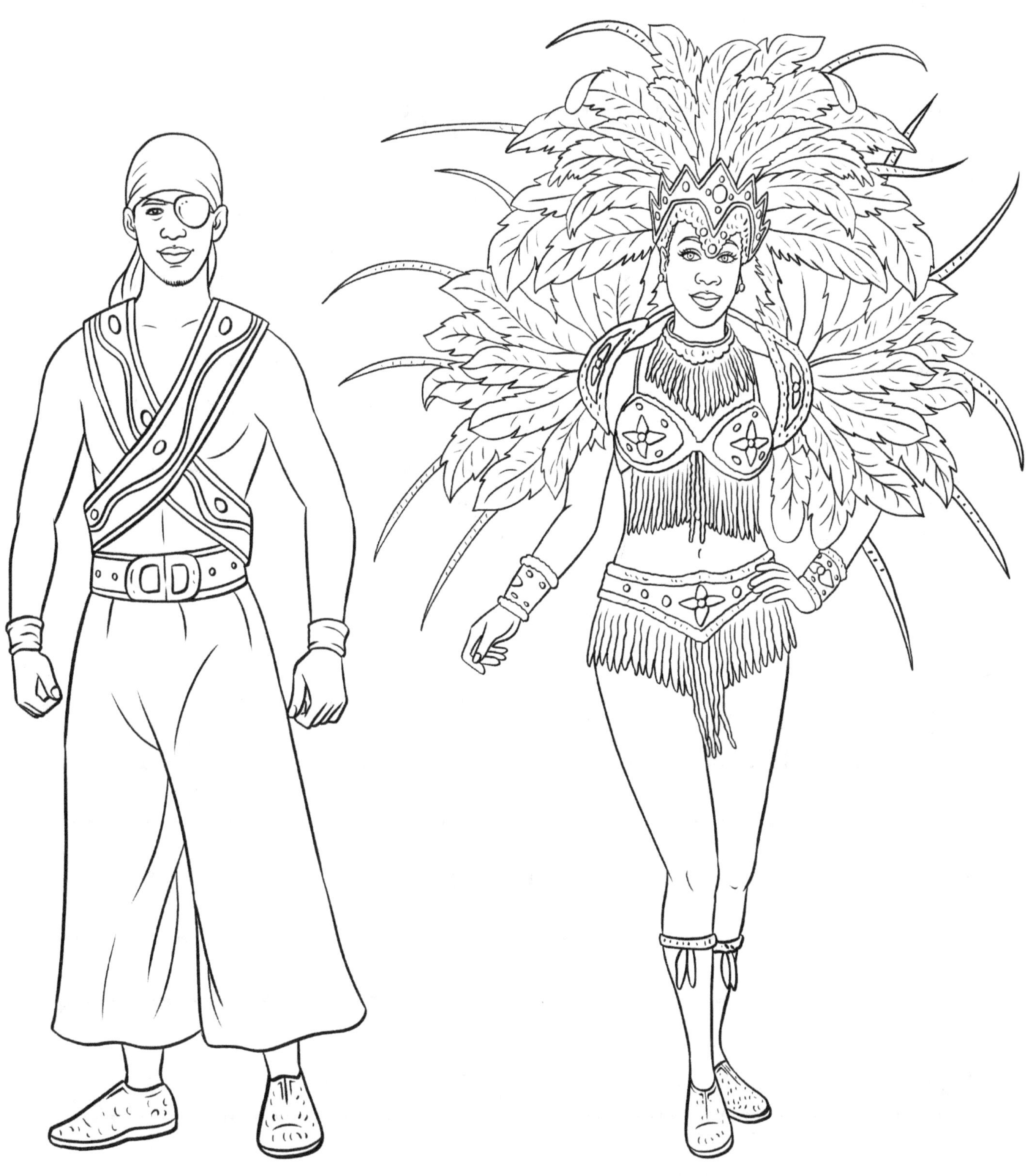

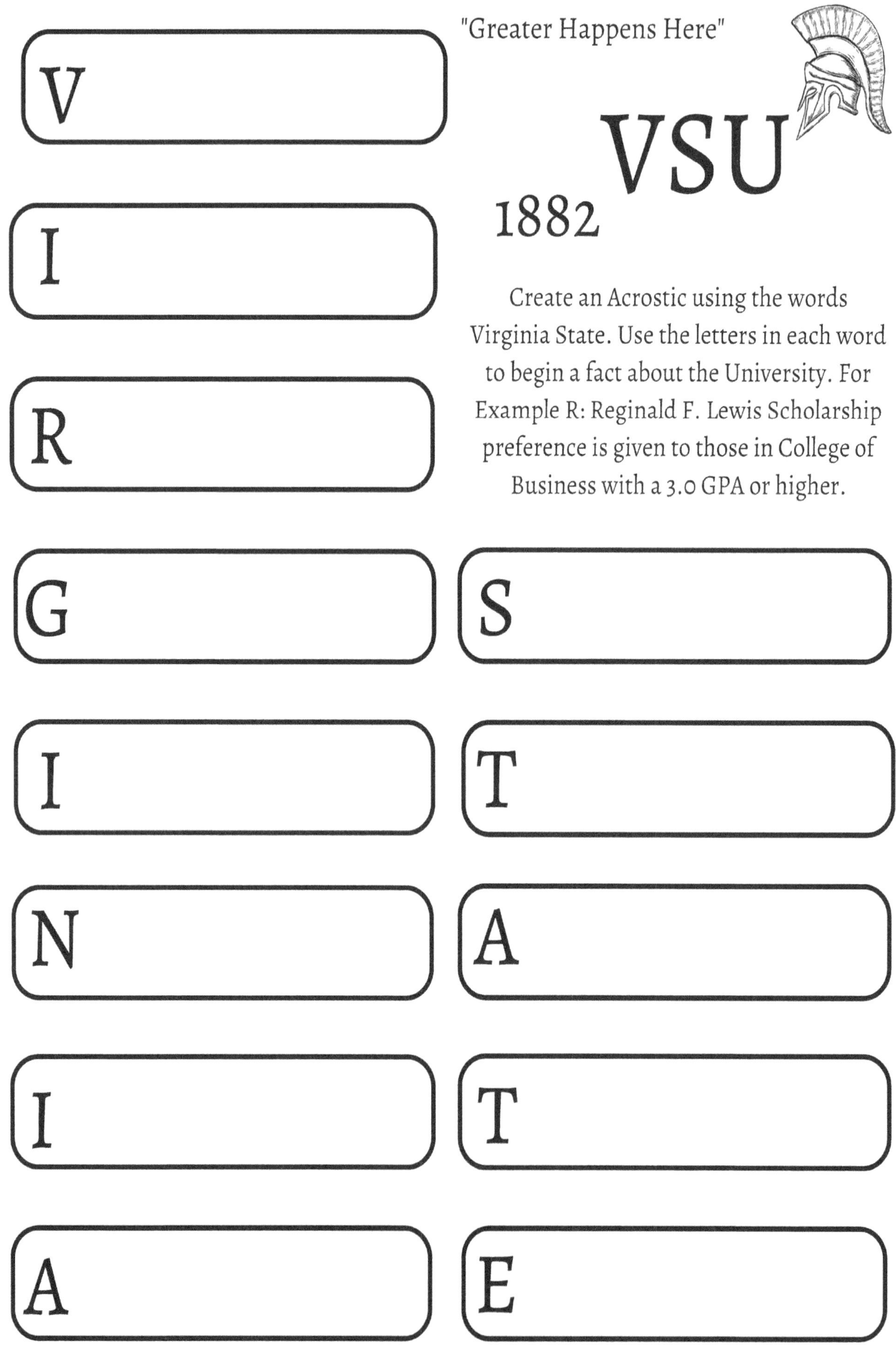

V
I
R
G
I
N
I
A
S
T
A
T
E
"Greater Happens Here"
VSU
1882
Create an Acrostic using the words Virginia State. Use the letters in each word to begin a fact about the University. For Example R: Reginald F. Lewis Scholarship preference is given to those in College of Business with a 3.0 GPA or higher.

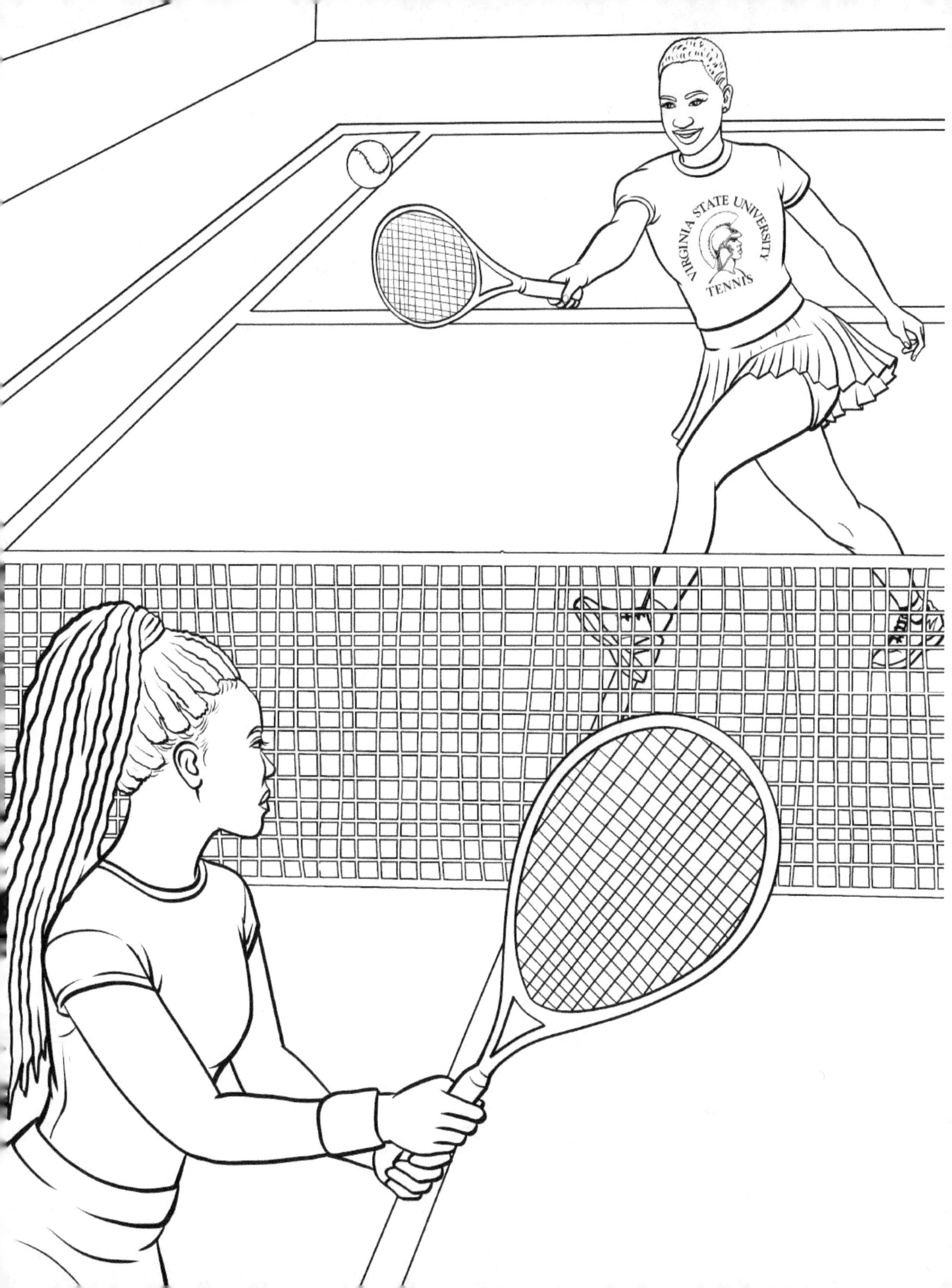

VIRGINIA STATE UNIVERSITY
TENNIS

Virginia Union University

True | **FALSE**

1. Student Activities & Leadership host PatherFest.

   D A

2. You cannot obtain a Doctorate of Ministry at VUU.

   B R

3. VUU is associated with the American Baptist Churches USA.

   W C

4. Ambassadors of Sound Marching Band is a part of the CIAA.

   O D

5. Cheerleading is considered a Women & Men's Athletic Sport at VUU.

   E T

6. School of Theology is named after 5th president Samuel Dewitt Proctor.

   I F

7. VUU is committed to serving veteran, military students and their dependents.

   D G

8. John Malcus Ellison was the second alumnus and African American to serve as president.

   H V

9. VUU Global is a new virtual learning program within the Center for the Study of HBCUs.

   P I

10. If you major in Business Analytics, you are a part of the Accounting & Finance Department.

    J H

11. You can receive both a Masters of Divinity from VCU & Masters in Patient Counseling from STVU.

    K L

12. The Evenlyn Reid Syphax School of Education has two departments: Teacher and Secondary Education.

    L I

13. If you are a first time freshman, you can potentially receive a Community, Culture, Research Scholarship.

    O M

14. Trio Upward Bound serves high school students and provides resources in preparation for college entrance.

    L N

15. Universidad Virginia Union goal is to increase retention and graduation rates for Latino/a & Indian Students.

    O E

16. The Hezekiah Walker Center for Sacred Music will allow students to enter the Gospel World with a competitive edge.

    L P

17. Legacy Awards & Scholarship Gala was created to raise revenue to help students overcome financial burdens associated with obtaining a degree.

    E Q

18. These 4 institutions merged and formed VSU : Richmond Theological Seminary, Wayland Seminary, Hartshorn Memorial College & Storer College.

    R S

Motto

___ ___ ___   ___ ___ ___   ___ ___ ___   ___ ___   ___ ___ ___ ___ ___ ___ ___
 5 10 15   16   4 18   1   3   6 11 14   9   2   13 8 12 7 17

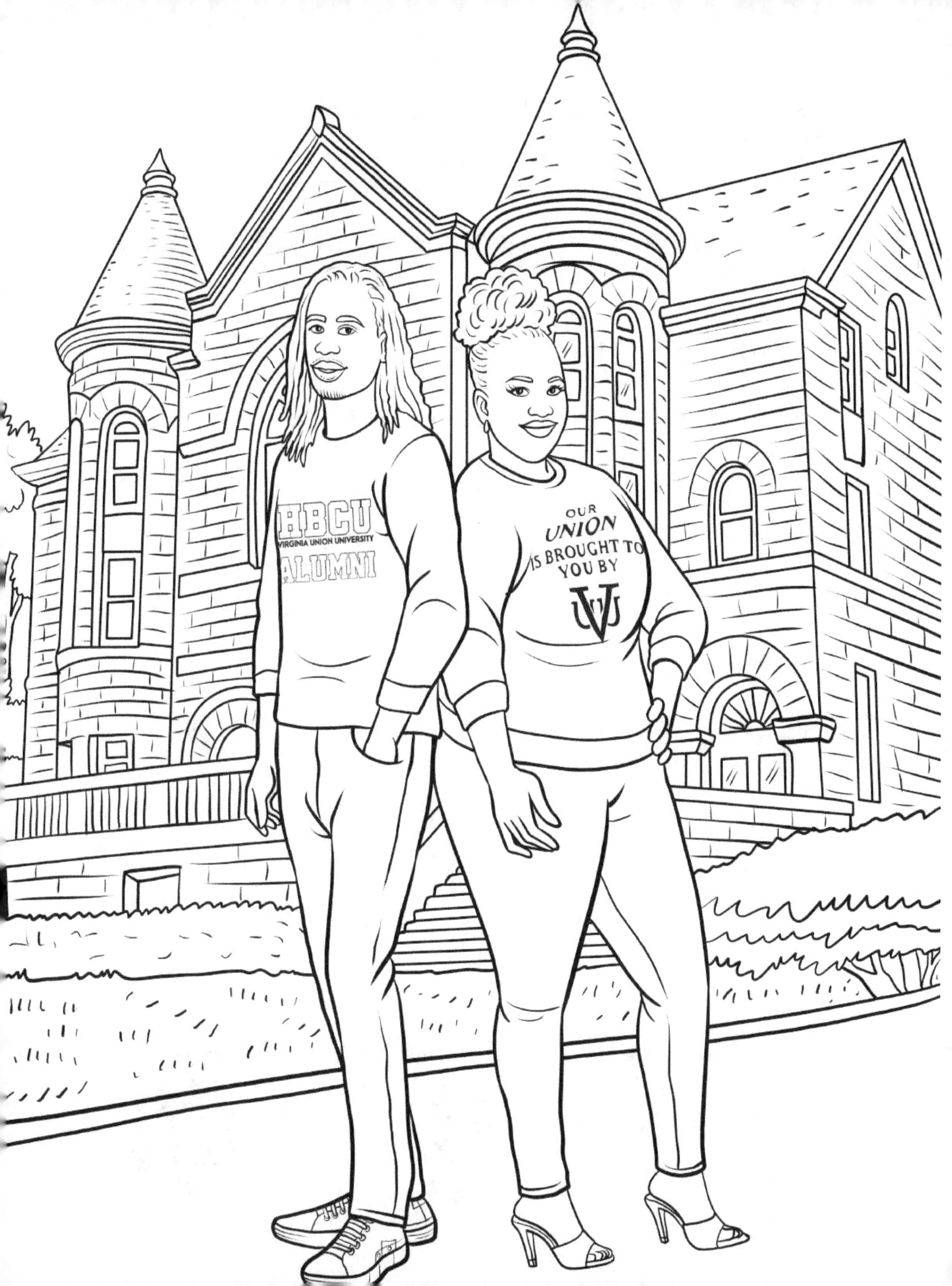
HBCU
VIRGINIA UNION UNIVERSITY
ALUMNI
OUR
UNION
IS BROUGHT TO
YOU BY
VU

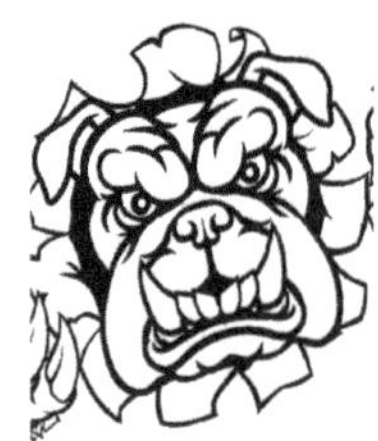

Wilberforce University

2 LIES AND 1 TRUTH
CIRCLE WHICH STATEMENT IS TRUE

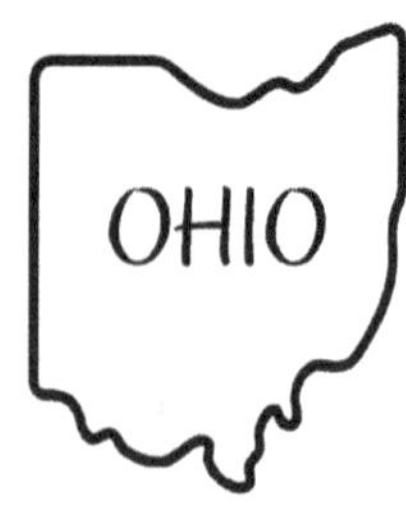

1. In 1863, The African Methodist Episcopal church purchased the college to ensure survival

a. Making it the first Black operated & owned in the nation

b. The Civil War caused student enrollment to increase

c. As a result the first board members were only Black

2. In the 1890s students from which African country were admitted :

a. Kenya

b. South Africa

c. Cameroon

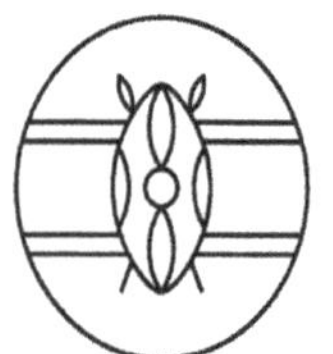
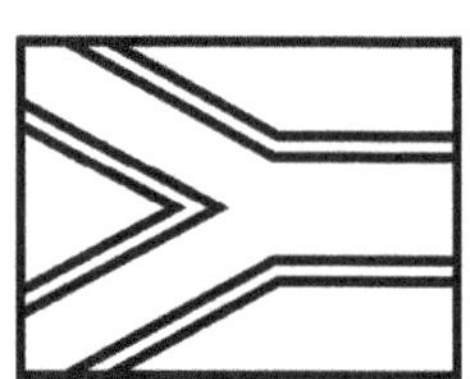
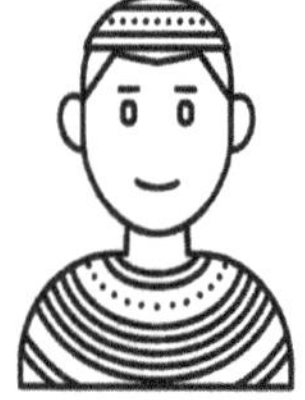

3. All students must participate in cooperative education, aka

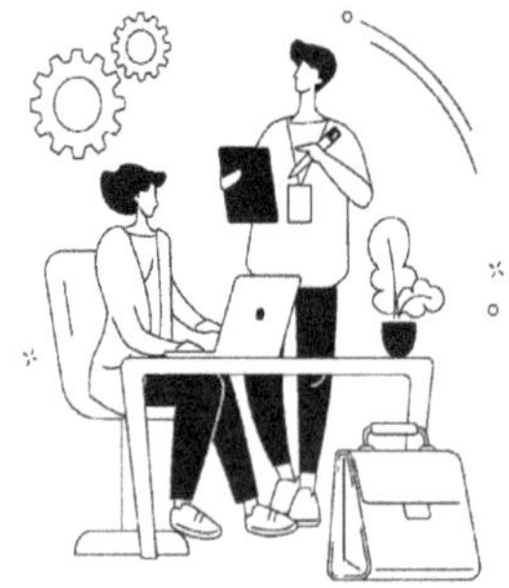

a. Final Group Project

b. International Service Learning Project

c. Internships that provide work experience

Did you know?
Know you Know

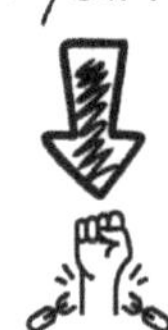

4. What is the Center Purpose:

a. S.T.E.M

b. Study Abroad

c. Entrepreneurship & Innovation

Founded in 1856, Wilberforce history began before the Civil War. As the Ohio underground railroad (a slave escape route for those going North to freedom) was being created, the university became a safe spot and was integral to the process.

5. American Mathematician whose work inspired movie Hidden Figures :

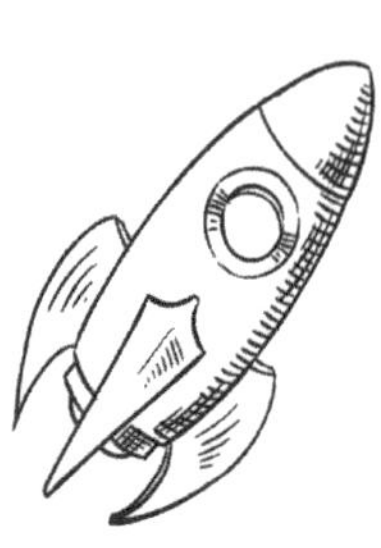

a. Lilian Hayman

b. Dorothy Vaughan

c. Shontel Brown

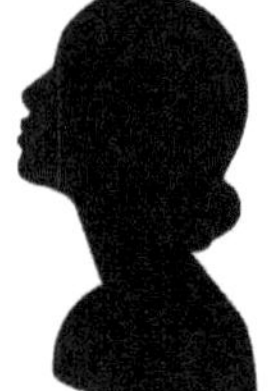
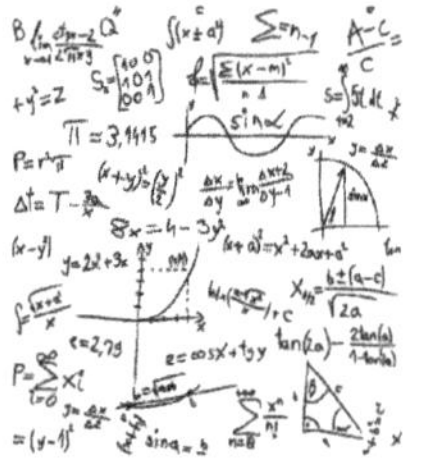
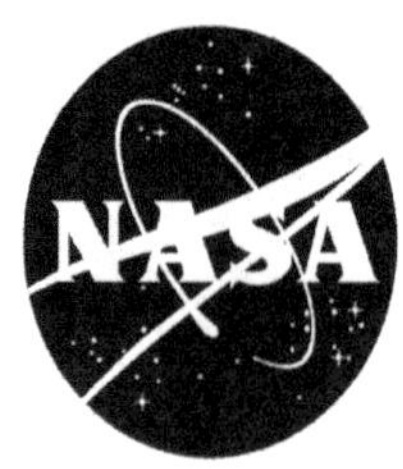

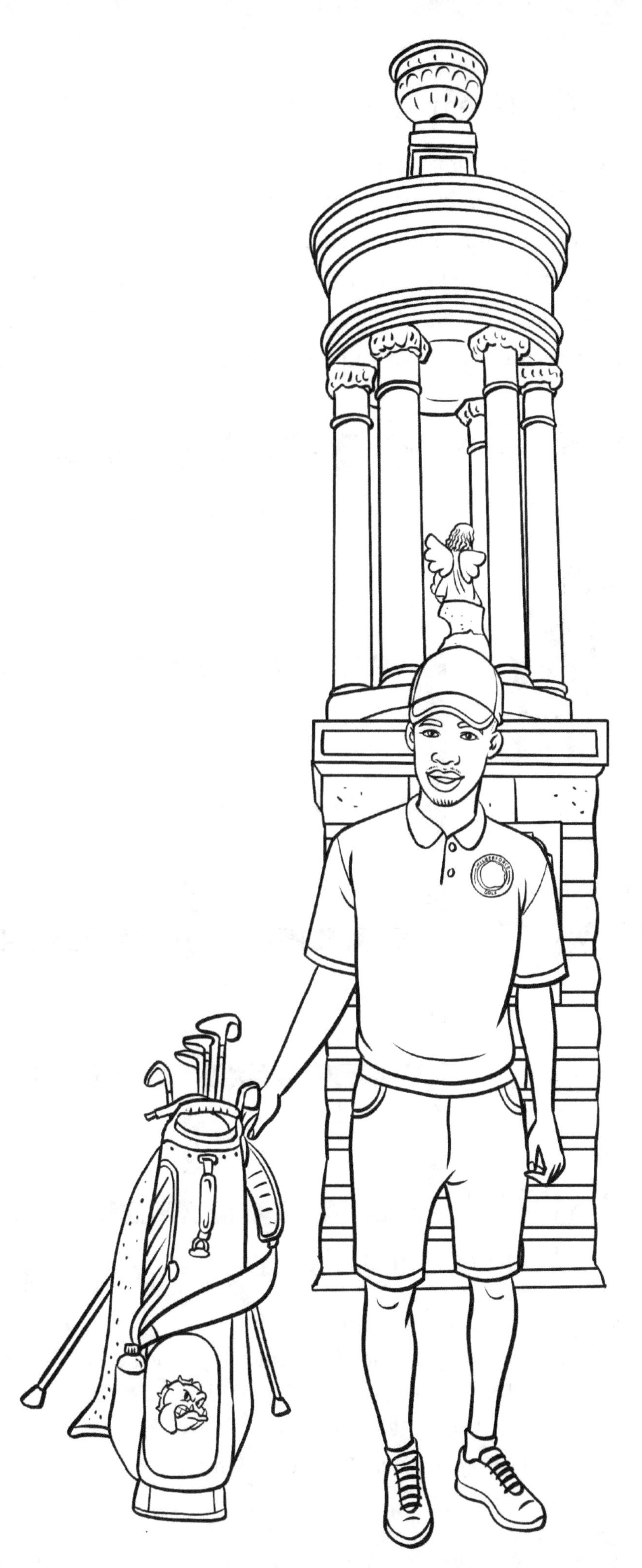

"The Great Debaters"

Melvin B. Tolson is known for being a professor, poet, coach & head of the debate team. In 1935, students Hobart Jarrett, Henry Heights, James Farmer, Jr. and Henrietta Bell (Wells) defeated the University of Southern California national debate team champions. This was unprecedented because of the Jim Crow laws at the time. In 2007, Denzel Washington directed and acted in a movie called, "The Great Debaters". He donated 1 million dollars to the Tolson/Washington Forensics Society scholarship to revive the debate team at Wiley College.

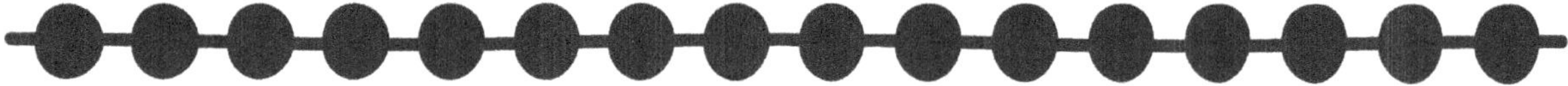

Directions: Create an opening statement & provide arguments for each statement below.

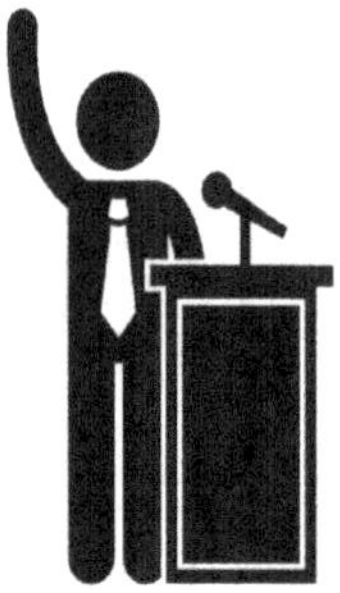

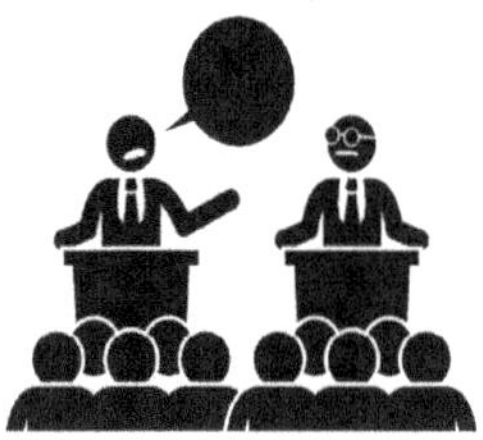

Arguments For	Arguments Against

Wiley College History

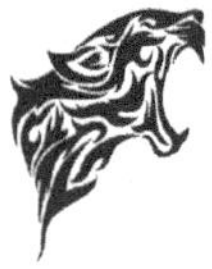

In 1873, Wiley College was founded in Marshall Texas. Although the college dealt with an atmosphere of hostility in the South, it managed to flourish in other ways. Such as expansion of school buildings, partnerships with the National Association for the Advancement of Colored People (NAACP) and the National Urban League. Wiley now offers degrees in the areas of Science, Education, Business & Technology and Social Sciences & Humanity.

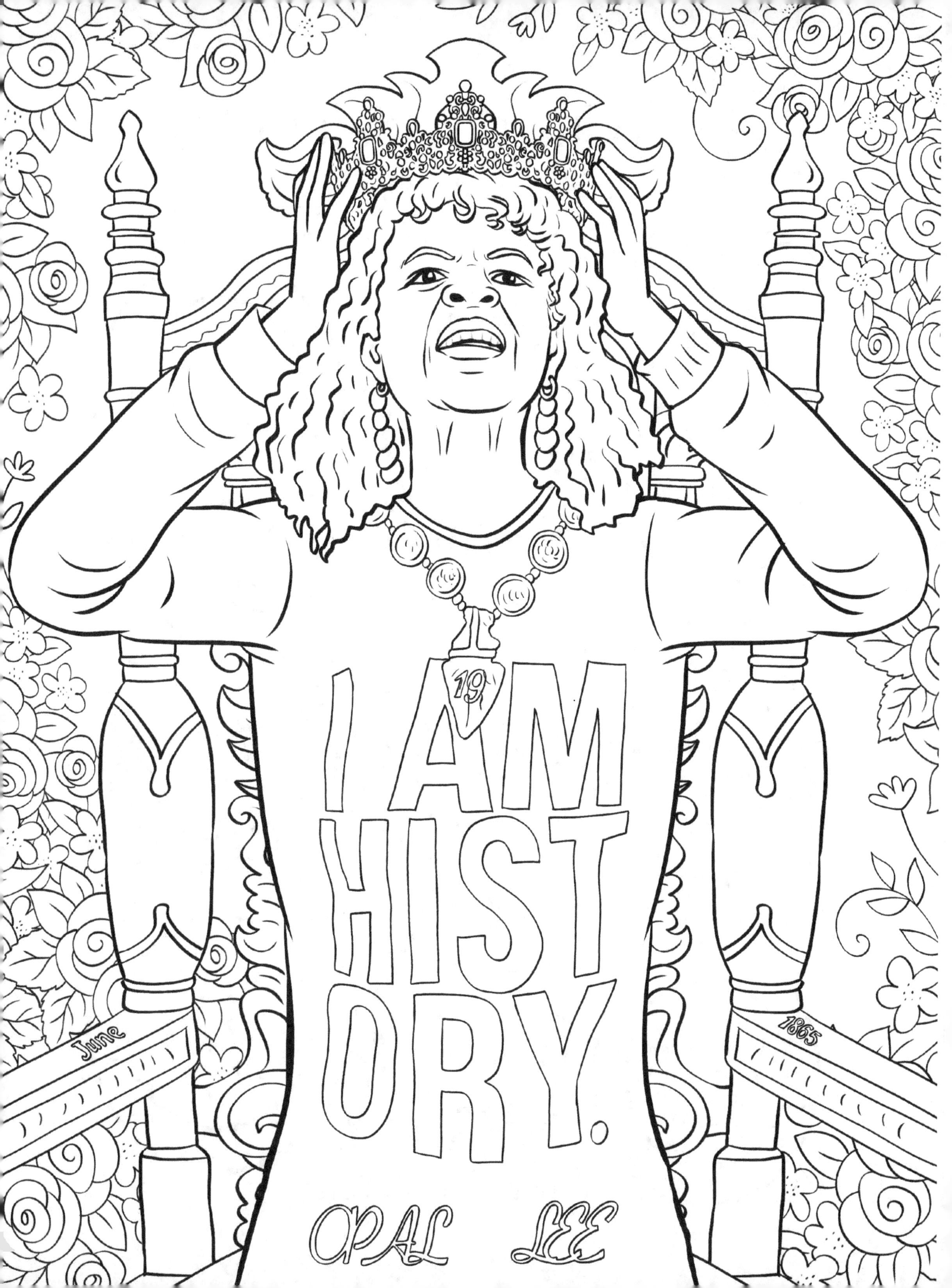

I AM HISTORY.
19
June
1865
OPAL LEE

Winston - Salem
Scavenger Hunt

18 State University 92

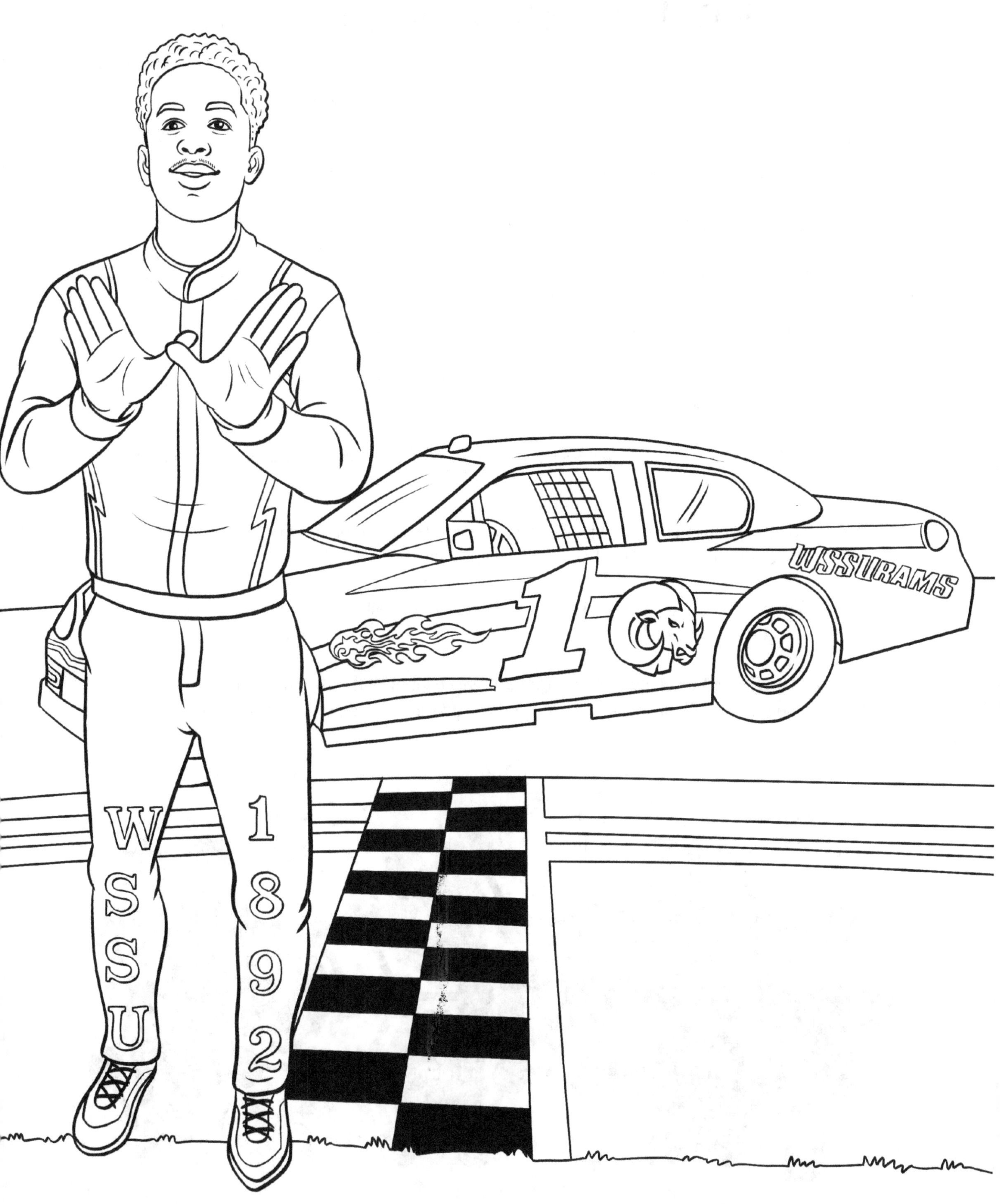

WSSURAMS
1
WSSU
1892

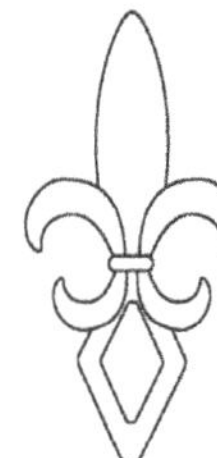 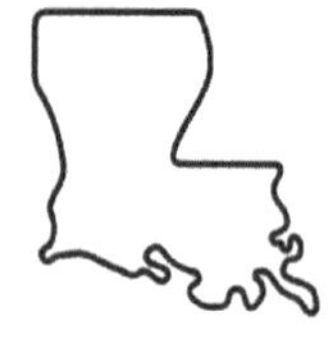

Xavier University of Louisiana

Unscramble the words and fill in the blanks below.

1. Xavier University is located in a ______ __________ known as "the Birthplace of Jazz".

2. Xavier was founded by the Sisters Of Blessed Sacraments and __________ __________

3. Institute for Black ______ Studies to strengthen their understanding of culture and faith.

4. Class of "97" alumni, was The first African-American female mayor of New Orleans.

5. Give ______ Xavier Day is an online event sponsored by alumni that helps raise funds for exemplary students.

6. College of __________ prepares students in the areas of patient counseling, drug therapy, care of pharmaceutics.

7. This program is a partnership between Xavier & High school students that focuses on increasing interest in STEM and biomedical fields.

8. The XULA ____________ Stories Program is for journalists & students examining critical problems such as mass incarceration, inequality in schools and more.

9. The Xavier University ________ Department collaborated with a multicultural toy company to create dolls to empower diversity within the competitive cheer sport.

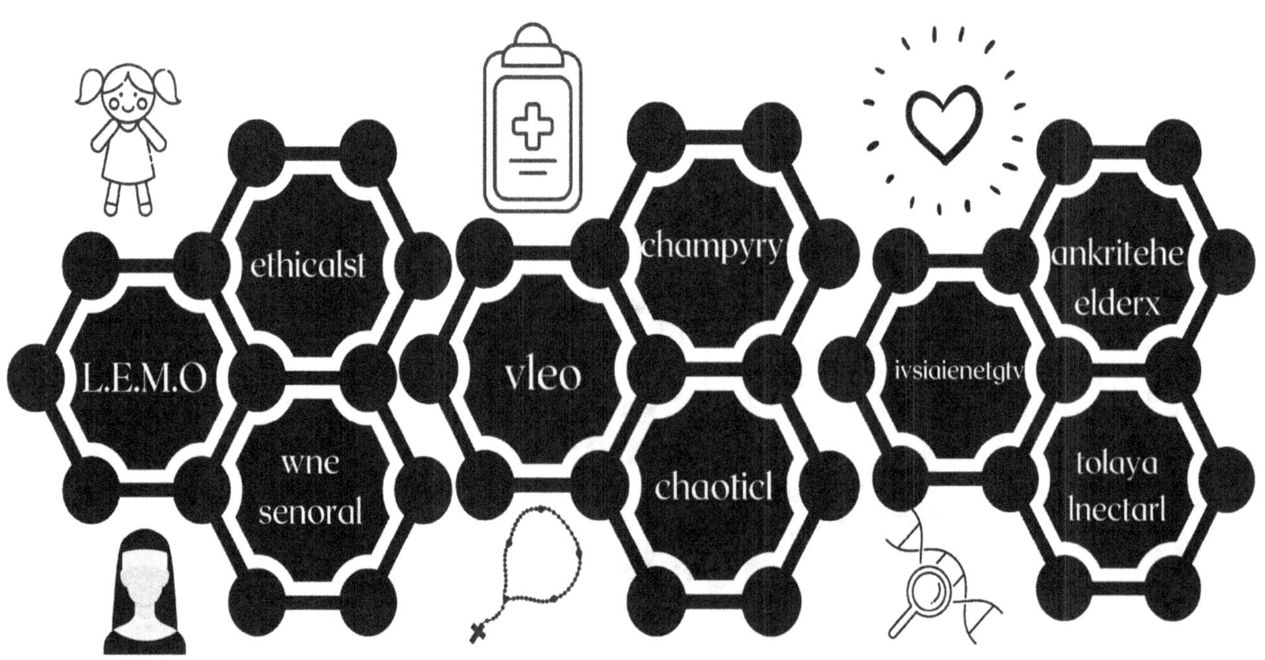

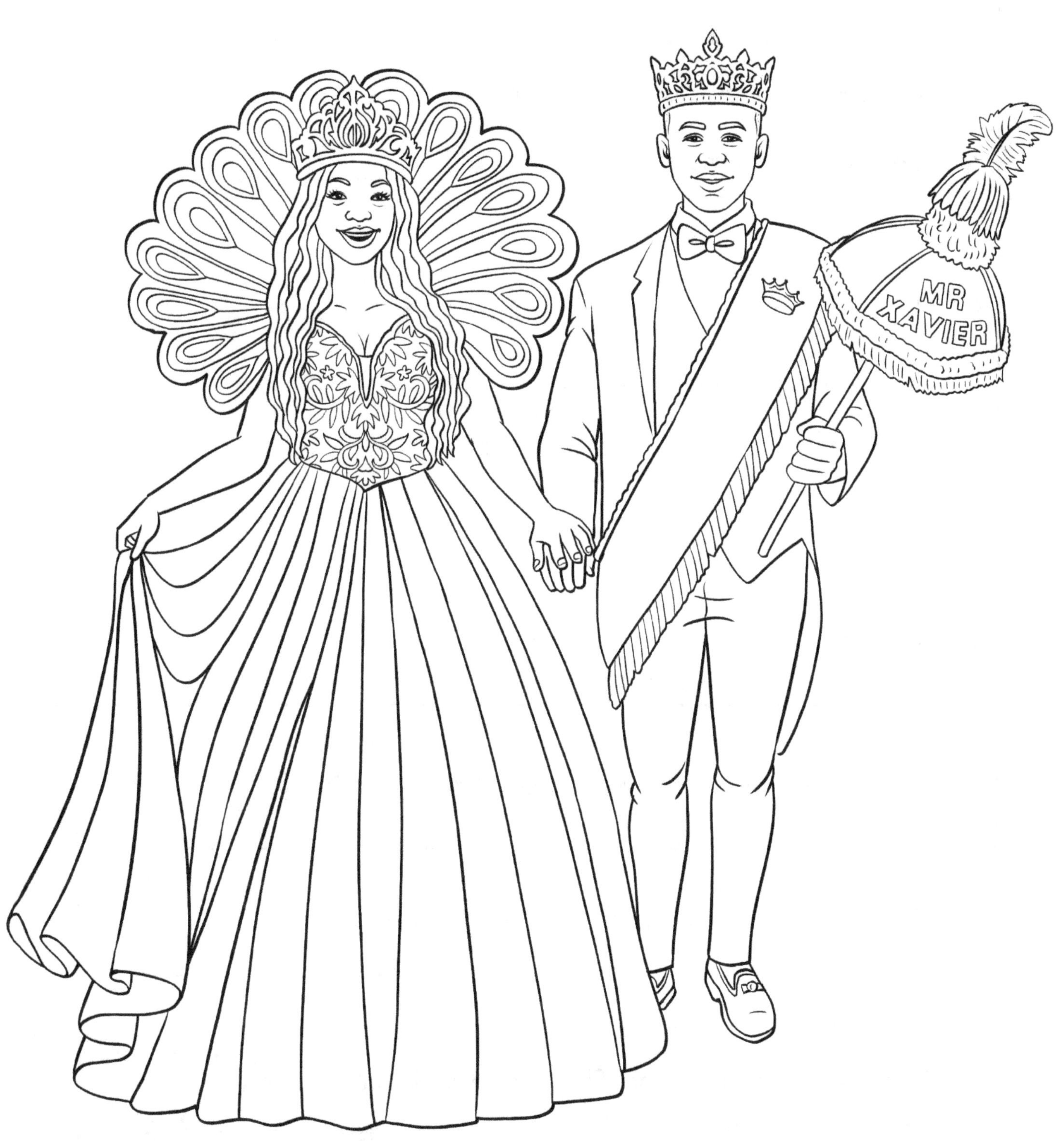

MR
XAVIER

1906

Alpha Phi Alpha Fraternity

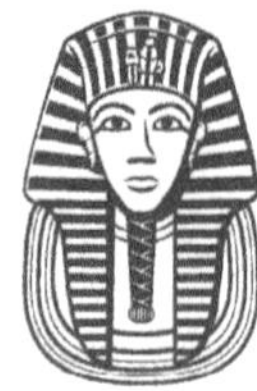

Find out more about the fraternity,by answering the questions below

1 What College campus was Alpha Phi Alpha founded on? _______________

2 The 7 founders are known as the _______________________

3 Alpha Phi Alpha was established on _______________________

4 This is the ▬▬ intercollegiate fraternity for African American men.

5 List four special initiatives that Alpha Phi Alpha participates in

① _______________________   ③ _______________________

② _______________________   ④ _______________________

6 What is the "Voteless People is a Hopeless People"?

____

7 Describe how the fraternity is involved with the Peace Corps.

____

8 What is Spinx Media and how do they disseminate info?

____

____

9 What is the focus of the Alpha Phi Alpha Education Foundation?

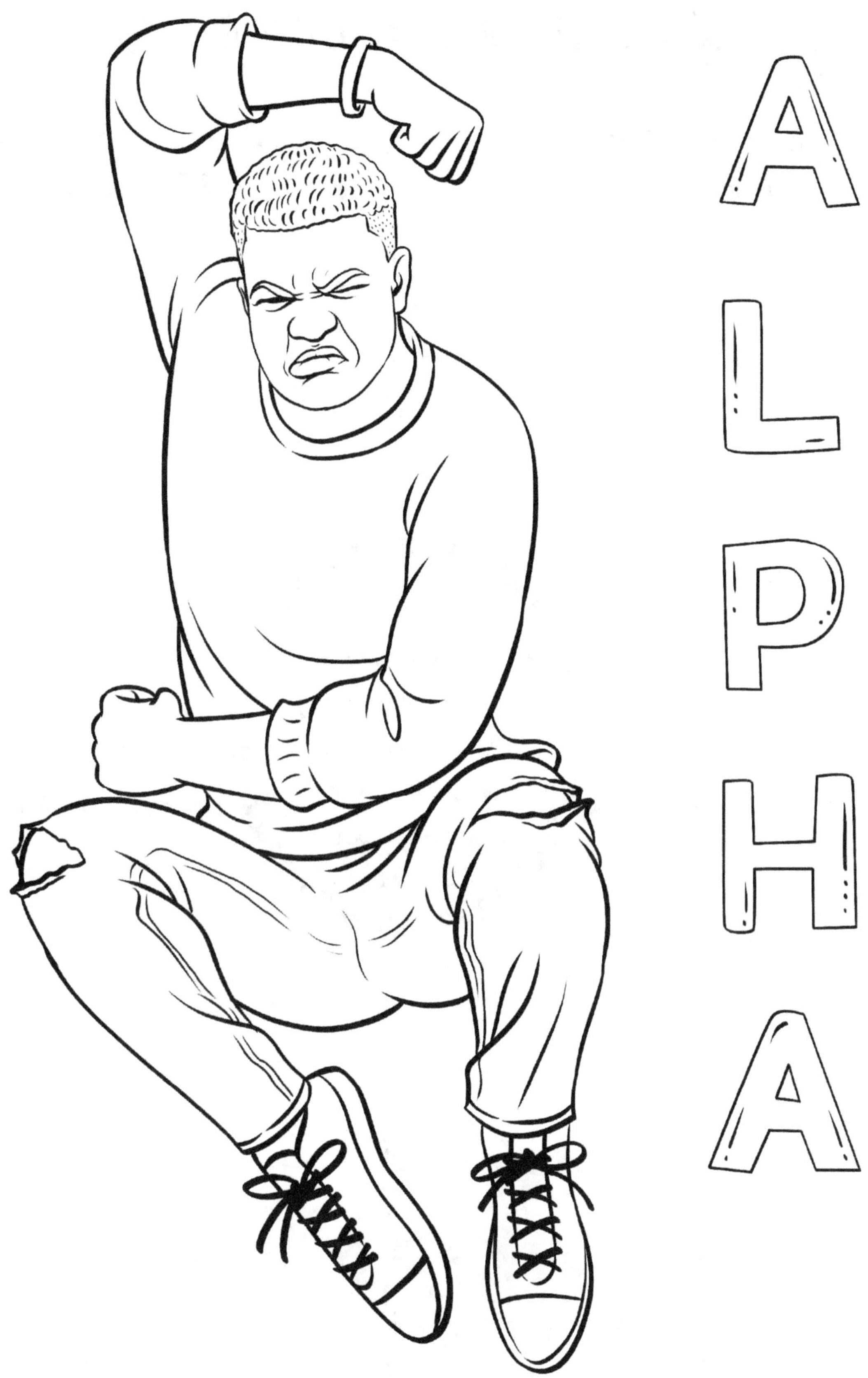

A
L
P
H
A

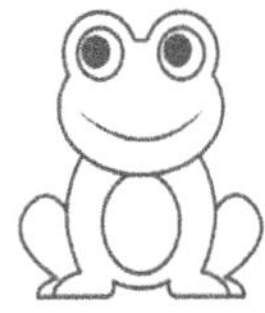 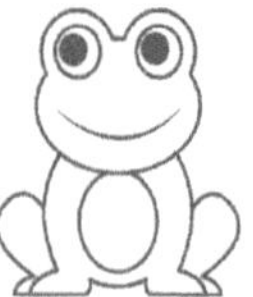# Alpha Kappa Alpha Sorority

Research & write about a founding member.

How does the sorority aim to target HBCU's for life?

Alpha Kappa Alpha is the first greek letter sorority. It was founded on January 1908 on the campus of Howard University.

Describe 3 Sorority Program Initiatives.

Name 5 famous AKA members

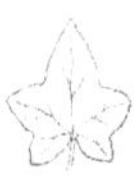

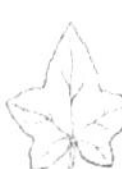

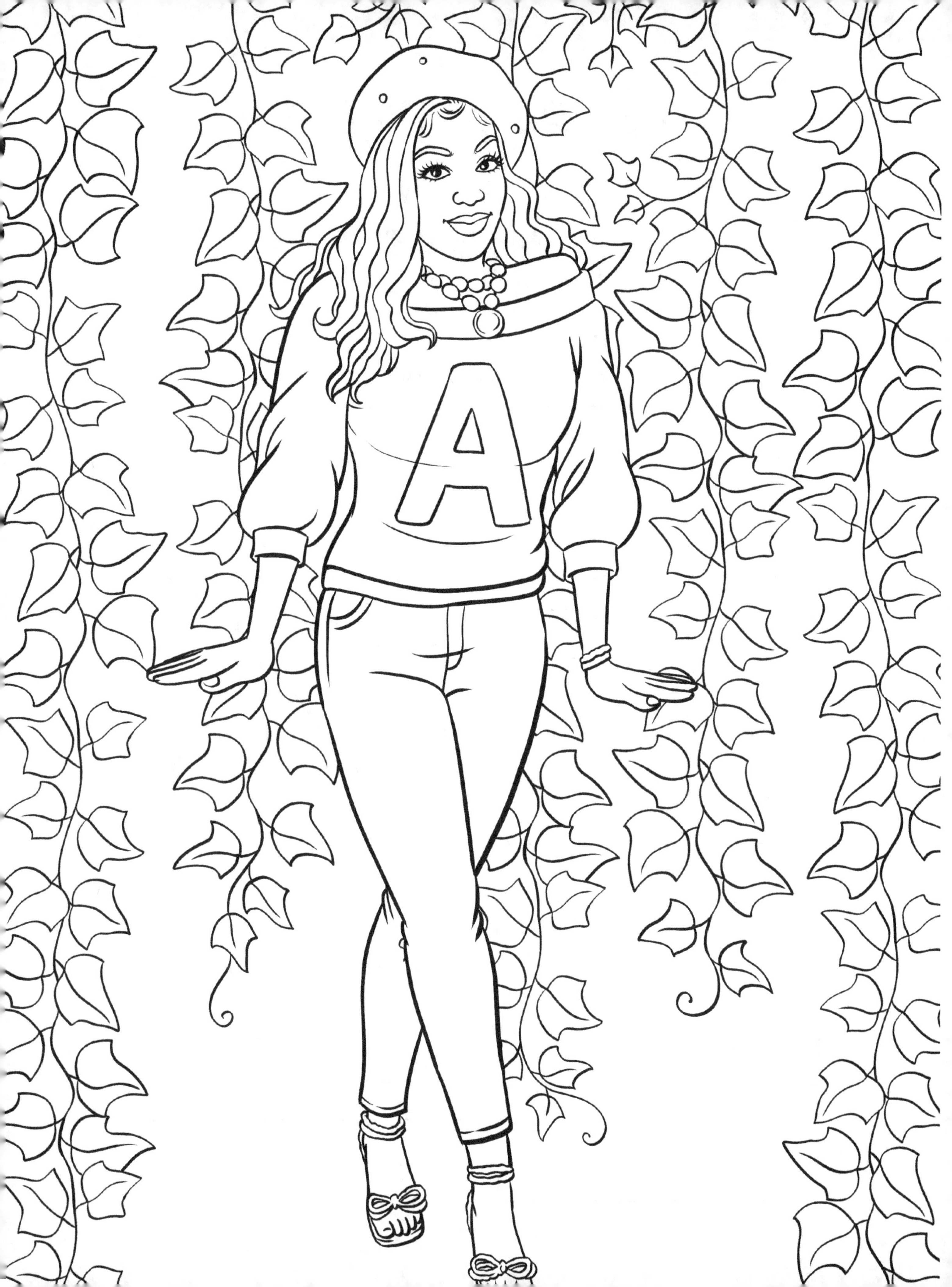

KAPPA ALPHA PSI

INDIANA

Fraternity

1911

UNIVERSITY

Name the 10 Founders

Provide a Brief History

____

____

____

____

What is the purpose of the Read to Room Program?

____

____

____

Create the Diamond

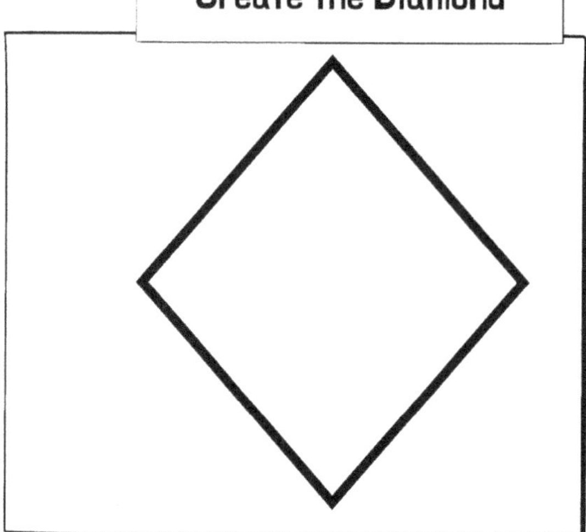

Draw the Canes

What are the core initiatives of the Guide Right National Service Program?

____

____

____

____

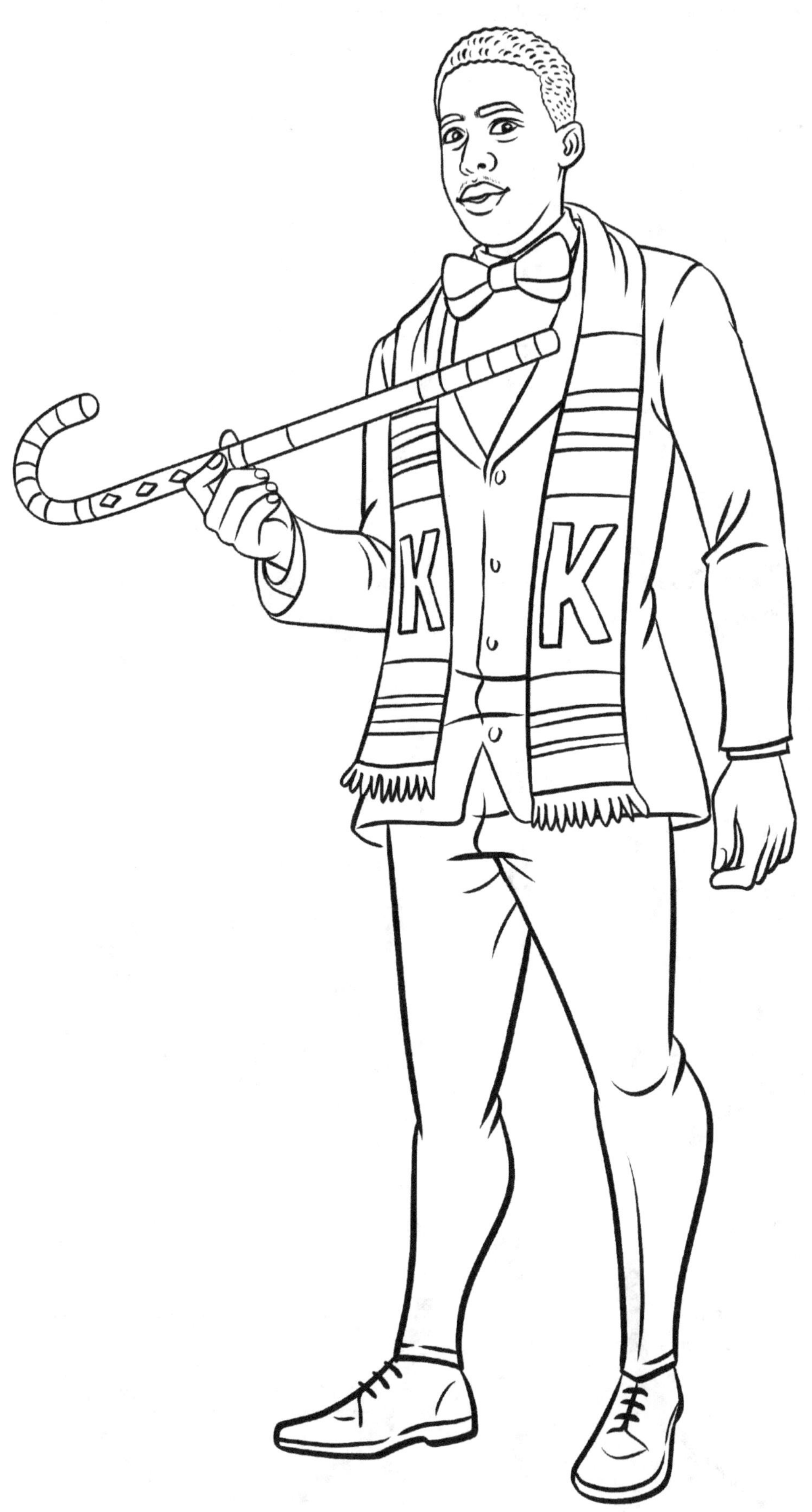
K
K

Omega Psi Phi was founded November 17, 1911 and was the first Greek fraternity to be founded on HBCU Campus of Howard University. Their motto, "friendship is essential to the soul".

O M E G A P S I P H I

Fraternity

Omega Psi Phi was founded by 3 undergraduates:

A) Edgar Amos Love
B) Ernest Everett Just
C) Oscar James Cooper

What are the cardinal principles of the organization?

A) Manhood
B) Good Character
C) Perseverance & Uplift

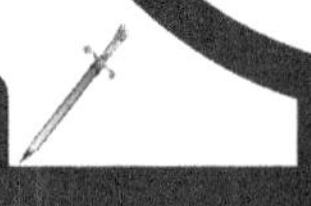

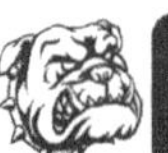

Project 1911- purpose is to raise donations for:

A) College Scholarship
B) University application/test fees
C) Informs African Americans how to act when stopped by law enforcement

The fraternity has International mandated programs:

A) College Endowment Fund- Giving funds to HBCUs
B) Voter Registration, Educational, Mobilization
C) International Prayer Call

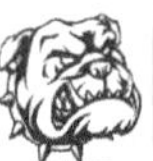

19

11

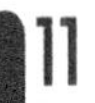

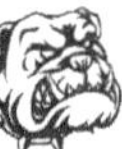

Notable Omegas

A) The Arts: Steve Harvey
B) Athletics: Shaquille O'neal
C) Business: Byron E. Lewis Sr.
D) Civil Rights: Jesse Jackson
E) Scientist: George Washington Carver

Brother, You're on my Mind is an initiative that would create dialogue amongst African American men and Mental Health. The 2 major goals include:
A) Distribute relevant materials at schools & health fairs
B) Importance of exploring options for mental health illness & reaching out to health care providers
C) Join efforts on educating Omega members, extended family & closely related communities

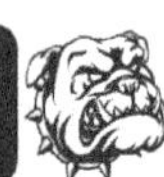

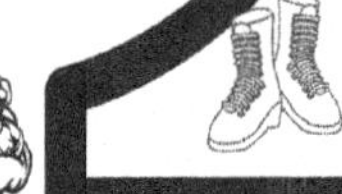

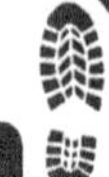

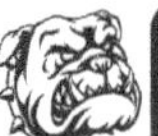

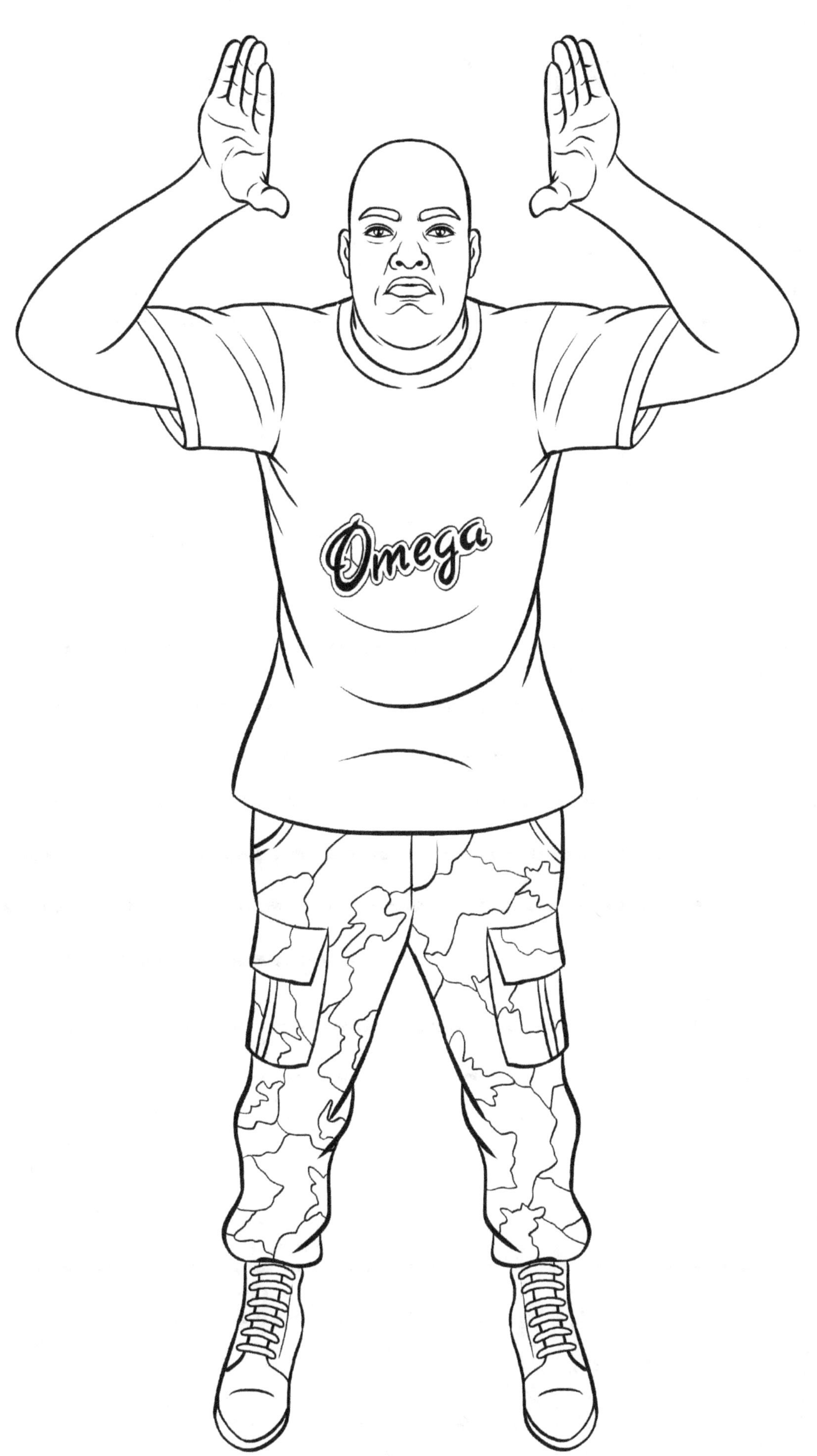
Omega

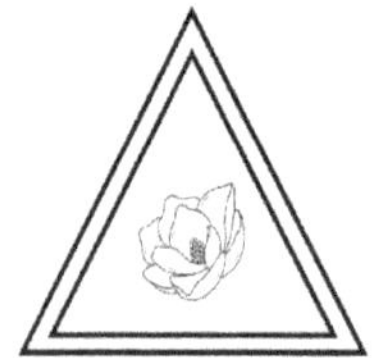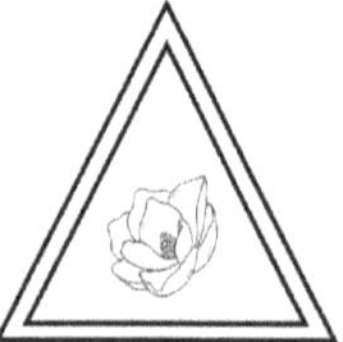

Delta Sigma Theta Sorority

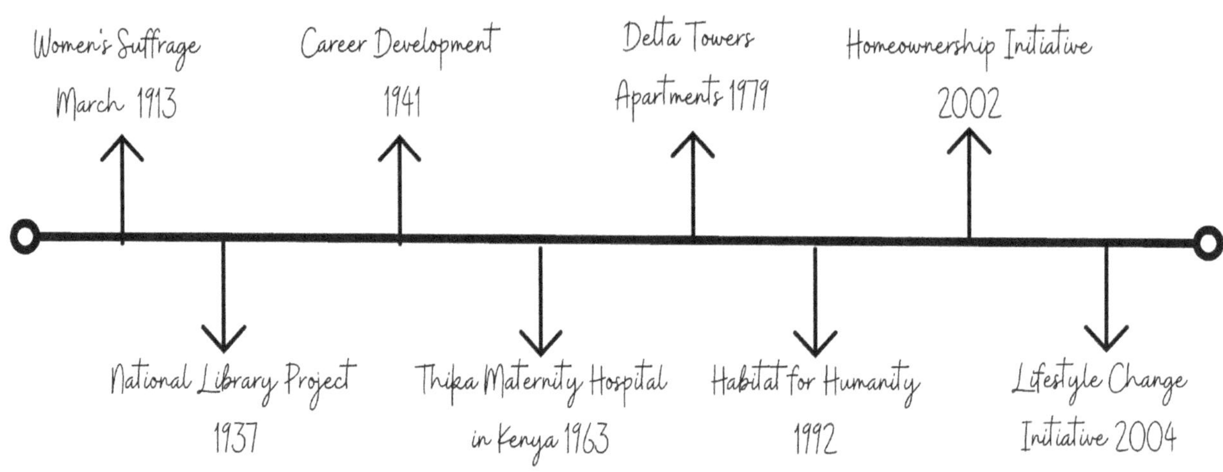

Identify what role Delta Sigma Theta played in each service project

1913 Women's Suffrage March

1937 National Library Project

1941 Career Development

1963 Thika Maternity Hospital

1979 Delta Towers Apartments

1992 Habitat for Humanity

2002 Homeownership Initiative

2004 Lifestyle Change Initiative

Describe in detail what volunteer program would you implement

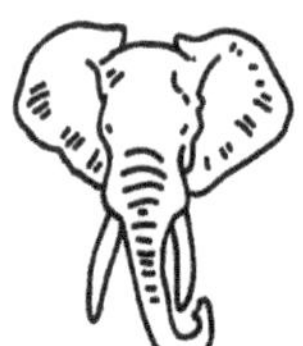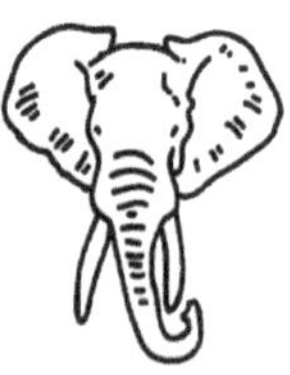

On January 13, 1913 Delta Sigma Theta was founded on the campus of Howard University, located in Washington, DC. They were founded by 22 African American college women.

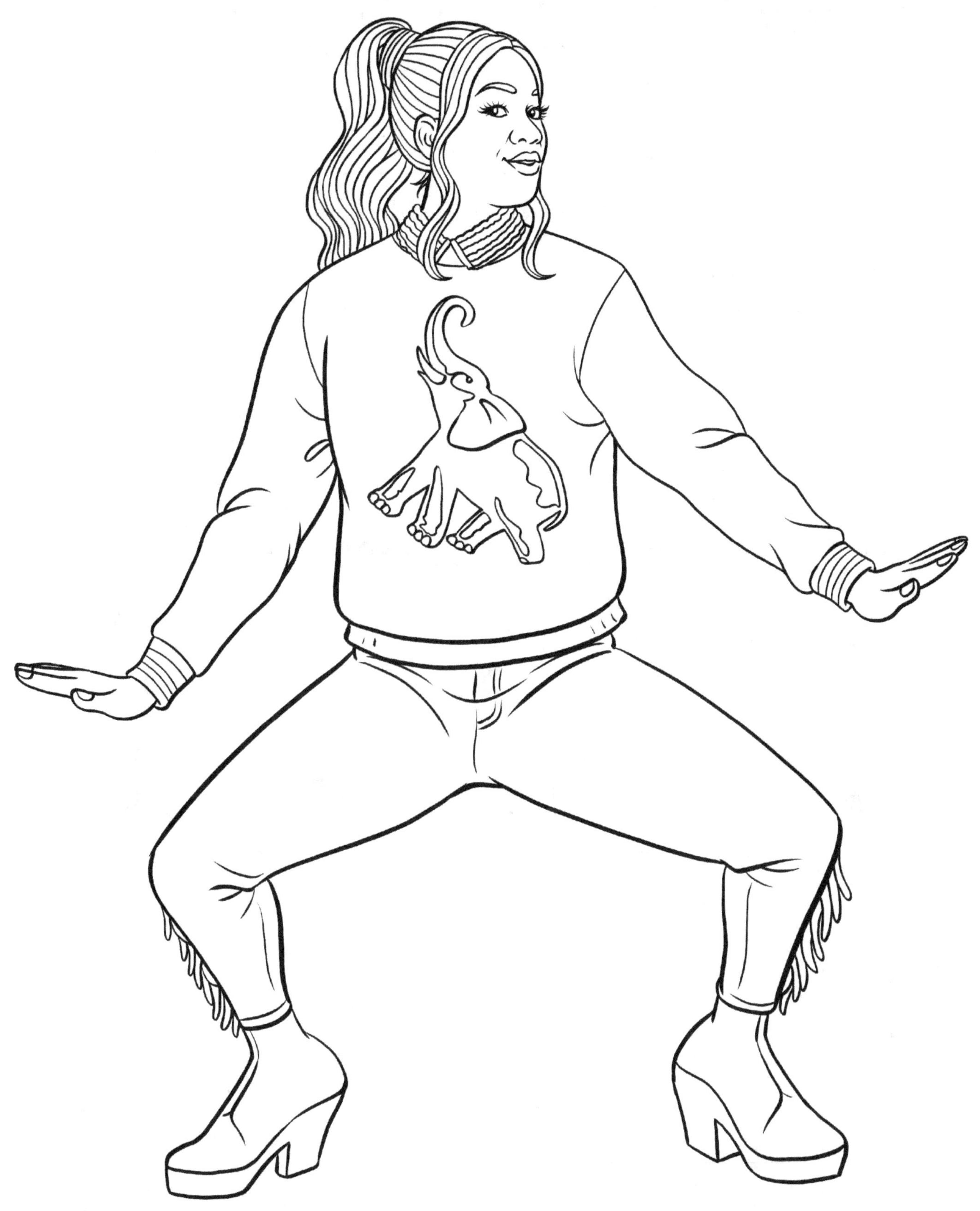

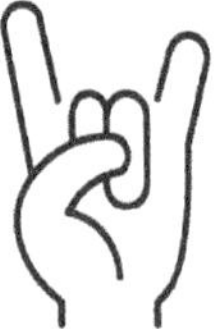 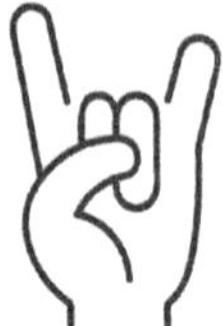

1914

Phi Beta Sigma was founded on the campus of _______________

Fraternity Motto: —————— For Service and Service For Humanity.

Phi Beta Sigma is _______________ bound to Zeta Phi Beta Inc.

In the 1950's —————— youth auxiliary was developed.

The Founders are Honorable A. Langston Taylor, Leonard. F Morse & ——————

Unscramble the Words

Beta

Famous Sigmas

Name the partner organizations

Φ   Β   Σ

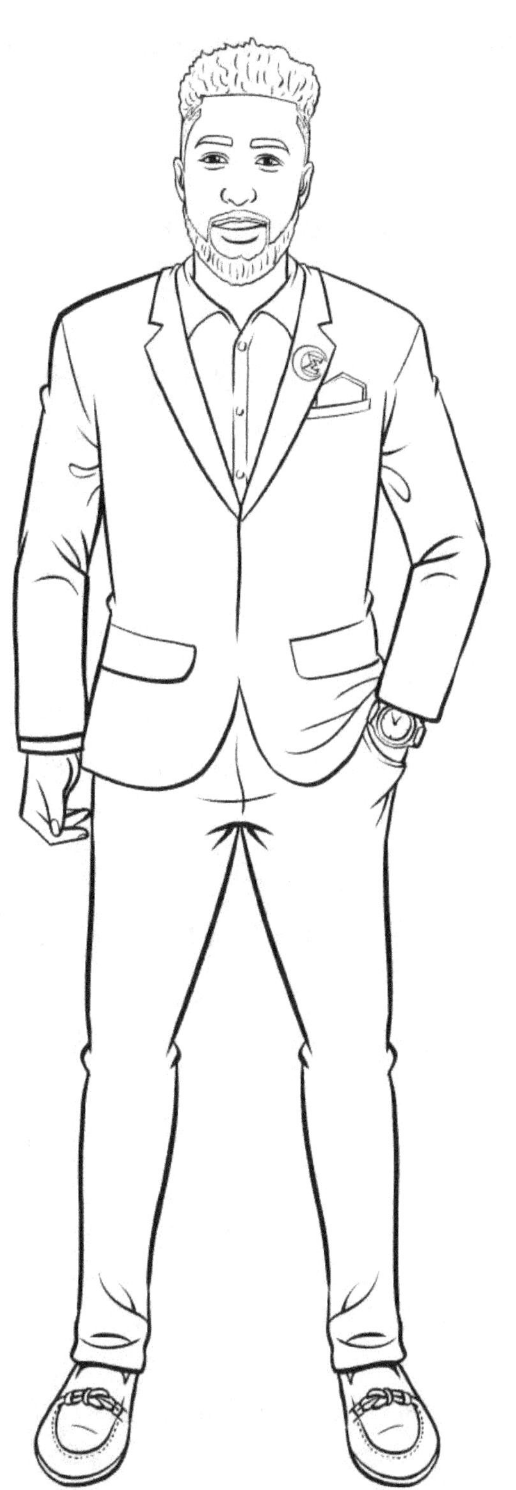

B
L
U
PHI

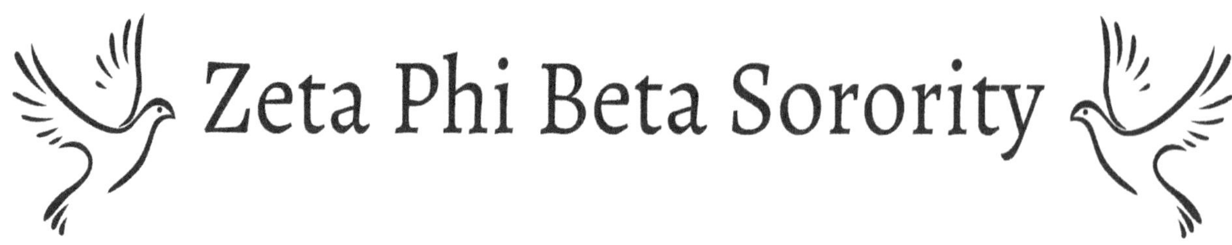

Zeta Phi Beta Sorority

Zeta Phi Beta was founded on January 16, 1920 on Howard University in Washington, DC. The 5 founders are Arizona Clever Stemons, Myrtle Tyler Faithful, Viola Tyler Goings, Fannie Pettie Watts, & Pearl Anna Neal.

Famous Zeta Phi Beta Members

Match the name to the description

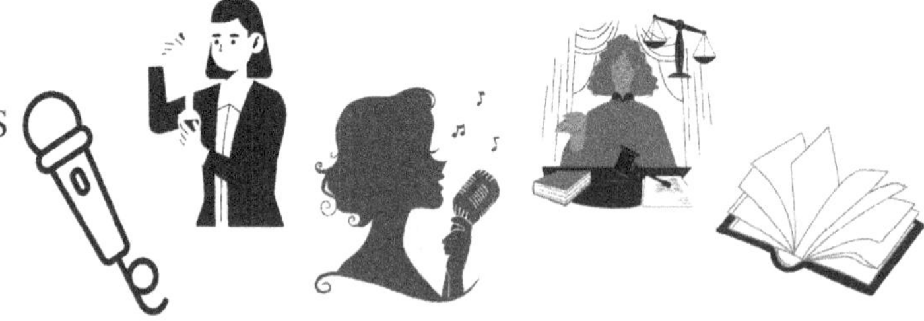

A.	Syleena Johnson	1	Author Best known for her book "Their Eyes were watching God".
B.	Sheryl Underwood	2	First African American to practice law before the US Supreme Court.
C.	Zora Neale Hurston	3	Comedian & 23rd International President of Zeta Phi Beta.
D.	Annie Turbo Malone	4	American Singer-Songwriter, Actress & TV Presenter.
E.	Violette Neatley Anderson	5	Business Owner, Inventor, First Black woman millionaire.

Fun Facts: Fill in the Blank

The official colors are royal _____ and pure _________

In 1948, they became the first sorority to charter a chapter in __________

Zetas helping other people excel (Z-Hope) serves to help people through Mind, ______ & Spirit.

The _______ group has not received a higher degree, but assists members with community activities.

Zeta Phi Beta & ___________ are the only constitutionally bound sorority & Fraternity in the NHPC.

EST. 1920

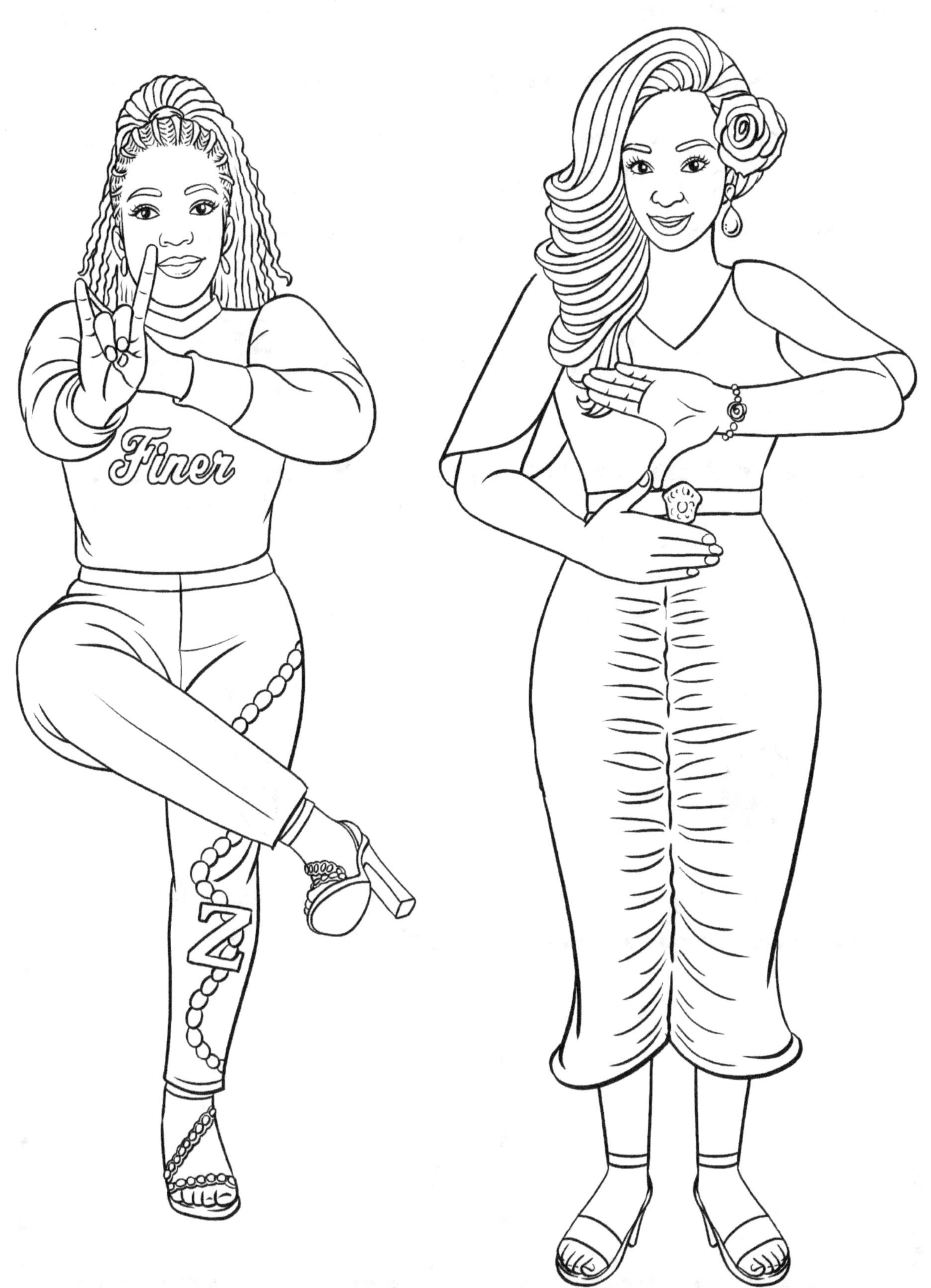
Finer
Z

Sigma Gamma Rho Sorority

Sigma Gamma Rho was founded and established at Butler University on November 12, 1922 by 7 young, female educators.

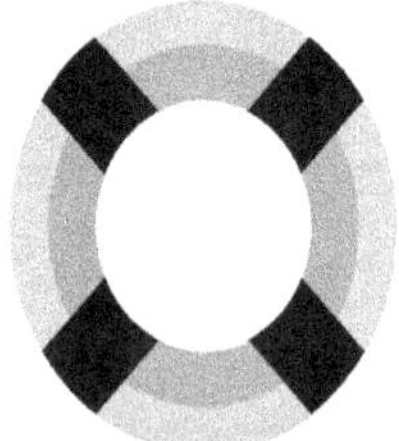 Swim 1922 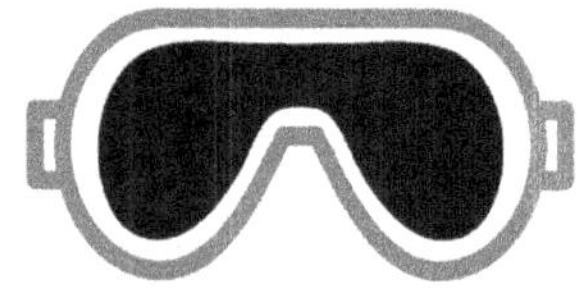

"Greater Service, Greater Progress". Swim 1922 was initiated after realizing that Black and Brown children do not know how to swim. This campaign addresses this need by having Olympians & members teach the community water safety & how to swim.

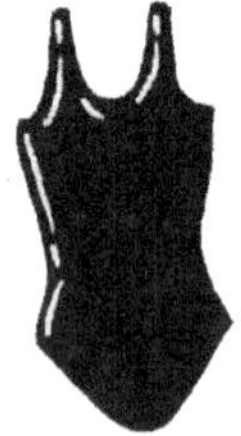

Draw a French Toy Poodle

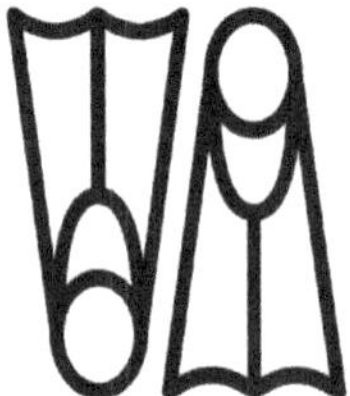

Draw a Yellow Tea Rose

National Mascot

Sorority Flower

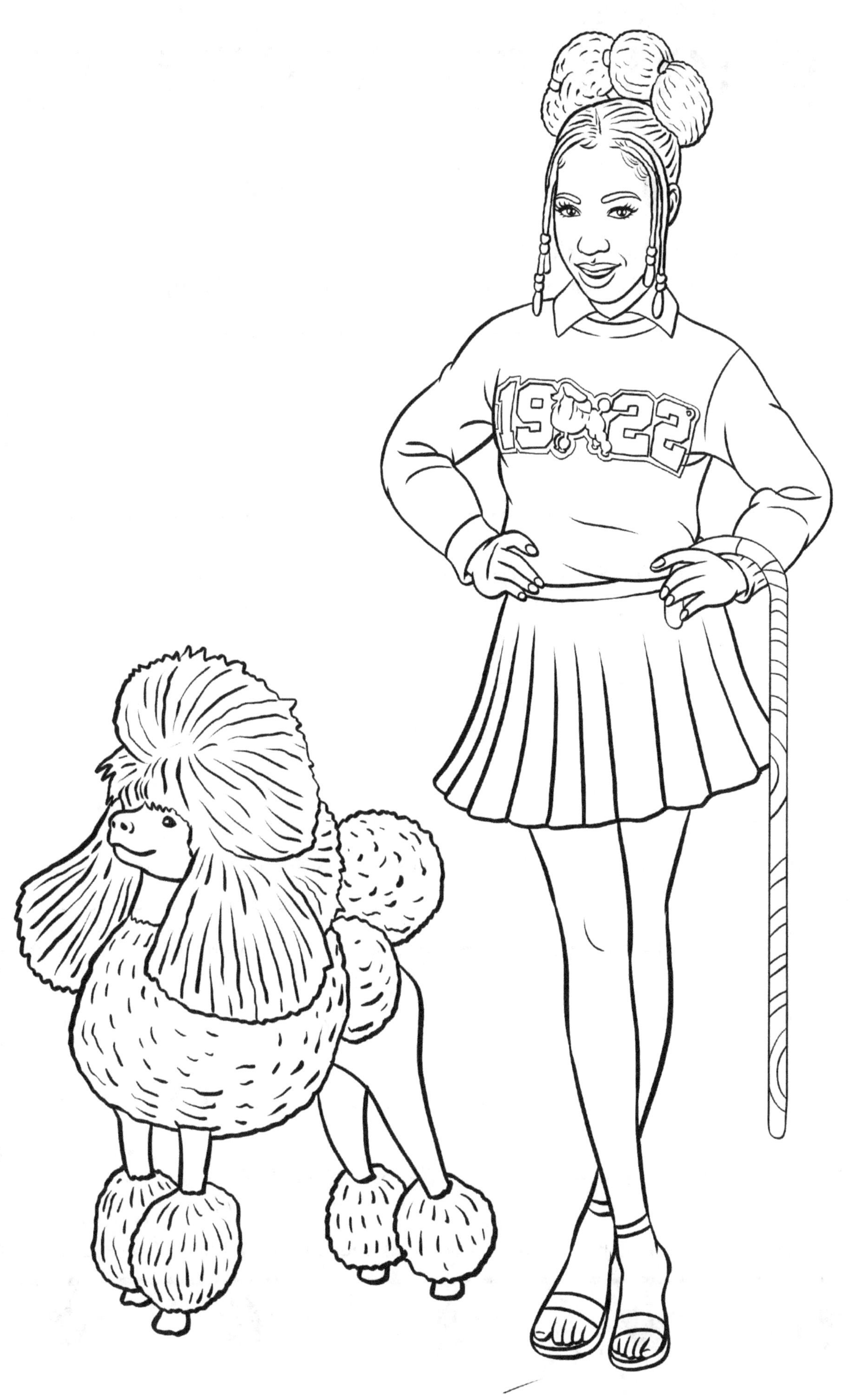
19 22

19 IOTA PHI THETA 63

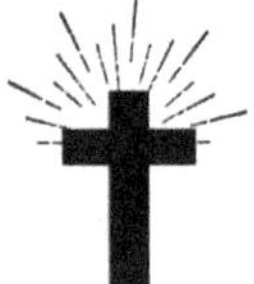  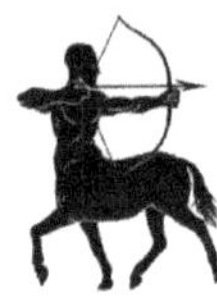

Iota Phi Theta Men's Health Program. Plan and provide details on a seminar
that would help make men more aware of common illnesses and early detection.

I.S.H.I.E.L.D. IOTAS Saving, Healing, Improving, Empowering Lives Daily
Provide additional details about this program below.

____

____

____

____

Fill in the blanks using one of the words below:

Tradition	Twelve	Eternal Sweetheart	Morgan State University

- The fraternity was founded on September 19, 1963, by _____________ founders.

- Iota Phi Theta was founded on the campus of _____________ Baltimore, Maryland.

- Motto: "Building a _____________ Not Resting Upon One".

- In support of Iota Phi Theta, Audrey Brooks has been given the title _____________

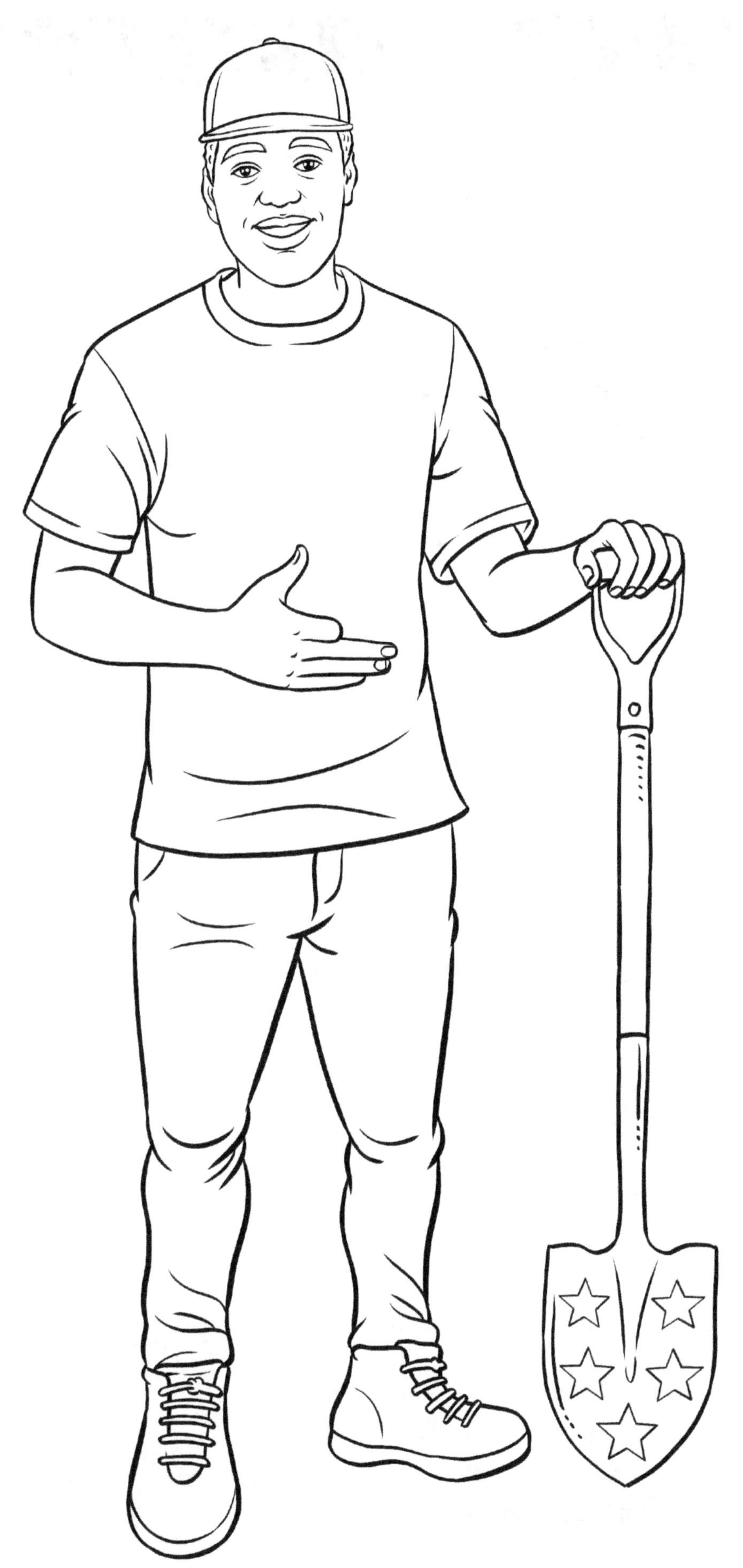

Offer of Admission

February 1, 2022

Dear

Congratulations! On behalf of the faculty and administration, I am excited to offer you admission to ____________ for the Fall 2023 academic year.

As an applicant, we are amazed at your character, personal accomplishments and intellectual ability. We know that you will make an impactful contributions to our college campus.

At ________________ University you will have the opportunity to learn about Africa, African diaspora and Black culture. During your academic career, you will become a changemaker that will prepare you to face real world challenges.

Furthermore, based on your application, we are are also pleased to offer you offer a full academic scholarship and book tuition. Please see your enclosed certificate for your reward amount.

Sincerely,

Director of Undergraduate Admissions

Directions: Fill in the blanks with your personal information and the college of your choice.

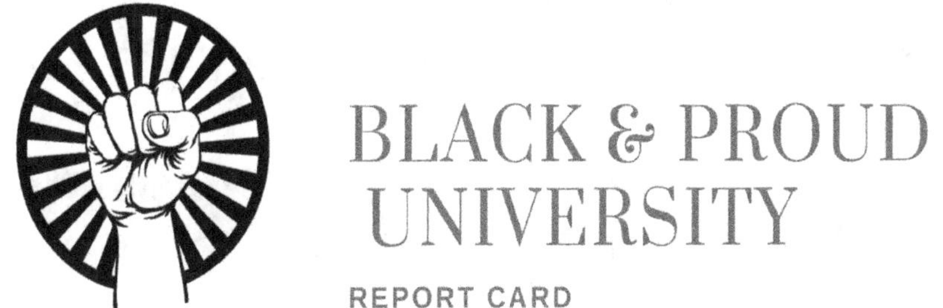

Student Name: ___________________

Student Number: ___________________

Major: ___________________

Minor: ___________________

Course Code:	Course Name:	Units:	Grade:
AFRO 005	**Intro to Africana Studies**	3	

Total Units
____

GRADING SYSTEM:

4.0: 93-100	2.7: 80-82	1.3: 67-69
3.7: 90-92	2.3: 77-79	1.0: 65-66
3.3: 87-89	2.0: 73-76	0.0: 64 & below
3.0: 83-86	1.7: 70-72	

Student Status
____

Semester Average
____

General Average
____

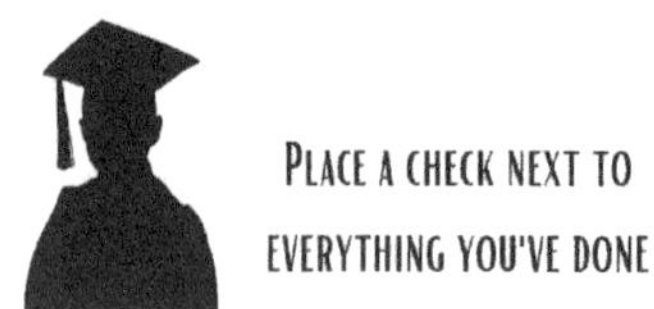

HBCU Bucket List

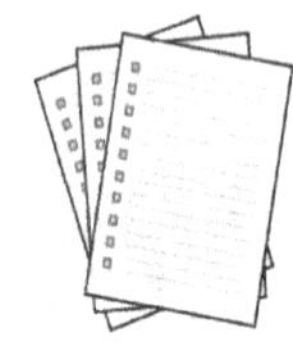

Date a classmate

Win an academic Scholarship

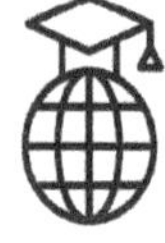

Network

Live in the freshman dorms

visit the A building often

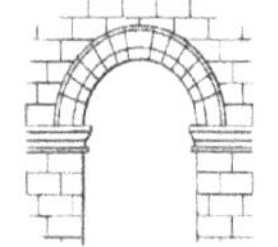

Swag surf at an event

Saw a celebrity at Homecoming

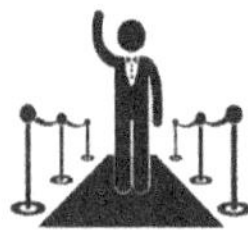

Road Trip with your Roomies

Apply to graduate school

Eat Soul Food on Thursdays in the Cafe

Graduate from your favorite HBCU

Join a Sorority or Fraternity

Study abroad in your favorite country

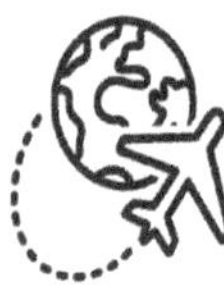

Be part of the Royal Court

Fall asleep during an 8 am class

Attend Chapel to hear the University Choir

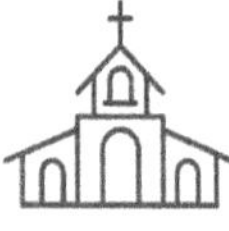

Editor for the school Newspaper

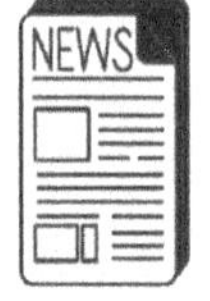

Chilling on the Quad on 1st Fridays

Meet Black people from all over the world

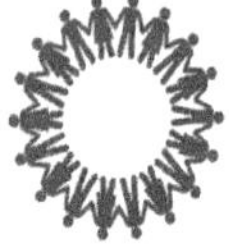

Apply to become a Resident Assistant

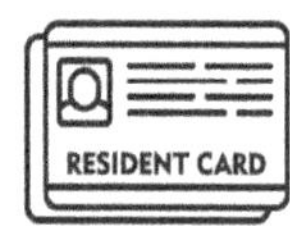

sign up for Alternative Spring Break

Summer internship with a prestigious company

Explore your college town with your friends

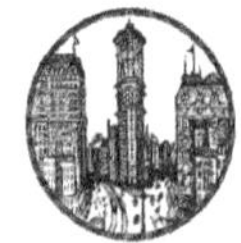

Show HBCU pride with school paraphernalia

Learn about Black history in all your classes

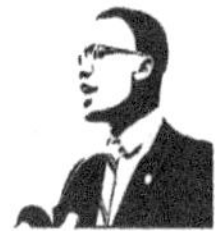

Attend homecoming game for half time show

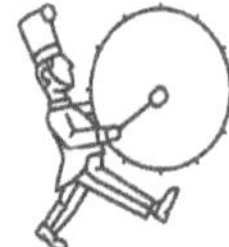

Find your best college buddies for life

Maintain a 3.5 GPA while joining an organization

Pull in all nighter with classmates in the library

Attend office hours with your favorite professor

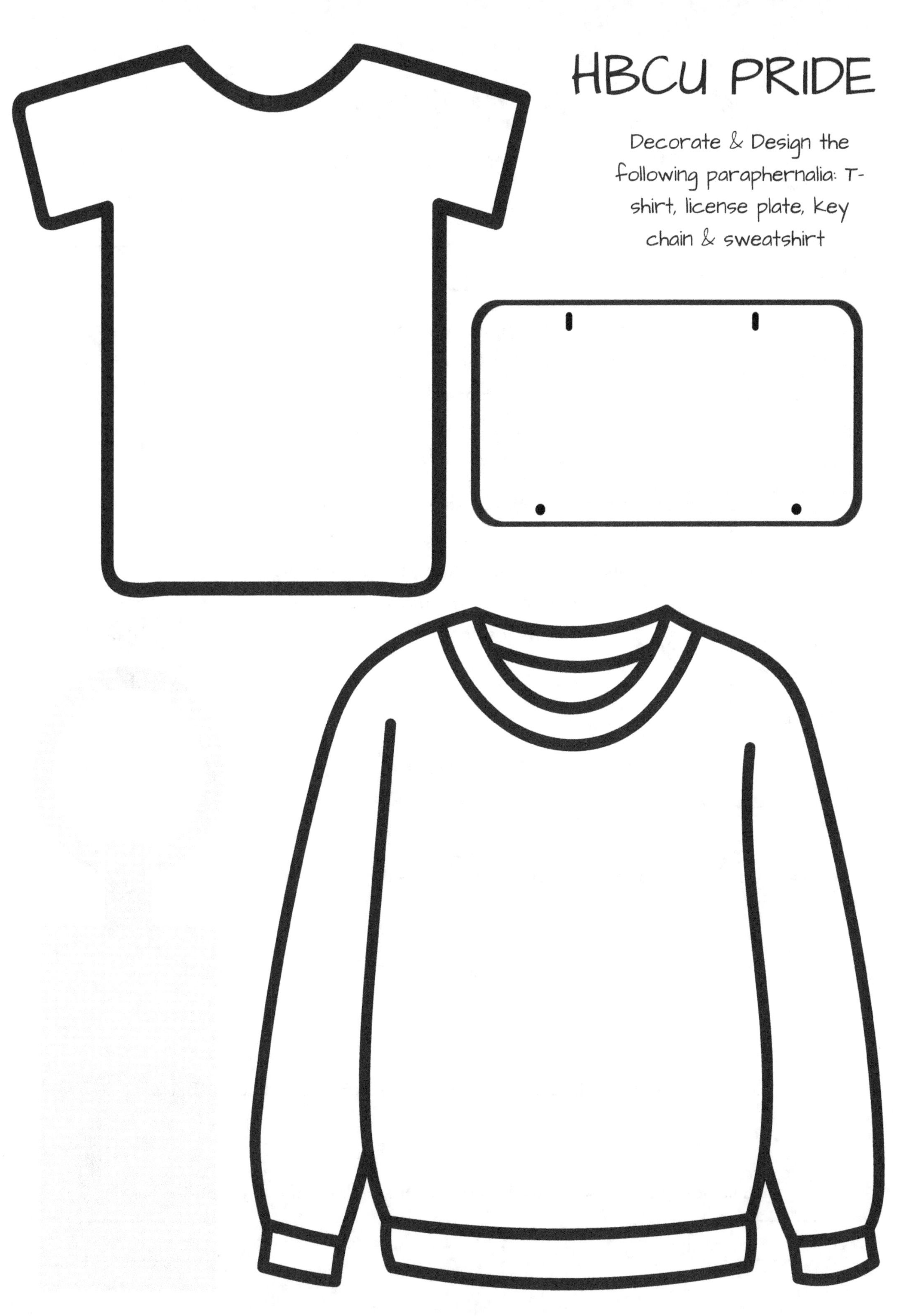
HBCU PRIDE
Decorate & Design the following paraphernalia: T-shirt, license plate, key chain & sweatshirt

HBCU BAND

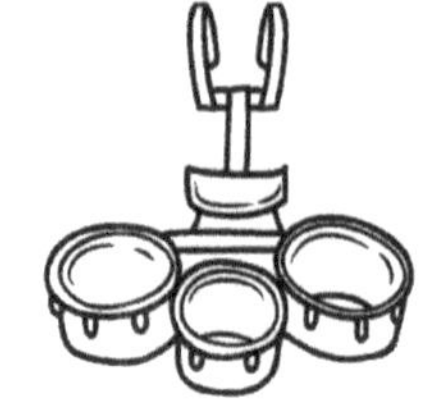

WRITE THE NAME OF EACH INSTRUMENT IN THE BOX

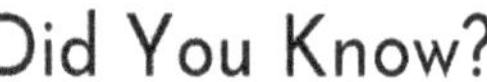

Did You Know?

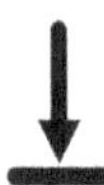

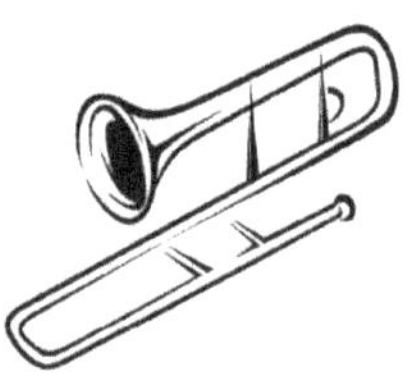

Black marching bands were formed as part of the military during the colonial era. In the late 19th century minstrel troupes began performing. During World War 1, many of the musicians joined Black colleges and universities.

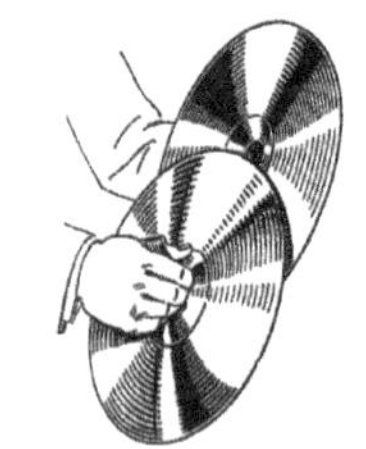

Currently, the bands showcase sportsmanship through high marching drum majors, soulful music and band members. Homecoming, parades, and even the big screen is where they shine the most.

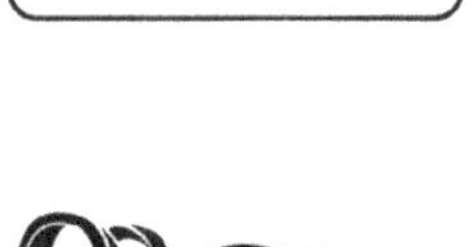

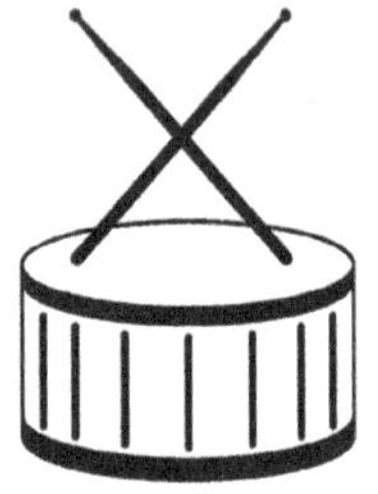

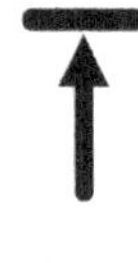

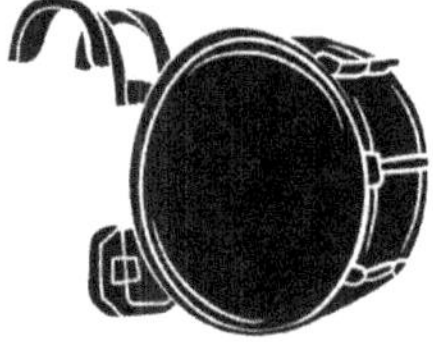

Fact OR Fiction

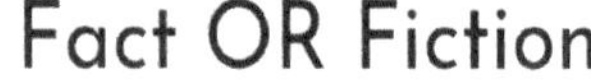

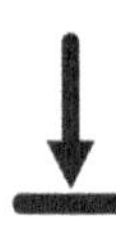

Majorette dancers perform alongside band members.

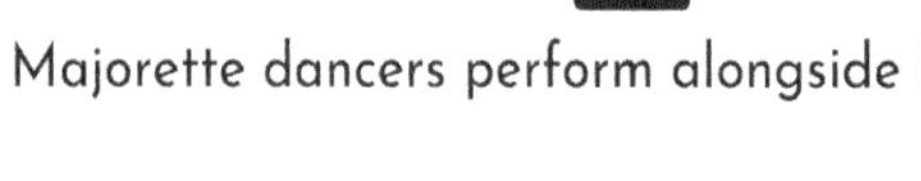

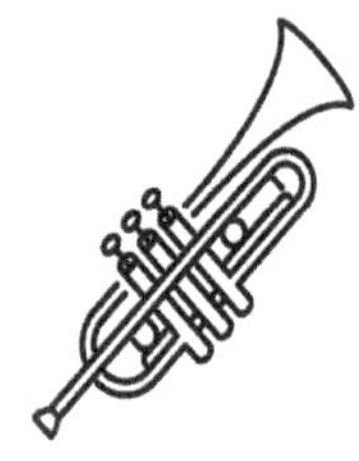

The first known HBCU Band was formed at Tuskegee Normal School.

Lincoln University Marching band is known as the Purple Crush Roaring Tigers.

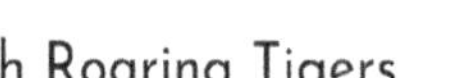

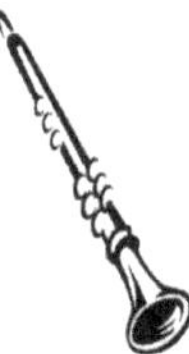

Tesla Battle of the bands was created to recognize the excellence of college marching bands.

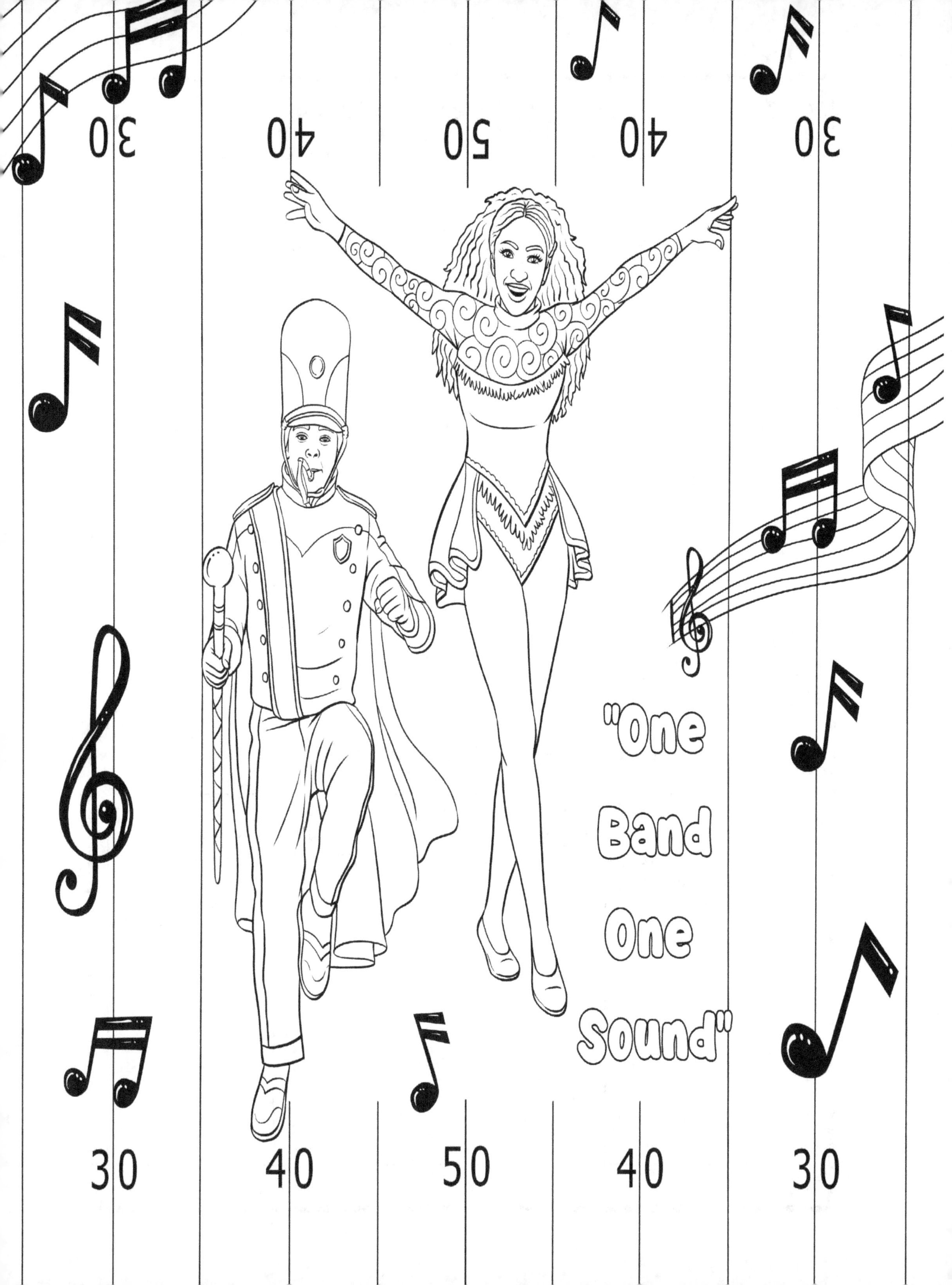

30
40
50
40
30
"One
Band
One
Sound"
30
40
50
40
30

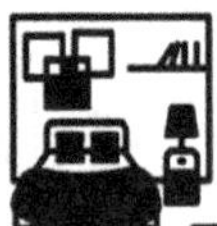 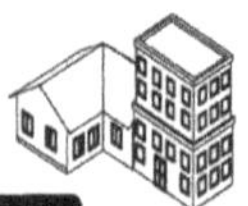

DORM EDITION

This   OR   That:

This	OR	That:
Dine at the Cafeteria		Eat dinner cooked by your suitemate
Live in the freshman dorms		Off campus housing with a teammate
Sneak in a guest after hours		Break curfew to go to bae house
Roommate that snores loudly		Roommate that always brings bf/gf over
Stuck outside after a fire drill in winter		Locked in dorm; sweltering heat with no AC

<u>Write down essentials that you will need for the dorm.</u>

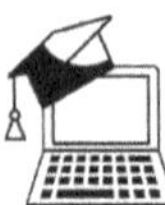

--------------------------- --------------------------- ---------------------------

___________________ ___________________ ___________________

___________________ ___________________ ___________________

--------------------------- --------------------------- ---------------------------

<u>How would you respond to the following real life residence issues?</u>

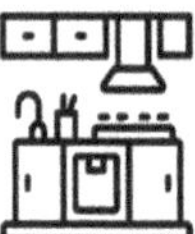

You are asleep after studying for a midterm. You are awakened by your drunk roommates after a night of partying.	You are going to cook dinner but realize, someone ate your chicken wings & potatoes.	Your roommate is messy: doesn't clean the shared bathroom, leaves dishes in the sink and has clothes everywhere.

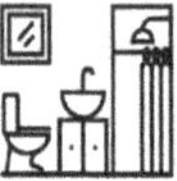

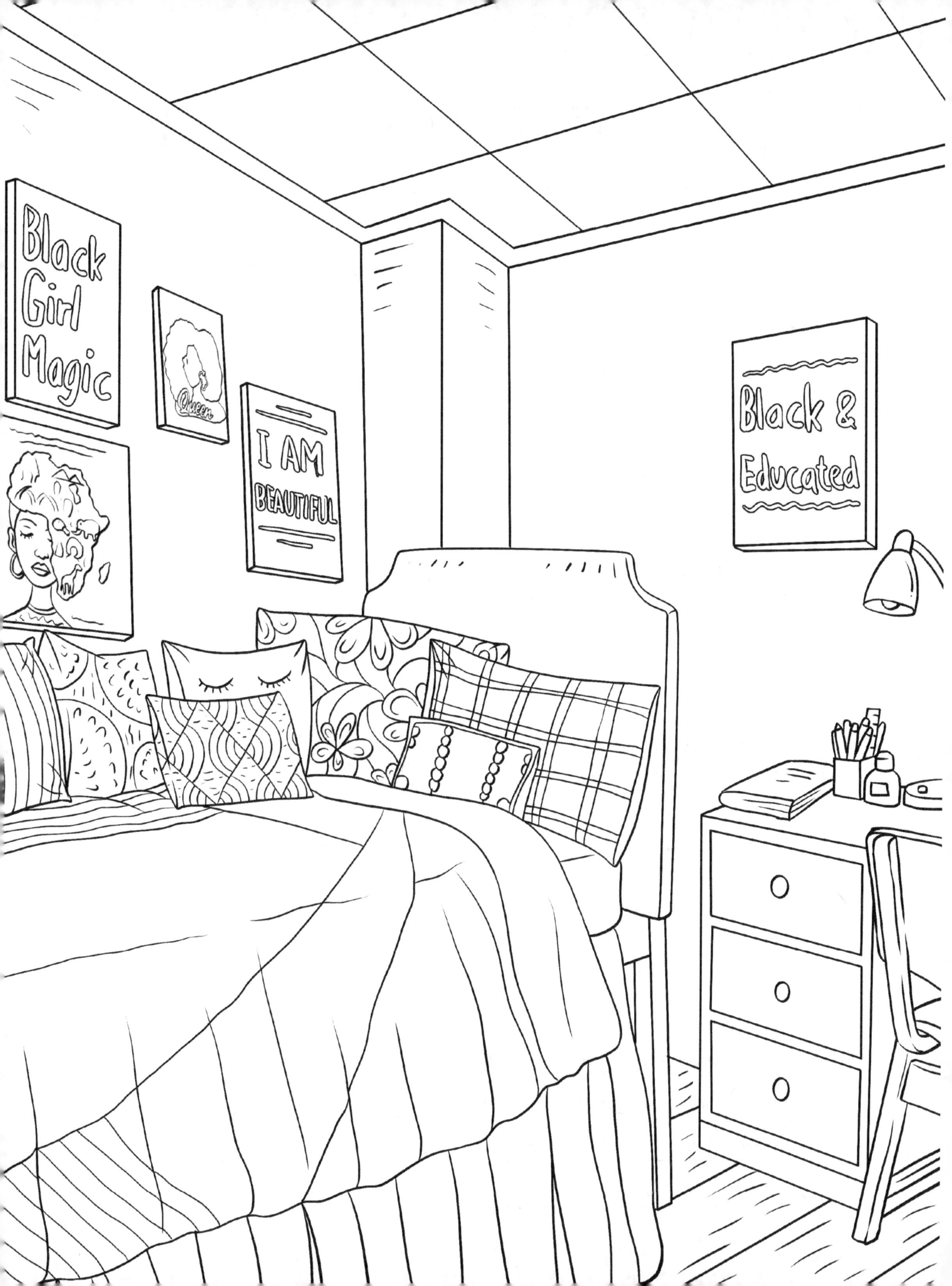

Black Girl Magic
Queen
I AM BEAUTIFUL
Black & Educated

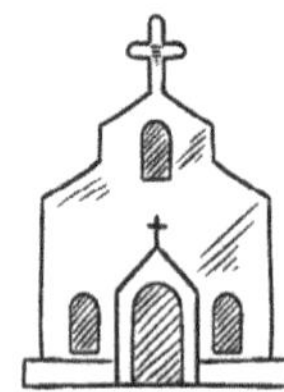

Faith & Education

Churches of varying denominations played a significant role in founding HBCUs

Name 3 vital ways in which the church helped to shape HBCUs?

✳ ____

✳ ____

✳ ____

Match the College with the founding Church

A	Bennett College	a	Catholic Church
B	Shaw University	b	Baptist Church
C	Voorhes College	c	Episcopal Church
D	Xavier University	d	United Church of Christ
E	Concordia College	e	United Methodist Church
F	Paul Quinn College	f	African Methodist Episcopal
G	Oakwood University	g	Evangelical Lutheran Church
H	LeMoyne-Owen College	h	Seventh-day Adventist Church

HBCU

Choose the College of your choice and complete

✳ What is a chapel assistant? _______________________________________

✳ Write your favorite scripture _______________________________________

✳ What worship service would you attend? _______________________________________

✳ What community projects are available? _______________________________________

✳ What scholarships does the chapel offer? _______________________________________

✳ Which religious program is most interesting? _______________________________________

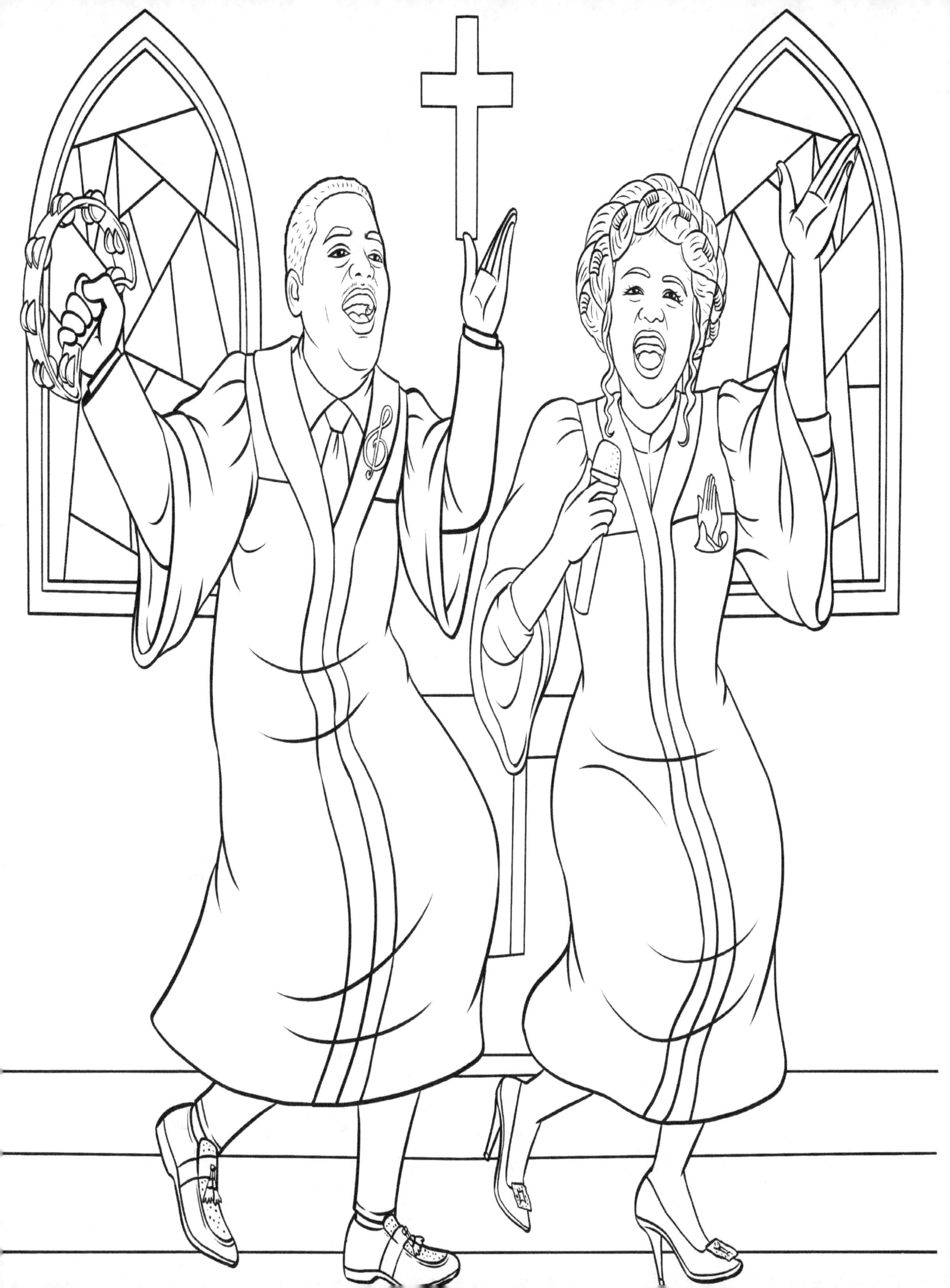

 # FOOD, FASHION & FELLOWSHIP 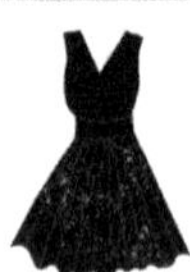

Favorite Memory with friends in the Cafe

____

____

Draw your favorite dish from Fried Chicken Wednesday, Soul Food Thursday or Catfish Friday

What style of fashion did you wear to the Cafe?

Draw a line to match some of your favorite food items from the cafeteria

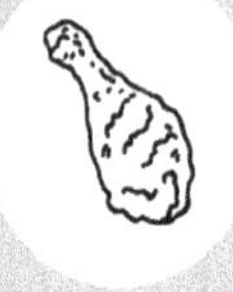

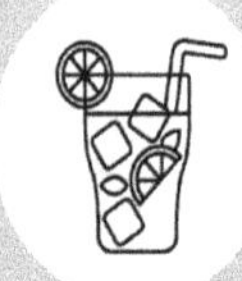

Cat Fish

Chocolate Cake

Lemonade

Fried Chicken

Sweet Potato

Mac & Cheese

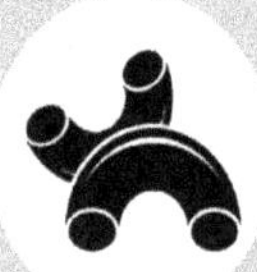
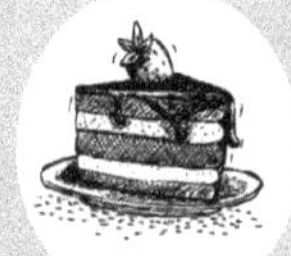
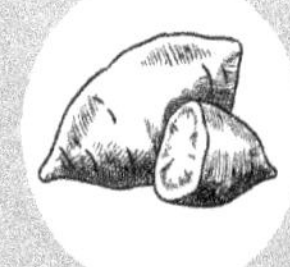

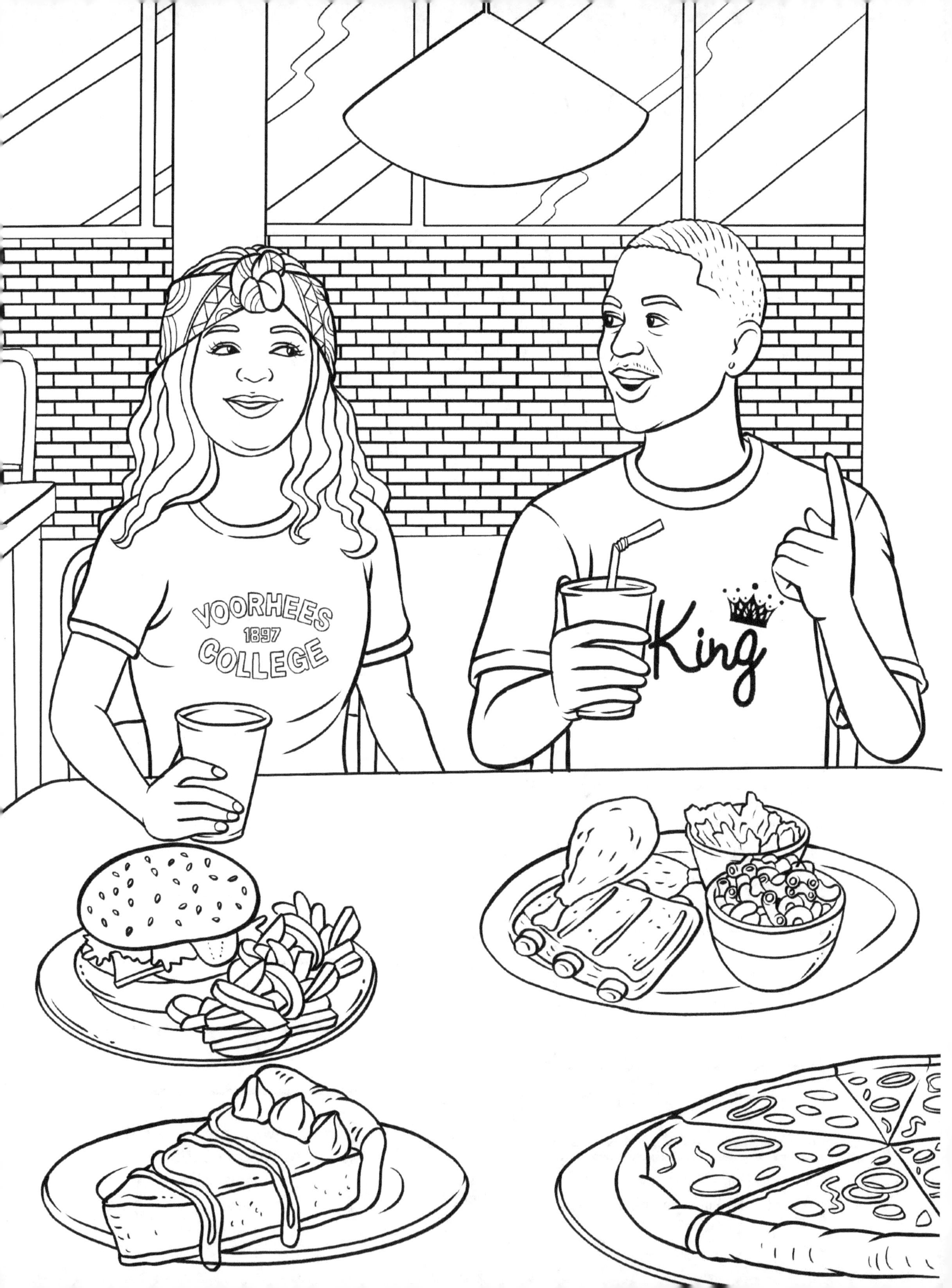

VOORHEES
1897
COLLEGE
King

Homecoming

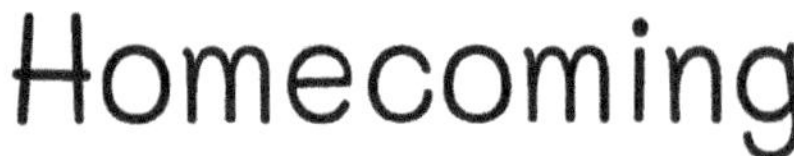

We are family, I have all my brothers and sisters with me!
Homecoming is essentially a family reunion. Everyone such
as alumni, current students and friends show up on their
favorite college campus for week-long festivities.

```
R O J A M M U R D C F S W S U M N F
G W O H S P E T S I A O L D E A O R
N O L I Y K Y F R W S U F M D R I A
E I S P S T P I Q Q H R L W A C N T
C M Q P R R N X Y B I Q L G R H U E
A B A A E M A U U E O B A N A I E R
W C P G U L B W D W N U B I P N R N
S U E L L C C M E S M T M N G Y I
K O A L O L H O M R H V E O Y B L T
X G R M E I A I N E O L K C B A I Y
A T E O C B T B T C W D S E O N M C
A D S K R F R A T C E G A M H D A Z
Y B E E L I G A V O W R B O I I F E
X N V A F L T N T I O C T H P H H A
A I H G I D G Y D I H F N Z H N I H
A J H A F E R Y O Y O V K E O T B P
I U T N O I T A C O V N O C P C Q D
S T U D E N T S Y S W A G S U R F H
```


Football Game or
Halftime Show?

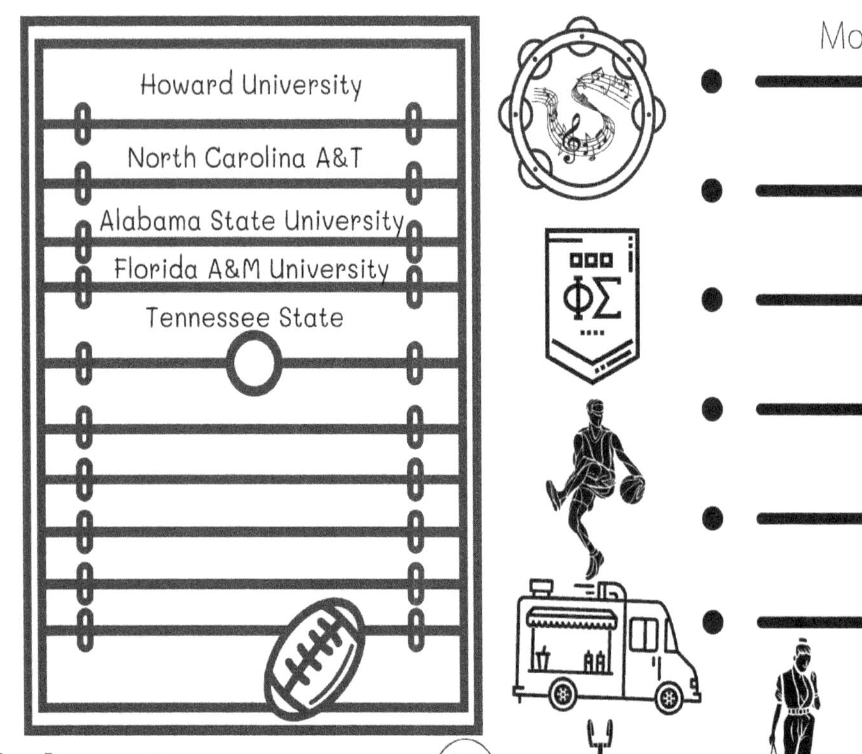

Top 10 Homecomings you must
attend. Fill in the blank.

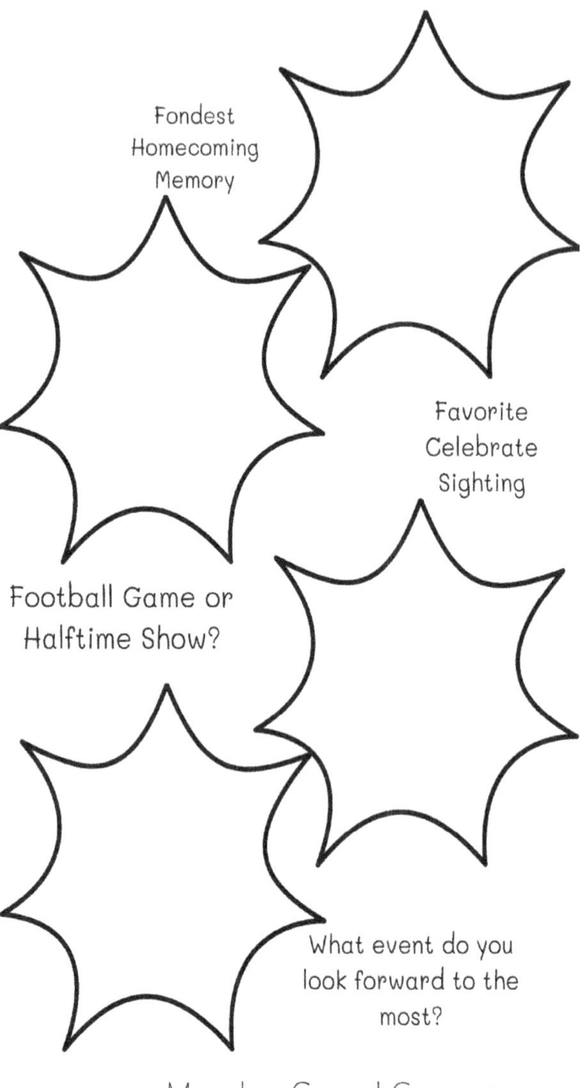

Monday: Gospel Concert

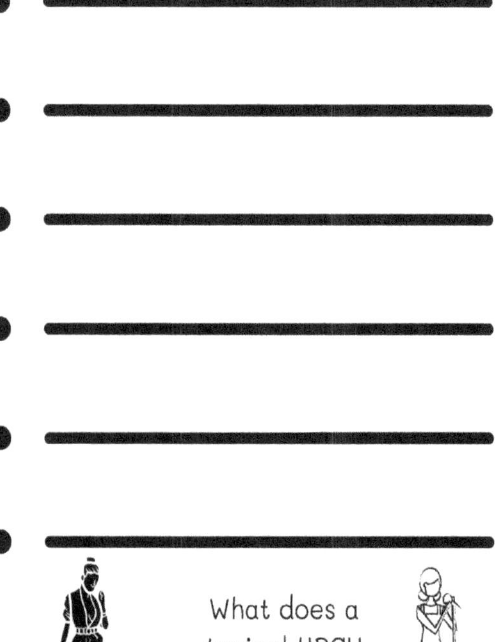

What does a
typical HBCU
week look
like?

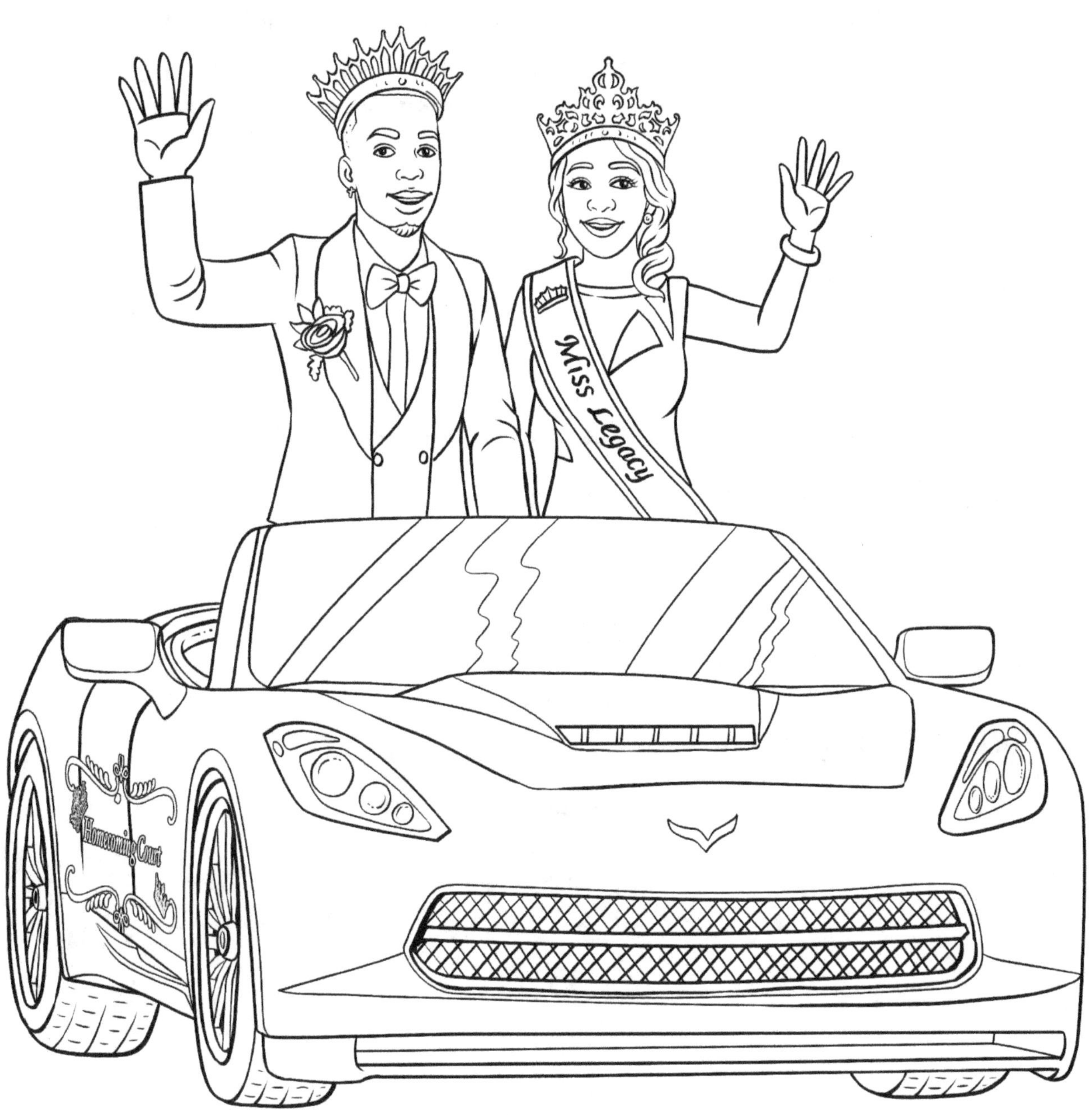

Miss Legacy
Homecoming Court

Music is good for the Soul

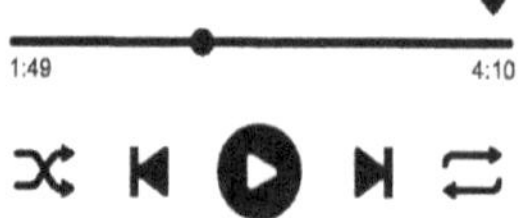

Black National Anthem:

"Lift Every Voice & Sing" is hymn with lyrics written by James Weldon Johnson & music by J. Rosamond Johnson. Write and sing along below.

In 2009, this popular song was created by F.L.Y.

Create a

Top 10 HBCU playlist

1. Before I let you Go
2.
3.
4.
5.
6.
7.
8.
9.
10.

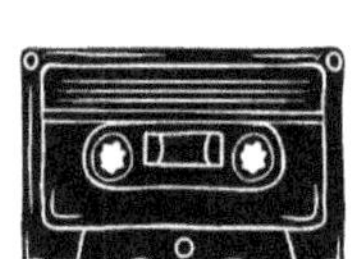

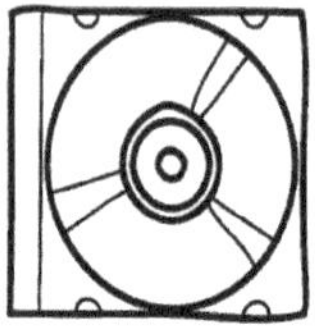

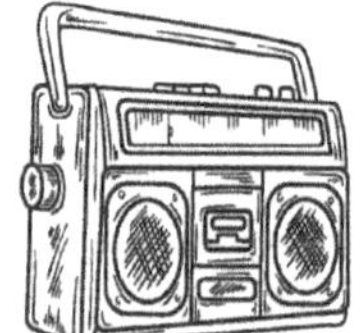

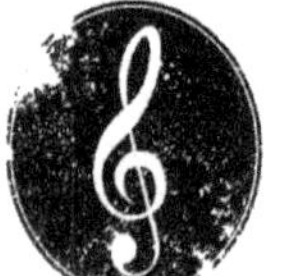

Gospel Songs

1.
2.
3.

Cover Songs by HBCU Bands

1.
2.
3.
4.
5.

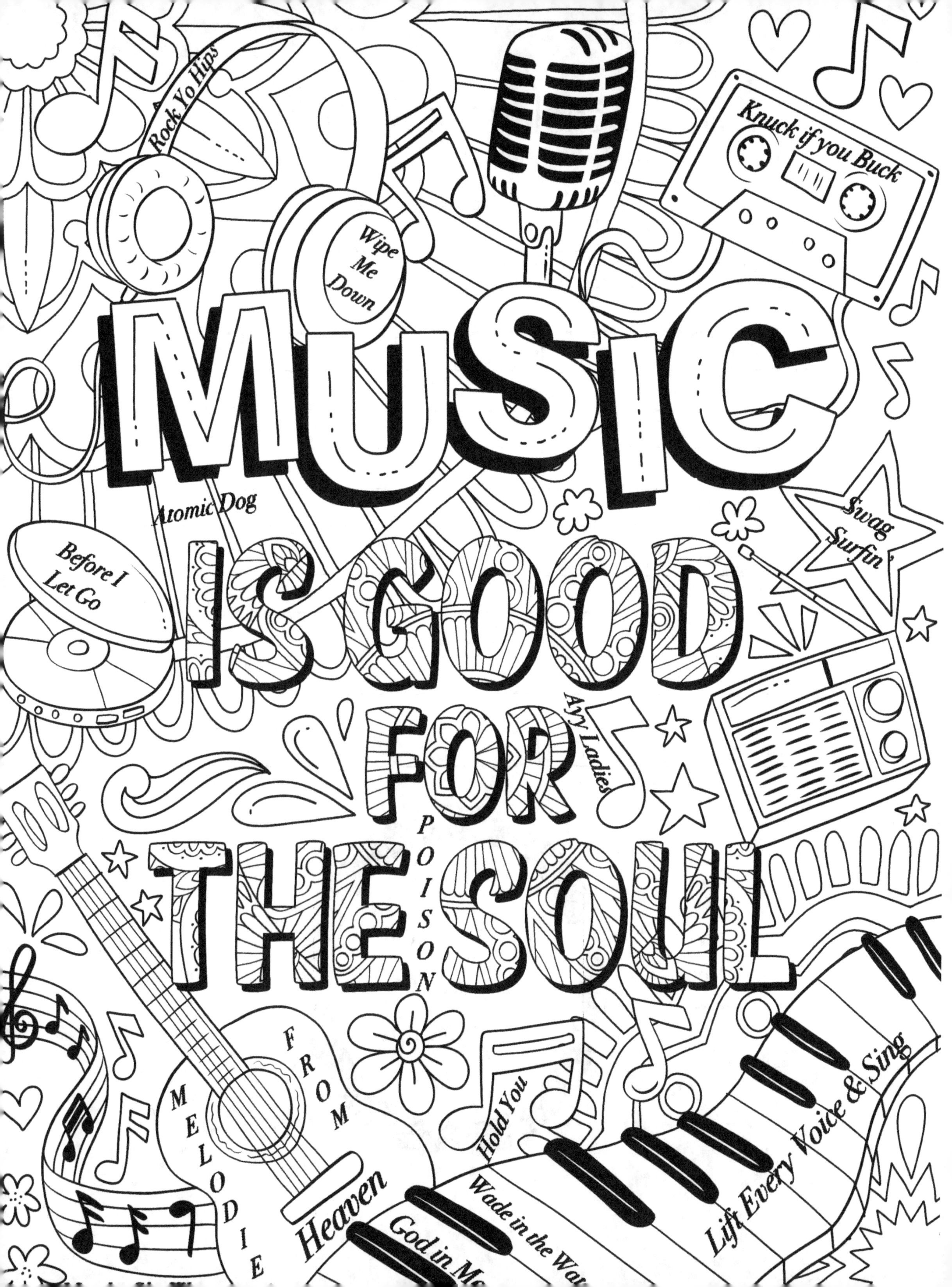

Rock Yo Hips
Wipe Me Down
Knuck if you Buck
MUSIC
Atomic Dog
Before I Let Go
IS GOOD
Swag Surfin'
FOR
Ayy Ladies
THE SOUL
POISON
MELODIE
FROM
Heaven
Hold You
God in Me
Wade in the Water
Lift Every Voice & Sing

HBCU Scholarship Scattergories

Directions: Find a scholarship related to the category on the left using the letter in the circle.

	(H)	(B)	(C)	(U)
Academic				
Athletic				
Community Service				
Extracurricular				
HBCU				
Hobbies				
Unique				

Create a Resume

Ways you can prepare for scholarships

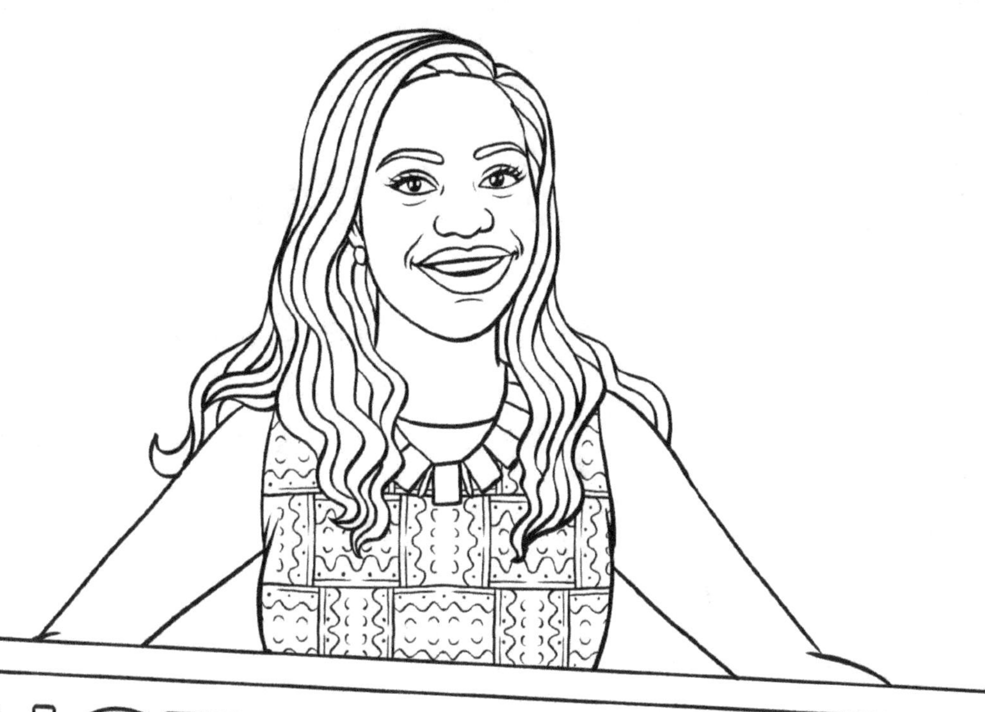

UNCF
6/30/38
Talore Hill
10,000
Ten Thousand and 00/100
Academic Scholarship
UNCF

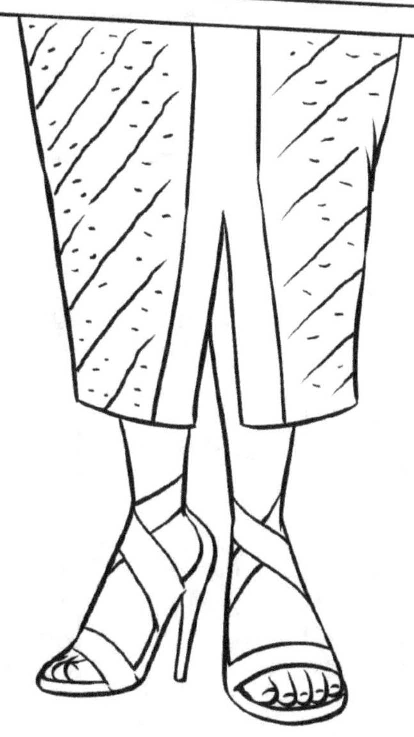

Study Abroad

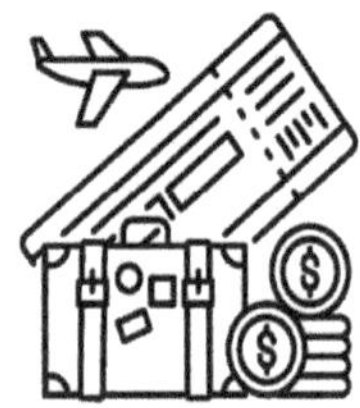

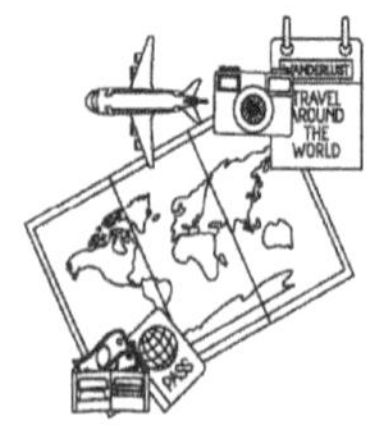

Study Abroad: when a student pursues their academic goals in a foreign country.

Advantages of traveling abroad

1.

2.

3.

**Translate the
the following
phrases.**

Choose a season to study

Fall

Winter

Spring

Summer

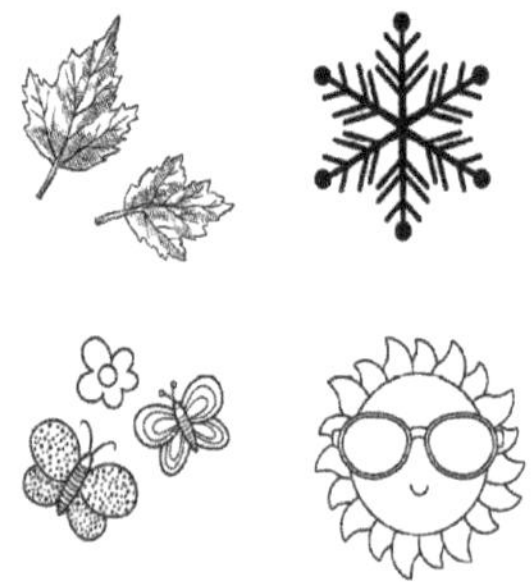

How do you plan to fund your study abroad program?

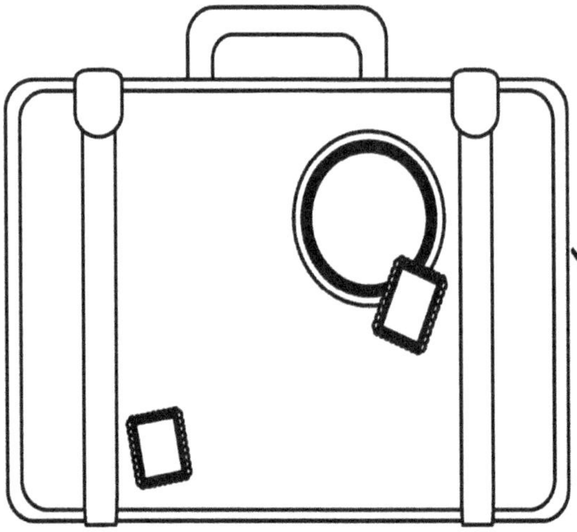

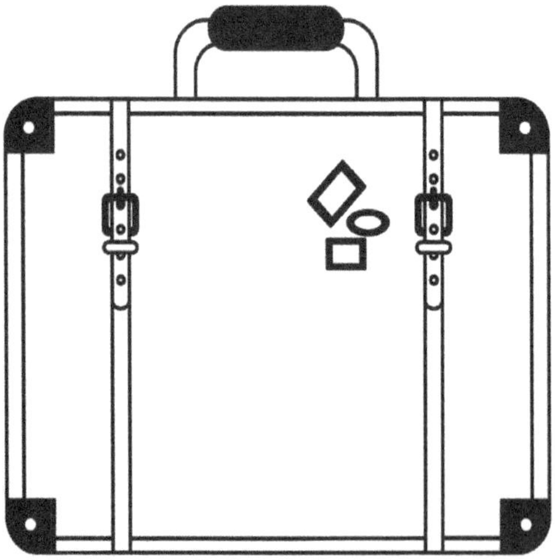

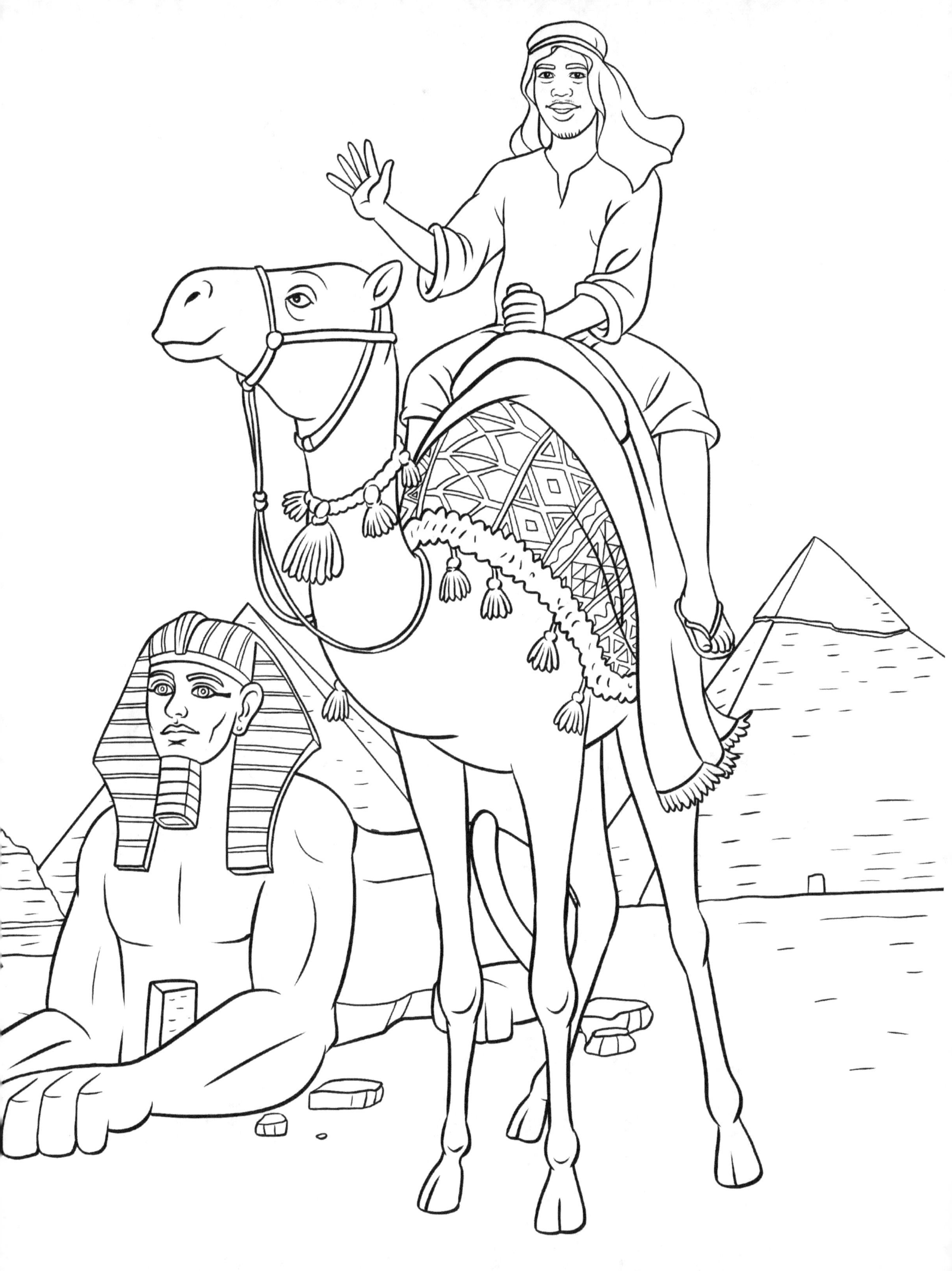

NAME	SPORT	COLLEGE	ACCOMPLISHMENT
WILMA RUDOLPH	TRACK & FIELD	TSU	WON 3 GOLD MEDALS AT THE 1960'S SUMMER OLYMPICS IN ROME, ITALY.
JERRY RICE	FOOTBALL	MVSU	WON 3 SUPER BOWLS, ELECTED PRO FOOTBALL HALL OF FAME, & NAMED BEST PLAYER OF ALL TIME

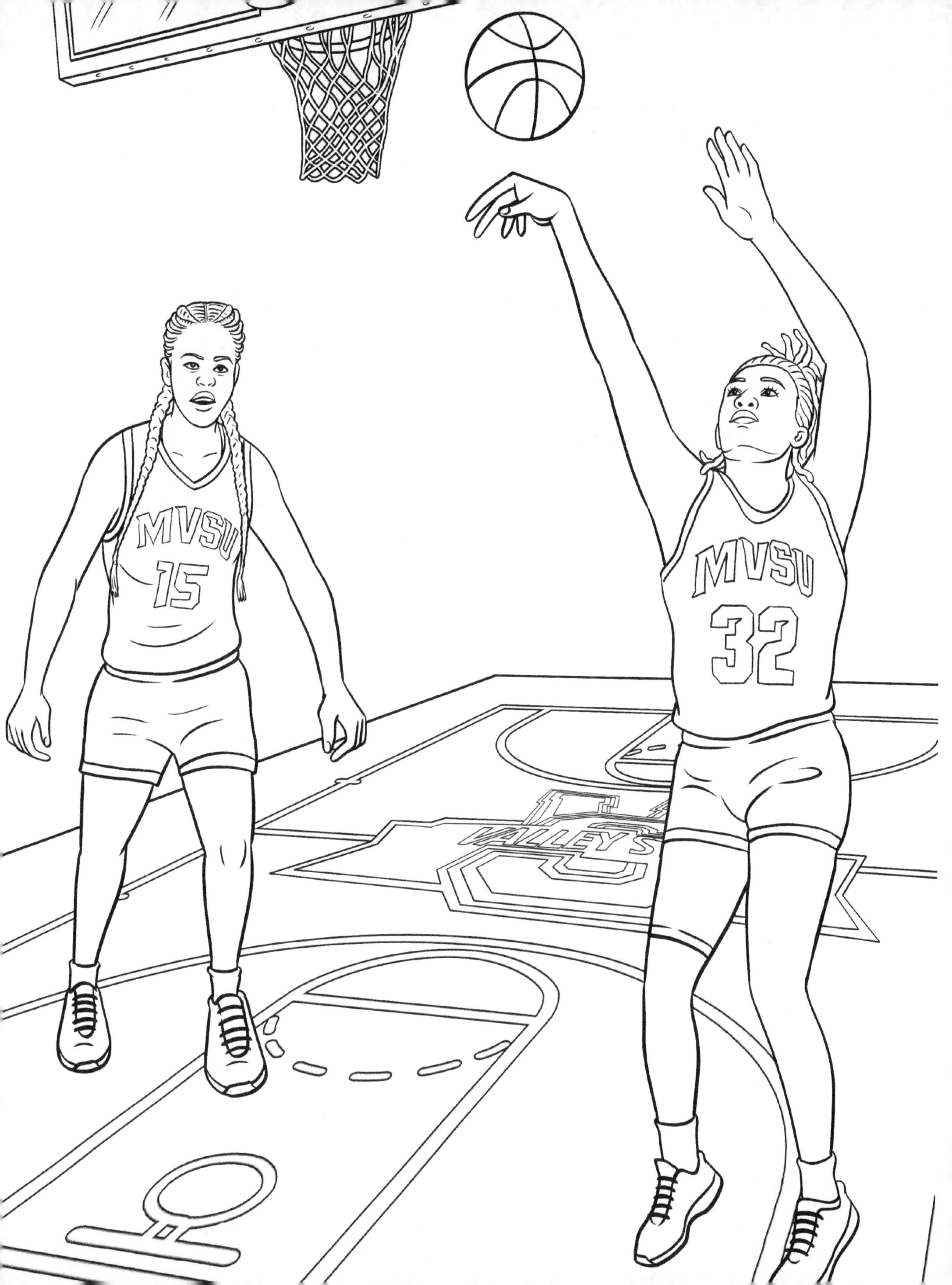

MVSU
15
MVSU
32
VALLEY S

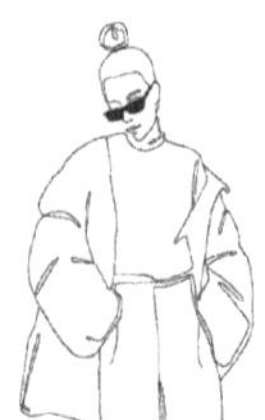 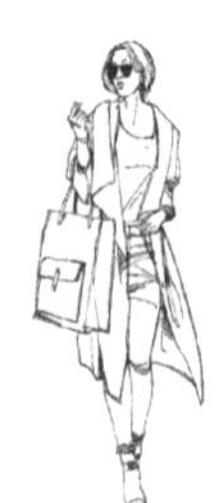

The yard is the heart and soul of an HBCU. Close your eyes and imagine Black people from around the world, with various fashion, hairstyles and dialect. Students, professors, alumni come to meet, think, organize, party and build legacies.

Directions: Create an Acrostic Poem. The first sentence of the poem must start with the given letter. In addition, incorporate words from the box.

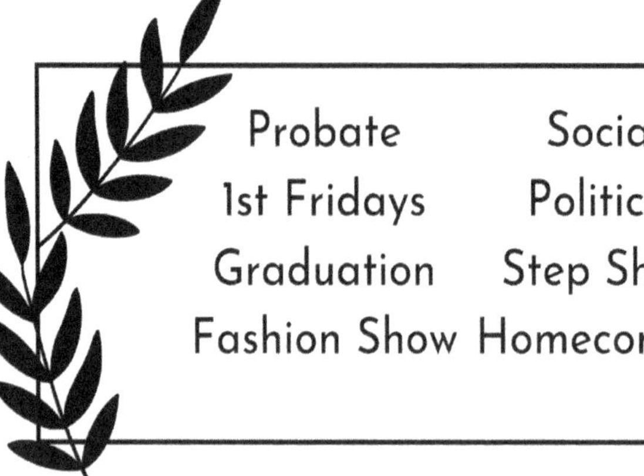

T

H

E

Y

A

R

D

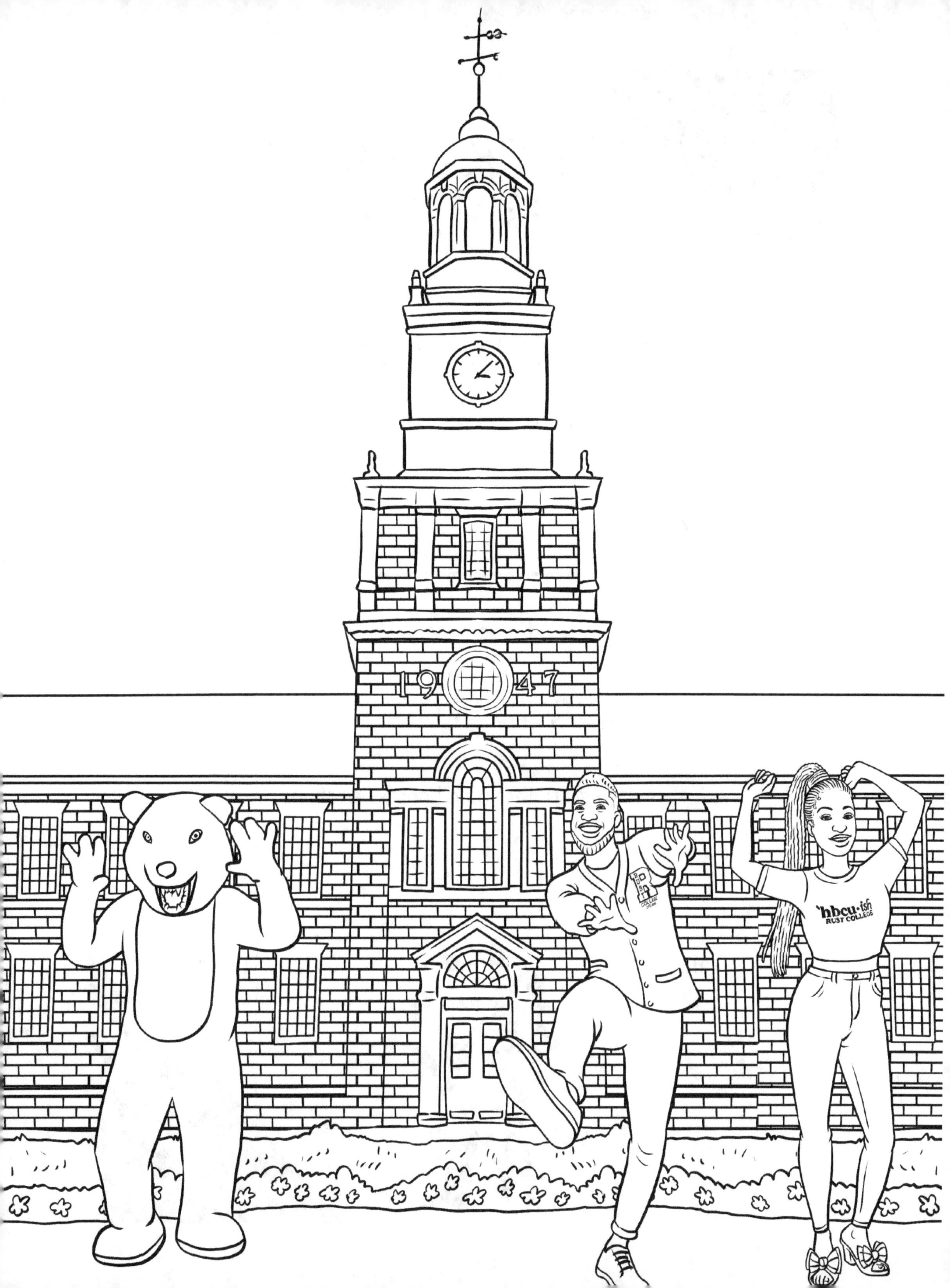
1947
RUST COLLEGE
'hbcu·ish
RUST COLLEGE

BLACK & PROUD UNIVERSITY

THE TRUSTEES OF BLACK & PROUD
UNIVERSITY HAVING FULFILLED THE
REQUIREMENTS AND HAVING BEING
RECOMMENDED BY THE FALCULTY

the degree of

Bachelor's of

With all the rights, privileges and honors pertaining thereto

Talore Hill
DEAN

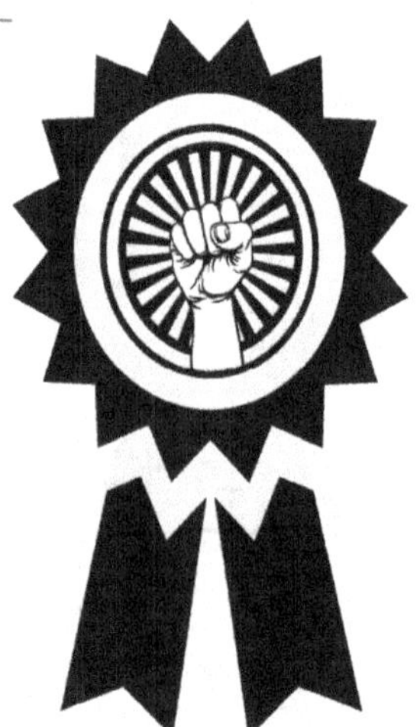

Tiffany Heard
President

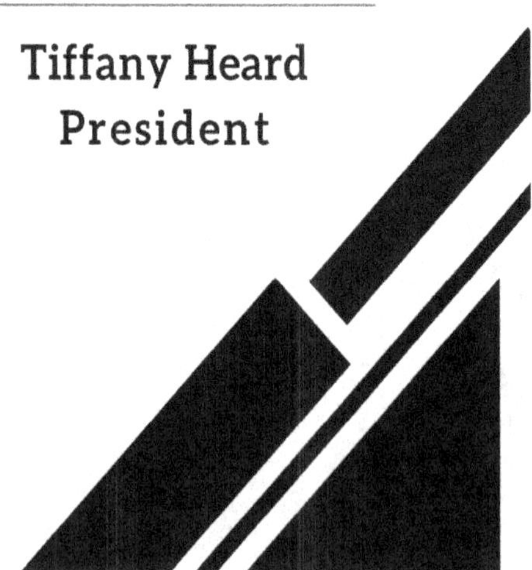

CONGRATULATIONS
HBCU MADE

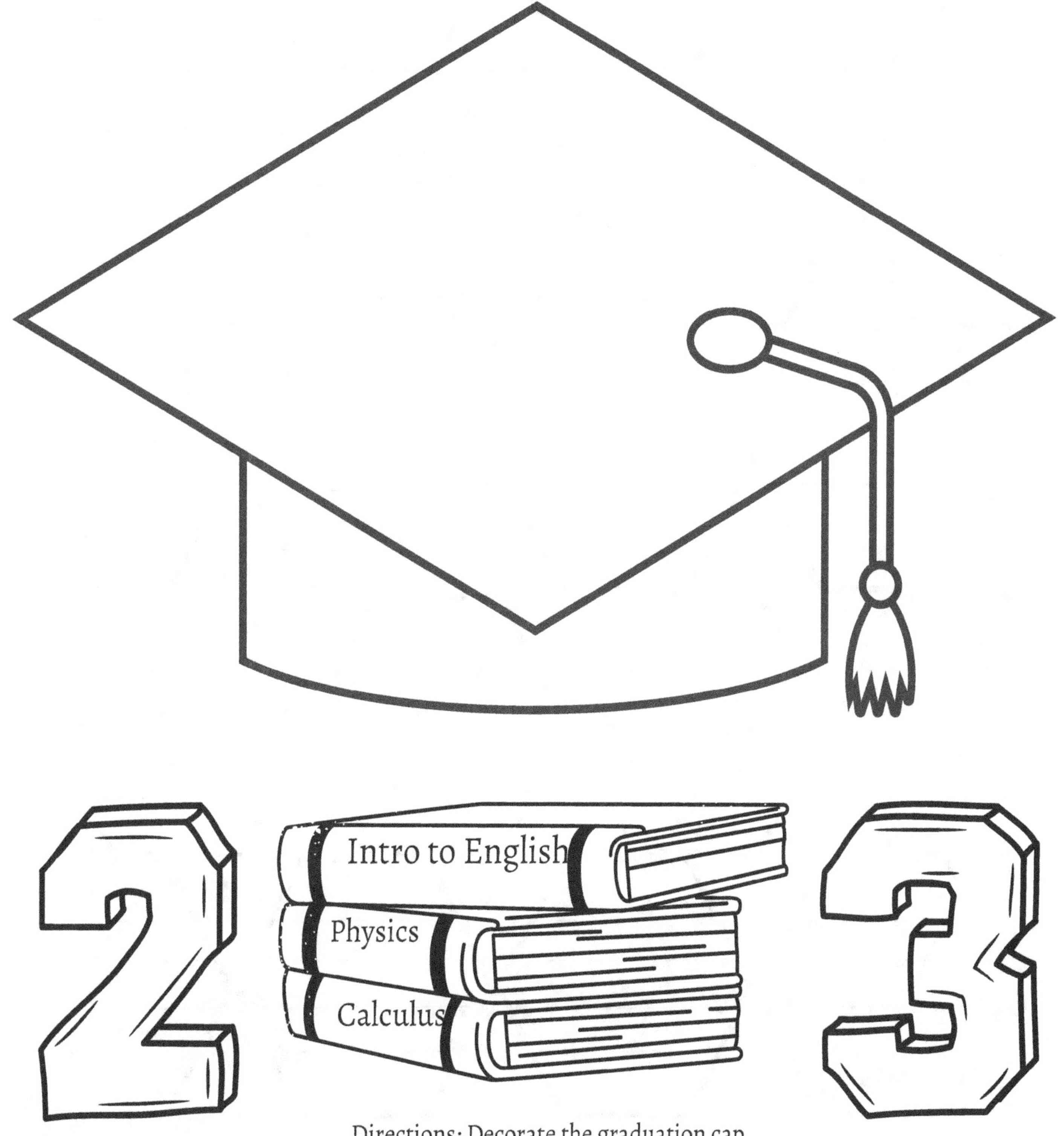

Directions: Decorate the graduation cap.

Notable HBCU Alumni

The cream of the crop come from HBCU's. Name some of your favorites.

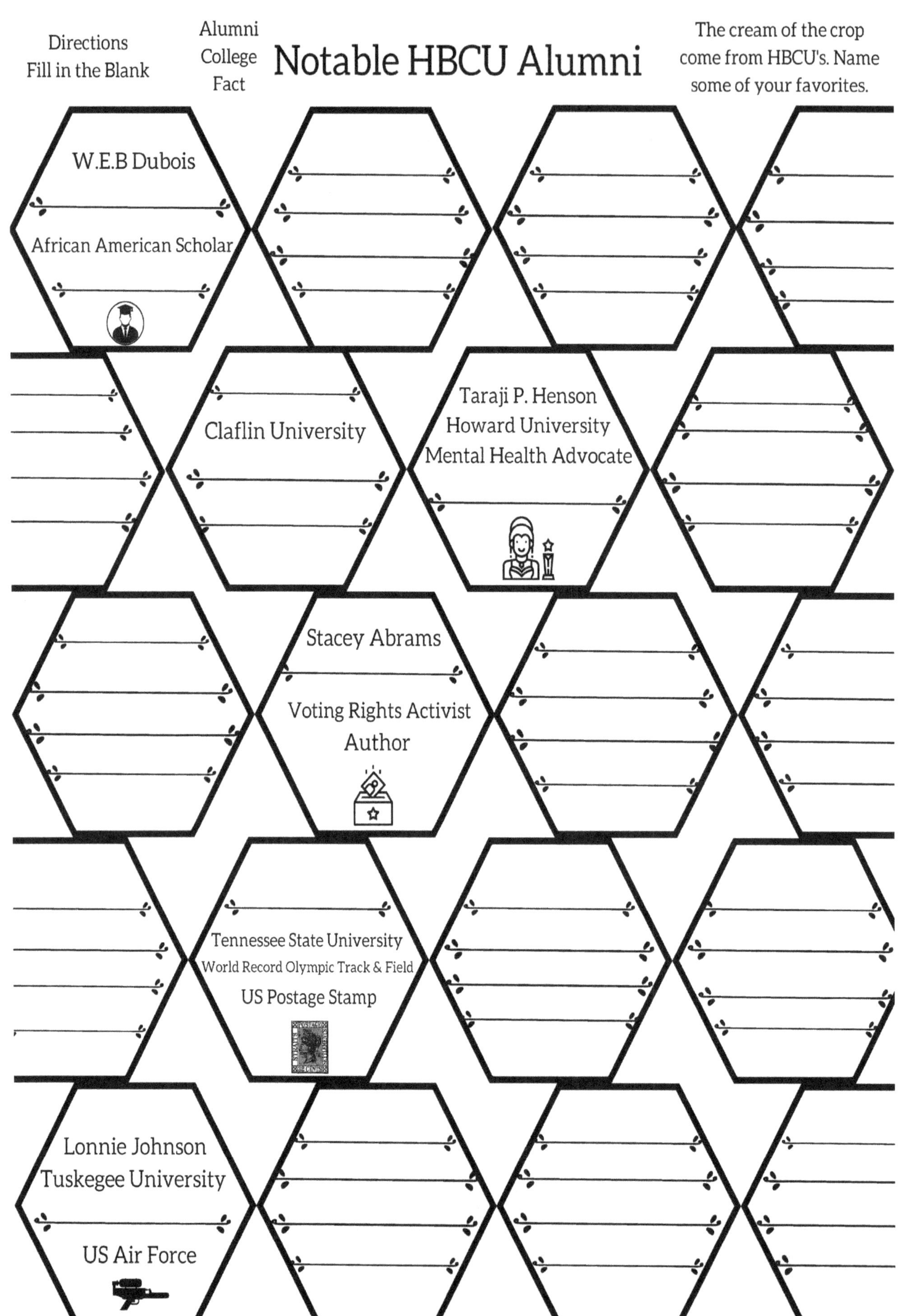

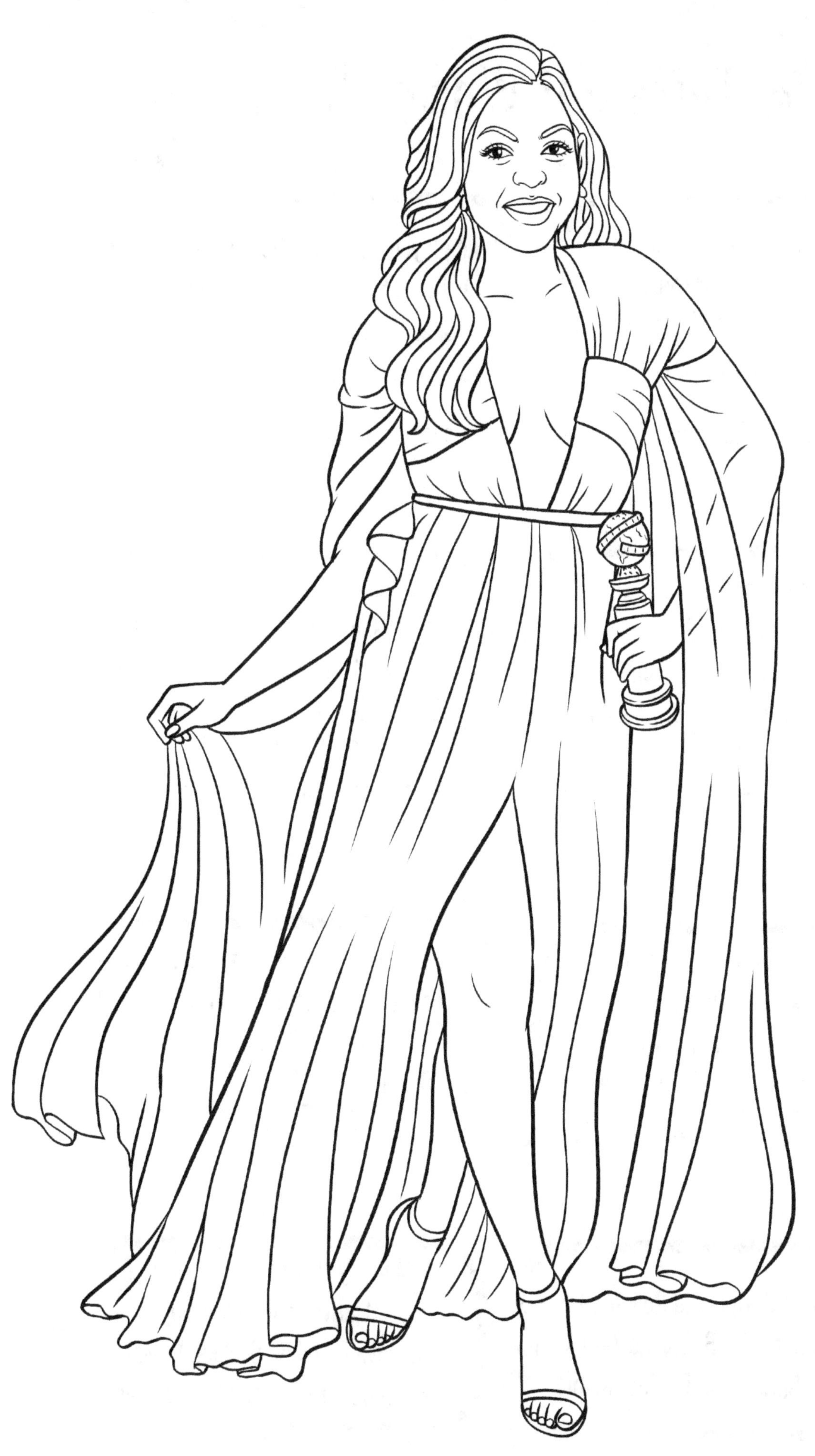

A "Different World" Trivia

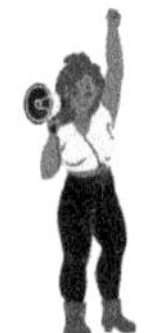
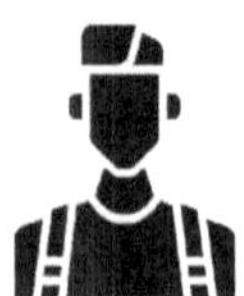

What fictional college was the show filmed at?
A. NYU B. Howard
C. Hillman D. Hampton

Who played Lena's ex- boyfriend Piccolo?
A. Tupac Shakur B. Heavy D
C. LL Cool J D. Biggie Smalls

According to Shazza and Freddie, how do humans give birth to themselves?

What famous singer was Jada Pinkett named after?
A. Billie Holiday B. Lena Horne
C. Mahalia Jackson D. Tina Turner

What was the name of Dwayne's internship & where did he relocate?
A. Tokai/Thailand B. Hirose/Laos
C. Kineshewa/Japan D. Akihiro/Bali

Who was your favorite character and why did they resonate with you?

"If I should die before I wake" Josie writes a speech for class on?
A. HIV/AIDS B. Apartheid
C. Voting Rights D. Discrimination

"Cat's in a Cradle" What did Ron & Dwayne encounter at a football game?
A. Robbery B. Police Brutality
C. Lying D. Racism

Did a "Different World" inspire you to attend an HBCU?

Which Fraternity did Ron join?
A. Kappa Lamda Nu B. Omega Zeta Alpha
C. Delta Rho Beta D. Phi Iota Sigma

In "Mammy Dearest" Kim Reese reads Ego Tripping" wrote by
A. Maya Angelou B. Nikki Giovanni
B. Audre Lorde C. Alice Walker

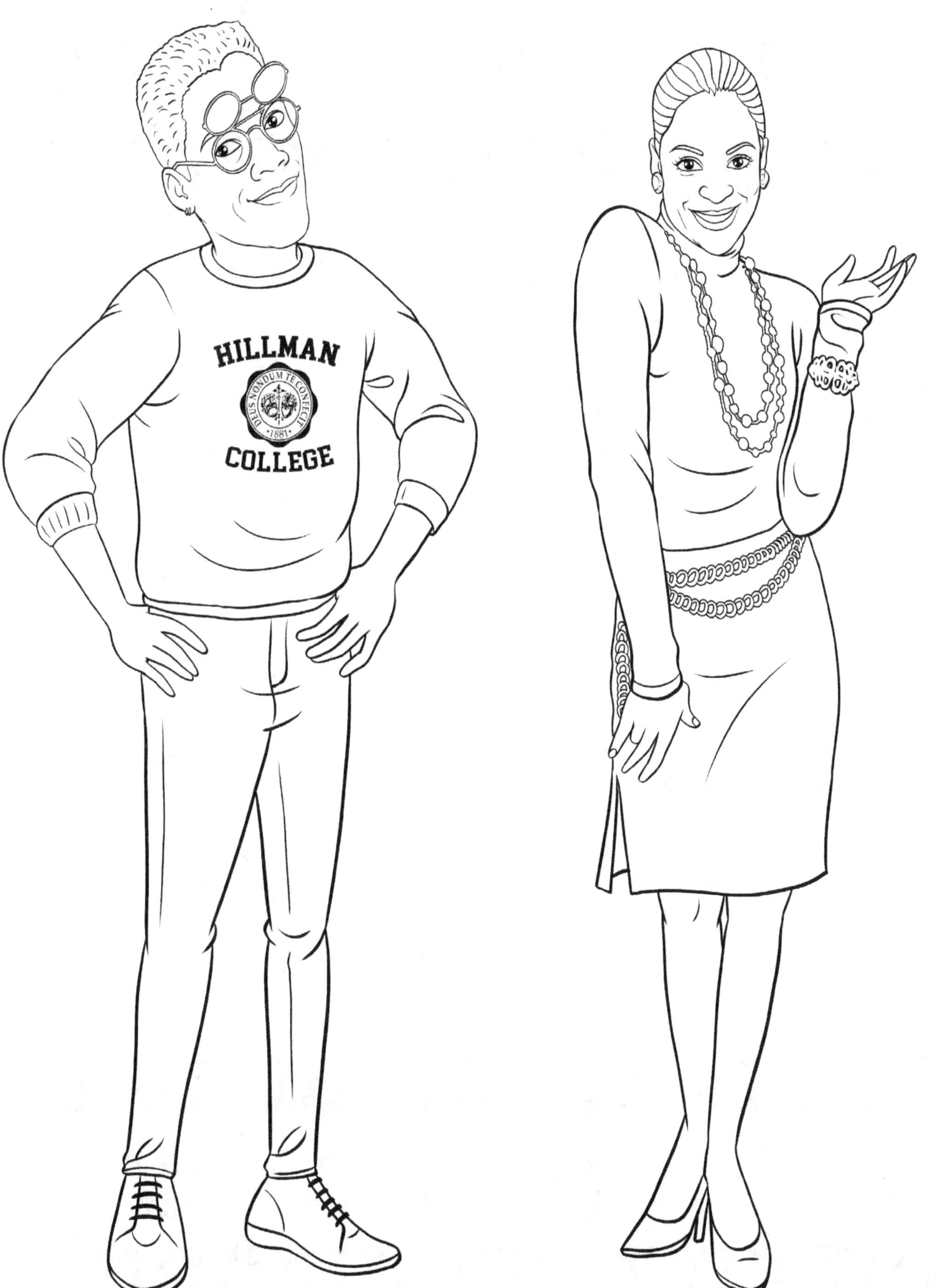

HILLMAN
DEUS NONDUM TE CONFECIT
·1881·
COLLEGE

| Tell Them We Are Rising | Beyonce Homecoming | A Different World | Girls Trip | College Hill |

It's not just about you. It's about us, we're a team.

"One band, one sound."

Black Colleges are where Black people are affirmed

We must never ever bow down before the tyranny of the majority.

Name that line from famous movie that depict HBCU Culture

Stop worrying about integrating and being accepted, and start thinking about building for yourself, for our people - so that we can provide a *future* for our children.

Learn to articulate, you juvenile delinquent!

This movie was filmed on Cheney University Campus

I am strong. I am powerful. I am beautiful.

| The Great Debaters | School Daze | Drumline | Stomp the Yard | Train Ride |

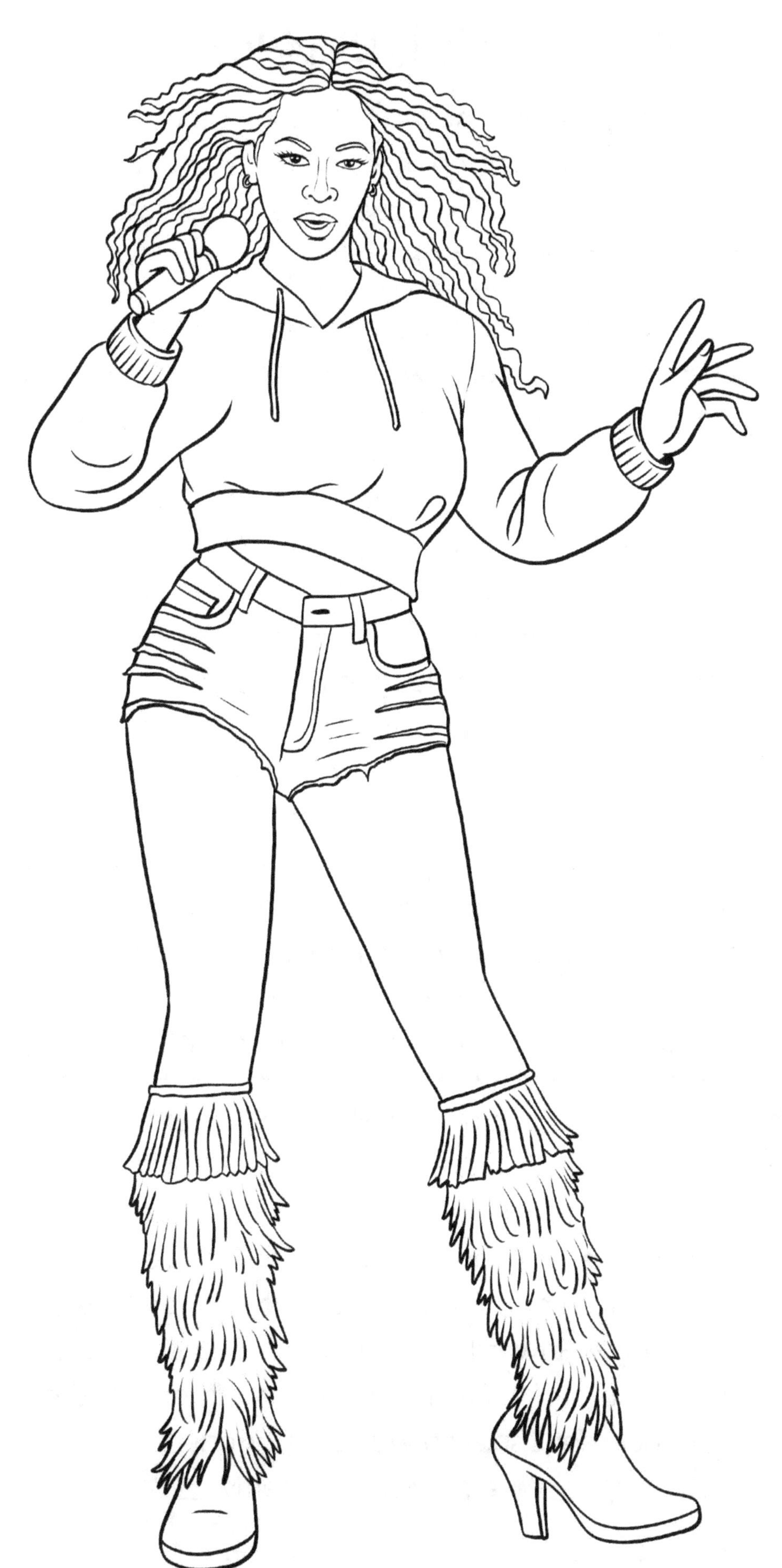

Tiffany attends Howard University

My name is Tiffany Heard. I moved to Washington, D.C. to pursue a Master of Social Work degree at Howard University. During college, I was very active on campus. I was the Student Council President of the School of Social Work.

Howard has one of the best homecomings. My first year, I served on the Gospel committee where I worked with Gospel Rapper "Da Truth." Gospel greats such as Marvin Sapp & Shirley Caesar also performed.

I served as a volunteer during Alternative Spring Break. In Chicago, we met with various elementary and high schools to fight against gun violence and taught Kwanzaa principles to students.

In South Africa, we met with colleagues & shadowed them at prisons, daycares, & various organizations. We had the opportunity to visit a safari, Robbin Island, Parliament and Cape Town University.

My fondest memory was delivering a short commencement speech to a crowd of thousands, including my supportive family cheering me on! My HBCU will forever hold a special place in my heart.

Write FA or FI next to each statement below

I lived in a dorm called the Towers ___
I was accepted into multiple HBCUs ___
I went to the cafe for soul food Thursdays __
My concentration was Displaced Populations ___
I received numerous academic scholarships ___
I went to Howard as an undergraduate student __
I had an internship working with immigrant children ___
Commencement speech was about transformation from a
caterpillar to a butterfly __

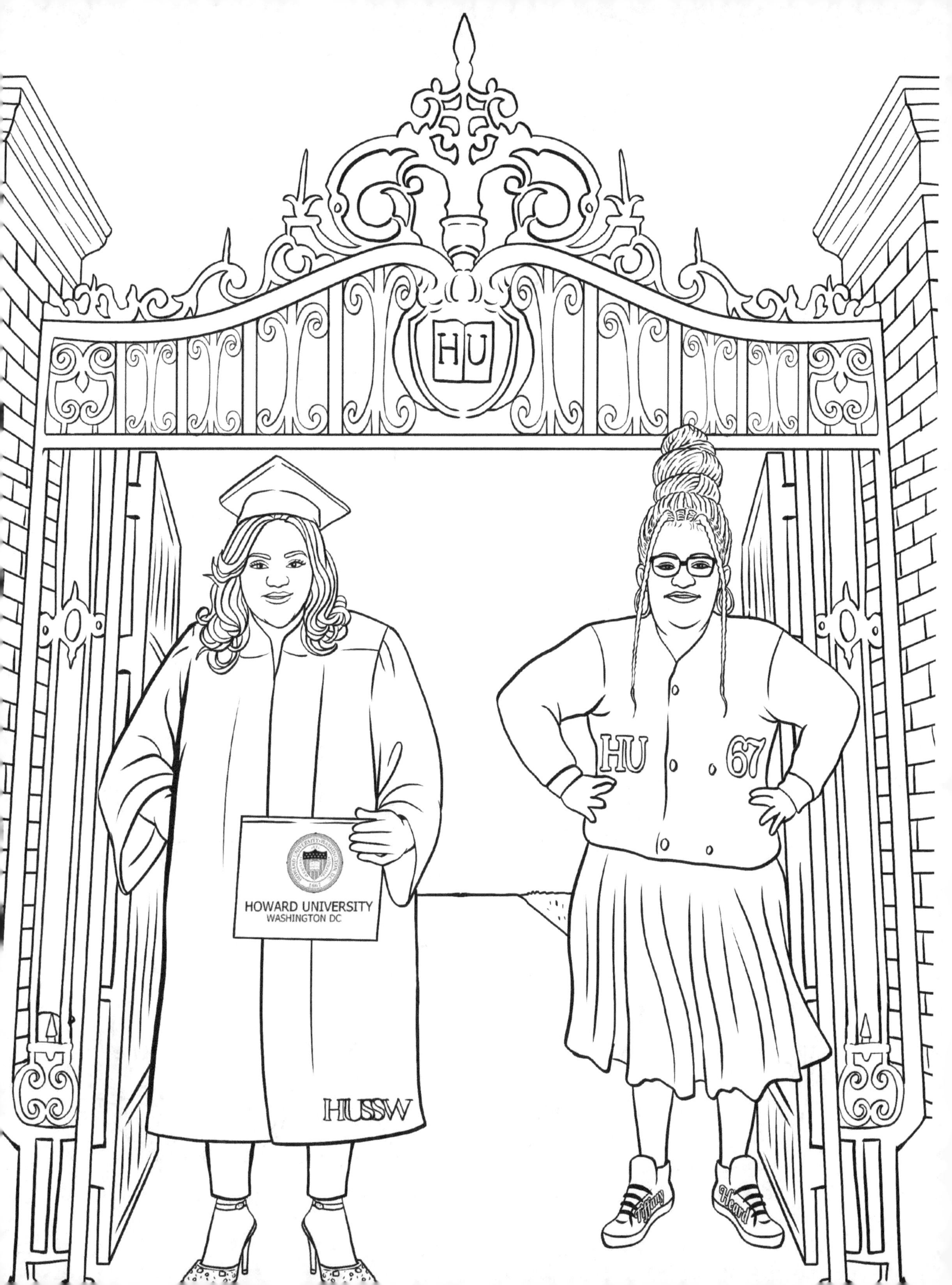

HU
HOWARD UNIVERSITY
WASHINGTON DC
HUSSW
HU
67

Historically Black College and University Project

Choose an HBCU of your choice & fill in the shapes with pertinent information

Motto:

1st & Current President

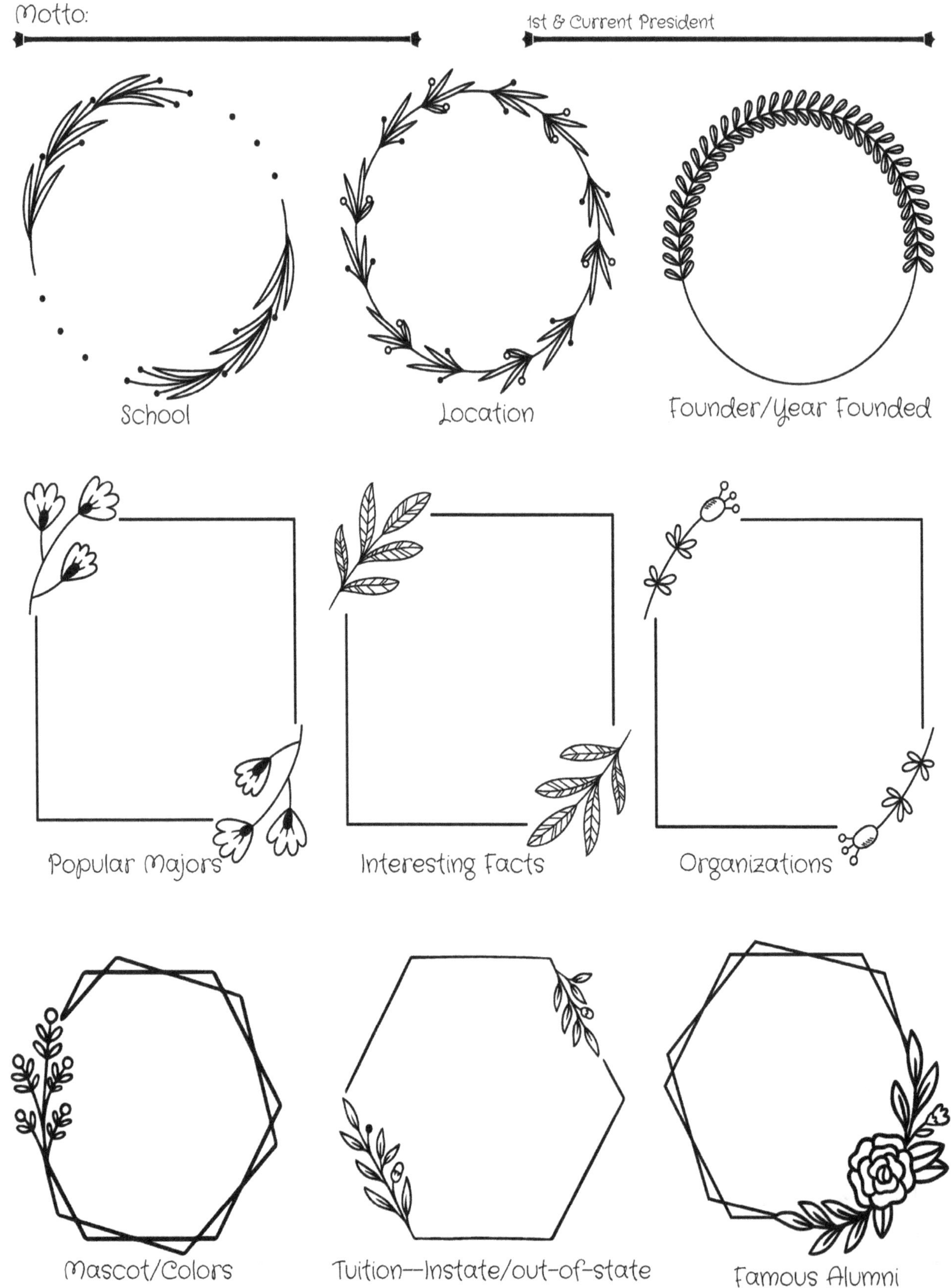

School

Location

Founder/Year Founded

Popular Majors

Interesting Facts

Organizations

Mascot/Colors

Tuition—Instate/out-of-state

Famous Alumni

HBCU Statistics

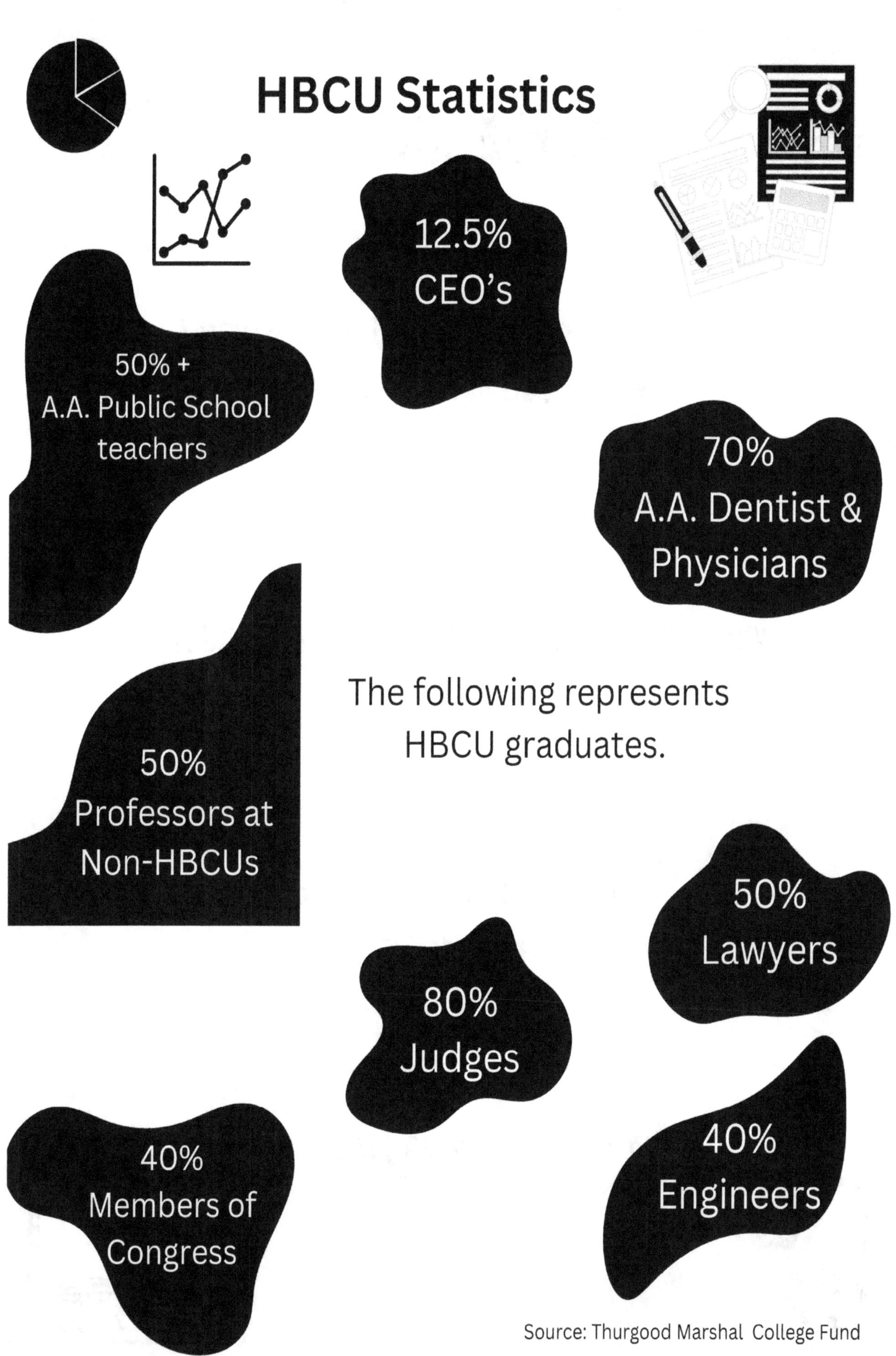

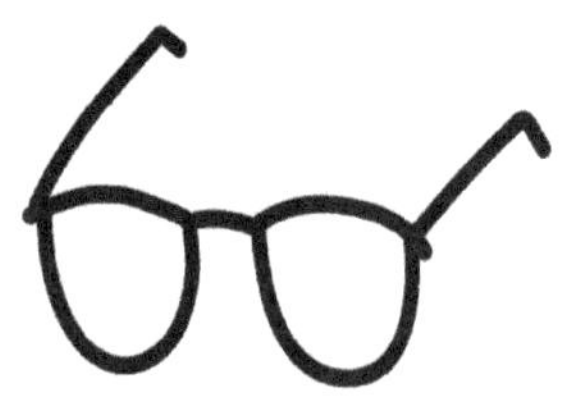 # Reflections 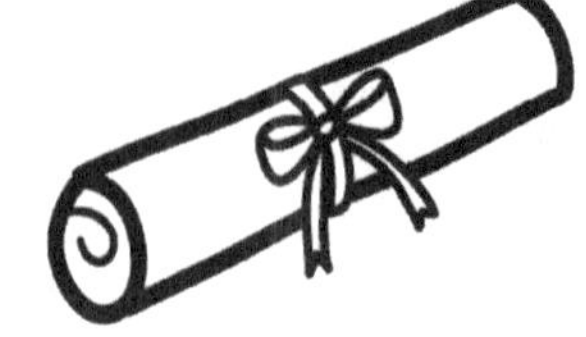

Which HBCU did **you graduate from**? Which HBCU
would **you like to** attend?

What did **you** already know about HBCUs?

Name 3 things **you** have
learned.

Favorite coloring page/ activity

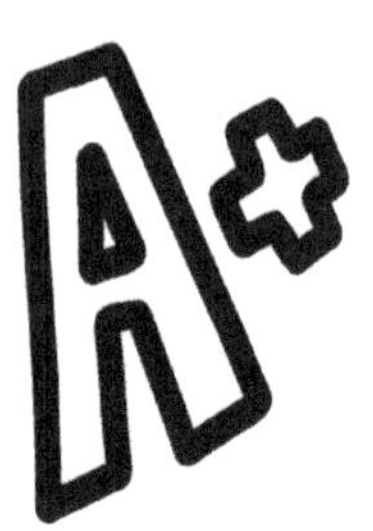

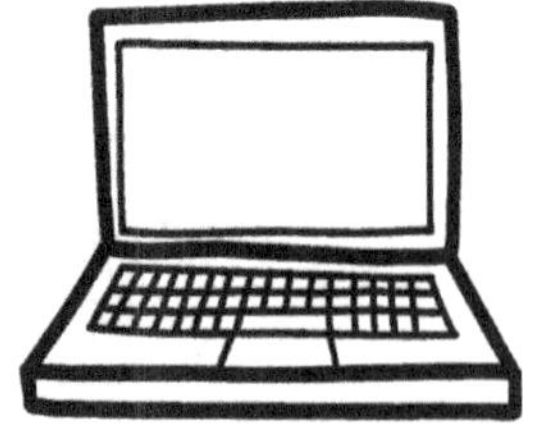

HUES OF HBCUS

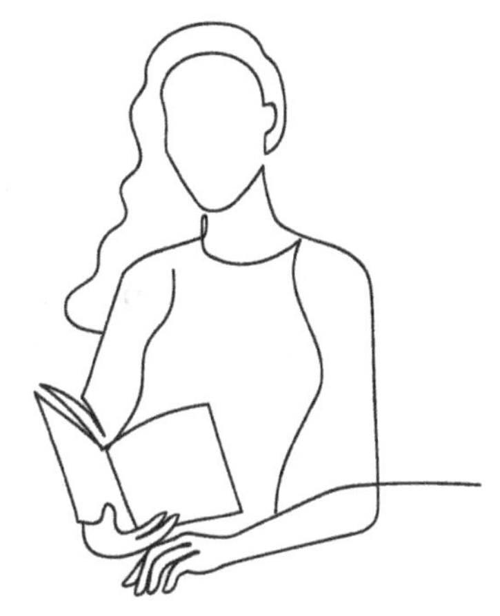

IF YOU ARE INTERESTED IN HAVING HUES OF HBCUS
NEAR YOU

CONTACT:
EMAIL: SWEETTIFFYSINSPIRATIONS@GMAIL.COM
WEBSITE: WWW.HUESOFAFRICA.COM
INSTAGRAM: @HUES_OF_AFRICA
YOUTUBE: WHERE IN THE HEARD IS TIFFANY

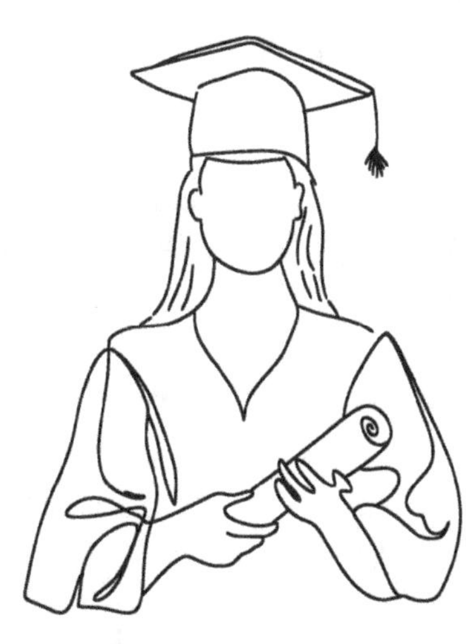

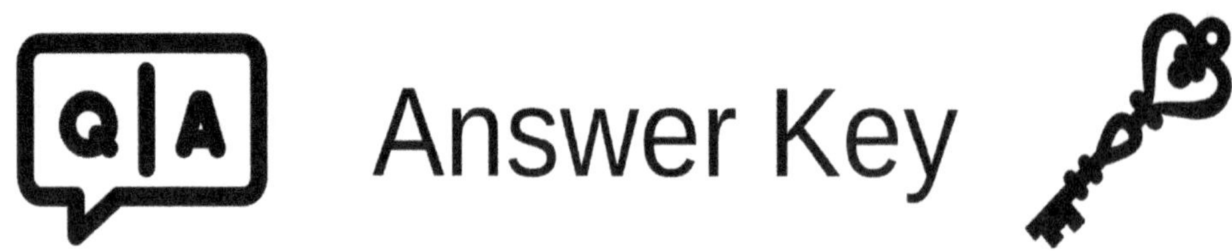

Answer Key

HBCU Geography

Alabama	(2)	Georgia	(10)	Missouri	(2)	Tennessee	(6)
Arkansas	(4)	Kentucky	(2)	North Carolina	(10)	Texas	(9)
California	(1)	Louisiana	(6)	Ohio	(2)	U.S. Virgin Islands	(1)
Delaware	(1)	Maryland	(4)	Oklahoma	(1)	Virginia	(5)
D.C	(2)	Michigan	(1)	Pennsylvania	(2)	West Virginia	(2)
Florida	(4)	Mississippi	(7)	South Carolina	(8)		

HBCU Jeopardy

HBCU History: Land, Education, Mary McLeod Bethune, North Carolina, HBCU History Course

Fraternity/Sorority: Alpha Phi Alpha, Sigma Gamma Rho, Zeta Phi Beta, Phi Beta, Sigma, Iota Phi Theta

Movies/ T.V. Shows: A Different World, Drum Line, School Daze, Great Debaters, College Hill

HBCU Names: Cheyney University, Morehouse College, Xavier University of Louisiana, Charles Drew University, University of the Virgin Islands

Famous People: Chadwick Boseman, Langston Hughes, Keshia Knight Pulliam, Yolanda Adams, 2 Chainz

Alabama A & M University

1) Dr. William Hooper Councill, 2) Alabama A & M University Choir, 3) B.S. in Construction Management, 4) PHD in Plant & Soil Science, 5) Ruben Studdard, 6) The Bulldog Times Magazine 7) Bulldog Strong 8) Harriet J. Terry Hall 9) Marching Maroon & White 10) Remote Sensing & GIS

Alabama State University

Ricky Smiley, ASU Honey Beez, Prosthetics & Orthotics

Alcorn State University

Hiram Revels, Farmers, Medgar Evers, Alex Haley, Accounting, Business, Recreation, Dynomite, Ensemble, Military, Agronomy, Music, Dr. Walters, Substance Abuse, "Where Knowledge And Character Matter"

University of Arkansas Pine Bluff

Aquaculture .Museum, Arkansawyer, Smokey, STEM

Benedict College

South Carolina, Bathsheba Benedict, Freed Slaves, Big House, Benedict College Rev. John J. Starks, Dr. Rosyln Clark Artis, Preachers, Band of Distinction

Bowie State University

1A, 2I, 3H, 4J, 5G, 6D, 7F, 8B, 9E, 10C

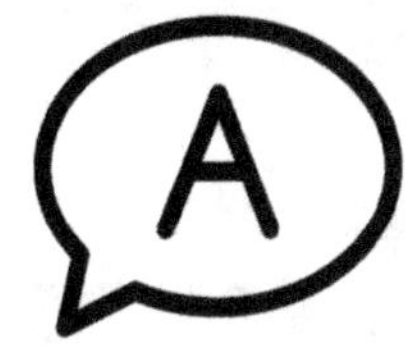 # Answer Key 

Bethune Cookman University
Fantasy, Fantasy, Reality, Fantasy, Reality

Cheyney University of Pennsylvania
Column Answers
The house of Julian Abele, Richard Humphreys, Quakers, Pennsylvania, Emlen Hall
Institute for Colored Youth, George Cheyney
Success Coaches, Dudley Centre, Fanny Coppin, Edward Bouchet,

Clark Atlanta University
Column Answers
Cancer, Africana, Experience
Consortium, Dubois, Methodist
(Left) Panther
(Down) Mighty Marching
(Right) Band

Coppin State University
1. False 2. False 3. True 4. True 5. True 6. False 7. True 8. False 9. True 10. True

Dillard State University
Bleu Devils, Louisiana, Theatre, Ray Charles, Psi Chi, Kimbrough, Follett, Kearny, Lawless, Hobley

Edward Waters University
B. Jacksonville, Florida C. African Methodist Episcopal Church

Elizabeth City University
Fest & Spirit Awards, Cross Country, Homeland Security, N.C. General Assembly, Bias
Mathematics, Interloan, Pace, Omari Salisbury, House Bill 383, B.S. in Unmanned Aircraft Systems

Fisk University
Ida B. Wells,1865, Nikki Giovanni
Jubilee Singers, Caribbean Student Association, Fisk Master Bonus
Bonus Question: Homeland Security

Florida A&M University (FAMU)
2. Excellence with Caring 3. Tallahassee, Florida 4. Innovation 5. Graphic design
6. Set Friday 7.Rattler Parent Engagement 9. Respiratory Therapy Cardiopulmonary Science
10. Bernard Kinsey 11. Study Abroad 12. Life Gets Better 13. Rattler Handshake 14. B.A Theatre
17. Center for Disability Access and Resources 18. K, Michelle 19. Entomology 20. Marching 100
21. Miami 22. Medical Marijuana Education Research 23.Carnegie Library
24. Leadership & Service Learning

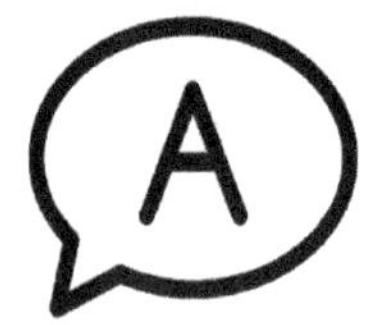 # Answer Key 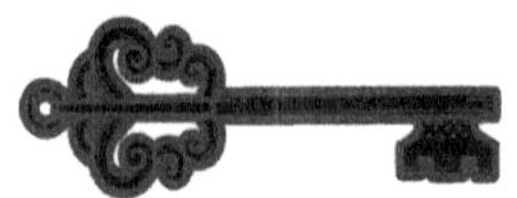

Fort Valley State University
Robins, Episcopal, Science, Organizational, FVSU, Veterinary, Agricultural, Health
Henry A. Hunt, Vault-Valley, Davison, Ham, Cheerleaders, ROTC, Blue Machine, Gospel Choir

Grambling University
Eddie, Brown, Marching, Johnson, Tiger Card, NCAA, Cybersecurity

Hampton University
B, A, C

Howard University
5 publications: The Hilltop, Howard Magazine, Howard University Bison Yearbook, The Journey of Negro Education, Capstone.
Radio Station: WHUR 96.3 FM   T.V Station: WHUT TV
Best HBCU: Homecoming   Fill in the Blank: Truth and Service

Jackson State University
Accounting, aerospace, Ayerhall, battalion, Blue bengals, Civilrights
Cleopatra, health policy, Jacksonstate, Jazzstudies, jsettes, jsuvibe
Mass choir, meteorology, Mississippi, missjsu, Socialwork, sonicboom
Sports media, SWAC, tigers, urban design, WEB Dubois, WJSU

Langston University
Down
1. Urban 3. Oklahoma 6. LU Gazette 7. mLion 9. Mccabe 10. Langston 12. Pride
Across
2. Goat 4. Lamar Harrison 5. College Hill 8. Zero 11. Cultural 13. Morrill

Lincoln University
1 c C
2 e F
3 f F
4 a B
5 d A
6 b D

Meharry Medical College
(Column Answers)
Nashville, Oral and Maxillofacial, Salt Wagon, Dr. Georgia E. L. Patton
Mr. Atwater, Ross Fitness & recreation center, Health, White Coats for black lives
Samuel Meharry, George W. Hubbard, Obstetrics & Gynecology, HBCU Wellness
Match day , M.S. Data Science, 1915, Hastings Kamuzu Banda

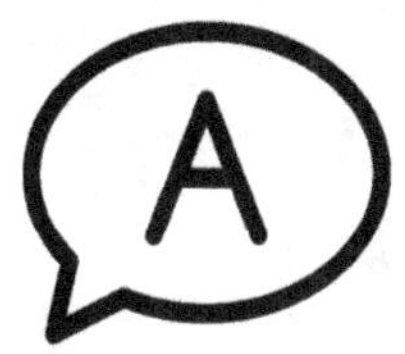 # Answer Key 

<u>Morehouse College</u>
A. Chinese B. Religion C. Journalism D. French

<u>North Carolina A& T</u>
Q & A
Sit in at White only counter
Silent Protest to End Segregation
February One
Commencement Speaker: Michelle Obama
Secret Code: Aggie Pride

<u>Prairie View</u>
Prairie View Produces Productive People

<u>Savannah State University</u>
Savannah State, Cyrus G. Wiley, Tiger Roar, Alternative Spring Break, Men & Women Golf, WHCJ 90.3 FM, Marine Science

<u>Selma University</u>
Factual, Factual, Factual, Deceptive, Factual, Factual, _

<u>Shaw University</u>
Row Answers
SNCC, Shirley Caesar, Masters of Divinity
B. A. Visual & Performing Arts, Woman as students, Active Minds
Platinum Sounds, Founder's Day, Center for Racial & Social Justice

<u>Spelman</u>
Rows Across
Minor in African Diaspora, College Glee Club, Oprah Winfrey, G-Stem
My Sister's Closet, True, Commuter Student Association, Wisdom LLC, Violence Prevention & Intervention Program
Girls going Global, Documentary Filmmaking, Stacey Abrams, CARE Team
Entrepreneurship Education, The Blue Record, LEADS, Spelman Serves, Food Studies
4/11/1881, Johnetta B. Cole, Wellness Center at Read Hall, Sisters Chapel

<u>Southern University and A & M College</u>
Column Answers
P. B. S. Pinchback, Theophile. T. Alain Henry Demas, Human Juke Box, LaCumba, David Banner
Nursing, Dr. Delores Spikes, Bayou, The Southern Digest,

 # Answer Key 

Texas Southern University
Houston, Education, Soul, Megan

Talladega College
We regard the education of our children and youth as vital to the preservation of our liberties

Tougaloo College
Tougaloo Mississippi, 1869, The American Missionary Association, The Jackson Civil Rights Movement, Sit in at the Woolworth Lunch Counter, Medgar Evers House

Tuskegee University
B, C, A
FI, FA, FI, FA, FA, FA, FI

University of the Virgin Islands
March 16, 1982, St. Thomas & St. Croix, Substance Abuse & HIV Prevention, WUVI 97.3, Ecology, False, UVI Institutional, Masters of Arts in School Counseling & Guidance, Mangrove Restoration, Paradise Jam, The Caribbean Writer, 1986, St. John, (President, Vice President, Treasure, Secretary), BSN Bachelor of Science in Nursing, Ricky Skerritt, Emerging Caribbean Scientists, The Buccaneer, BUCS Fitness Center, B.S. Criminal Justice, Yes, 6:2, Miss UVI, PHD in Creative Leadership for Innovation and Change, UVI Carnival Troupe

University of the District of Columbia
Fill in the Blank:
Miner, City, Washington, D.C, Columbia, Public
College of Agriculture, Urban Sustainability & Environmental Sciences (CAUSES)
College of Arts & Sciences (CAS)
School of Business & Public Administration (SBPA)
School of Engineering and Applied Sciences (SEAS)
David A. Clarke School of Law
Research and Graduate Studies
University of the District of Columbia Community College (UDC-CC)
UDC Campus: Bertie Backus, Congress Heights, Reagan National Airport, Hangar #2

Virginia State Union
True, False, True, True, False, True, True, False, True
False, False, False, True, True, False, True, True, True,

Wilberforce University
1. a) first black operated & owned 2. b) South Africa 3. c) Internship 4. c) Entrepreneurship & Innovation 5. b) Dorothy Vaughan

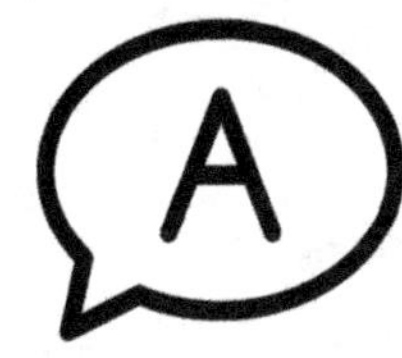 # Answer Key 

Wilberforce University
1. a) first black operated & owned 2. b) South Africa 3. c) Internship 4. c) Entrepreneurship & Innovation 5. b) Dorothy Vaughan

Xavier University
New Orleans, Katherine Drexal, Catholic, LaToya Cantrell, Love, Pharmacy, M.O.L.E, Investigative, Athletics

Alpha Phi Alpha
Fill in the Blank
Cornell University, Jewels, December 4, 1906, oldest
Initiatives
Boy Scouts of America, Peace Corps, Big Brother/Big Sister of America, Leadership Development Institute, World Policy Council

Kappa Alpha Psi
10 Founders
Elder Watson Diggs, Byron Kenneth Armstrong, Ezra D. Alexander, Henry Tourner Asher, Marcus Peter Blakemore, Paul Waymond Caine, George Wesley Edmonds,Guy Levis Grant, Edward Giles Irvin, John Milton Lee

Omega Psi Phi
Column
B, A, E
B, C, A

Phi Beta Sigma
Fill in the Blank:
Howard University, Culture, Constitutionally, Sigma Beta Club, Charles Brown
Unscramble: Service, Crescent, Brotherhood, Royal Blue, Pure White,

Zeta Phi Beta
Matching: A4, B3, C1, D5, E2
Fill in the Blank : Blue & White, Africa, Body, Zeta Amicae, Phi Beta Sigma

Iota Phi Theta
Fill in the Blank
Twelve, Morgan State University, Tradition, Eternal Sweetheart

HBCU Band
Fact, Fact, Fiction, Fiction

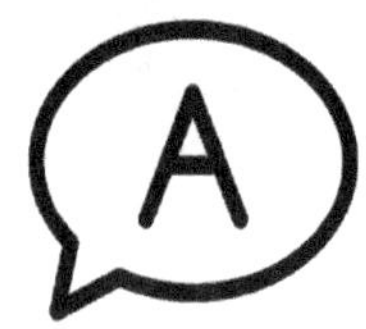 # Answer Key 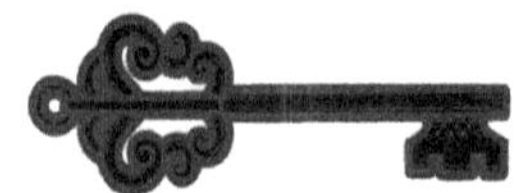

Faith & Education
Matching Answers
Ae, Bb, Cc, Da, Eg, Ff, Gh, Hd

HBCU Sports
Unscramble: Band, Golf, Dance, Sailing, Baseball, Triathlon, Volleyball, Gymnastics, Cheerleading, Track & Field
Athletic Conferences: MEAC, SWAC, SIAC, CIAA, GCAC
Bayou Classic: Grambling State University & Southern University

A Different World Trivia
Column Answers
C, B, A, A
A, C, D, B

Movies
Row Answers
Stomp the Yard, Drum Line, Tell them we are Rising
The Great Debaters, A Different World
School Daze, Train Ride, Girls Trip

Tiffany
FA, FI, FA, FA, FI, FI, FA, FA

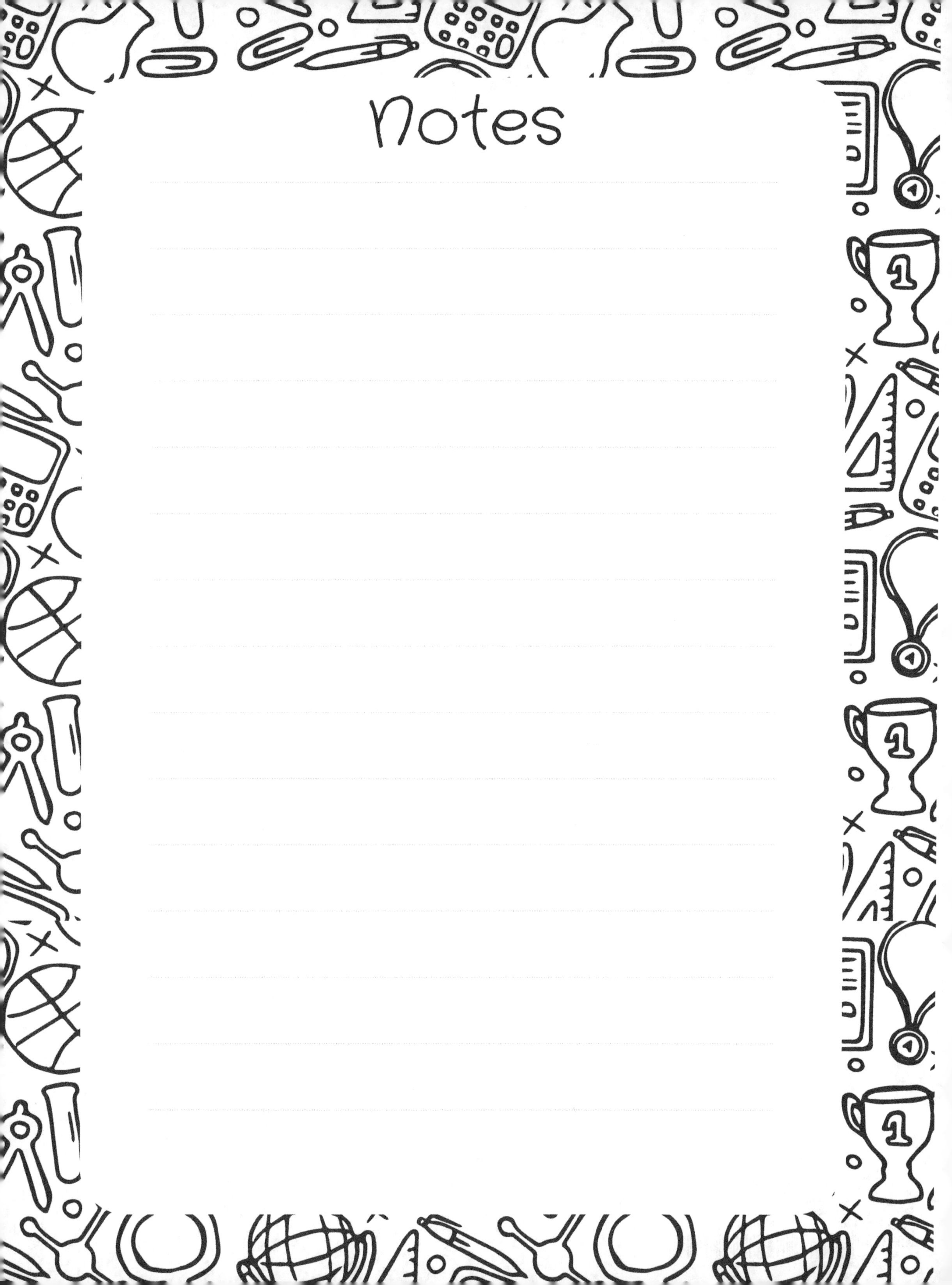

Notes